BARRON'S

Pass Key to the SAT*

ELEVENTH EDITION

Sharon Weiner Green, M.A.
Former Instructor in English
Merritt College, Oakland, California

Ira K. Wolf, Ph.D.
Former High School Teacher, College Professor,
and University Director of Teacher Preparation

Brian W. Stewart, M.Ed.
Founder and President
BWS Education Consulting, Inc.

*SAT is a registered trademark of the College Board, which was not
involved in the production of, and does not endorse, this product.

© Copyright 2017, 2016, 2012, 2010, 2008, 2006, 2005, 2001, 1998, 1994
by Barron's Educational Series, Inc.

Adapted from Barron's *SAT*, © 2017 by Barron's Educational Series, Inc.

All inquiries should be addressed to:
Barron's Educational Series, Inc.
250 Wireless Boulevard
Hauppauge, New York 11788
www.barronseduc.com

ISSN: 2154-3232

ISBN: 978-1-4380-0997-1

PRINTED IN CANADA
9 8 7 6 5 4 3 2 1

Contents

Preface

You have in your hands *Barron's Pass Key to the SAT*, the compact version of Barron's classic *SAT* review book. Small enough to toss in your backpack, portable enough to read on the bus, this short course in SAT preparation provides you with the basic tips and strategies you need to cope with the SAT.

If you feel unready for the SAT, if you don't quite know what to expect on it, *Pass Key* may be just the eye-opener you need.

It offers you dozens of specific tips that will help you attack every type of SAT question, and provides you with practice exercises.

It offers you the exclusive SAT Concise Word List, your best chance to acquaint yourself with the whole range of college-level vocabulary you will face on the SAT.

It not only gives you all of the math facts and formulas you need to know, it provides more than a dozen special tactics (all illustrated with sample problems) to show you how to answer every type of SAT math question.

It thoroughly covers the writing skills section of the SAT, providing you with useful tips for dealing with the multiple-choice questions, as well as showing you how to tackle writing a 50-minute essay.

Best of all, it offers you the chance to take not one, but two complete practice SAT exams that correspond to the SAT in content, format, and level of difficulty. Each test has an answer key and complete solutions and explanations.

Read the tips. Go over the strategies. Do the practice exercises. *Then* take the practice SATs and see how you score. Study the answer explanations, especially those for questions you were unsure of or answered incorrectly. You'll come out feeling far more secure about what it will be like to take the SAT.

SAT Format and Test Dates

▲▼▲▼▲▼▲▼▲▼▲▼▲▼▲▼▲▼▲▼▲▼▲▼▲▼▲▼▲▼▲▼▲▼

SAT FORMAT

Total Time: 3 hours, plus 50 minutes for the Optional Essay	
Section 1: Reading **52 Questions** *Time—65 minutes*	5 Reading Passages, including 1 paired passage
Section 2: Writing and Language **44 Questions** *Time—35 minutes*	4 Passages
Section 3: Math, No Calculator **20 Questions** *Time—25 minutes*	15 Multiple Choice, 5 Grid-in
Section 4: Math, Calculator **38 Questions** *Time—55 minutes*	30 Multiple Choice, 8 Grid-in
Optional Essay **1 Question** *Time—50 minutes*	Write an essay analyzing how the author of a given passage has made his or her argument. Evaluated on reading, analysis, and writing.

You can register to take the SAT at *sat.collegeboard.org*.

SAT TEST DATES

Test Dates	Registration Deadlines	
	Regular	Late
2017–2018 School Year*		
October 7, 2017		
November 4, 2017		
December 2, 2017		
March 10, 2018		
May 5, 2018		
June 2, 2018		
2018–2019 School Year*		
August 25, 2018		
October 6, 2018		
November 3, 2018		
December 1, 2018		
March 9, 2019		
May 4, 2019		
June 1, 2019		

*As of press time, exam dates for the 2017–2018 and 2018–2019 school years are approximate. Check *collegeboard.org* periodically to confirm the anticipated test dates and the registration and late registration deadlines.

Acknowledgments

The authors gratefully acknowledge the following copyright holders for permission to reprint material used in reading passages:

Pages 207–208: From *Mortal Lessons: Notes on the Art of Surgery* by Richard Selzer. Copyright © 1974, 1975, 1976, 1987 by Richard Selzer.

Pages 210–211: From *The Press and the Presidency* by John Tebbel and Sarah Miles Watts. Copyright © 1985, Oxford University Press, New York.

Page 211: From *An Analysis of the President-Press Relationship in Solo and Joint Press Conferences in the First Term of President George W. Bush, A Thesis Submitted to the Graduate Faculty of the Louisiana State University and Agricultural and Mechanical College in partial fulfillment of the requirements for the degree of Master of Mass Communication in The Manship School of Mass Communication*, by Susan Billingsley, May 2006.

Pages 214–215: From "The facts behind the frack: Scientists weigh in on the hydraulic fracturing debate," by Rachel Ehrenberg, *Science News*, 24 August 2012. Reprinted with permission of Science News for Students.

Pages 309–310: Excerpt from pp. 141–142 from *I Love Paul Revere, Whether He Rode or Not* by Richard Shenkman. Copyright © 1991 by Richard Shenkman.

Pages 313–314: From "Sleep: The Brain's Housekeeper?" by Emily Underwood, *Science*, 18 October 2013. Reprinted with permission from AAAS.

Pages 320–322: From "Dinosaur metabolism neither hot nor cold, but just right," by Michael Balter, *Science*, 13 June 2014. Reprinted with permission from AAAS.

About the SAT

COMMONLY ASKED QUESTIONS ABOUT THE SAT

What Is the SAT?

The SAT is a standardized exam that most high school students take before applying to college. Generally, students take the SAT for the first time as high school juniors. If they are happy with their scores, they are through. If they want to try to improve their scores, they can take the test a second or even a third time.

The SAT covers two areas: English and Math. The English Test consists of two sections: one is Evidence-Based Reading; the other, Writing and Language. In addition, there is an optional essay. Each time you take the SAT, you receive several scores and subscores. On each of the two main areas, English and Math, you receive a score between 200 and 800. You also receive a composite score, a number between 400 and 1600, which is the sum of your two area scores. If you write the optional essay, two readers will evaluate it. Each reader will award a score between 1 and 4 on each of three criteria. Those scores will be added together, so you will receive essay scores between 2 and 8 on each of three domains.

What Types of Questions Are in the Evidence-Based Reading Section?

The evidence-based reading section consists of five long reading passages, with each passage followed by ten or eleven questions. All the questions in this section are multiple-choice questions, with four answer choices. These evidence-based reading questions test your ability to understand what you read—both content and technique. The questions ask about the passage's main idea or specific details, the author's attitude to the subject, the author's logic and techniques, the author's use of evidence to support claims made in the passage, the implications of the discussion, or the meaning of specific words. Some passages are paired: you will be asked to answer two or three questions that compare the viewpoints of two passages on the same subject.

What Types of Questions Are in the Language and Writing Skills Section?

There are 44 questions on the Writing and Language Test of the SAT.

Below is one typical writing and language test format for the new SAT. You should expect to see something similar to this on test day, although likely in a different order:

44-Question Writing and Language Test (35 minutes)

Questions 1–11	career-related topic
Questions 12–22	humanities
Questions 23–33	social studies
Questions 34–44	science

One or two of these will be informative/explanatory texts, one or two of these will be arguments, and one will be a narrative.

One or two passages on your test will be accompanied by an infographic—a table, chart, graph, map, or some combination of graphics.

Of the 44 questions on your test, 24 will be about expression of ideas (improving the quality of the author's message) and 20 will be about standard English conventions (grammar, usage, and mechanics). Eight questions will test your command of evidence (some with the infographics and some based on the text), and 8 questions will test words in context (e.g., determining the correct "fit" given the rhetorical goal). The writing and language questions are in a random order of difficulty.

What About the Essay?

The SAT essay is optional. It asks you to *analyze an argument.* This section comes at the end of the test. The argument will be on a general topic and written for a broad audience—you will not need any background knowledge on the subject to formulate your response. You will have *50 minutes* to respond to a source text and question.

What Types of Questions Are on the Math Sections?

The math part of the SAT has a total of 58 questions divided into two sections, each of which has its own format.

- The 25-minute section, during which calculators may not be used, has 20 questions: 15 multiple-choice questions and 5 grid-in questions.

- The 55-minute section, during which calculators may be used, has 38 questions: 30 multiple-choice questions and 8 grid-in questions.

Multiple-Choice Questions

On the math part of the SAT, 45 of the 58 questions are multiple-choice questions. Although you have certainly taken multiple-choice tests before, the SAT uses a few different types of questions, and you must become familiar with all of them. By far, the most common type of question is one in which you are asked to solve a problem. The straightforward way to answer such a question is to do the necessary work, get the solution, look at the four choices, and choose the one that corresponds to your answer.

Grid-in Questions

On the math part of the SAT, 13 of the 58 questions are what the College Board calls student-produced response questions. Since the answers to these questions are entered on a special grid, they are usually referred to as *grid-in* questions. Except for the method of entering your answer, this type of question is probably the one with which you are most familiar. In your math class, most of your homework problems and test questions require you to determine an answer and write it down, and this is what you will do on the grid-in problems. The only difference is that, once you have figured out an answer, it must be recorded on a special grid so that it can be read by a computer.

How Is the SAT Scored?

First, the machine that grades your SAT will calculate a *raw score* for both parts of the test (English and math). On the SAT every question is worth exactly the same amount: 1 raw score point. A correct answer to a difficult math question on which you may have to spend two or three minutes is worth no more than a correct answer to an easy question that you can answer in a few seconds.

Your raw score on the math part of the SAT, which is the total number of correct answers you have on both math sections, is converted to a *scaled score* between 200 and 800 points. On the English part of the SAT, your raw scores for the reading section and the language and writing section are calculated separately. Each one is then converted to a test score between 10 and 40. Those two scores are added together, yielding a score between 20 and 80, which is then multiplied by 10 to come up with an English score between 200 and 800. Finally, your math and English scaled scores are added together to give you an SAT score between 400 and 1600.

On both the English part and the math part the median score is about 500, meaning that the median SAT score is approximately 1000. How many correct answers (i.e., raw score points) do you need to earn a scaled score of 500 or more? Not as many as you might think. The chart below is an excerpt of an SAT conversion table.

MATH CONVERSION TABLE (MAXIMUM RAW SCORE, 58 POINTS)	
Raw Score	Scaled Score
29	530
28	520
27	510
26	500

On each part of the test, if you earn a raw score of *half* the number of points possible, you will wind up with a scaled score of more than 500. That means that you do *not* have to attempt all, or even most, of the questions on the test to come up with a good score. In fact, unless you are in the top 5 percent of all students, and think that you might score over 700 on one of the parts, you shouldn't even attempt to finish that part. *Working slowly and carefully will undoubtedly earn you higher scores.* If you aren't going to finish a section, take your final 10 seconds to bubble in an answer to every question you don't get to. Be sure to bubble in an answer to every question on the SAT.

How Important Is the SAT?

In addition to your application form, the essays you write, and the letters of recommendation that your teachers and guidance counselor write, colleges receive two important pieces of numerical data. One is your high school transcript, which shows the grades you have earned in all your courses in 3½-*years*. The other is your SAT scores, which show how well you performed in 3 or 4 *hours* one Saturday morning. Which is more important? Your transcript, by far. However, your scores on the SAT definitely do count, and it is precisely because you want your SAT scores to be as high as possible that you purchased this book. If you use this book wisely, you will not be disappointed.

How Can This Book Help You Score High on the SAT?

This book is packed full with review materials, practice exercises, and test-taking strategies. Use them: They'll prepare you to do well on the SAT. The vocabulary list will help boost your word power. Chapter 5 will give you practical advice on essay-writing, advice that will help you not only on the SAT but also on every other essay test you have to take. Chapter 6 will pinpoint the important math facts and formulas you need to know and show you how to handle each type of math question. The dozens of testing tips and strategies will teach you how to make the most of what you learn.

After going through this review and taking the practice tests at the end of the book, you will know exactly what to expect on the SAT. You will be ready to face the test with confidence, knowing you have done your best to prepare yourself.

2 | Tips and Strategies for the SAT

The easiest way to answer a question correctly is to know the answer. If you understand what the author is saying in a paragraph in the reading section, you won't have any trouble choosing the right answer. If you know exactly how to solve a mathematics question and you don't make any mistakes in arithmetic, you won't have any trouble choosing the right answer. But you won't always be absolutely sure of the right answer. Here are some suggestions that may help you. (You'll find specific strategies and tips for each type of question in later chapters of the book.)

GUESSING

The rule is this: if you have worked on a problem, you should be able to eliminate at least one of the choices. This is what is called an *educated* guess. You are not guessing wildly, marking answers at random. You are working on the problem, ruling out answers that make no sense. The more choices you can rule out, the better your chance is of picking the right answer and earning one more point.

You should almost always be able to rule out some answer choices. Most math questions contain at least one or two answer choices that are absurd (for example, negative choices when you know the answer must be positive). In the critical reading section, once you have read a passage, you can always eliminate some of the answer choices. Cross out any choices that you *know* are incorrect, and go for that educated guess.

Of course, if you truly have no idea, make a wild guess. *Whenever you are about to run out of time, quickly guess at all of the remaining questions.*

TIMING

You have only a limited amount of time in which to complete each section of the test, and you don't want to waste any of it. So here are three suggestions.

1. Memorize the directions for each type of question. They appear in the practice tests, later in this book. They present the same information that you will find on the SAT. However, the time you spend reading directions at the actual test is test time. If you don't have to read the directions, you have that much more time to answer the questions.

2. By the time you get to the actual test, you should have a fair idea of how much time to spend on each question. If a question is taking too long, make a guess and go on to the next question. This is no time to try to show the world that you can stick to a job no matter how long it takes.

3. It makes no sense to miss a few questions at the beginning of a section by going too fast, only to have a few more minutes to work on the last few questions in that section. On each of the four sections, it is better to go slower and not finish than to go faster and attempt to answer all the questions and make careless mistakes along the way. *Just be sure to bubble in an answer for every question that you don't get to.*

Unless you expect to score over 700 on one of the parts of the test, if you are attempting all the questions in that part, you are probably going too fast. *You will increase your score by slowing down and attempting fewer questions.*

HOW TO USE THIS BOOK

To help you make the best use of your time before the SAT, we have created two possible study plans to follow. Select the plan that best reflects your situation, and feel free to modify it as necessary.

7-Day Study Plan

With only seven days to go before the SAT, your best bet is to concentrate on working through our practice tests. Use the following schedule:

Day 1

Get a general overview of what to expect by reading the general test-taking strategies in Chapter 2, the pointers on evidence-based reading questions in Chapter 3, and the tips on writing skills multiple-choice questions in Chapter 5. Quickly scan the pointers on essay-writing in Chapter 5 as well. Look over the mathematics tips in Chapter 6, in particular the list of mathematical formulas. Pay particular attention to the formulas you already know: This is not the time to try to master something new.

Day 2

Take Practice Exam 1 under simulated test conditions. Complete the exam in one sitting. Use a clock or timer. Allow precisely 65 minutes each for section 1, 35 minutes for section 2, 25 minutes for section 3, and 55 minutes for section 4. If you are doing the optional essay, take 50 minutes. After each section, give yourself a five-minute break. When you have finished the exam, check your answers against the answer key.

Day 3

Go through the answer explanations for Practice Exam 1, concentrating on the explanations to any questions you answered incorrectly. Refer to the tips in Chapters 3, 5, and 6 as necessary.

Day 4

Based on your performance on Practice Exam 1, decide which area of study you most need to review. Turn to that chapter, reread the introduction and specific tips, and work through the practice exercises that follow. Review your answers.

Day 5

In the essay section in Chapter 5, reread the "Tips to Help You Cope" and the section "Putting it All Together." Take 50 minutes and write a response to one of the sample prompts at the end of the chapter. Check your practice essay against the essay rubric in Chapter 5 to evaluate your performance.

Day 6

Take Practice Exam 2 under simulated test conditions, following the directions given for Day 2. Once again, when you have finished the exam, check your answers against the answer key.

Day 7

Go through the answer explanations for Practice Exam 2, concentrating on the explanations to any questions you answered incorrectly.

30-Day Study Plan

With a full month to go before the SAT, you have plenty of time to review the tips on critical reading, writing, and mathematical reasoning in Chapters 3, 5, and 6, to increase your familiarity with frequently tested vocabulary terms, and to work your way through our practice tests. Use the following schedule:

Day 1

Get a general overview of what to expect by reading the general test-taking strategies in Chapter 2. Pay particular attention to the tips on guessing and timing.

Day 2

Take Practice Exam 1 under simulated test conditions. Complete the exam in one sitting. Use a clock or timer. Allow precisely 65 minutes for section 1, 35 minutes for section 2, 25 minutes for section 3, and 55 minutes for section 4. If you are doing the optional essay, take 50 minutes. After each section, give yourself a five-minute break. When you have finished the exam, check your answers against the answer key.

Day 3

Go through the answer explanations for Practice Exam 1, concentrating on the explanations to any questions you answered incorrectly.

Day 4

Study the first 30 words on the SAT Concise Word List in Chapter 4. Pay special attention to words with multiple meanings and to words that are unfamiliar to you.

Day 5

Read the introduction to the mathematical reasoning sections in Chapter 6, including the guidelines for using a calculator. Review the list of important formulas and key facts, refreshing your memory of concepts you have covered in school.

Day 6

Study the second group of 30 words on the SAT Concise Word List in Chapter 4. Again, pay special attention to words with multiple meanings and to words that are unfamiliar to you.

Day 7

Read the general introduction to the evidence-based reading section in Chapter 3. Then study the specific tips on answering evidence-based reading questions and do Practice Exercise A. Check your answers.

Day 8

Study the third group of 30 words on the SAT Concise Word List in Chapter 4.

Day 9

In Chapter 6, read Mathematical Reasoning Tips 1–5 on working with diagrams. Then review Tips 6–9 on how to improve your speed and accuracy in answering these questions.

Day 10

In Chapter 6, do the Practice Exercises following Tip 9 and review your answers.

Day 11

Study the fourth group of 30 words on the SAT Concise Word List in Chapter 4.

Day 12

Review grammar rules and writing and language tips in Chapter 5.

Day 13

Study the fifth group of 30 words on the SAT Concise Word List in Chapter 4.

Day 14

Work through the practice writing and language exercises in the second half of Chapter 5.

Day 15

In Chapter 5, read the introduction to writing an essay. Review the essay rubric, the first sample essay, and the student response.

Day 16

In Chapter 6, read Mathematical Reasoning Tips 10–14 on answering multiple-choice questions. Then do the Practice Exercises that follow Tip 14 and review your answers.

Day 17

Study the sixth group of 30 words on the SAT Concise Word List in Chapter 4.

Day 18

In the essay section in Chapter 5, read the tips to help you cope and the section "Putting it All Together" to learn about the whole process of writing your essay step by step.

Day 19

Study the seventh group of 30 words on the SAT Concise Word List in Chapter 4.

Day 20

Practice outlining two of the additional prompts for practice in Chapter 5.

Day 21

Study the eighth group of 30 words on the SAT Concise Word List in Chapter 4.

Day 22

In Chapter 5, write a full-length response to one of the additional prompts for practice. Evaluate the quality of your *reading, analysis,* and *writing* based on the essay rubric.

Day 23

In Chapter 6, study Mathematical Reasoning Tips 15–16 on handling grid-in questions. Then do the Practice Exercises that follow Tip 16 and review your answers.

Day 24

In Chapter 3, review the introduction and the specific tips on handling evidence-based reading questions and do Practice Exercises B and C. Check your answers.

Day 25

Study the ninth group of 30 words on the SAT Concise Word List in Chapter 4.

Day 26

Write another full-length essay response to one of the additional prompts for practice in Chapter 6. Evaluate the quality of your *reading, analysis,* and *writing* based on the essay rubric.

Day 27

Study the tenth and final group of words on the SAT Concise Word List in Chapter 4.

Day 28

Take Practice Exam 2 under simulated test conditions. Complete the exam in one sitting. Use a clock or timer. Allow precisely 65 minutes for section 1, 35 minutes for section 2, 25 minutes for section 3, and 55 minutes for section 4. If you are doing the optional essay, take 50 minutes. After each section, give yourself a five-minute break. When you have finished the exam, check your answers against the answer key.

Day 29

Go through the answer explanations for Practice Exam 2, concentrating on the explanations to any questions you answered incorrectly. Refer to the tips in Chapters 3, 5, and 6 as necessary. In Chapter 6, once again review the list of important formulas and key facts, this time concentrating on those concepts that gave you difficulty when you took your practice exams.

Day 30

Follow the instructions below, Before the Test. Do not study. Just relax, knowing you have done a good job preparing yourself to take the SAT.

BEFORE THE TEST

1. If the test location is unfamiliar to you, drive there before the test day so that you will know exactly where you're going on the day you take the test.
2. Set out your test kit the night before. You will need your admission ticket, a photo ID (a driver's license or a non-driver picture ID, a passport, or a school ID), your calculator, four or five sharp No. 2 pencils (with erasers), plus a map or directions showing how to get to the test center.
3. Get a good night's sleep so you are well rested and alert.
4. Wear comfortable clothes. Dress in layers. Bring a sweater in case the room is cold.
5. Bring an accurate watch—not one that beeps—in case the room has no clock. You'll want to use the same watch or small clock that you've been using during your practice sessions.

6. Don't be late. Allow plenty of time for getting to the test site. You want to be in your seat, relaxed, before the test begins.

DURING THE TEST

1. **Do not waste any time reading the directions or looking at the sample problems** at the beginning of every section. You already know all of the rules for answering each question type that appears on the SAT. They will not change.
2. **Pace yourself.** Don't work so fast that you start making careless errors. On the other hand, don't get bogged down on any one question.
3. **Make educated guesses.** If you attempt a question, but aren't sure of the correct answer, eliminate as many choices as possible, and then guess.
4. **Make wild guesses.** If you are running out of time on a section, take your last 10 seconds and quickly guess at all of the remaining questions.
5. **Watch out for eye-catchers,** answer choices that are designed to tempt you into guessing wrong.
6. **Change answers only if you have a reason for doing so;** don't change them on a last-minute hunch or whim.
7. **Check your assumptions.** Make sure you are answering the question asked and not the one you *thought* was going to be asked.
8. **Remember that you are allowed to write in the test booklet.** Use it to do your math computations and to draw diagrams. Underline key words and phrases in the reading passages. Cross out any answer choices you are *sure* are wrong. Circle questions you want to return to.
9. **Check frequently to make sure you are answering the questions in the right spots.**
10. **Remember that you don't have to attempt every question to do well.**

3 | The Evidence-Based Reading Section: Strategies, Tips, and Practice

In this chapter you'll learn how best to handle the different types of evidence-based reading questions on the SAT using strategies and tips that have helped thousands of SAT-takers before you. You'll also find practice exercises for many of these question types. After doing the exercises, you'll feel confident taking the exam because you'll be familiar with the types of questions on it.

⚸ GENERAL TIPS FOR ANSWERING EVIDENCE-BASED READING QUESTIONS

1. When you are answering the evidence-based reading questions, remember that the test is looking for the best answer, the most likely answer. This is not the time to try to show how clever you can be by imagining exotic situations that would justify different answers. If you can imagine a weird situation that would make one of the reading questions correct—forget it! This test is scored by a machine, which has absolutely no imagination or sense of humor; an imaginative answer is a wrong answer. Stick to the most likely answer.

2. Remember also that sprinkled throughout the evidence-based reading sections are easy "vocabulary-in-context" questions. If you get bogged down answering time-consuming questions and forget about the time, you may never get to the easy questions up ahead.

3. Consider secondary meanings of words. If none of the answer choices seem right to you, take another look. A word may have more than one meaning.

THE EVIDENCE-BASED READING TEST

SAT evidence-based reading questions test your ability to understand what you read—both content and technique. Each reading test will contain four single passages and one set of paired passages, for a total of 3,250 words. Each of the single passages or paired sets of passages will be 500–750 words long.

The Reading Test will include:

- One passage from a classic or contemporary work of U.S. or world literature.
- One passage or pair of passages from either a U.S. founding document (Declaration of Independence, Gettysburg Address) or a text in the great global conversation that they inspired or that inspired them (Mary Wollstonecraft's *A Vindication of the Rights of Woman*; speeches by Nelson Mandela, Mahatma Gandhi, and so on).
- One passage or pair of passages about economics, psychology, sociology, or some other social science.
- Two science passages (or one passage and one passage pair) that examine foundational concepts and developments in Earth science, biology, chemistry, or physics.

There will be one or two informational graphics included with one of the history/social sciences passages and with one of the science passages. (Graphics are tables, charts, and graphs that convey information relevant to the content of the passage.)

There will be 52 questions in the reading section, with 10 or 11 questions on each passage or set of paired passages. Ten of these 52 questions will be vocabulary questions (two per passage). Ten more will be command-of-evidence questions (two per passage). All questions will be multiple-choice, with four answer choices.

Vocabulary questions ask you to:

- Use context clues in a passage to figure out which meaning of a word or phrase the author intends.
- Determine how an author's choice of words influences a passage's tone and meaning.

Command of Evidence questions ask you to:

- Find evidence in a passage (or pair of passages) that best supports the answer to a previous question or that functions as the basis upon which you can make a reasonable conclusion.
- Identify how writers use evidence to support the claims they make.
- Find a relationship between an informational graphic and the passage with which it is paired.

The questions that come after each passage are not arranged in order of difficulty. They are arranged to suit the way the passage's content is organized. (A question based on information found at the beginning of the passage generally will come before a question based on information at the passage's end.) If you are stumped by a tough reading question, do not skip the other questions on that passage. A tough question may be just one question away from an easy one.

⚷ TIPS TO HELP YOU COPE

1. When you have a choice, tackle a passage with a familiar subject before one with an unfamiliar one. It is hard to concentrate when you read about something wholly unfamiliar to you. Give yourself a break. When there are several passages in a section, first tackle the one that most interests you or that deals with a topic that you know well.

2. In tackling the reading passages, be flexible in your approach. Students often ask whether it is better to read the passage first or the questions first. The answer is, there is no one true way. It depends on the passage, and *it depends on you*.

   The Questions First Approach

   Read the italicized introduction and the opening sentence of the passage, and then head straight for the questions. As you read a question, be on the lookout for key words, either in the question itself or among the answer choices. Then run your eye down the passage, looking for those key words or their synonyms. When you locate your key word, read that sentence and a couple of sentences around it and see whether you can confidently answer the question based on just that small portion of the passage. If you can't, be flexible: skim the entire passage and choose your answer.

   The Passage First Approach

   Read the entire passage quickly but with understanding and then turn to the questions. You do not have to remember *everything* in the passage; you just need to get a general sense of the points that are being made. Again, be flexible: if you are having trouble reading a passage, turn to the questions before you finish the passage. The wording of the questions may help you understand what the passage is talking about. You can test both approaches as you work through the practice exercises at the end of this chapter. Try some passages tackling the questions one at a time, each time reading the question first before turning to the passage to find the correct answer. Try others reading through the entire passage before you answer the questions. See which approach works better for you.

3. Read as rapidly as you can with understanding, but do not force yourself. Do not worry about the time element. If you worry about not finishing the test, you will begin to take short cuts and miss the correct answer in your haste.

4. Make use of the italicized introductions to acquaint yourself with the text. As you read the italicized introductory material and tackle the passage's opening sentences, try to anticipate what the passage will be about. You'll be in a better position to understand what you read.

5. As you continue reading, try to remember in which part of the passage the author makes major points. In that way, when you start looking for the phrase or sentence which will justify your choice of answer, you will be able to save time by going to that section of the passage immediately rather than having to reread the entire section.

6. When you tackle the questions, <u>go back to the passage</u> to verify your choice of answer. Do not rely on your memory alone.

7. Watch out for words or phrases in the question that can alert you to the kind of question being asked.

   Questions asking for information stated in the passage:
   the author asserts
   according to the passage
   according to the author

   Questions asking you to draw a conclusion:
   it can be inferred
   would most likely
   is best described
   it can be argued
   suggests that
   the author implies
   the author probably considers
   would probably

   Questions asking about the main idea of the passage:
   main point of the passage
   chiefly concerned with
   passage as a whole
   primary purpose

   Questions asking about contextual meaning:
   as used in line 15, . . . most nearly means
   what the author means in saying
   in context, the word/phrase
   in the context of the passage

   Questions asking about the author's use of evidence:
   which choice provides the best evidence

8. When asked to find the main idea, be sure to check the opening and summary sentences of each paragraph. Authors typically provide readers with a sentence that expresses a paragraph's main idea succinctly. Although such <u>topic sentences</u> may appear anywhere in the paragraph, readers customarily look for them in the opening or closing sentences.

9. When asked to make inferences, take as your answer what the passage logically suggests, not what it states directly. Look for clues in the passage; then choose as your answer a statement which is a logical development of the information the author has provided.

10. When asked to determine the questions of attitude or tone, look for words that convey emotion, express values, or paint pictures. These images and descriptive phrases get the author's feelings across.

11. When asked to give the meaning of a word or phrase, look for nearby context clues. Words in the immediate vicinity of the word you are trying to define will often give you a sense of the meaning of the word.

12. Familiarize yourself with the technical terms used to describe a passage's organization. Words like *assertion, hypothesis,* and *generalization* turn up again and again. Be sure you know what they mean.

13. Use the line numbers in the questions to be sure you've gone back to the correct spot in the passage. Fortunately, the lines are numbered in the passages, and the questions often refer you to specific lines in the passage by number. It takes less time to locate a line number than to spot a word or phrase.

14. Try to answer all the questions on a particular passage. Don't let yourself get bogged down on any one question. Skip the one that's got you stumped, but make a point of coming back to it later, after you've answered one or two more questions on the passage. Often, working through other questions on the same passage will provide you with information you can use to answer questions that stumped you the first time around.

15. When dealing with double passages, tackle them one at a time. After reading the lines in italics introducing both passages, read Passage 1; then jump straight to the questions, and answer all those based on Passage 1. Next read Passage 2; then answer all the questions based on Passage 2. Finally, tackle the two or three questions that refer to both passages. Go back to both passages as needed.

16. When dealing with graphic interpretation questions, use only the evidence in the graphic and in the passage. Pay close attention to the graph labels and axes to avoid careless mistakes. Use this system to deal with the graph interpretation questions on the test.

Size Up the Question

Look over the question stem to spot key words or concepts that will help you pinpoint the precise parts of the graph with answers to the question.

Explore the Infographic

Check out the graph, identifying all labels and units of measurement used. Pay special attention to any title provided for the infographic.

Anticipate the Answer

Before looking at the answer choices, see whether you can come up with an answer to the question solely on the basis of what you find in the infographic.

Eliminate Wrong Answers

Go through each answer choice to see whether it is supported by evidence in the infographic or in the passage. For an answer to be correct, it must be supported directly by evidence in the graph or in the passage.

17. Scan all the questions on a passage to spot the command-of-evidence questions coming up. They ask: "Which choice provides the best evidence for the answer to the previous question?" Pay special attention as you answer the question immediately before a command-of-evidence question. If you do it right, you'll be answering two questions, not just one.

PRACTICE EXERCISES

Answers given on page 36.

Each passage below precedes questions based on its content. Answer all questions following a passage based on what that passage <u>states</u> directly or <u>implies</u>.

Exercise A
Short Passages

Try these questions based on short passages in order to familiarize yourself with some common question types.

MAIN IDEA/PURPOSE

Question 1 is based on the following passage.

The passage below is excerpted from Somerset Maugham's The Moon and Sixpence, *first published in 1919.*

The faculty for myth is innate in the human race. It seizes with avidity upon any incidents, surprising or mysterious, in the career of those who have at all distinguished themselves from their fellows, and invents a legend. It is the
Line   protest of romance against the commonplace of life. The incidents of the legend
(5)   become the hero's surest passport to immortality. The ironic philosopher reflects with a smile that Sir Walter Raleigh is more safely enshrined in the memory of mankind because he set his cloak for the Virgin Queen to walk on than because he carried the English name to undiscovered countries.

1. In lines 5–8, the author mentions Sir Walter Raleigh primarily to

    (A) emphasize the importance of Raleigh's voyages of discovery.
    (B) mock Raleigh's behavior in casting down his cloak to protect the queen's feet from the mud.
    (C) illustrate how legendary events outshine historical achievements in the public's mind.
    (D) distinguish between Raleigh the courtier and Raleigh the seafarer.

Question 2 is based on the following passage.

The passage below is excerpted from a text on marine biology.

Consider the humble jellyfish. Headless, spineless, without a heart or brain, it has such a simple exterior that it seems the most primitive of creatures. Unlike its sessile (attached to a surface, as an oyster is attached to its shell)
Line relatives whose stalks cling to seaweed or tropical coral reefs, the free-
(5) swimming jellyfish or medusa drifts along the ocean shore, propelling itself by pulsing, muscular contractions of its bell-shaped body. Yet beneath the simple surface of this aimlessly drifting, supposedly primitive creature is an unusually sophisticated set of genes, as recent studies of the invertebrate phylum Cnidaria (pronounced nih-DARE-ee-uh) reveal.

2. Which assertion about jellyfish is supported by the passage?

    (A) They move at a rapid rate.
    (B) They are lacking in courage.
    (C) They attach themselves to underwater rock formations.
    (D) They are unexpectedly complex.

Question 3 is based on the following passage.

The passage below is excerpted from an article on Florida's Everglades National Park.

Pioneering conservationist Marjory Stoneman Douglas called it the River of Grass. Stretching south from Lake Okeechobee, fed by the rain-drenched Kissimmee River basin, the Everglades is a water marsh, a slow-moving river
Line of swamps and sawgrass flowing southward to the Gulf of Mexico. It is a
(5) unique ecosystem, whose enduring value has come from its being home to countless species of plants and animals: cypress trees and mangroves, wood storks and egrets, snapping turtles and crocodiles. For the past 50 years, however, this river has been shrinking. Never a torrent, it has dwindled as engineering projects have diverted the waters feeding it to meet agricultural
(10) and housing needs.

3. The author of this passage cites the conservationist Marjory Stoneman Douglas in order to

    (A) present a viewpoint.
    (B) challenge an opinion.
    (C) introduce a metaphor.
    (D) correct a misapprehension.

Question 4 is based on the following passage.

The following passage is taken from a brochure for a museum exhibit.

How does an artist train his eye? "First," said Leonardo da Vinci, "learn perspective; then draw from nature." The self-taught eighteenth century painter George Stubbs followed Leonardo's advice. Like Leonardo, he studied
Line anatomy, but, unlike Leonardo, instead of studying human anatomy, he
(5) studied the anatomy of the horse. He dissected carcass after carcass, peeling away the five separate layers of muscles, removing the organs, baring the veins and arteries and nerves. For 18 long months he recorded his observations, and when he was done he could paint horses muscle by muscle, as they had never been painted before. Pretty decent work, for
(10) someone self-taught.

4. The primary purpose of the passage is to

    (A) explain a phenomenon.
    (B) describe a process.
    (C) urge a course of action.
    (D) argue against a practice.

Question 5 is based on the following passage.

The following passage is an excerpt from an article on Lady Mary Wortley Montagu, known best today for her travel writings.

In 1979, when the World Health Organization declared that smallpox had finally been eradicated, few, if any, people recollected the efforts of an eighteenth-century English aristocrat to combat the then-fatal disease. As a
Line young woman, Lady Mary Wortley Montagu had suffered severely from
(5) smallpox. In Turkey, she observed the Eastern custom of inoculating people with a mild form of the pox, thereby immunizing them, a practice she later championed in England. The Turks, she wrote home, even held house parties during which inoculated youngsters played together happily until they came down with the pox, after which they convalesced together.

5. The primary purpose of the passage is to

(A) celebrate the total eradication of smallpox.
(B) challenge the actions of Lady Mary Wortley Montagu.
(C) demonstrate that smallpox was a serious problem in the eighteenth century.
(D) call attention to a neglected historical figure.

VOCABULARY IN CONTEXT

Questions 6 and 7 are based on the following passage.

The passage below is excerpted from Somerset Maugham's The Moon and Sixpence, *first published in 1919.*

The faculty for myth is innate in the human race. It seizes with avidity upon any incidents, surprising or mysterious, in the career of those who have at all distinguished themselves from their fellows, and invents a legend. It is the
Line   protest of romance against the commonplace of life. The incidents of the
(5)   legend become the hero's surest passport to immortality. The ironic philosopher reflects with a smile that Sir Walter Raleigh is more safely enshrined in the memory of mankind because he set his cloak for the Virgin Queen to walk on than because he carried the English name to undiscovered countries.

6. As used in line 1, "faculty" most nearly means

(A) capacity.
(B) authority.
(C) teaching staff.
(D) branch of learning.

7. As used in line 6, "reflects" most nearly means

(A) mirrors.
(B) exhibits.
(C) muses.
(D) casts back.

Question 8 is based on the following passage.

The passage below is excerpted from a text on marine biology.

Consider the humble jellyfish. Headless, spineless, without a heart or brain, it has such a simple exterior that it seems the most primitive of creatures. Unlike its sessile (attached to a surface, as an oyster is attached to its shell)
Line   relatives whose stalks cling to seaweed or tropical coral reefs, the free-
(5)   swimming jellyfish or medusa drifts along the ocean shore, propelling itself by pulsing, muscular contractions of its bell-shaped body. Yet beneath the simple surface of this aimlessly drifting, supposedly primitive creature is an

unusually sophisticated set of genes, as recent studies of the invertebrate phylum Cnidaria (pronounced nih-DARE-ee-uh) reveal.

8. As used in line 8, "sophisticated" most nearly means

(A) worldly.
(B) complex.
(C) suave.
(D) aware.

Questions 9 and 10 are based on the following passage.

The passage below is excerpted from an article on Florida's Everglades National Park.

Pioneering conservationist Marjory Stoneman Douglas called it the River of Grass. Stretching south from Lake Okeechobee, fed by the rain-drenched Kissimmee River basin, the Everglades is a water marsh, a slow-moving river of
Line swamps and sawgrass flowing southward to the Gulf of Mexico. It is a unique
(5) ecosystem, whose enduring value has come from its being home to countless species of plants and animals: cypress trees and mangroves, wood storks and egrets, snapping turtles and crocodiles. For the past 50 years, however, this river has been shrinking. Never a torrent, it has dwindled as engineering projects have diverted the waters feeding it to meet agricultural and housing needs.

9. As used in line 5, "enduring" most nearly means

(A) tolerating.
(B) long-suffering.
(C) hard-won.
(D) lasting.

10. As used in line 9, "meet" most nearly means

(A) encounter.
(B) assemble.
(C) satisfy.
(D) join.

Question 11 is based on the following passage.

The passage below is excerpted from Willa Cather's classic novel My Antonia, *first published in 1918.*

Mrs. Harding was short and square and sturdy-looking, like her house. Every inch of her was charged with an energy that made itself felt the moment she entered a room. Her face was rosy and solid, with bright, twinkling eyes and a
Line stubborn little chin. She was quick to anger, quick to laughter, and jolly from
(5) the depths of her soul. How well I remember her laugh; it had in it the same

sudden recognition that flashed into her eyes, was a burst of humor, short and intelligent. Her rapid footsteps shook her own floors, and she routed lassitude and indifference wherever she came.

11. As used in line 2, "charged with" most nearly means

(A) accused of.

(B) billed for.

(C) entrusted with.

(D) filled with.

Questions 12 and 13 are based on the following passage.

The passage below is taken from Senate History, 1964–Present, June 10, 1964, Civil Rights Filibuster Ended.

At 9:51 on the morning of June 10, 1964, Senator Robert C. Byrd completed an address that he had begun 14 hours and 13 minutes earlier. The subject was the pending Civil Rights Act of 1964, a measure that occupied the Senate for 57 working days, including six Saturdays. A day earlier, Democratic Whip
Line
(5) Hubert Humphrey, the bill's manager, concluded he had the 67 votes required at that time to end the debate.

The Civil Rights Act provided protection of voting rights; banned discrimination in public facilities—including private businesses offering public services—such as lunch counters, hotels, and theaters; and established equal
(10) employment opportunity as the law of the land.

As Senator Byrd took his seat, House members, former senators, and others— 150 of them—vied for limited standing space at the back of the chamber. With all gallery seats taken, hundreds waited outside in hopelessly extended lines.

Georgia Democrat Richard Russell offered the final arguments in opposition.
(15) Minority Leader Everett Dirksen, who had enlisted the Republican votes that made cloture a realistic option, spoke for the proponents with his customary eloquence. Noting that the day marked the 100th anniversary of Abraham Lincoln's nomination to a second term, the Illinois Republican proclaimed, in the words of Victor Hugo, "Stronger than all the armies is an idea whose time
(20) has come." He continued, "The time has come for equality of opportunity in sharing in government, in education, and in employment. It will not be stayed or denied. It is here!"

Never in history had the Senate been able to muster enough votes to cut off a filibuster on a civil rights bill. And only once in the 37 years since 1927 had
(25) it agreed to cloture for any measure.

The clerk proceeded to call the roll. When he reached "Mr. Engle," there was no response. A brain tumor had robbed California's mortally ill Clair Engle of his ability to speak. Slowly lifting a crippled arm, he pointed to his eye, thereby signaling his affirmative vote. Few of those who witnessed this
(30) heroic gesture ever forgot it. When Delaware's John Williams provided the

decisive 67th vote, Majority Leader Mike Mansfield exclaimed, "That's it!" Richard Russell slumped; Hubert Humphrey beamed. With six wavering senators providing a four-vote victory margin, the final tally stood at 71 to 29. Nine days later the Senate approved the act itself—producing one of the 20th
(35) century's towering legislative achievements.

12. As used in line 3, "occupied" most nearly means

(A) inhabited.
(B) engaged.
(C) invaded.
(D) held.

13. As used in line 5, "concluded" most nearly means

(A) finished.
(B) arranged.
(C) stated.
(D) judged.

Question 14 is based on the following passage.

The following passage is excerpted from an article in a natural history journal.

When I found out about the nesting habits of the Marbled Murrelet, I could see why they've become endangered—it's amazing they survive at all. The only places they nest are in old-growth redwoods or Douglas firs within thirty miles of
Line the ocean—although to call it 'nesting' is a bit of a stretch. The female lays an
(5) egg in a depression on a large branch a hundred-fifty feet or more off the ground. And that branch has to be a fair distance below the crown of the tree, so that the egg will be concealed from above, because the eggs and young chicks are especially susceptible to crows, jays, and other predatory birds. Add to this the fact that adult birds mate for life, and don't nest every year, and the odds against
(10) survival seem almost insurmountable. The only way these birds have kept going as a species is because they're extremely secretive. Even the experts almost never actually see them in their nesting habitats. Most 'sightings'—somewhere around ninety-five percent—are from having *heard* them.

14. In line 4, "stretch" most nearly means

(A) expanse.
(B) period.
(C) elasticity.
(D) exaggeration.

Question 15 is based on the following passage.

The following passage is excerpted from Phoenix Fire, *a novel by Tim O'Laughlin.*

Fort Bragg had once been a major fishing town, but the catch was way down from what it had been in the past. Commercial fishing was yet another casualty of unsound forestry practices that had gone unchecked for
Line generations. The problem had resulted from the massive amount of earth-
(5) moving and excavation, not to mention the denuded hillsides the loggers left behind. In the early days of logging, berms of soft earth had been mounded up to provide a soft landing for the huge redwoods, to keep the brittle wood from splintering when they fell. At first, no one had known the effect that the highly erosive logging practices would have on local fisheries—that the
(10) salmon and steelhead population would be decimated, as streams and rivers became warmer from their exposure to the sun, and silt covered the spawning beds. Even after scientists discovered the connection between logging and the decline of the salmon population, the legislature was horrendously slow to act to protect the fishing industry.

15. As used in line 1, "catch" most nearly means a

   (A) concealed drawback.
   (B) quantity of something caught.
   (C) device for securing motion.
   (D) desirable prospect.

Exercise B
Full-Length Passages

Questions 1–10 are based on the following passage.

The following passage is an excerpt from the short story "Clay" in Dubliners *by James Joyce. In this passage, tiny, unmarried Maria oversees tea for the washerwomen, all the while thinking of the treat in store for her: a night off with her younger brother and his family.*

The matron had given her leave to go out as soon as the women's tea was over and Maria looked forward to her evening out. The kitchen was spick and span: the cook said you could see yourself in the big copper boilers. The fire
Line was nice and bright and on one of the side-tables were four very big
(5) barmbracks. These barmbracks seemed uncut; but if you went closer you would see that they had been cut into long thick even slices and were ready to be handed round at tea. Maria had cut them herself.
Maria was a very, very small person indeed but she had a very long nose and a very long chin. She talked a little through her nose, always soothingly:
(10) "Yes, my dear," and "No, my dear." She was always sent for when the women

quarreled over their tubs and always succeeded in making peace. One day
the matron had said to her:

"Maria, you are a veritable peace-maker!"

And the sub-matron and two of the Board ladies had heard the compliment.
(15) And Ginger Mooney was always saying what she wouldn't do to the dummy
who had charge of the irons if it wasn't for Maria. Everyone was so fond of
Maria.

When the cook told her everything was ready, she went into the women's
room and began to pull the big bell. In a few minutes the women began to
(20) come in by twos and threes, wiping their steaming hands in their petticoats and
pulling down the sleeves of their blouses over their red steaming arms. They
settled down before their huge mugs which the cook and the dummy filled up
with hot tea, already mixed with milk and sugar in huge tin cans. Maria
superintended the distribution of the barmbrack and saw that every woman got
(25) her four slices. There was a great deal of laughing and joking during the meal.
Lizzie Fleming said Maria was sure to get the ring and, though Fleming had
said that for so many Hallow Eves, Maria had to laugh and say she didn't want
any ring or man either; and when she laughed her grey-green eyes sparkled
with disappointed shyness and the tip of her nose nearly met the tip of her
(30) chin. Then Ginger Mooney lifted her mug of tea and proposed Maria's health
while all the other women clattered with their mugs on the table, and said she
was sorry she hadn't a sup of porter to drink it in. And Maria laughed again till
the tip of her nose nearly met the tip of her chin and till her minute body nearly
shook itself asunder because she knew that Mooney meant well though, of
(35) course, she had the notions of a common woman.

1. The author's primary purpose in the second paragraph is to

   (A) introduce the character of a spinster.
   (B) describe working conditions in a public institution.
   (C) compare two women of different social classes.
   (D) illustrate the value of peace-makers in society.

2. It can be inferred from the passage that Maria would most likely view the
   matron as which of the following?

   (A) An inept administrator
   (B) A benevolent superior
   (C) A demanding taskmaster
   (D) An intimate friend

3. Which choice provides the best evidence for the answer to the previous
   question?

   (A) Lines 11–13 ("One day . . . peace-maker")
   (B) Line 14 ("And the sub-matron . . . compliment")
   (C) Lines 18–19 ("When the cook . . . bell")
   (D) Lines 23–25 ("Maria superintended . . . slices")

4. It can most reasonably be inferred from the care with which Maria has cut the barmbracks (lines 5–7) that

   (A) she fears the matron.
   (B) she is not in a hurry to leave.
   (C) it is a dangerous task.
   (D) she takes pride in her work.

5. As used in line 16, "charge" most nearly means

   (A) responsibility.
   (B) accusation.
   (C) attack.
   (D) fee.

6. The language of the passage most resembles the language of

   (A) a mystery novel.
   (B) an epic.
   (C) a fairy tale.
   (D) a sermon.

7. Which choice provides the best evidence for the answer to the previous question?

   (A) Lines 2–3 ("The kitchen . . . boilers")
   (B) Lines 8–9 ("Maria . . . chin")
   (C) Lines 19–21 ("In a few . . . arms")
   (D) Lines 30–32 ("Then Ginger . . . drink it in")

8. As used in line 35, "common" most nearly means

   (A) united.
   (B) widespread.
   (C) usual.
   (D) coarse.

9. Which of the following traits least characterizes Maria?

   (A) A deferential nature
   (B) Eagerness for compliments
   (C) Respect for authority
   (D) Reluctance to compromise

10. During the course of the final paragraph, the omniscient narrator's focus shifts from

    (A) evaluation of laundry women's working conditions to reflection on personal disappointments of the main character.

    (B) depiction of an average working day to an explanation of the protagonist's importance to her community.

    (C) portrayal of interactions within a group to description of the main character's reactions to the conversation.

    (D) recounting of a current group activity to a flashback to an earlier scene.

Questions 11–20 are based on the following passage.

This passage is adapted from Frederick E. Hoxie, This Indian Country: American Indian Political Activists and the Place They Made, *published in 2012.*

Sarah Winnemucca spoke out against the morality of American expansion just as federal officials were embarking on a national campaign to "civilize" all American Indians. Of course missionaries had striven to convert and "uplift"
Line
(5) Indian people from the seventeenth century forward, but it was not until the middle of the nineteenth century, when the U.S. conquest of the continent became complete, that federal officials and the general public shifted the bulk of their attention from extending the nation's borders to creating a comprehensive system for incorporating indigenous communities into the nation. They hoped to integrate these individuals into the lower rungs of a modern industrial state.
(10) The centrality of domestic reform to the Indian civilization effort had been apparent even in prewar proposals to establish reservations, but those ideas were given new life after the Civil War by reformers such as Lydia Maria Child, who sought to extend the promise of American civilization from newly freed slaves to Indians. A former abolitionist, Child declared in 1870 that "human
(15) nature is essentially the same in all races and classes of men," adding, "My faith never wavers that men can be made just by being treated justly, honest by being dealt with honestly, and kindly by becoming objects of kindly sympathy." Women like Child and Amelia Stone Quinton, who had taught newly freed African Americans in the South immediately after the Civil War, were at the
(20) forefront of this effort. Their commitment to "all races and classes of men" inspired them to press for Indian schools and Indian citizenship. In 1879 Quinton founded the Women's National Indian Association, a forerunner of the later male-led Indian Rights Association. This activity inspired younger women, such as the anthropologist Alice Cunningham Fletcher and the popular author
(25) Helen Hunt Jackson, to join the effort.

These women saw domestic reform aimed at civilization (education, traditional marriage, and individual landownership) as a solution for Native communities increasingly surrounded by land-hungry whites. Fletcher became an early advocate of replacing reservations with individual landownership and
(30) a firm supporter of the nation's growing network of boarding schools. Helen

Hunt Jackson offered her prescriptions in the form of popular essays and stories. Her most famous effort was a romance set in the Mission Indian communities of southern California. Published in 1884, *Ramona* portrayed the struggle of a Christian Indian woman striving to establish a household for her

(35) pious husband and son. Jackson's account of the heroine Ramona's homemaking in the face of racial hostility and rampant lawlessness echoed the domestic images in Harriet Beecher Stowe's more famous *Uncle Tom's Cabin* and other works that illustrated the nuclear family's ability to protect individuals from hostile outsiders. For Jackson, as for Fletcher and Stowe, a

(40) civilized home managed by a Christian matron could be both a refuge from lawlessness and a vehicle for transporting its members to a better place.

In 1883, with the publication of *Life among the Piutes*, Winnemucca attacked the heart of this national campaign of uplift and domestic reform. As early as 1870, she had argued from her post at Camp McDermitt that the solution to

(45) Indian suffering was "a permanent home on [the Indians'] own native soil." Thirteen years later, in *Life among the Piutes*, she proposed the same solution. Winnemucca's angry words were hurled at a uniform set of self-serving popular attitudes and a rapidly hardening government policy: Indians represented the past, treaties were obsolete, native cultures must yield, and

(50) the incorporation of conventional American domestic behaviors was the surest recipe for civilization. Her speeches and writing, coming from an eloquent, self-confident woman, challenged that mind-set and proposed an alternative scenario in which Indian communities consolidated and progressed on their own within protected enclaves inside America's borders. Rooted in

(55) the story of herself and her family and aimed at establishing "homes to live in" for her community, the book was intended as a public testimonial that would provide a guide for Indian survival that challenged alien definitions of Native private life and civilization. The common thread of her activist career was the dignity of Indian communities and the role within them of powerful

(60) Indian women who upheld the best standards of their tribal traditions.

11. The primary purpose of the passage is to

   (A) explain that reservations are not an ideal way to uplift the Indians.
   (B) show that women share strong bonds, even though they have different backgrounds.
   (C) explain the establishment of the Women's National Indian Association.
   (D) explain one woman's resistance to a major reform movement.

12. It can most reasonably be inferred from the passage that the author would likely agree with the idea that

   (A) American Indians needed to be civilized.
   (B) the majority would inevitably have prevailed.
   (C) women authors helped bring about social and political change.
   (D) women were more effective political advocates than were men.

13. As used in line 21, "press" most nearly means

   (A) flatten.
   (B) weigh heavily.
   (C) urge insistently.
   (D) squeeze affectionately.

14. What view did domestic reformers such as Helen Hunt Jackson promote through novels, essays, and other works?

   (A) Adherence to family structure and gender roles that conformed to the dominant American culture would help Indians integrate into society more effectively.
   (B) Adherence to tribal traditions was necessary to prevent complete assimilation and to force the United States government to honor treaty obligations.
   (C) Human nature manifests itself in the same manner in all races.
   (D) The Mission Indians deserved their own reservation in southern California.

15. Which choice best provides the best evidence for the answer to the previous question?

   (A) Lines 28–30 ("Fletcher . . . schools")
   (B) Lines 30–32 ("Helen Hunt Jackson . . . stories")
   (C) Lines 33–35 ("Published . . . son")
   (D) Lines 39–41 ("For Jackson, . . . to a better place")

16. As used in line 31, "prescriptions" most nearly means

   (A) medicine to be administered.
   (B) changes to be considered.
   (C) punishments to be endured.
   (D) reforms to be instituted.

17. The role played by the Women's National Indian Association with regard to the Indian Rights Association can best be described as

   (A) adversarial.
   (B) concurrent.
   (C) cooperative.
   (D) foundational.

18. Over which major issue did Sarah Winnemucca's views clash with those of the other women reformers?

   (A) The proper form of Indian land ownership
   (B) Use of the term "Indian"
   (C) The importance of literary works in social and political movements
   (D) The role of women in politics

19. *Life among the Piutes* may be most aptly characterized as

    (A) a captivating romance.
    (B) an autobiographical testimonial.
    (C) a moralizing historical novel.
    (D) a traditional Native American legend.

20. According to the passage, what was the major change that occurred in the mid-nineteenth century?

    (A) A change in United States government policy from expansion of territory to consolidation of control over people within that territory
    (B) A change in the focus of reformers from abolition to prohibition
    (C) A change in the focus of reformers from men to women
    (D) A change in Indian policy toward the United States government from cooperation to resistance

Exercise C

The questions that follow the two passages in this section relate to the content of both, and to their relationship. The correct response may be stated outright in the passages or merely suggested.

Questions 1–11 are based on the following passages.

The following passages are excerpted from works that discuss the survival of the city in our time. Passage 1 was written by the literary critic and scholar A. Bartlett Giamatti; Passage 2, by the urban planner and sociologist William H. Whyte.

Passage 1

    When musing on cities over time and in our time, from the first (whenever it was) to today, we must always remember that cities are artifacts. Forests, jungles, deserts, plains, oceans—the organic environment is born and dies
Line
(5)   and is reborn endlessly, beautifully, and completely without moral constraint or ethical control. But cities—despite the metaphors that we apply to them from biology or nature ("The city dies when industry flees"; "The neighborhoods are the vital cells of the urban organism"), despite the sentimental or anthropomorphic devices we use to describe cities—are artificial. Nature has never made a city, and what Nature makes that may
(10) seem like a city—an anthill, for instance—only *seems* like one. It is not a city.
    Human beings made and make cities, and only human beings kill cities, or let them die. And human beings do both—make cities and unmake them—by the same means: by acts of choice. We enjoy deluding ourselves in this as in other things. We enjoy believing that there are forces out there completely
(15) determining our fate, natural forces—or forces so strong and overwhelming as to be like natural forces—that send cities through organic or biological

phases of birth, growth, and decay. We avoid the knowledge that cities are at best works of art, and at worst ungainly artifacts—but never flowers or even weeds—and that we, not some mysterious force or cosmic biological system, (20) control the creation and life of a city.

We control the creation and life of a city by the choices and agreements we make—the basic choice being, for instance, not to live alone, the basic agreement being to live together. When people choose to settle, like the stars, not wander like the moon, they create cities as sites and symbols of (25) their choice to stop and their agreement not to separate. Now stasis and proximity, not movement and distance, define human relationships. Mutual defense, control of a river or harbor, shelter from natural forces—all these and other reasons may lead people to aggregate, but once congregated, they then live differently and become different.

(30) A city is not an extended family. That is a tribe or clan. A city is a collection of disparate families who agree to a fiction: They agree to live *as if* they were as close in blood or ties of kinship as in fact they are in physical proximity. Choosing life in an artifact, people agree to live in a state of similitude. A city is a place where ties of proximity, activity, and self-interest assume the role of (35) family ties. It is a considerable pact, a city. If a family is an expression of continuity through biology, a city is an expression of continuity through will and imagination—through mental choices making artifice, not through physical reproduction.

Passage 2

It is because of this centrality [of the city] that the financial markets have (40) stayed put. It had been widely forecast that they would move out en masse, financial work being among the most quantitative and computerized of functions. A lot of the back-office work has been relocated. The main business, however, is not record keeping and support services; it is people sizing up other people, and the center is the place for that.

(45) The problems, of course, are immense. To be an optimist about the city, one must believe that it will lurch from crisis to crisis but somehow survive. Utopia is nowhere in sight and probably never will be. The city is too mixed up for that. Its strengths and its ills are inextricably bound together. The same concentration that makes the center efficient is the cause of its crowding and (50) the destruction of its sun and its light and its scale. Many of the city's problems, furthermore, are external in origin—for example, the cruel demographics of peripheral growth, which are difficult enough to forecast, let alone do anything about.

What has been taking place is a brutal simplification. The city has been (55) losing those functions for which it is no longer competitive. Manufacturing has moved toward the periphery; the back offices are on the way. The computers are already there. But as the city has been losing functions it has been reasserting its most ancient one: a place where people come together, face-to-face.

(60)   More than ever, the center is the place for news and gossip, for the creation of ideas, for marketing them and swiping them, for hatching deals, for starting parades. This is the stuff of the public life of the city—by no means wholly admirable, often abrasive, noisy, contentious, without apparent purpose.

But this human congress is the genius of the place, its reason for being, its
(65)   great marginal edge. This is the engine, the city's true export. Whatever makes this congress easier, more spontaneous, more enjoyable is not at all a frill. It is the heart of the center of the city.

1. The author's purpose in Passage 1 is primarily to

    (A) identify the sources of popular discontent with cities.
    (B) define the city as growing out of a social contract.
    (C) illustrate the difference between cities and villages.
    (D) compare cities with blood families.

2. The author cites the sentence "The neighborhoods are the vital cells of the urban organism" (lines 6–7) as

    (A) a paradox with ironic implications.
    (B) a straightforward statement of scientific fact.
    (C) a momentary digression from his central thesis.
    (D) an example of one type of figurative language.

3. The author's attitude toward the statements quoted in lines 6–7 is

    (A) approving.
    (B) ambivalent.
    (C) pragmatic.
    (D) skeptical.

4. According to the author of Passage 1, why is an ant hill by definition unlike a city?

    (A) It can be casually destroyed by human beings.
    (B) It exists on a far smaller scale than any city does.
    (C) It is the figurative equivalent of a municipality.
    (D) It is a work of instinct rather than of imagination.

5. Mutual defense, control of waterways, and shelter from the forces of nature (lines 26–27) are presented primarily as examples of motives for people to

    (A) move away from their enemies.
    (B) build up their supplies of armaments.
    (C) gather together in settlements.
    (D) redefine their family relationships.

6. As used in line 25, "stop" most nearly means

    (A) bring to an end.
    (B) come to a halt.
    (C) prevent.
    (D) cease.

7. By saying a city "is a considerable pact" (line 35), the author primarily stresses its

    (A) essential significance.
    (B) speculative nature.
    (C) moral constraints.
    (D) surprising growth.

8. Underlying the forecast mentioned in lines 40–42 is the assumption that

    (A) the financial markets are similar to the city in their need for quantitative data.
    (B) computerized tasks such as record keeping can easily be performed at remote sites.
    (C) the urban environment is inappropriate for the proper performance of financial calculations.
    (D) either the markets would all move or none of them would relocate.

9. As used in line 50, "scale" most nearly means

    (A) series of musical tones.
    (B) measuring instrument.
    (C) relative dimensions.
    (D) thin outer layer.

10. The author of Passage 2 differs from the author of Passage 1 in that he

    (A) disapproves of relocating support services to the city's outskirts.
    (B) has no patience with the harshness inherent in public life.
    (C) believes that in the long run the city as we know it will not survive.
    (D) is more outspoken about the city's difficulties.

11. Compared to Passage 1, Passage 2 is

    (A) more lyrical and less pragmatic.
    (B) more impersonal and less colloquial.
    (C) more objective and less philosophical.
    (D) more practical and less detached.

Answer Key

Exercise A

1. C	5. D	9. D	13. D
2. D	6. A	10. C	14. D
3. C	7. C	11. D	15. B
4. C	8. B	12. B	

Exercise B

1. A	6. C	11. D	16. D
2. B	7. B	12. C	17. D
3. A	8. D	13. C	18. A
4. D	9. D	14. A	19. B
5. A	10. C	15. D	20. A

Exercise C

1. B	4. D	7. A	10. D
2. D	5. C	8. B	11. C
3. D	6. B	9. C	

Answer Explanations

Exercise A

Short Passages

1. **(C)**

The fact that Raleigh is remembered more for a romantic, perhaps apocryphal, gesture than for his voyages of exploration *illustrates how legendary events outshine historical achievements in the public's mind.*

2. **(D)**

The final sentence of the passage maintains that, contrary to expectation, the jellyfish has a sophisticated or *complex* genetic structure. Beware of eye-catchers. Choice (B) is incorrect. "Spineless" (line 1) here means invertebrate, lacking a backbone or spinal column. It does not mean lacking in courage or cowardly.

3. **(C)**

The author refers to Douglas in order to introduce Douglas's metaphoric description of the Everglades as the "River of Grass."

4. **(C)**

The author is describing the process by which Stubbs taught himself to draw horses.

5. **(D)**

The opening sentence of the passage states that few, if any, people recalled Lady Mary's effort to fight smallpox. Her efforts have largely been forgotten. Thus, the purpose of the passage is to *call attention to a neglected historical figure.*

6. **(A)**

The human faculty for myth is the *capacity* or ability of people to invent legends.

7. **(C)**

An ironic philosopher (someone who looks on the world with wry or amused detachment) might well reflect or *muse* about the irony of Raleigh's being remembered more for his romantic gesture than for his grueling voyages.

8. **(B)**

The final sentence of the passage maintains that, contrary to expectation, the jellyfish has a sophisticated or *complex* genetic structure. Note the use of "Yet" here. It is a contrast signal, alerting you to be on the lookout for an antonym. The jellyfish has a simple surface, but that simple surface conceals an unusually *complex* set of genes.

9. **(D)**

Enduring value is value that *lasts*. The *lasting* value of the Everglades is that it provides a habitat for endangered species.

10. **(C)**

The engineering projects have diverted water away from the Everglades in order to meet or *satisfy* the water needs of Florida's farms and housing developments.

11. **(D)**

In saying that "Every inch of [Mrs. Harding] was charged with an energy that made itself felt the moment she entered a room," the author is asserting that Mrs. Harding's body was *filled with* this extraordinarily vital energy. Although "charged" can mean *accused* ("charged with murder"), *billed* ("charged for shipping"), or *entrusted* ("charged with the task"), that is not how it is used here.

12. (B)

The Civil Rights Act of 1964 was a law or measure that had *engaged* the senators (that is, kept them busy) for nearly two whole months. Although "occupied" can mean *inhabited* ("occupied an apartment"), *invaded* ("Nazis occupied Poland"), or *held* ("occupied a top position"), that is not how it is used here.

13. (D)

Humphrey came to the conclusion or *judged* that the measure's supporters had enough votes that it would pass. Although "concluded" can mean *finished* ("the lecture concluded"), *arranged* ("they concluded a ceasefire"), or *stated* ("'That's all, Folks,' Porky Pig concluded"), that is not how it is used here.

14. (D)

The author is emphasizing the implausibility of describing the location in which these birds lay their eggs as a proper nest. When birds nest, they find or make a secluded, safe place where they can shelter their young. The Marbled Murrelet's nesting place, however, is not particularly safe. To call what they do "nesting," therefore, is something of an *exaggeration*, stretching the definition beyond its reasonable limits. Although "stretch" can mean *expanse* ("a bumpy stretch of road"), *period* ("long stretches of time"), or *elasticity* ("the rubber band lost its stretch"), that is not how it is used here.

15. (B)

Note that the passage opens with the statement that "Fort Bragg had once been a major fishing town." The catch referred to is the *quantity of* fish *caught* by the local fishermen. Although "catch" can mean a *concealed drawback* ("Watch out, there's a catch in it!"), *device for securing motion* ("Fasten the window catch"), or *desirable prospect* ("Prince William was quite a catch!"), that is not how it is used here.

Exercise B

Full-Length Passages

1. (A)

Throughout the second paragraph, the author pays particular attention to Maria's appearance, her behavior, and her effect on others. If she had been *introduced* previously in the text, there would be no need to present these details about her at this point in the passage.

2. (B)

The passage mentions the matron twice: once, in the opening line, where she gives Maria permission to leave work early; once, in lines 11–13, where she pays Maria a compliment. Given this context, we can logically infer that Maria views the matron positively, finding her a *benevolent* or kindly *supervisor*. Choices (A) and (C) are incorrect. Nothing in the passage suggests Maria has a negative view of the matron. Choice (D) is incorrect. Given Maria's relatively menial position, it is unlikely she and the matron would be close or intimate friends.

3. **(A)**

In this sentence, the matron, Maria's supervisor at her place of employment, pays Maria a compliment, calling her a peacemaker. Maria appears to cherish this compliment. Thus, it seems likely that she would regard the matron as *a benevolent superior*.

4. **(D)**

To slice loaves so neatly and invisibly takes a great deal of care. The author specifically states that Maria has cut the loaves. Not only that, he emphasizes the importance of her having done so by placing this statement at the end of the paragraph (a key position). As the subsequent paragraphs point up, Maria is hungry for compliments. Just as she takes pride in her peacemaking, she takes pride in her ability to slice barmbracks evenly.

5. **(A)**

To have charge of the irons is to have the *responsibility* for looking after them. Although "charge" can mean *accusation* ("a charge of murder"), *attack* ("Charge!"), or *fee* ("a charge for admission"), that is not how it is used here.

6. **(C)**

The descriptions of the bright and shiny kitchen where you "could see yourself in the big copper boilers" and of tiny, witch-like Maria with her long nose and long chin belong to the realm of the fairy tale.

7. **(B)**

With her pointy nose that almost touches her pointy chin, Maria resembles a creature straight out of a fairy tale. Thus, this physical description provides the best evidence to support the answer to the previous question.

8. **(D)**

From Maria's perspective, Mooney is a common woman: she is *coarse* and vulgar, liking a glass of porter (dark brown bitter beer, originally made as a drink for luggage-handlers) and drinking her tea out of a mug rather than a teacup. Although common can mean *united* ("a common defense"), *widespread* ("common knowledge"), or *usual* ("a common mistake"), that is not how it is used here.

9. **(D)**

Although the passage indicates that Maria has helped others to compromise or become reconciled, nothing in the passage suggests that she herself is reluctant or unwilling to compromise. In fact, given her respect for authority, willingness to compromise might well be a trait that characterizes her.

Use the process of elimination to answer this question. The passage suggests that choice (A), *a deferential nature*, characterizes Maria. It depicts Maria speaking soothingly and respectfully, paying special attention to her superior's words. Therefore, choice (A) is incorrect. The passage suggests that choice (B), *eagerness for compliments*, characterizes Maria. Maria's pleasure that the sub-matron and Board ladies had heard the matron's compliment shows how greatly she values any complimentary notice that comes her way. Therefore, choice (B) is incorrect. The passage suggests that choice (C), *respect for authority*, characterizes Maria. Maria's obedience to the cook and her deference to the matron show her respect for authority. Therefore, choice (C) is incorrect.

Clearly, of the choices given, choice (D), *reluctance to compromise*, least characterizes Maria.

10. **(C)**

The final paragraph begins with the workers gathering for their tea. They settle down, they laugh and joke and tease Maria, who has served the sliced fruit bread. This is a *portrayal of interactions within a group*. It is followed by an account of how Maria feels about being teased and of what she thinks about Ginger Mooney, who has proposed a toast to her health. Thus, during the course of the final paragraph, the narrator's focus shifts from *portrayal of interactions within a group* to *description of main character's reactions to the conversation*.

11. **(D)**

The passage focuses on the political activism of Sarah Winnemucca against the background of a national campaign to "civilize" all American Indians, showing that she rejected many of the assumptions adopted by other reformers of the day, including women reformers such as Lydia Maria Child, Amelia Stone Quinton, Alice Cunningham Fletcher, and Helen Hunt Jackson. Choice (D) is the best answer.

Choice (A) is incorrect because it contradicts Sarah Winnemucca's view. According to the other reformers portrayed in the account, the best way to incorporate American Indians into society was through promotion of private property, the nuclear family, and cultural assimilation. Winnemucca, in contrast, felt that the United States government should honor its treaty obligations with the Indians and accord to them collective control over their own lands in protected reservations. Choice (B) conveys an idea that was one of the main assumptions of the women reformers but is not a main point of the passage. Choice (C) refers to one political accomplishment of the women reformers whose methods and goals Winnemucca criticized.

12. **(C)**

The passage addresses two groups of influential reformers who were concerned about the welfare of American Indians and their place in the United States of the late nineteenth century and whose writings helped bring about needed social and political change: on the one hand, concerned non-American Indian women such as Lydia Maria Child, Amelia Stone Quinton, Alice Cunningham Fletcher, and Helen Hunt Jackson, and on the other hand, the American Indian woman activist Sarah Winnemucca. Choice (C) is the best answer.

Choice (A) is incorrect because the passage suggests that some of the efforts to "civilize" American Indians were detrimental to them and were opposed by Winnemucca, with whose views the author generally agrees. Choice (B) is outside the scope of the passage; however, the fact that individual reformers were able to shape subsequent history suggests that no one result was inevitable. Choice (D) cannot be the correct answer because the passage, while it focuses on the effective political action of women, makes no comparison of their effectiveness with that of men.

13. **(C)**

To press for Indian schools and Indian citizenship is to *urge insistently* that schools for Indians should be founded and that Indians should be granted their full rights as citizens of the United States. Choices (A), (B), and (D) are incorrect. Although press can mean *flatten* ("she pressed her slacks"), *weigh heavily* ("the heavy yoke pressed down on his shoulders"), or *squeeze affectionately* ("she pressed his hand"), that is not how it is used here.

14. **(A)**

According to the passage, domestic reform formed an important part of efforts to civilize the American Indians, and women reformers such as Alice Cunningham Fletcher and Helen Hunt Jackson advocated the adoption of traditional norms, institutions, social roles prescribed by "American civilization," including monogamy and the nuclear family, on the part of native Americans. Choice (A) is the best answer. Choice (B) is incorrect because it represents the views of Winnemucca as opposed to those of

Fletcher and Jackson. Choice (C) represents the views attributed to Lydia Maria Child and Amelia Stone Quinton in paragraph 2. Fletcher and Jackson may have shared these views, but that is not the focus of paragraph 3, which treats Jackson's writings. Choice (D) is incorrect because Jackson and other similar reformers favored private land ownership over the establishment of reservations.

15. **(D)**

Choice (D) states explicitly the ideas conveyed by Jackson in her works regarding the prescribed roles she thought American Indian women should play. Choice (A) is incorrect because it focuses on Fletcher rather than Jackson and on schools rather than writings. Choice (B) is incorrect because it merely reports that Hunt conveyed her ideas through essays and literary works. Choice (C) is not as good an answer as choice (D) because it describes the overall plot of the 1884 novel *Ramona* without presenting the specific points that it conveys.

16. **(D)**

The prescriptions in question are the recommendations that Helen Hunt Jackson provides for domestic *reform* of the Native communities. The best answer is choice (D). Choice (A) is incorrect because, as used in the passage, "prescriptions" have nothing to do with medicine, but rather are "prescribed courses of action." Choice (B) is incorrect because the changes in question are not options suggested for consideration but rather directives that are presented as obligatory. Choice (C) is incorrect because the idea of punishment does not appear in the context.

17. **(D)**

The Women's National Indian Association is described as the forerunner of the Indian Rights Association, suggesting that there is a causal link between the two: the former organization led up to, or contributed to, the founding of the latter. The adjective "foundational" conveys that causal connection, for it means that the Women's National Indian Association laid the foundation or provided the basis for the Indian Rights Association. Choice (D) is the best answer. Choices (A), (B), and (C) are all incorrect because they do not capture the chronological order and causal connection between the two organizations.

18. **(A)**

Choice (A) is the best answer. There are several issues regarding which of Sarah Winnemucca's views clashed with those of the other women reformers mentioned, but the only one that appears in the answer choices is the question of *Indian land ownership*. The women reformers advocated private land ownership, whereas Winnemucca advocated Indian sovereignty and collective ownership of large territories, in accordance with treaties the United States government had concluded with various Native American nations. Choice (B) is incorrect because the passage never discusses the use of the term "Indian." Choice (C) is incorrect. Given that Winnemucca and the other women reformers both wrote influential works promoting their social and political agenda, they evidently shared a belief in the importance of literary works in social and political movements. Winnemucca and the other woman reformers would also have agreed that women should play an active role in politics; thus, choice (D) also is incorrect.

19. **(B)**

Choice (B) is the best answer. *Life among the Piutes* has *autobiographical* elements, for it draws on Sarah Winnemucca's experience of growing up among her people under rapidly changing circumstances. It is also a *testimonial*, for it reports events of the past as she witnessed them firsthand and is meant to serve as evidence of the injustices that were done to the Piutes and other American Indians.

20. **(A)**

The opening paragraph makes clear that United States government policy shifted in the mid-nineteenth century. After the United States extended control over a large part of the North American continent and secured the borders, both government officials and the American public devoted their efforts to the incorporation of Native American communities into the nation. Choice (A) is the best answer.

Choice (B) must be incorrect because the passage does not mention prohibition, though it does mention abolition. Choice (C) is incorrect because, although the passage does mention men and women, it maintains a focus on women and does not mention any shift in focus from men to women. Choice (D) is incorrect because the passage does not focus on the policy of American Indians toward the United States government. Furthermore, all American Indians did not uniformly cooperate with the United States government prior to the mid-nineteenth century and then shift to resistance afterward.

Exercise C

1. **(B)**

Throughout Passage 1 the author reiterates that human beings make cities, that the creation of a city is an act of choice, that a city is the result of an agreement or pact. In all these ways, he *defines the city as growing out of a social contract* by which human beings choose to bind themselves.

2. **(D)**

The sentences quoted within the parenthesis are illustrations of the sort of metaphors we use in describing cities. Thus, they are examples *of one type of figurative language*.

3. **(D)**

Insisting that cities are not natural but artificial, the author rejects these metaphors as inaccurate. His attitude toward the statements he quotes is clearly *skeptical* (disbelieving).

4. **(D)**

An ant hill is the work of insects rather than of human beings. *It is a work of instinct rather than of imagination*, human intelligence, and choice; therefore, by the author's definition, it is not like a city.

5. **(C)**

The author cites these factors as "reasons (that) may lead people to aggregate" or *gather together in settlements*.

6. **(B)**

Look at the entire sentence in which "stop" appears. "When people choose to settle, like the stars, not wander like the moon, they create cities as sites and symbols of their choice to stop and their agreement not to separate." The nomads' choice to stop is their choice to cease wandering and settle down. In other words, they have chosen to *come to a halt* and put down roots. Choices (A), (C), and (D) are incorrect. Although stop can mean *bring to an end* ("Stop this racket!"), *prevent* ("Stop accidents before they happen"), or *cease* ("The rain stopped"), that is not how it is used here.

7. **(A)**

The author clearly is impressed by the magnitude of the choice people make when they agree to live as if mere geographical links, "ties of proximity," can be as strong as blood relationships. In proclaiming a city "a considerable pact," he stresses the *essential significance* or weightiness of this agreement.

8. **(B)**

One would predict such a mass exodus of financial firms only if one assumed that the firms could do their work just as well at distant locations as they could in the city. Thus, the basic assumption underlying the forecast is that *computerized tasks such as record keeping* (the major task of most financial institutions) *can easily be performed at remote sites*.

9. **(C)**

The city's concentration of people necessitates the enormous size of its buildings. These outsized buildings destroy the scale or *relative dimensions* of the city as originally envisioned by its planners. Choices (A), (B), and (D) are incorrect. Although scale can mean a *series of musical tones* ("practicing piano scales"), a *measuring instrument* ("postage scale"), or a *thin outer layer* ("snake scales"), that is not how it is used here.

10. **(D)**

The author of Passage 1 talks in terms of abstractions that keep people dwelling together in cities (the city as pact, the city as an expression of will and imagination); the author of Passage 2 openly mentions the concrete ills that threaten the city: overcrowding, overbuilding of outsized skyscrapers that block the sun, loss of businesses to the suburbs (with the attendant loss of tax revenues). Given his perspective as an urban planner and sociologist, he is inevitably moved to talk *about the city's difficulties.*

11. **(C)**

The author of Passage 1 muses about the nature of the city, defining it and dwelling on its significance. He is *philosophical.* Without romanticizing the city, the author of Passage 2 discusses both its strengths and weaknesses. Though he emphasizes the importance of the city, he tries to be impartial or *objective.* Compared to Passage 1, Passage 2 is *more objective and less philosophical.*

Building Your Vocabulary

4

Recognizing the meaning of words is essential to comprehending what you read. The more you stumble over unfamiliar words in a text, the more you have to take time out to look up words in your dictionary, the more likely you are to wind up losing track of what the author has to say.

To succeed in college, you must develop a college-level vocabulary. The time you put in now learning vocabulary-building techniques for the SAT will pay off later, and not just on the day of the test. In this chapter you will find a fundamental tool that will help you build your vocabulary: Barron's SAT Concise Word List.

No matter how little time you have before you take the SAT, you can familiarize yourself with the sort of vocabulary you will be facing on the test. Look over the words on our SAT Concise Word List. These words range from everyday ones like *abstract* and *innovation* to less commonly known ones like *anomaly* and *viability*. Many of them have appeared in reading passages or as question words on recently released copies of the new SAT.

Not only will looking over the SAT Concise Word List reassure you that you *do* know some SAT-type words, but also it may well help you on the actual day of the test. These words have turned up on recently released tests; some of them may turn up on the test you take.

For those of you who intend to work your way through the *entire* SAT Concise Word List and feel the need for a plan, we recommend that you follow the procedures described below in order to use the list most profitably:

1. Divide the list into groups of twenty words.
2. Allot a definite time each day for the study of a group.
3. Devote at least one hour to each group.
4. First go through the group looking at the short, simple-looking words (6 letters at most). Mark those you don't know. In studying, pay particular attention to them.
5. Go through the group again looking at the longer words. Pay particular attention to words with more than one meaning and familiar-looking words which have unusual definitions that come as a surprise to you. Study these secondary definitions.

6. List unusual words on index cards that you can shuffle and review from time to time. (Study no more than 5 cards at a time.)
7. Use the illustrative sentences as models and make up new sentences of your own.
8. In making up new sentences, use familiar examples and be concrete: the junior high school band tuning up sounds *discordant*, the wicked queen in "Snow White" is *malicious*.

For each word, the following is provided:

1. The word (printed in heavy type).
2. Its part of speech (abbreviated).
3. A brief definition.
4. A sentence illustrating the word's use.
5. Whenever appropriate, related words are provided, together with their parts of speech.

The word list is arranged in strict alphabetical order.

SAT CONCISE WORD LIST

A

abridge V. condense or shorten. Because the publishers felt the public wanted a shorter version of *War and Peace*, they proceeded to *abridge* the novel.

abstract ADJ. theoretical; not concrete; nonrepresentational. To him, hunger was an *abstract* concept; he had never missed a meal.

abstruse ADJ. obscure; profound; difficult to understand. Baffled by the *abstruse* philosophical texts assigned in class, Dave asked Lexy to explain Kant's *Critique of Pure Reason*.

academic ADJ. related to education; not practical or directly useful. When Sharon applied for the faculty position, the department head inquired about her *academic* qualifications. Seismologists' studies about earthquakes are not of purely *academic* interest, for seismology is the major tool for assessing the danger of potential earthquakes.

accessible ADJ. easy to approach; obtainable. We asked our guide whether the ruins were *accessible* on foot.

acclaim V. applaud; announce with great approval. The NBC sportscasters *acclaimed* every American victory in the Olympics and decried every American defeat. also N.

accommodate V. oblige or help someone; provide with housing; adapt to. Mitch always tried to *accommodate* his elderly relatives. When they visited New

York, he would *accommodate* them in his small apartment. His home felt cramped, but he did his best to *accommodate* himself to the situation.

acknowledge V. recognize; admit. Although I *acknowledge* that the Beatles' tunes sound pretty dated today, I still prefer them to the "gangsta rap" songs my brothers play.

adopt V. legally take a child as one's own; choose to follow an approach or idea; assume a position or attitude; formally accept (a suggestion or report). Tom *adopted* a daughter, who told him about a new weight-loss plan that her foster mother had *adopted*. In response, Tom *adopted* a patronizing tone, saying that fad diets never worked. Was the committee's report *adopted* unanimously, or did anyone abstain?

adversary N. opponent. The young wrestler struggled to defeat his *adversary*. adversarial, ADJ.

adversity N. misfortune; distress. In *Up from Slavery*, young Booker T. Washington shows courage and perseverance in his struggles with *adversity*.

advocate V. urge; plead for. The abolitionists *advocated* freedom for the slaves. also N.

aesthetic ADJ. artistic; dealing with or capable of appreciation of the beautiful. The beauty of Tiffany's stained glass appealed to Alice's *aesthetic* sense. aesthete, N.

affirmation N. positive assertion; confirmation; solemn pledge by one who refuses to take an oath. Despite Tom's *affirmations* of innocence, Aunt Polly still suspected he had eaten the pie.

alleviate V. relieve. This should *alleviate* the pain; if it does not, we shall have to use stronger drugs.

aloof ADJ. apart; reserved. Shy by nature, she remained *aloof* while all the rest conversed.

altercation N. heated dispute or quarrel. In that hot-tempered household, no meal ever ended peacefully; the inevitable *altercation* might even end in blows.

altruistic ADJ. unselfishly generous; concerned for others. In providing tutorial assistance and college scholarships for hundreds of economically disadvantaged youths, Eugene Lang performed a truly *altruistic* deed. altruism, N.

ambiguous ADJ. unclear or doubtful in meaning. His *ambiguous* instructions misled us; we did not know which road to take. ambiguity, N.

ambivalence N. the state of having contradictory or conflicting emotional attitudes. Torn between loving her parents one minute and hating them the next, she was confused by the *ambivalence* of her feelings. ambiv-alent, ADJ.

analogous ADJ. comparable. Some feminists contend that a woman's need for a man is *analogous* to a fish's need for a bicycle. analogy, N.

anecdote N. short account of an amusing or interesting event. At the wedding rehearsal dinner, the best man embarrassed the groom by telling *anecdotes* about their undergraduate escapades.

animosity N. active enmity; ill will. The recent killings on the West Bank have sharpened the longstanding *animosity* between the Palestinians and the Israelis.

antagonism N. hostility; active resistance. Barry showed *antagonism* toward his new stepmother by ignoring her whenever she tried talking to him. antag-onistic, ADJ.

antipathy N. dislike; aversion. Tom's extreme *antipathy* for quarreling keeps him from getting into arguments with his hot-tempered wife.

antithesis N. direct opposite to. Stagnation is the *antithesis* of growth.

apathy N. lack of caring; indifference. A firm believer in democratic govern-ment, she could not understand the *apathy* of people who never bothered to vote. apathetic, ADJ.

application N. request; act of putting something to use; diligent attention; relevance. Jill submitted her scholarship *application* to the financial aid office. Martha's research project is purely academic; it has no practical *application*. Pleased with how well Tom had whitewashed the fence, Aunt Polly praised him for his *application* to the task. Unfortunately, John's experience in book publishing had little or no *application* to the e-publish-ing industry.

apprehension N. fear of future evil; understanding; arrest (of a criminal). Despite the *apprehension* many people feel about black bears, these bears are generally more afraid of humans than humans are of them. Our *appre-hension* of the present inevitably is based upon our understanding of the past. Inspector Javert's lifelong ambition was to bring about the *apprehen-sion* and imprisonment of Jean Valjean.

arbitrary ADJ. unreasonable or capricious; randomly selected without any reason; based solely on one's unrestricted will or judgment. The coach claimed the team lost because the umpire made some *arbitrary* calls.

arrogance N. pride; haughtiness. Convinced that Emma thought she was better than anyone else in the class, Ed rebuked her for her *arrogance*.

articulate ADJ. effective; distinct. Her *articulate* presentation of the advertising campaign impressed her employers. also V.

artifact N. object made by human beings, either handmade or mass-produced. Archaeologists debated the significance of the *artifacts* discovered in the ruins of Asia Minor but came to no conclusion about the culture they represented.

aspire V. seek to attain; long for. Because he *aspired* to a career in professional sports, Philip enrolled in a graduate program in sports management. aspiration, N.

astute ADJ. wise; shrewd; keen. The painter was an *astute* observer, noticing every tiny detail of her model's appearance and knowing the exact importance of each one.

attribute V. ascribe; explain. I *attribute* her success in science to the encouragement she received from her parents.

augment V. increase; add to. Armies *augment* their forces by calling up reinforcements; teachers *augment* their salaries by taking odd jobs.

authoritarian ADJ. favoring or exercising total control; nondemocratic. The people had no control over their own destiny; they were forced to obey the dictates of the *authoritarian* regime. also N.

autonomous ADJ. self-governing. Although the University of California at Berkeley is just one part of the state university system, in many ways Cal Berkeley is *autonomous*, for it runs several programs that are not subject to outside control. autonomy, N.

aversion N. firm dislike. Bert had an *aversion* to yuppies; Alex had an *aversion* to punks. Their mutual *aversion* was so great that they refused to speak to one another.

B

belie V. contradict; give a false impression. His coarse, hard-bitten exterior *belied* his inner sensitivity.

benevolent ADJ. generous; charitable. Mr. Fezziwig was a *benevolent* employer who wished to make Christmas merrier for young Scrooge and his other employees. benevolence, N.

bolster V. support; reinforce. The debaters amassed file boxes full of evidence to *bolster* their arguments.

brevity N. conciseness. *Brevity* is essential when placing a phone call from an airplane; you are charged for every minute.

C

calculated ADJ. deliberately planned; likely. Lexy's choice of clothes to wear to the debate tournament was carefully *calculated*. Her conventional suit was *calculated* to appeal to the conservative judges.

candor N. frankness; open honesty. Jack can carry *candor* too far: when he told Jill his honest opinion of her, she nearly slapped his face. candid, ADJ.

capacity N. greatest amount or number that something can hold; amount that something can produce; power to understand or to perform; specified role or position. This thermos container has a one-liter *capacity*. Management has come up with a plan to double the factory's automobile production *capacity*. I wish I had the mental *capacity* to understand Einstein's theory of relativity. Rima traveled to Japan in her *capacity* as director of the Country Dance & Song Society.

capricious ADJ. fickle; incalculable. The storm was *capricious* and changed course constantly.

catholic ADJ. wide-ranging in interests. Her musical tastes are surprisingly *catholic*: she enjoys everything from the Anonymous Four to Lady Gaga.

censorious ADJ. critical. *Censorious* people delight in casting blame.

censure V. blame; criticize. The senator was *censured* for behavior inappropriate to a member of Congress. also N.

charismatic ADJ. compellingly charming; magnetic. The late Steve Jobs, former CEO of Apple, who commanded a rock-star-like following, was more than once called "the model of a *charismatic* leader."

cite V. refer to or quote, especially to justify a position; praise; summon someone before a court. When asked to support her position on the need to vaccinate children against polio, Rosemary *cited* several reports of dangerous new outbreaks of this once nearly eliminated disease. The mayor *cited* the volunteers of Hook & Ladder Company 1 for their heroism in extinguishing the recent fire. Although Terry was *cited* for contempt of court, he never went to jail.

coercion N. use of force to get someone to obey. The inquisitors used both physical and psychological *coercion* to force Joan of Arc to deny that her visions were sent by God. coerce, V.

compile V. assemble; gather; accumulate. We planned to *compile* a list of the words most frequently used on SAT examinations.

complement N. something that completes or fills up; number or quantity needed to make something complete. During the eighteenth century, fashionable accessories became an important *complement* to a lady's attire; without her proper fan and reticule, her outfit was incomplete. Gomer had the usual *complement* of eyes and ears, two of each.

compliance N. readiness to yield; conformity in fulfilling requirements. When I give an order, I expect *compliance*, not defiance. The design for the new school had to be in *compliance* with the local building code. comply, V.

comprehensive ADJ. thorough; inclusive. This book provides a *comprehensive* review of verbal and math skills for the SAT.

concede V. admit; yield. Despite all the evidence Monica had assembled, Mark refused to *concede* that she was right.

concentration N. (action of focusing one's total attention; gathering of people or things close to one another; relative amount of a substance (in a mixture, solution, volume of space, etc.). As Ty filled in the bubbles on his answer sheet, he frowned in *concentration*. Oakland has one of the largest *concentrations* of Tagalog speakers in California. Fertilizers contain high *concentrations* of nitrogen to help promote the growth of crops.

concise ADJ. brief and compact. When you define a new word, be *concise*; the shorter the definition, the easier it is to remember.

concrete ADJ. physical or material in nature, as opposed to abstract; real; specific. The word "boy" is *concrete*; the word "boyhood" is abstract. Unless the police turn up some *concrete* evidence of his guilt, we have no case against him. I don't have time to listen to vague pitches; come up with a *concrete* proposal, and then we can talk.

concur V. agree. Did you *concur* with the decision of the court or did you find it unfair?

conducive ADJ. contributing to; favorable. Rest and proper diet are *conducive* to good health.

conformity N. state of obeying regulations, standards; behavior that matches the behavior of most others in a group. In *conformity* with the by-laws of the society, I am calling for a special election. Be grateful for the oddballs who defy convention and break through the culture of *conformity* to go their own unique way.

confound V. confuse; puzzle. No mystery could *confound* Sherlock Holmes for long.

consensus N. general agreement. After hours of debate, the *consensus* of the group was that we should approve the executive director's proposal.

consistency N. absence of contradictions; dependability; degree of thickness. Sherlock Holmes judged puddings and explanations of their *consistency*: he liked his puddings without lumps and his explanations without improbabilities. Show up every day and do your job: *consistency* in performance is the mark of a good employee. If the pea soup is too thick, add some stock until it reaches the *consistency* you want.

constraint N. compulsion; repression of feelings. Because he trusted his therapist completely, he discussed his feelings openly with her without feeling the least *constraint*. constrain, V.

contend V. assert earnestly; struggle; compete. Sociologist Harry Edwards *contends* that young black athletes are exploited by some college recruiters.

contention N. angry disagreement; point made in a debate or argument; competition. Some people are peacemakers; others seek out any excuse for quarrels and *contention*. It is our *contention* that, if you follow our tactics, you will boost your score on the SAT. Through his editor, Styron learned that he was in *contention* for the National Book Award.

contract V. compress or shrink; make a pledge; catch a disease. Warm metal expands; cold metal *contracts*. During World War II, Germany *contracted* an alliance with Italy and Japan. To pay for his college education, James *contracted* a debt of $20,000. If you think you have *contracted* an infectious disease, see your doctor.

conviction N. strongly held belief. Nothing could shake his *conviction* that she was innocent. (secondary meaning)

corroborate V. confirm. Unless we find a witness to *corroborate* your evidence, it will not stand up in court.

credulity N. belief on slight evidence. Con artists take advantage of the *credulity* of inexperienced investors to swindle them out of their savings. credulous, ADJ.

criterion N. standard used in judging. What *criterion* did you use when you selected this essay as the prizewinner? criteria, PL.

cryptic ADJ. mysterious; hidden; secret. Thoroughly baffled by Holmes's *cryptic* remarks, Watson wondered whether Holmes was intentionally concealing his thoughts about the crime.

cursory ADJ. casual; hastily done. Because a *cursory* examination of the ruins indicates the possibility of arson, we believe the insurance agency should undertake a more extensive investigation of the fire's cause.

D

deference N. courteous regard for another's wish; respect owed to a superior. In *deference* to the minister's request, please do not take photographs during the wedding service. As the Bishop's wife, Mrs. Proudie expected the wives of the lesser clergy to treat her with due *deference*. defer, V.

definition N. statement of a word's exact meaning; clarity of sound or image being reproduced; distinctness of outlines, boundaries. This word list gives three *definitions* for the word "*definition*." The newest flat screen monitors have excellent resolution and amazing color *definition*. The gym's fitness program includes specific exercises to improve *definition* of the abdominal muscles.

delineate N. portray. He is a powerful storyteller, but he is weakest when he attempts to *delineate* character. delineation, N.

denounce V. condemn; criticize. The reform candidate *denounced* the corrupt city officers for having betrayed the public's trust. denunciation, N.

depict V. portray. In this sensational exposé, the author *depicts* Beatle John Lennon as a drug-crazed neurotic. Do you believe in the accuracy of this *depiction* of Lennon?

deprecate V. express disapproval of; protest against; belittle. A firm believer in old-fashioned courtesy, Miss Post *deprecated* the modern tendency to address new acquaintances by their first names. deprecatory, ADJ.

deride V. ridicule; make fun of. The critics *derided* his pretentious dialogue and refused to take his play seriously. derision, N.

derivative ADJ. unoriginal; derived from another source. Although her early poetry was clearly *derivative* in nature, the critics thought she had promise and eventually would find her own voice.

detachment N. emotional remoteness; group sent away (on a military mission, etc.); process of separation. Psychoanalysts must maintain their professional *detachment* and stay uninvolved with their patients' personal lives. The plane transported a *detachment* of Peace Corps volunteers heading for their first assignment abroad. Retinal *detachment*, in which the retina and optic nerve separate, causes severe vision loss.

determination N. firmness of purpose; calculation; decision. Nothing could shake his *determination* that his children would get the best education that money could buy. Thanks to my calculator, my *determination* of the answer to the problem took only seconds. In America's system of government, the president and Congress must heed the Supreme Court's *determination* of constitutional issues.

deterrent N. something that discourages; hindrance. Does the threat of capital punishment serve as a *deterrent* to potential killers? deter, V.

detrimental ADJ. harmful; damaging. The candidate's acceptance of major financial contributions from a well-known racist ultimately proved *detrimental* to his campaign, for he lost the backing of many of his early grass-roots supporters. detriment, N.

devious ADJ. roundabout; erratic; not straightforward. The Joker's plan was so *devious* that it was only with great difficulty we could follow its shifts and dodges.

devise V. think up; invent; plan. How clever he must be to have *devised* such a devious plan! What ingenious inventions might he have *devised* if he had turned his mind to science and not to crime.

diffuse ADJ. wordy and poorly organized; spread out (like a gas). If you pay authors by the word, you tempt them to produce *diffuse* manuscripts rather than brief ones. When a cloud covers the sun, the lighting is *diffuse*, or spread evenly across the entire sky overhead. diffusion, N.

digression N. wandering away from the subject. Nobody minded when Professor Renoir's lectures wandered away from their official theme; his *digressions* were always more fascinating than the topic of the day. digress, V.

diligence N. steadiness of effort; persistent hard work. Her employers were greatly impressed by her *diligence* and offered her a partnership in the firm. diligent, ADJ.

discerning ADJ. mentally quick and observant; having insight. Because he was considered the most *discerning* member of the firm, he was assigned the most difficult cases. discern, V. discernment, N.

disclose V. reveal. Although competitors offered him bribes, he refused to *disclose* any information about his company's forthcoming product. disclosure, N.

discordant ADJ. not harmonious; conflicting. Nothing is quite so *discordant* as the sound of a junior high school orchestra tuning up.

discount V. minimize the significance of; reduce in price. Be prepared to *discount* what he has to say about his ex-wife; he is still very bitter about the divorce. Sharon waited to buy a bathing suit until Macy's fall sale, when the department store *discounted* the summer fashions.

discrepancy N. lack of consistency; difference. The police noticed some *discrepancies* in his description of the crime and did not believe him.

discriminating ADJ. treating people of different classes unequally; able to see differences. The firm was accused of *discriminating* hiring practices that were biased against women. A superb interpreter of Picasso, she was sufficiently *discriminating* to judge the most complex works of modern art. (secondary meaning) discrimination, N.

disdain V. view with scorn or contempt. The bookish student *disdained* fashion models for their lack of intellectual interests. also N.

disinclination N. unwillingness. Some mornings I feel a great *disinclination* to get out of bed.

dismiss V. let go from employment; refuse to accept or consider. To cut costs, the store manager *dismissed* all the full-time workers and replaced them with part-time employees at lower pay. Because Tina believed in Tony's fidelity, she *dismissed* the notion that he might be having an affair.

disparage V. belittle. Do not *disparage* anyone's contribution; these little gifts add up to large sums. disparaging, ADJ.

disparity N. difference; condition of inequality. Their *disparity* in rank made no difference at all to the prince and Cinderella.

disperse V. scatter. The police fired tear gas into the crowd to *disperse* the protesters.

disputatious ADJ. argumentative; fond of argument. People avoided discussing contemporary problems with him because of his *disputatious* manner.

disseminate V. distribute; spread; scatter (like seeds). By their use of the Internet, propagandists have been able to *disseminate* their pet doctrines to new audiences around the globe.

dissent V. disagree. In the recent Supreme Court decision, Justice Sotomayor *dissented* from the majority opinion. also N.

divergent ADJ. differing; deviating. The two witnesses presented the jury with remarkably *divergent* accounts of the same episode. divergence, N.

diversity N. variety. Home to people of many different ethnic and religious backgrounds, the city of Oakland prides itself on the *diversity* of its population.

doctrine N. teachings, in general; particular principle (religious, legal, etc.) taught. He was so committed to the *doctrines* of his faith that he was unable to evaluate them impartially. The Monroe *Doctrine* declared the Western Hemisphere off-limits to European attempts at colonization.

document V. provide written evidence to support statements; create a detailed record. She kept all the receipts from her business trip in order to *document* her expenses for the firm. As a young photographer, Johnny Seal *documented* the Occupy Oakland demonstrations in his hometown. also N.

dogmatic ADJ. opinionated; arbitrary; doctrinal. We tried to discourage Doug from being so *dogmatic*, but never could convince him that his opinions might be wrong.

dubious ADJ. questionable; filled with doubt. Many critics of the SAT contend the test is of *dubious* worth. Jay claimed he could get a perfect 1600 on the SAT, but Ellen was *dubious*: she knew he hadn't cracked a book in three years.

E

economy N. national condition of monetary supply, goods production, etc.; prudent management of resources; efficiency or conciseness in use of words, etc. The president favors tax cuts to stimulate the *economy*. I need to practice *economy* when I shop: no more impulse buying for me! I admire the *economy* of Pope's verse: in a few words, he conveys worlds of meaning.

eloquence N. expressiveness; persuasive speech. The crowds were stirred by Martin Luther King's *eloquence*. eloquent, ADJ.

elusive ADJ. evasive; baffling; hard to grasp. Trying to pin down exactly when the contractors would be done remodeling the house, Nancy was frustrated by their *elusive* replies. elude, V.

embrace V. include; hug; adopt or espouse. The Encyclopedia of the Middle Ages *embraces* a wide variety of subjects, with articles on everything from agricultural implements to zodiac signs. Clasping Maid Marian in his arms, Robin Hood *embraced* her lovingly. In joining the outlaws in Sherwood Forest, she had openly *embraced* their cause.

emulate V. imitate; rival. In a brief essay, describe a person you admire, someone whose virtues you would like to *emulate*.

encounter N. meeting. I will always remember my *encounter* with Bishop Tutu. also V.

endorse V. approve; support. Everyone waited to see which one of the rival candidates for the city council the mayor would *endorse*. (secondary meaning) endorsement, N.

engage V. pledge to do something (especially, to marry); hire someone to perform a service; attract and keep (attention); induce someone to participate; take part in; attack (an enemy). When Tony and Tina became *engaged*, they decided to *engage* a lawyer to write up a pre-nuptial agreement. Tony's job *engages* him completely. When he's focused on work, not even Tina can *engage* him in conversation. Instead, she *engages* in tennis matches, fiercely *engaging* her opponents.

enhance V. increase; improve. You can *enhance* your chances of being admitted to the college of your choice by learning to write well; an excellent essay can *enhance* any application.

enigma N. puzzle. Despite all attempts to decipher the code, it remained an *enigma*.

enmity N. ill will; hatred. At Camp David, President Carter labored to bring an end to the *enmity* that prevented the peaceful coexistence of Egypt and Israel.

equivocal ADJ. ambiguous; intentionally misleading. Rejecting the candidate's *equivocal* comments on tax reform, the reporters pressed him to state clearly where he stood on the issue. equivocate, V.

erroneous ADJ. mistaken; wrong. I thought my answer was correct, but it was *erroneous*.

erudite ADJ. learned; scholarly. Though his fellow students thought him *erudite*, Paul knew he would have to study many years before he could consider himself a scholar.

exacerbate V. worsen; embitter. The problem with flooding was *exacerbated* by several additional inches of rain.

execute V. put into effect; carry out; put to death (someone condemned by law). The United States Agency for International Development is responsible for *executing* America's development policy and foreign assistance. The ballet master wanted to see how well Margaret could *execute* a pirouette. Captured by the British while gathering military intelligence, Nathan Hale was tried and *executed* on September 22, 1776.

exemplary ADJ. serving as a model; outstanding. At commencement the dean praised Ellen for her *exemplary* behavior as class president.

exemplify V. serve as an example of; embody. For a generation of ballet goers, Rudolf Nureyev *exemplified* the ideal of masculine grace.

exhaustive ADJ. thorough; comprehensive. We have made an *exhaustive* study of all published SAT tests and are happy to share our research with you.

expedient ADJ. suitable; practical, politic. A pragmatic politician, he was guided by what was *expedient* rather than by what was ethical. expediency, N.

expedite V. hasten. Because we are on a tight schedule, we hope you will be able to *expedite* the delivery of our order.

explicit ADJ. totally clear; definite; outspoken. Don't just hint around that you're dissatisfied; be *explicit* about what's bugging you.

exploit V. make use of, sometimes unjustly. Cesar Chavez fought attempts to *exploit* migrant farmworkers in California. exploitation, N.

extraneous ADJ. not essential; superfluous. No wonder Ted can't think straight! His mind is so cluttered up with *extraneous* trivia, he can't concentrate on the essentials.

F

fabricate V. manufacture or build; make up to mislead or deceive. Motawi Tileworks *fabricates* distinctive ceramic tiles in the Arts and Crafts style. The defense lawyer accused the arresting officer of *fabricating* evidence against her client.

facilitate V. help bring about; make less difficult. Rest and proper nourishment should *facilitate* the patient's recovery.

facility N. natural ability to do something with ease; ease in performing; something (building, equipment) set up to perform a function. Morgan has always displayed a remarkable *facility* for playing basketball. Thanks to years of practice, he handles the ball with such *facility* that as a twelve-year-old he can outplay many students at the university's recreational *facility*.

faculty N. inherent mental or physical power; teaching staff. As he grew old, Professor Twiggly feared he might lose his *faculties* and become unfit to teach. Once he'd lost his *faculties*, he would have no place on the *faculty*.

fallacious ADJ. false; misleading. Paradoxically, *fallacious* reasoning does not always yield erroneous results: even though your logic may be faulty, the answer you get may nevertheless be correct. fallacy, N.

fanaticism N. excessive zeal; extreme devotion to a belief or cause. When Islamic fundamentalists demanded the death of Salman Rushdie because his novel questioned their faith, world opinion condemned them for their *fanaticism*.

feasible ADJ. practical. Construction of a new stadium hardly seems *feasible* in these difficult economic times. feasibility, N.

figurative ADJ. not literal, but metaphorical; using a figure of speech. "To lose one's marbles" is a *figurative* expression; if you're told that Jack has lost his marbles, no one expects you to rush out to buy him a replacement set.

friction N. rubbing against; clash of wills. If it were not for the *friction* between the tires and the pavement, driving a car would be like sliding all over an ice rink. The *friction* between Aaron Burr and Alexander Hamilton intensified over time until it culminated in their famous duel.

frugality N. thrift; economy. In economically hard times, anyone who doesn't practice *frugality* risks bankruptcy. frugal, ADJ.

furtive ADJ. stealthy; sneaky. The boy gave a *furtive* look at his classmate's test paper.

G

generalization N. broad, general statement derived from specific instances; vague, indefinite statement. It is foolish to make *generalizations* based on insufficient evidence: that one woman defrauded the welfare system of thousands of dollars does not mean all welfare recipients are cheats. I would rather propose solutions to problems than make vague *generalizations*.

graphic ADJ. pertaining to visual art; relating to visual images; vividly portrayed. The illustrator Jody Lee studied the *graphic* arts at San Francisco's Academy of Art. In 2016 the SAT began to include reading questions that required students to interpret *graphic* information from charts and diagrams. The description of the winter storm was so *graphic* that you could almost feel the hailstones.

gratify V. please. Lori's parents were *gratified* by her outstanding performance on the SAT.

gratuitous ADJ. given freely; unwarranted; uncalled for. Quit making *gratuitous* comments about my driving; no one asked you for your opinion.

gravity N. seriousness. We could tell we were in serious trouble from the *gravity* of her expression. (secondary meaning) grave, ADJ.

guile N. deceit; duplicity; wiliness; cunning. Iago uses considerable *guile* to trick Othello into believing that Desdemona has been unfaithful.

gullible ADJ. easily deceived. He preyed upon *gullible* people, who believed his stories of easy wealth.

H

hamper V. obstruct. The minority party tried their best to *hamper* the president's efforts to pass legislation.

hardy ADJ. sturdy; robust; able to stand inclement weather. We asked the gardening expert to recommend particularly *hardy* plants that could withstand our harsh New England winters.

heresy N. opinion contrary to popular belief; opinion contrary to accepted religion. Galileo's assertion that the earth moved around the sun directly contradicted the religious teachings of his day; as a result, he was tried for *heresy*. heretic, N.

hierarchy N. arrangement by rank or standing; authoritarian body divided into ranks. To be low man on the totem pole is to have an inferior place in the *hierarchy*.

hinder V. slow down or make (something) difficult; prevent. Although the operation was successful, an infection *hindered* the recovery of the patient, who remained hospitalized for an additional week. Gordon was determined not to let anyone *hinder* him from achieving his goal.

homogeneous ADJ. of the same kind. Educators try to put pupils of similar abilities into the same classes because they believe that this *homogeneous* grouping is advisable. homogeneity, N.

hypocritical ADJ. pretending to be virtuous; deceiving. I resent his *hypocritical* posing as a friend for I know he is interested only in his own advancement. hypocrisy, N.

hypothetical ADJ. based on assumptions or hypotheses. Why do we have to consider *hypothetical* cases when we have actual case histories that we can examine? hypothesis, N.

I

idiosyncrasy N. individual trait, usually odd in nature; eccentricity. One of Richard Nixon's little *idiosyncrasies* was his liking for ketchup on cottage cheese. One of Hannibal Lecter's little *idiosyncrasies* was his liking for human flesh.

illusory ADJ. deceptive; not real. Unfortunately, the costs of running a concession stand were so high that Tom's profits proved *illusory*.

immutable ADJ. unchangeable. All things change over time; nothing is *immutable*.

impair V. injure; hurt. Drinking alcohol can *impair* your ability to drive safely; if you're going to drink, don't drive.

impeccable ADJ. faultless. The uncrowned queen of the fashion industry, Diana was acclaimed for her *impeccable* taste.

impede V. hinder; block; delay. A series of accidents *impeded* the launching of the space shuttle.

implausible ADJ. unlikely; unbelievable. Though her alibi seemed *implausible*, it turned out to be true.

implement N. piece of equipment. We now own so many rakes, hoes, and hedge clippers that we need a tool shed in which to store all our gardening *implements*.

implement V. put into effect; supply with tools. The mayor was unwilling to *implement* the plan until she was sure it had the governor's backing. also N.

implication N. something hinted at or suggested; likely consequence; close involvement. When Miss Watson said that she hadn't seen her purse since the last time Jim was in the house, her *implication* was that Jim had taken it. This had potentially serious *implications* for Jim. If his *implication* in a theft were proved, he'd be thrown into jail.

implicit ADJ. understood, but not stated. Jack never told Jill he adored her; he believed his love was *implicit* in his actions.

imposition N. applying or enforcement; unwelcome burden or demand. After the riots, we expected the *imposition* of a curfew. Bob asked to stay with us for two weeks, if that wouldn't be too much of an imposition.

impudence N. impertinence; insolence. Kissed on the cheek by a perfect stranger, Lady Catherine exclaimed, "Of all the nerve! Young man, I should have you horse-whipped for your *impudence*."

inadvertent ADJ. unintentional; careless or heedless. Elizabeth, I am sure your omission from the guest list was *inadvertent*: Darcy would never intentionally slight you so.

incisive ADJ. cutting; sharp. The commentator's report was clear and *incisive*: it cut to the heart of the matter.

incite V. arouse to action. The demagogue *incited* the mob to take action into its own hands.

inclusive ADJ. tending to include all. The comedian turned down the invitation to join the Players' Club, saying any club that would let him in was too *inclusive* for him.

incompatible ADJ. so opposed in nature as to be unable to coexist; unable to work together in combination. Their political views were clearly *incompatible*, and yet they remained good friends despite their differences. The Dragon Naturally Speaking dictation program worked on my PC but was *incompatible* with my iMac.

incongruous ADJ. not fitting; absurd. Dave saw nothing *incongruous* about wearing sneakers with his tuxedo; he couldn't understand why his date took one look at him and started to laugh. incongruity, N.

inconsistent ADJ. self-contradictory; lacking uniformity. The witness's testimony was *inconsistent*: at times she appeared to contradict herself.

indifferent ADJ. unmoved; lacking concern. Because she felt no desire to marry, she was *indifferent* to his constant proposals.

indiscriminate ADJ. not marked by making careful distinctions; done at random. Mother disapproved of Junior's *indiscriminate* television viewing; she wished he'd be a little more selective in his choice of shows. The newspaper editorial denounced the terrorists for their *indiscriminate* killing of civilians.

induce V. persuade; bring about. After the quarrel, Tina said nothing could *induce* her to talk to Tony again. Drinking a glass of warm milk before bedtime can help *induce* sleep. inducement, N.

inert ADJ. inactive; lacking power to move. If you surround hot metals with chemically *inert* argon, you can protect the metals from potential oxidation by oxygen in the air. Pneumonia left her so tired that she could only lie on the sofa, totally *inert*.

ingenious ADJ. clever; resourceful. Kit admired the *ingenious* way in which her new smartphone incorporated the latest technology. ingenuity, N.

inherent ADJ. firmly established by nature or habit. Katya's *inherent* love of justice caused her to champion anyone she considered treated unfairly by society.

innate ADJ. inborn. Mozart's parents soon recognized young Wolfgang's *innate* talent for music.

innocuous ADJ. harmless. An occasional glass of wine with dinner is relatively *innocuous* and should have no ill effect on you.

innovation N. change; introduction of something new. She loved *innovations* just because they were new. innovate, V.

instigate V. urge; start; provoke. Rumors of police corruption led the mayor to *instigate* an investigation into the department's activities.

integrity N. uprightness; wholeness. Lincoln, whose personal *integrity* has inspired millions, fought a civil war to maintain the *integrity* of the Republic, that these United States might remain undivided for all time.

intervene V. come between. When close friends get into a fight, be careful if you try to *intervene*; they may join forces to gang up on you.

intimate V. hint; suggest. When Dick asked Jane whether she'd like a breath mint, was he *intimating* that she had bad breath?

intimidate V. frighten. I'll learn karate and then those big bullies won't be able to *intimidate* me any more.

intrepid ADJ. fearless. For her *intrepid* conduct nursing the wounded during the war, Florence Nightingale was honored by Queen Victoria.

ironic ADJ. resulting in an unexpected and contrary manner. It is *ironic* that his success came when he least wanted it.

L

lament V. grieve; express sorrow. Even advocates of the war *lamented* the loss of so many lives in combat. lamentation, N.

latent ADJ. potential, but undeveloped; dormant. Sometimes *latent* tuberculosis becomes active years later.

levity N. lack of seriousness; lightness. Stop giggling and wriggling around in your seats; such *levity* is improper in church.

linger V. loiter or dawdle; continue or persist. Hoping to see Juliet pass by, Romeo *lingered* outside the Capulet house for hours. Though Mother made stuffed cabbage on Monday, the smell *lingered* around the house for days.

listless ADJ. lacking in spirit or energy. We had expected him to be full of enthusiasm and were surprised by his *listless* attitude.

lofty ADJ. very high. Though Barbara Jordan's fellow students used to tease her about her *lofty* ambitions, she rose to hold one of the highest positions in the land.

M

magnitude N. greatness of extent; great importance; size. Seismologists use the Richter scale to measure the *magnitude* of earthquakes. Mexico's Bicentennial Celebration was an event of such *magnitude* that it had a lasting positive impact on the country's economy. When students work with very large numbers (millions and billions), they need to understand the *magnitude* of these numbers.

malicious ADJ. hateful; spiteful. Jealous of Cinderella's beauty, her *malicious* stepsisters expressed their spite by forcing her to do menial tasks. malice, N.

materialism N. preoccupation with physical comforts and things. By its nature, *materialism* is opposed to idealism, for where the *materialist* emphasizes the needs of the body, the idealist emphasizes the needs of the soul.

medium N. means of doing something; substance in which an organism lives; form or material employed by an artist, author, or composer. M.I.T.'s use of the Internet as a *medium* of education has transformed the university into a global enterprise. Ty's experiment involved growing bacteria in a nutrient-rich *medium*. Johnny's favorite artistic *medium* is photography; he hopes to become a photojournalist.

methodical ADJ. systematic. An accountant must be *methodical* and maintain order among his financial records.

meticulous ADJ. excessively careful; painstaking; scrupulous. Martha Stewart was a *meticulous* housekeeper, fussing about each and every detail that went into making up her perfect home.

miserly ADJ. stingy; mean. The *miserly* old man hoarded his coins not out of prudence but out of greed. miser, N.

mitigate V. appease. Nothing he did could *mitigate* her wrath; she was unforgiving.

mundane ADJ. worldly as opposed to spiritual; everyday. Uninterested in philosophical questions, Tom talked only of *mundane* matters such as the latest basketball results.

N

negate V. cancel out; nullify; deny. A sudden surge of adrenalin can *negate* the effects of fatigue: there's nothing like a good shock to wake you up.

nonchalance N. indifference; lack of concern; composure. Cool, calm, and collected under fire, James Bond shows remarkable *nonchalance* in the face of danger.

noncommittal ADJ. uncommunicative; undecided; neutral. Her *noncommittal* reply surprised us, because we had been led to believe she was in favor of our proposal.

notoriety N. disrepute; ill fame. To the starlet, any publicity was good publicity: if she couldn't have a good reputation, she'd settle for *notoriety*. notorious, ADJ.

novelty N. something new; newness. First marketed in 1977, home computers were no longer a *novelty* by 1980. After the first couple of months at college, Johnny found that the *novelty* of living in a dormitory had worn off.

nurture V. nourish; educate; foster. The Head Start program attempts to *nurture* pre-kindergarten children so that they will do well when they enter public school. also N.

O

objective ADJ. not influenced by personal feelings or prejudices; able to be perceived by the senses. Andrea loved her little son so much that it was impossible for her to be *objective* about his behavior. Nurses gather *objective* data about a patient by taking the patient's temperature or measuring the patient's height and weight.

objective N. goal; aim. Morgan's *objective* is to play basketball so well that he can be a starter on the varsity team.

oblivion N. obscurity; forgetfulness. After a decade of popularity, Hurston's works had fallen into *oblivion*; no one bothered to read them anymore. oblivious, ADJ.

obscure V. darken; make unclear. We had hoped to see Mount Rainier, but Seattle's ever-present cloud cover *obscured* our view. At times he seemed purposely to *obscure* his meaning, preferring mystery to clarity.

obstinate ADJ. stubborn. We tried to persuade him to give up smoking, but he was *obstinate* and refused to change.

ominous ADJ. threatening. These clouds are *ominous*; they suggest a severe storm is on the way.

opaque ADJ. not transparent; hard to understand or explain. The *opaque* window shade kept the sunlight out of the room. The language of the federal income tax forms was so *opaque* that I had to turn to an accountant for help. opacity, N.

opportunist N. individual who sacrifices principles for expediency by taking advantage of circumstances. Forget ethics! He's such an *opportunist* that he'll vote in favor of any deal that will give him a break.

optimist N. person who looks on the good side. The pessimist says the glass is half-empty; the *optimist* says it is half-full.

orator N. public speaker. The abolitionist Frederick Douglass was a brilliant *orator* whose speeches centered on the evils of slavery.

P

partisan ADJ. one-sided; prejudiced; committed to a party. On certain issues of conscience, she refused to take a *partisan* stand. also N.

peripheral ADJ. marginal; outer. The struggles, challenges, dysfunctions, dreams, and accomplishments of families in the past are not *peripheral* to historical inquiry, but central to it. Rather than live in the crowded city center, we chose to buy a house in one of the *peripheral* suburbs ringing the metropolis.

perpetuate V. make something last; preserve from extinction. Some critics attack *The Adventures of Huckleberry Finn* because they believe Twain's book *perpetuates* a false image of African-Americans. In environments where resources are unstable, large numbers of organisms are produced quickly on the chance that some will survive to *perpetuate* the species.

pervasive ADJ. permeating; spread throughout every part. Despite airing them for several hours, she could not rid her clothes of the *pervasive* odor of mothballs that clung to them. pervade, V.

pessimism N. belief that life is basically bad or evil; gloominess. Considering how well you've done in the class so far, you have no real reason for such *pessimism* regarding your final grade.

phenomena N., PL. observable facts; subjects of scientific investigation. We kept careful records of the *phenomena* we noted in the course of these experiments.

plastic ADJ. able to be molded. When clay dries out, it becomes less *plastic* and loses its malleability.

pragmatic ADJ. practical (as opposed to idealistic); concerned with the practical worth or impact of something. This coming trip to France should provide me with a *pragmatic* test of the value of my conversational French class.

preclude V. make impossible; eliminate. The fact that the band was already booked to play in Hollywood on New Year's Eve *precluded* their accepting the New Year's Eve gig in London they were offered.

predator N. creature that seizes and devours another animal; person who robs or exploits others. A wide variety of *predators*—cats, owls, hawks—catch mice for dinner. A carnivore is by definition *predatory*, for he *preys* on weaker creatures.

pressing ADJ. urgent; critical; acute. The refugees' most *pressing* need was for shelter.

prevalent ADJ. widespread; generally accepted. A radical committed to social change, Reed had no patience with the conservative views *prevalent* in the America of his day.

profound ADJ. deep; not superficial; complete. Freud's remarkable insights into human behavior caused his fellow scientists to honor him as a *profound* thinker. profundity, N.

profusion N. abundant quantity. Along the Mendocino coast, where there is enough moisture, wildflowers flourish in great *profusion*.

proliferation N. rapid growth; spread; multiplication. Times of economic hardship inevitably encourage the *proliferation* of countless get-rich-quick schemes. proliferate, V.

prolific ADJ. abundantly fruitful. She was a *prolific* writer and wrote as many as three books a year.

provincial ADJ. pertaining to a province; limited in outlook; unsophisticated. As *provincial* governor, Sir Henry administered the Queen's law in his remote corner of Canada. Caught up in local problems, out of touch with London news, he became sadly *provincial*.

prudent ADJ. cautious; careful. A miser hoards money not because he is *prudent* but because he is greedy. prudence, N.

Q

qualified ADJ. limited; restricted. Unable to give the candidate full support, the mayor gave him only a *qualified* endorsement. (secondary meaning)

quandary N. dilemma. When both Harvard and Stanford accepted Laura, she was in a *quandary* as to which school she should attend.

R

ramble V. wander aimlessly (physically or mentally). Listening to the teacher *ramble*, Judy wondered whether he'd ever get to his point.

ratify V. approve formally; verify. Before the treaty could go into effect, it had to be *ratified* by the president.

rebuttal N. refutation; response with contrary evidence. The defense lawyer confidently listened to the prosecutor sum up his case, sure that she could answer his arguments in her *rebuttal*.

reciprocate V. repay in kind. The Olivers invited us to dinner last month; we should *reciprocate* and have them over for a meal.

recount V. narrate or tell; count over again. A born storyteller, my father loved to *recount* anecdotes about his early years in New York. Because the vote for class president was so close, we had to *recount* all the ballots before we were sure that Johnny was the winner.

rectify V. set right; correct. You had better *rectify* your accounting errors before the auditors arrive.

redundant ADJ. superfluous; excessively wordy; repetitious. Your composition is *redundant*; you can easily reduce its length. redundancy, N.

reflect V. think seriously about; represent faithfully; show a physical image; create a good or bad impression. Mr. Collins *reflected* on Elizabeth's rejection of his proposal. Did it *reflect* her true feelings, he wondered. Looking at his image *reflected* in the mirror, he refused to believe that she could reject such a fine-looking man. Such behavior *reflected* badly upon her.

refute V. disprove. In Scottoline's latest mystery, a young defense attorney runs into trouble as she tries to come up with new evidence to *refute* the evidence against her client.

relegate V. banish to an inferior position; delegate; assign. After Ralph dropped his second tray of drinks that week, the manager swiftly *relegated* him to a minor post cleaning up behind the bar.

replenish V. fill up again. Before she could go on another backpacking trip, Carla had to *replenish* her stock of freeze-dried foods.

reprove V. censure; rebuke. The principal *reproved* the students when they became unruly in the auditorium. reproof, N.

reservation N. qualification or doubt about approving something; land set aside for Native Americans or for Australian aborigines; booking (a room or seat). Jill thought it would be great to go bungee-jumping, but I had strong *reservations* about the whole idea. Only about 20 percent of American Indians and Alaskan Natives still live on reservations or trust lands. We just booked a *reservation* to go see The Book of Mormon.

reserve N. backup supply; body of troops not part of the regular military forces; place set aside for specific purpose; formal but distant manner. Australia supplies much of the world's uranium from its abundant uranium *reserves*. Reluctant to enlist in the regular army, Don considered joining the *reserves*. On their African safari, Tom and Susan visited some fascinating big game *reserves*. Although Mark's air of *reserve* attracted some girls, it put off Judy, who felt his formality showed a lack of warmth.

resigned ADJ. unresisting; patiently submissive. *Resigned* to his downtrodden existence, the day laborer was too meek to protest his supervisor's bullying. resignation, N.

resolution N. firmness of purpose; formal expression of intent; solving of a problem. Nothing could shake Philip's *resolution* that his children would get the best education that money could buy. The symphony board passed a *resolution* to ban cell phone use during concerts. Friar Laurence hoped for a peaceful *resolution* of the conflict between the feuding Montagues and Capulets.

restraint N. moderation or self-control; controlling force; restriction. Control yourself, young lady! Show some *restraint*!

reticence N. reserve; uncommunicativeness; inclination to silence. Fearing his competitors might get advance word about his plans from talkative staff members, Hughes preferred *reticence* from his employees to loquacity.

retract V. withdraw; take back. He dropped his libel suit after the newspaper finally *retracted* its statement. retraction, N.

rhetorical ADJ. pertaining to effective communication; insincere in language. To win his audience, the speaker used every *rhetorical* trick in the book.

rudimentary ADJ. undeveloped; elementary. Echidnas lack external ears; their tails are, at best, *rudimentary*.

S

sanction V. approve; ratify. Nothing will convince me to *sanction* the engagement of my daughter to such a worthless young man.

satirical ADJ. mocking. The humor of cartoonist Gary Trudeau often is *satirical*; through the comments of the Doonesbury characters, Trudeau ridicules political corruption and folly.

scanty ADJ. meager; insufficient. Thinking his helping of food was *scanty*, Oliver Twist asked for more.

scrupulous ADJ. conscientious; extremely thorough. Though Alfred is *scrupulous* in fulfilling his duties at work, he is less conscientious about his obligations to his family and friends.

scrutinize V. examine closely and critically. Searching for flaws, the sergeant *scrutinized* every detail of the private's uniform.

simulate V. imitate or reproduce in appearance; pretend to feel. The director had the cast members put on false beards to *simulate* the appearance of age. Jack appeared to be devoted to his wealthy aunt, but he was only *simulating* affection for her in the hope that she'd leave him her fortune.

skeptic N. doubter; person who suspends judgment until the evidence supporting a point of view has been examined. I am a *skeptic* about the new health plan; I want some proof that it can work. skepticism, N.

solution N. act of solving (a problem, difficult situation, etc.); liquid mixture whose components are uniformly distributed. If you get a foreign object in your eye, one possible *solution* to the problem is to try to flush the object out of your eye with clean water or a saline *solution*.

speculate V. form a theory about something, often without sufficient evidence; assume a financial risk in hopes of gain. Students of the stock market *speculate* that the seeds of the financier's downfall were planted when he *speculated* heavily in junk bonds.

sporadic ADJ. occurring irregularly. Although you can still hear *sporadic* outbursts of laughter and singing outside, the big Halloween parade has passed; the party's over till next year.

squander V. waste. If you *squander* your allowance on candy and comic books, you won't have any money left to buy the new video game you want.

stagnant ADJ. motionless; stale; dull. The *stagnant* water was a breeding ground for disease. stagnate, V.

static ADJ. unchanging; lacking development. Why watch chess on TV? I prefer watching a game with action, not something *static* where nothing seems to be going on. stasis, N.

submissive ADJ. yielding; timid. Crushed by his authoritarian father, Will had no defiance left in him; he was totally *submissive* in the face of authority.

subordinate ADJ. occupying a lower rank; inferior; submissive. Bishop Proudie's wife expected the *subordinate* clergy to behave with great deference to her.

subside V. settle down; descend; grow quiet. The doctor assured us that the fever would eventually *subside*.

substantiate V. establish by eidence; verify; support. These endorsements from satisfied customers *substantiate* our claim that Barron's *SAT* is the best SAT-prep book on the market.

succinct ADJ. brief; terse; compact. Don't bore your audience with excess verbiage: be *succinct*.

suffragette N. advocate of voting rights for women. In recognition of her efforts to win the vote for women, Congress authorized coining a silver dollar honoring the *suffragette* Susan B. Anthony.

superficial ADJ. on the surface; not thorough. Justin's fall left him with *superficial* scrapes and bruises that healed quickly. To revise a textbook properly, you must do more than make a few *superficial* changes to the manuscript.

superfluous ADJ. excessive; overabundant; unnecessary. Please try not to include so many superfluous details in your report; just give me the bare facts. superfluity, N.

surpass V. exceed. Her SAT scores *surpassed* our expectations.

susceptible ADJ. impressionable; easily influenced; having little resistance, as to a disease; receptive to. Said the patent medicine man to his very *susceptible* customer: "Buy this new miracle drug, and you will no longer be *susceptible* to the common cold."

sustain V. experience; support. He *sustained* such a severe injury that the doctors feared he would be unable to work to *sustain* his growing family.

symmetry N. arrangement of parts so that balance is obtained. Something lopsided by definition lacks *symmetry*.

synthesis N. combination of different parts (ideas, styles, genres) to create a connected whole; chemical production of a more complex substance from simpler ones; electronic production of sounds. Combining their owners' Catholicism with their own West African beliefs, Haitian slaves created a *synthesis* now known as Voodoo. The *synthesis* of aspirin involves the reaction of salicylic acid and acetic anhydride in the presence of a catalyst. Using digital tools, musicians mix sounds from different instruments, creating a *synthesis* of new musical sounds.

synthetic ADJ. made by combining different substances; (of an action or emotion) not genuine. Tires, once manufactured from rubber plants, nowadays are made from *synthetic* materials produced from crude oil. Although the dean strongly condemned the actions of the campus police, we felt his outrage was *synthetic*: he took no action against the police for their brutal treatment of the demonstrators.

T

taciturn ADJ. habitually silent; talking little. The stereotypical cowboy is a *taciturn* soul, answering lengthy questions with a "Yep" or "Nope."

temper V. moderate or tone down; toughen (steel). Not even her supervisor's grumpiness could *temper* Nancy's enthusiasm for her new job. Heated in a forge and then *tempered*, stainless steel blades hold an edge well.

tentative ADJ. provisional; experimental. Phil had a *tentative* plan for organizing the camping trip; he just needed to think through a few more details before he was ready to share his ideas.

terse ADJ. concise; abrupt; pithy. There is a fine line between speech that is *terse* and to the point and speech that is too abrupt.

thesis N. statement advanced as a premise to be supported; long essay. In her speech, Lexy made a convincing argument, supporting her *thesis* with statistics as well as anecdotal evidence. In graduate school, she wrote a doctoral *thesis*, which was later published to great reviews.

thrive V. prosper; flourish. Despite the impact of the recession on the restaurant trade, Philip's cafe *thrived*.

transient ADJ. momentary; temporary; staying for a short time. Ann's joy at finding the perfect Christmas gift for Phil was *transient*; she still had to find presents for her cousins. Located near the airport, this hotel caters to a largely *transient* trade.

trite ADJ. hackneyed; commonplace. The *trite* and predictable situations in many television programs turn off many viewers, who, in turn, turn off their sets.

turbulence N. state of violent agitation. We were frightened by the *turbulence* of the ocean during the storm.

turmoil N. great commotion and confusion. Lydia running off with a soldier! Mother fainting at the news! The Bennet household was in *turmoil*.

U

undermine V. weaken; sap. The recent corruption scandals have *undermined* many people's faith in the city government. The recent torrential rains have washed away much of the cliffside; the deluge threatens to *undermine* the pillars supporting several houses at the edge of the cliff.

underscore V. emphasize. Addressing the jogging class, Kim *underscored* the importance of good nutrition.

uniformity N. sameness; monotony. After a while, the *uniformity* of TV situation comedies becomes boring.

unprecedented ADJ. groundbreaking; unheard of; unparalleled. For a first novel, Margaret Mitchell's *Gone with the Wind* was an *unprecedented* success.

unwarranted ADJ. unjustified; groundless; undeserved. We could not understand Martin's *unwarranted* rudeness to his mother's guests.

usurp V. seize another's power or rank. The revolution ended when the victorious rebel general succeeded in his attempt to *usurp* the throne.

V

vacillate V. waver; fluctuate. Uncertain which suitor she ought to marry, the princess *vacillated*, saying now one, now the other. The boss likes his staff to be decisive. When he asks for your opinion, whatever you do, don't *vacillate*. vacillation, N.

venerate V. revere. Many film stars and celebrities *venerate* Tibet's spiritual leader, the Dalai Lama.

verbose ADJ. wordy. This article is too *verbose*; we must edit it.

viable ADJ. having a reasonable chance of success; capable of living or growing into something living. The plan to build a new stadium, though lacking a few details, is *viable* and stands a good chance of winning popular support. By definition, a fetus is *viable* once it has reached the stage of being capable of living, under normal conditions, outside the uterus or womb.

vigor N. active strength. Although he was over seventy years old, Jack had the *vigor* of a man in his prime. vigorous, ADJ.

vindicate V. clear from blame; exonerate; justify or support. The lawyer's goal was to *vindicate* her client and prove him innocent on all charges. The critics' extremely favorable reviews *vindicate* my opinion that *Hamilton* is a brilliant musical.

volatile ADJ. changeable; explosive; evaporating rapidly. The political climate today is extremely *volatile*; no one can predict what the electorate will do next. Ethyl chloride is an extremely *volatile* liquid; it evaporates instantly.

W

warrant V. give adequate grounds for; give a warranty for a product. No matter how irritated Warren was, that did not *warrant* his rudeness to his mother's guests. The Honda dealership *warranted* the condition of our new van.

Y

yield N. amount produced. An experienced farmer can estimate the annual *yield* of his acres with surprising accuracy. also V.

Z

zealot N. fanatic; person who shows excessive zeal. Though Glenn was devout, he was no *zealot*; he never tried to force his beliefs on his friends.

The Writing and Language and Essay Sections: Strategies, Tips, and Practice

5

In this chapter you'll learn how best to tackle the types of writing and language questions you'll encounter on the SAT and how best to approach the optional timed essay-writing portion of the test. You'll find practice exercises plus a selection of SAT-style essay prompts for your practice essays. After working through this chapter, you'll be thoroughly familiar with the contents of these sections on the SAT.

The SAT Writing and Language Test is a part of the "Evidence-Based Reading and Writing" half of the test. The writing test is set up as follows:

- 1 section with 4 passages
- 35 minutes long
- 11 questions per passage, with 44 questions total
- Questions in a random order of difficulty

GENERAL TIPS FOR ANSWERING WRITING AND LANGUAGE QUESTIONS

1. Take your time. Most students will have no trouble finishing the SAT Writing and Language test. Although your fellow test takers may be rushing along, do not get caught up in that. If you are going to edit well, you must be very thorough.
2. Pace yourself to finish when time is called. It is much more likely that you will pick up on a grammar issue if you do the questions one time well as opposed to rushing to the end so that you can double-check your work. You will have nearly 9 minutes for each passage—you may want to plan on checking your pace at the end of each passage so that you don't go too quickly or too slowly.

3. Underline and circle key information as you read long questions. If you miss even one word on one of the writing and language questions that actually asks you a direct question, you may very well miss the entire point of what is being asked. Take advantage of the fact that you can write all over the test. So underline and circle anything that seems especially important as you read through the questions.

4. Try to "hear" as you read by silently mouthing things. One of the best ways to edit a paper is to hear what is written as opposed to reading it only visually. Mouthing what is written will help you pick up on a variety of things, such as necessary pauses for punctuation, parallel phrasing, and proper idiom usage. Hearing the words will help you tap into your intuitive knowledge about what *sounds right* in the English language. You simply need to answer the question correctly; there is no need to justify why you have chosen your answer. Do be careful that while hearing it, you are not too casual in your tone. The SAT Writing and Language test will be more formal, so the style may at times differ from the way you may talk informally. For example, "I knew it was she" is correct while "I knew it was her" is not. While the writing you find will be more formal, it will not be stuffy. For example, you should say, "The teacher tried to stop the fight," as opposed to "The teacher endeavored to terminate the belligerence."

5. Think about the meaning. Many writing errors involve small-scale issues, like punctuation and subject-verb agreement. Other errors will involve large-scale issues, like conforming to a given writing objective or making an appropriate transition. As a result, it is essential that you focus not only on looking for minor grammar errors but also carefully consider how you can make the meaning of what is written as logical as possible. The SAT Writing and Language test is more about *editing* than just *proofreading*, so be sure you consider the big picture.

6. Consider relevant context. You must consider the context surrounding potential grammar issues to analyze a number of possible problems, such as logical transitions, tense agreement, and tone consistency. Sometimes you may need to read quite a bit beyond what is highlighted in the question so that your answer will be consistent with what follows. When in doubt about whether a selection is consistent with the rest of the passage, take the time to check it out.

COMMON GRAMMAR AND USAGE ERRORS

Sentence Basics

A **_sentence_** expresses a complete thought with both a subject and a predicate, i.e., a subject and a verb. A subject is a noun—a person, place, or thing—or a pronoun. The predicate includes a verb—a word that expresses an *action*, such as "is," "were," "do," "drove," "eat," or "sat." Here are some examples of complete sentences:

> *Who won the game?*
> *The sky is falling.*
> *The flag is waving in the wind.*
> *Don went to see the latest movie at the theater last night.*

A **_sentence fragment_** expresses an incomplete thought. It lacks a subject and/or a predicate. Here are some examples of sentence fragments:

> *Need the latest results from the survey.*
> *As soon as the sun set.*
> *A cup of coffee with my breakfast.*
> *The United Kingdom of Great Britain and Northern Ireland, also known as the U.K.*

Here are some possible ways the above sentence fragments can be fixed:

> **You** *need the latest results from the survey.*
> **Go** *to my house.*
> **I like** *a cup of coffee with my breakfast.*
> *The United Kingdom of Great Britain and Northern Ireland* **is** *also known as the U.K.*

A **_run-on sentence_** consists of two or more complete sentences that are <u>not</u> joined together with appropriate punctuation or transitions. Here are some examples of run-on sentences. Can you figure out where the first sentence ends?

> *Dan worked diligently on his computer his son read a book.*
> *You don't take out the trash, I will be very angry.*
> *The forecast was for a tornado, we headed to the basement.*
> *It was a long time ago, an ocean covered what is now a modern city.*

Here are some possible ways the above run-ons can be fixed:

> *Dan worked diligently on his computer* **while** *his son read a book.*
> **If** *you don't take out the trash, I will be very angry.*
> *The forecast was for a* **tornado; we** *headed to the basement.*
> **A long time ago,** *an ocean covered what is now a modern city.*

Wordiness

Quality writing demands clear descriptions, but a longer sentence is not necessarily a better one. Repetitive and irrelevant wording must be removed.

Example	Correction (if needed)
I am going to run for the distance of 3 miles.	I am going to run for ~~the distance of~~ 3 miles. (A mile is widely known to be a unit of distance, so this wording is extra.)
Teachers who educate people often have to work long hours grading papers and planning lessons.	Teachers ~~who educate people~~ often have to work long hours grading papers and planning lessons. (A teacher by definition educates people, so this information is unnecessary.)
Quantitative easing, the process in which a central bank increases the money supply, can be used to stimulate the economy.	Fine as is. Since "quantitative easing" is a specialized term, clarifying its meaning is helpful.

Parallelism

Excellent writing requires more than just the necessary information. The information must be presented in a way that is consistent, flowing, and parallel.

Incorrect	Correct*
Eating sandwiches and to drink milk are my lunchtime mainstays.	Eating sandwiches and **drinking** milk are my lunchtime mainstays.
Neither the dog or the cat made a mess.	Neither the dog **nor** the cat made a mess.
Respond to the essay question quickly and with thoroughness.	Respond to the essay question quickly and **thoroughly**.

*These sentences can be fixed in multiple ways.

Modifier Placement

Place descriptions in logical spots in the sentence so that the object of discussion is clear. Clarify vague or dangling modifiers.

Incorrect	Correct*
The student's work was subpar, not complete all the requirements.	The student's work was subpar, **because he did** not complete all the requirements.
My friend pensively enjoyed his dinner, chewing quietly.	My friend**, chewing quietly,** pensively enjoyed his dinner.

Incorrect	Correct*
Once the movie was over, unsatisfied about the ending was I.	Once the movie was over, **I was** unsatisfied about the ending.
When driving through the city, many pedestrians jaywalked.	**Many pedestrians jaywalked when I was** driving through the city.
Michael Jordan is regarded as the best basketball player of all time, winner of 6 World Championships.	Michael Jordan**, winner of 6 World Championships,** is regarded as the best basketball player of all time.
After eating the whole pizza, ready to take a nap was John.	**After he ate the whole pizza, John was ready to take a nap**. (This places "John" in a more logical spot.)
About to get out of bed, the covers were removed.	About to get out of bed, **he removed the covers**. (This clarifies who was ready to get out of bed.)

*These sentences can be fixed in multiple ways.

Logical Comparisons

Make sure that the sentence compares the correct number and types of things so that the comparison is logical.

Incorrect	Correct*
Your locker is always neater than me.	Your locker is always neater than **mine**. (Compare a locker to a locker, not a locker to a person.)
The president of the steel company is more qualified than the computer company.	The president of the steel company is more qualified than **the president of** the computer company. (Compare a president to a president, not a president to a company.)
My sister is better than everybody at solving differential equations.	My sister is better than everybody **else** at solving differential equations. (Clarify that the sister is not a part of the group to which she is being compared.)

*These sentences can be fixed in multiple ways.

Coordination and Subordination

Parts of sentences must coordinate and subordinate. In other words, the parts of sentences must be joined by logical connecting words.

Incorrect	Correct*
The newspaper delivery didn't come, and we watched television news.	The newspaper delivery didn't come, **so** we watched television news.
She finished her homework, she is going to play video games.	**Since** she finished her homework, she is going to play video games.
Mary loves to go for bike rides, and she loves the wind rushing through her hair.	Mary loves to go for bike rides, **for** she loves the wind rushing through her hair.

*These sentences can be fixed in multiple ways.

Verb Use and Tense

This table summarizes some of the basic conjugation patterns of verbs.

Past	Present	Future
He was	He is	He will
They were	They are	They will
She tasted	She tastes	She will taste
We washed	We wash	We will wash
Past Perfect	**Present Perfect**	**Future Perfect**
I had been	I have been	I will have been
They had been	They have been	They will have been
She had tasted	She has tasted	She will have tasted
We had washed	We have washed	They will have washed

Be sure that the tense, mood, and voice of all verbs are properly used.

Incorrect	Correct*
In the 19th century, Phillip has been a naval officer before he becomes a pirate.	In the 19th century, Phillip <u>had</u> been a naval officer before he <u>became</u> a pirate. (This was in the 19th century, so it took place in the past. Use the past perfect, "had been," to indicate that an event preceded another past event, "became.")
The gift was purchased by you.	<u>You purchased</u> the gift. (Use active voice rather than passive voice.)
If he was winning, he would be much more satisfied.	If he <u>were</u> winning, he would be much more satisfied. (Use the subjunctive mood to indicate situations that are contrary to fact.)

*These sentences can be fixed in multiple ways.

Singular and Plural Agreement

Matching subjects and verbs would be easy if they were always placed next to one another. On the SAT, determining correct number agreement among nouns, pronouns, adjectives, and verbs will often be challenging. The following table includes some examples.

Incorrect	Correct*
The pilot who has flown many planes are captaining our flight.	The pilot who has flown many planes is captaining our flight. ("Pilot" is the singular subject.)
Either the table or the chair need to be fixed.	Either the table or the chair needs to be fixed. (When using "either … or," treat each item in the pair as a unique object. In this case, each item will be fixed separately.)
The union of carpenters advocate for better pay.	The union of carpenters advocates for better pay. (The subject is the singular group "union" not the "carpenters.")
Each person need to perform their best if we are going to succeed.	Each person needs to perform his or her best if we are going to succeed. (The sentence refers to each person individually. Collective words like "each," "anyone," and "everybody" are singular.)
Every dress for the bridesmaids were the same.	Every dress for the bridesmaids was the same. (This is another example of a collective word. "Every" is referring to each dress by itself, so a singular verb is needed.)
If you need to find a book, one should seek assistance from a librarian.	If you need to find a book, you should seek assistance from a librarian. (Keep the pronouns consistent. The sentence could also be changed to "If one needs to find a book, one should.")
Andy and Tanner were thrilled to drive on his boat.	Andy and Tanner were thrilled to drive on Andy's boat. (The pronoun "his" is vague. The pronoun needs to be clarified so we know whose boat it is.)

*These sentences can be fixed in multiple ways.

Diction (Proper Wording)

The SAT will assess your abilities to distinguish between commonly confused words and to recognize proper idiomatic expressions. This table clarifies the correct usage of many commonly confused words.

Confused Words	General Rules	Examples of Proper Use
Accept vs. Except	*accept*: receive *except*: excluding	My teacher will <u>accept</u> my work, <u>except</u> when it is late.
Affect vs. Effect	*affect*: typically a verb *effect*: typically a noun	The biggest <u>effect</u> of the policy was how it <u>affected</u> immigration.
Allude vs. Elude	*allude*: indirectly refer to *elude*: escape from	The novelist <u>alluded</u> to how the robber could <u>elude</u> the police.
Amount vs. Number	*amount*: usually not countable *number*: usually countable	It took a great <u>amount</u> of courage to round up the necessary <u>number</u> of votes.
Beside vs. Besides	*beside*: next to *besides*: in addition to	<u>Besides</u> riding the roller coaster, I am going to ride the carousel <u>beside</u> the park entrance.
Between vs. Among	*between*: comparing one thing at a time, typically just two objects *among*: comparing nondistinct items or comparing three or more objects	Keeping this <u>between</u> you and me, I think she has <u>among</u> the most lovely smiles I have ever seen. ("You" and "me" are mentioned one at a time, whereas "smiles" is not mentioning the individual smiles.)
Choose vs. Chose	*choose*: present tense *chose*: past tense	After I <u>chose</u> poorly last time I went to the restaurant, I will be much more careful what I <u>choose</u> today.
Complement vs. Compliment	*complement*: complete something *compliment*: flattery	When the coach recognized how my skills <u>complemented</u> those of my teammates, she gave me a very nice <u>compliment</u>.
Elicit vs. Illicit	*elicit*: evoke or obtain *illicit*: illegal	The detective tried to <u>elicit</u> information from the witnesses about the <u>illicit</u> activity in their neighborhood.
Have vs. Of	*have*: verb (action word) *of*: preposition (connecting word)	I would <u>have</u>. NOT "I would <u>of</u>."
I vs. Me	*I*: subject *me*: object	<u>I</u> love it when my friend talks to <u>me</u>.

Confused Words	General Rules	Examples of Proper Use
Its vs. It's	*its*: possession *it's*: "it is"	It's important that when you purchase a phone, you are certain to check its warranty.
Less/much vs. Fewer/many	*less/much*: usually not countable *fewer/many*: usually countable	There is less anger and much contentment. There are fewer criminals and many law-abiding citizens.
Lie vs. Lay	*lie*: recline (present tense) *lay*: place (present tense)	Lay the pillow on the bed before you lie down to go to sleep.
Lose vs. Loose	*lose*: suffer a loss *loose*: not tight fitting	If your pants are too loose, you may lose your wallet.
Principal vs. Principle	*principal*: high-ranking person or primary *principle*: rule or belief	Our high school principal is very serious about following his principles.
Than vs. Then	*than*: for comparisons *then*: for time	I had more time back then but less time than I probably will have next year.
There vs. Their vs. They're	*there*: place *their*: possession *they're*: "they are"	When we travel over there to our friends' house, their hospitality is remarkable. In fact, they're the best hosts I know.
To vs. Too vs. Two	*to*: connecting preposition *two*: number *too*: comparisons	Go to the store, buy two apples, and be sure they aren't too old.
Which vs. That	*which*: nonrestrictive (extra information) *that*: restrictive (essential information)	The house that was on fire burned to the ground, which was unfortunate.
Who vs. Whom	*who*: subject *whom*: object (use "who" when you would use "he," and use "whom" when you would use "him")	Who is going to the movie? From whom did you purchase the ticket?
Whose vs. Who's	*whose*: possession *who's*: "who is"	Who's going to determine whose bike that is?
Your vs. You're	*your*: possession *you're*: "you are"	You're very nice; you must have learned that from your parents.

Punctuation

Although there are many specific punctuation rules, the most important guidelines for the grammar tested on the SAT are given in the tables that follow.

Commas

General Guideline	Appropriate Use
Separate a phrase (dependent clause) from a complete sentence (independent clause).	Once you have completed your homework, you may watch your favorite television show.
Join two complete sentences when there is a transitional word, like the "FANBOYS": *for, and, nor, but, or, yet,* and *so.*	The shark seemed excited about all the fish in the water, but the scuba divers were worried about all the activity.
Separate extra information (parenthetical phrases) from the rest of the sentence.	My history textbook, which I have had since the beginning of the year, occupies a special shelf in my locker.
Separate items in a list with commas.*	My favorite forms of punctuation include commas, semicolons, and dashes.
Do not use commas to separate parts of a sentence if everything in the sentence is needed to make it clear and logical.	A car that is speeding away from the police poses a danger to the community. (In this case, you must specify that a speeding car is the type of car that is a danger to the community. So a comma must not be used.)
Just because a sentence is long does not mean that it needs a comma. Look more at the structure of the sentence than at its length.	The European Organization for Nuclear research has used its world-class particle accelerators to make significant strides in particle physics.
A clarifying phrase (appositive) needs to be separated with commas. The name is sufficient to know who the person is, so commas are needed to separate the description. If the description is too vague to narrow down the item precisely, then no commas should separate descriptive phrases.	George Washington, the first President of the United States, has the U.S. capital named after him. (Alternatively, consider a sentence like this: *"President George Washington was elected."* The title "President" is not specific enough to narrow it down. However, the title "first President of the United States" is specific enough in the example above, so this phrase needs to be separated.)

*The SAT has traditionally preferred the serial or "Oxford" comma (i.e., having a comma between the second-to-last and last items in a list). Since there is not a universally accepted rule about whether the serial comma should be used, it is extremely unlikely that the SAT would include a test question about it.

Semicolons

General Guideline	Appropriate Use
You can use a semicolon to separate two complete, related sentences.	I am excited to go to the amusement park; I can't wait to ride the big roller coaster.
Use a semicolon to separate items in a list when at least one of the items has a comma or commas within it.	John's rock band traveled to New York, Boston, and Hartford in the Northeast; Chicago, Columbus, and Cleveland in the Midwest; and Orlando, Charleston, and Birmingham in the South.

Colons

General Guideline	Appropriate Use
Use a colon after a complete sentence to set off a list.	When you go to the store, please pick up the following items: soap, gum, and batteries.
Use a colon after a complete sentence to set off a clarification.	We were shocked to learn who the true villain in the film was: the seemingly friendly storekeeper.

Dashes

A dash, —, is longer than a hyphen. In contrast, a hyphen, -, is used to make compound words.

General Guideline	Appropriate Use
Although other punctuation can often work, the dash can provide variety in your writing when you need to indicate an interruption or change of thought.	Be careful when crossing that street—it is not very safe. (In this case, a colon or semicolon could work instead of the dash.)
A dash can be used to interrupt a sentence and provide a change of voice.	We lost the game—hardly a surprise given our terrible effort—but at least our dreadful season was over.
Dashes can set off a parenthetical phrase. If you start with a dash at one end of the phrase, you need to use a dash at the other end for consistency.	Test anxiety—something that affects many students—can be managed by setting realistic expectations for test performance.

Apostrophes

General Guideline	Appropriate Use
Use an apostrophe before the "s" to indicate that a singular entity possesses something.	The toy's instructions were rather confusing.
Use an apostrophe after the "s" to indicate that a plural entity possesses something.	All players' equipment must be within the rules.
Use an apostrophe to indicate a contraction with pronouns (they're, it's, you're, who's) and no apostrophe to indicate possession (their, its, your, whose).	It's a good idea to talk to your doctor if you're concerned that friends shared their cold when you visited them. No matter whose cold it was, they're going to be glad that you found out if you show its symptoms. Who's going to argue with that?
Use an apostrophe before the "s" to indicate possession after a noun that is already plural.	The women's restroom is next to the men's.

QUANTITATIVE GRAPH ANALYSIS

An important part of the SAT Writing and Language Test is the analysis of graphs. You can expect that a few questions will assess your ability to determine what claims can be made based on the information in a graph. The graphs can take a variety of forms—several possible presentations are given below. When you encounter graph analysis questions, keep these tips in mind:

- These questions will be about your quantitative reasoning, not about your mastery of grammar.
- Look carefully at the key/legend, axis labels, and units. Allow yourself enough time to become acquainted with the graph's organization.
- Since the questions will usually ask you to pick an accurate interpretation of the graph, take a glance at what the choices are generally stating so that you have a feel for what they are after. Then, as best as you can, try to come up with an answer of your own before jumping to a given answer.

Practice

Determine whether the following claims are supported or not supported based on the information in the graph.

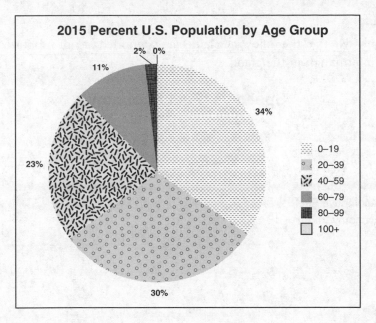

Source: *http://www.census.gov/population/international/data/worldpop/tool_population.php*

1. *Supported or NOT Supported*: The majority of the 2015 U.S. population is under 40 years of age.
2. *Supported or NOT Supported*: It is about three times as likely that a randomly selected U.S. citizen is in his or her 40s or 50s as it is that he or she is in his or her 60s or 70s.
3. *Supported or NOT Supported*: Women represent a slight minority of the overall U.S. population.

Answers

1. Supported. Adding the 0–19 age group and the 20–39 age group gives us 34% + 30% for a total of 64%, which is clearly a majority of the population.
2. NOT Supported. 40–59 year olds represent 23% of the population, and 60–79 year olds represent 11% of the population. 23 is not three times 11. Instead, 23 is closer to twice 11, making this claim incorrect.
3. NOT Supported. The graph gives information only about the relative percentages of age groups. No information is given about gender breakdown. So this claim cannot be justified based on the information in the graph.

Practice

Determine whether the following claims are supported or not supported based on the information in the graph.

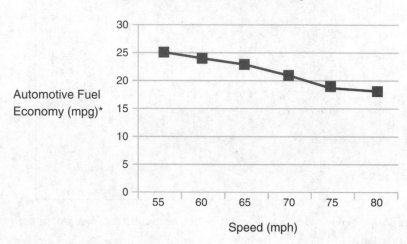

Speed vs. Fuel Economy

Source: *http://www.mpgforspeed.com*

1. *Supported or NOT Supported*: Automotive speed and fuel economy, when considering speeds between 55 and 80 miles per hour, have an inverse relationship.
2. *Supported or NOT Supported*: An increase in wind speed causes a proportional decrease in fuel efficiency because of an increase in wind resistance and friction.
3. *Supported or NOT Supported*: A car like one tested by the researchers who made this graph will likely have a fuel efficiency of approximately 22 miles per gallon at a speed of approximately 77 miles per hour.

Answers

1. Supported. The graph shows a steady decline in fuel efficiency as automotive speed increases, making for an inverse relationship.
2. NOT Supported. Although this is an accurate scientific statement, it is outside the scope of the information presented in the graph. So the graph cannot make an accurate claim about the statement.
3. NOT Supported. Read the statement closely—if it had said 67 miles per hour instead of 77, the statement would be correct. At 77 miles per hour, the fuel efficiency is close to 18 miles per gallon.

⚷ TIPS TO HELP YOU COPE

1. Consider reading the passage through once before answering the questions. With nearly 9 minutes per passage and a little under 1 minute per question, you should have plenty of time to work through the problems. Rather than having time at the end of the Writing and Language test to double-check and possibly do nothing, you can instead use your time to read the passage with an eye on its overall flow and meaning. This will enable you to do well on questions involving big-picture analysis of the passage and proper transitions.

2. Try to create your own answer before looking at the choices. All of the choices on the SAT Writing and Language test will be well written, and many will be quite persuasive. Prior to jumping into the choices, do your best to come up with a general idea of what you think the answer should be. This will put you in control rather than letting the test control you. If you are having trouble developing an idea for an answer, use the differences among the choices to pinpoint the type of error in question. That way, you can at least narrow down your thoughts before making a decision.

3. Do not hesitate to come back to questions. If you are having difficulty figuring out the answer to a question, let your subconscious mind take over while you consciously move on to other problems. While you are working through the other problems, your subconscious mind will likely piece together what makes the most sense on the problem you skipped. Then, with fresh eyes, you can come back to the question you previously skipped, and it will likely seem much easier than before.

4. Use similarities among the answers to eliminate choices. If you have a multiple-choice question with these choices, what is the answer?

   (A) %
   (B) %
   (C) $
   (D) %

The answer is choice (C), because it is different from the other options. Similarly, if you have an SAT Writing and Language question with choices like these,

   (A) Additionally
   (B) Also
   (C) In contrast
   (D) Moreover

you can use the similarities among the answers to eliminate possibilities. "Additionally," "also," and "moreover" mean that you are giving further discussion or examples along the same lines as before. However, "in contrast" means you have something that is the opposite of what came previously. So the answer must be choice (C). This technique can be particularly helpful in sorting out wordiness, punctuation, and transitions, among other things. Use this technique as a useful supplement to thinking through the question, not as your primary approach.

5. If you must guess, be smart about it. There is no penalty for guessing on questions as there was in the past. So be certain you have filled in an answer for every question. Instead of picking a random answer, keep the following tips in mind:

- The SAT will often have a few of the same answer choices in a row. Do not avoid picking an answer choice simply because you have used it on the previous question.

- "No Change" has just as much of a chance of being right as do the other options. Do not feel that you must make edits to every single question.

- Once you have made a thoughtful decision, don't second-guess. Read the context, consider the answers carefully, and pick the best option. If you have done these things, be comfortable picking your answer and moving on.

6. Realize that these are grammar rules, not merely grammar preferences. You have likely had a teacher who has had certain "pet peeves" about how you should write your essays. Maybe you have had a teacher who insisted you use only the formal third person voice in your essays; maybe your teacher marked off points for starting sentences with "but" or "because." The SAT does not care about such things. Any issues you encounter will be clear problems. The answers will be based on widespread English practice, not the personal preferences of particular editors. As a result, don't overthink what you encounter on the SAT Writing and Language test.

7. Give the SAT the benefit of the doubt. The College Board has invested tremendous resources into making the SAT error free. Do not waste time looking for mistakes on the test, because it is <u>extremely</u> unlikely there will be any. Instead, realize that this is a well-crafted assessment that demands you demonstrate your editing skills. The questions are not about whether what is given is true—they are simply about what is grammatically correct. The questions do not have tricks or gimmicks. If you are picking an answer because of some trick (e.g., thinking the SAT always

prefers short answers), you will be incorrect. If you pick an answer because it represents well-written English, you will be right.

PRACTICE EXERCISES

On the SAT Writing and Language test, you will have 4 passages from the following different content areas: careers, history and social studies, humanities, and science. One of each of these passage categories is presented below, giving you the same number of passages and questions you will have on the actual SAT Writing and Language test. Detailed answer explanations follow each passage.

Answers given on page 104.

Exercise A

The Doctor Is In

According to the United States Department of Labor, the 2012 median pay for veterinarians ❶ <u>were approximately</u> $85,000 annually, with the top ten percent earning more than $140,000. The job outlook is about average, so Doctors of Veterinary Medicine have to compete for jobs ❷ <u>by differentiating themselves through past experience and specialization.</u> Although private practice is expected to grow with more pet owners attending regular visits and animal medical care expanding into cancer treatments and organ transplants, the number of graduating veterinarian students is higher than ever—a trend that ❸ <u>continue to keeps</u> jobs scarce.

1. (A) NO CHANGE
   (B) has been approximately
   (C) had been approximately
   (D) was approximately

2. Which choice would most logically complete the sentence?

   (A) NO CHANGE
   (B) as people in a wide variety of professions must do on a regular basis.
   (C) by considering what other career paths may be most interesting to them.
   (D) with research scientists, project engineers, and computer specialists, all of whom have technical expertise.

3. (A) NO CHANGE
   (B) continues to keep
   (C) continue to keep
   (D) continues to keeping

Prospective veterinarians should pursue a ❹ <u>bachelors</u> degree in an area of science like biology, chemistry, or animal science and maintain a high G.P.A. to gain admission into a veterinary program, ❺ <u>where</u> they will spend three years in classrooms and labs, followed by a year in clinical rotations. After completing the doctorate, veterinarians have to pass federal and state licensing examinations before being allowed to practice. Still, even with accredited licensing, many veterinarians choose to enter one-year internships so they can later compete for higher-paying positions.

❻ <u>Eventually, vets will research, diagnose, and treat</u> medical conditions of pets, livestock, and other animals. Some will specialize in companion animals and work in private clinics and hospitals, while others will choose to work with farm animals or in research facilities. These vets usually travel back and forth between offices and farms or ranches to care for and perform surgeries on livestock. Those involved in food safety and inspection may spend their workdays in slaughterhouses and food-processing plants in an effort to prevent the spread of disease. Many others choose to stay at the university and teach. ❼ <u>Irregardless</u> of the work environment a veterinarian chooses, the job resembles that of a normal physician in its expanse; it is interdisciplinary, unpredictable, and constantly changing with new medical discoveries.

4. (A) NO CHANGE
   (B) bachelors'
   (C) bachelor's
   (D) bachelor is

5. (A) NO CHANGE
   (B) that
   (C) which
   (D) in

6. (A) NO CHANGE
   (B) Eventually, vets will research diagnose, and treat
   (C) Eventually vets will research diagnose and treat
   (D) Eventually vets will research, diagnose and treat

7. (A) NO CHANGE
   (B) With regards
   (C) Regarding
   (D) Regardless

A rare **⑧** <u>acception</u> to the usual veterinarian routines may be best exemplified in someone like Luke Gamble, a British vet who founded Worldwide Veterinary Services and Mission Rabies to support global initiatives to help animals **⑨** <u>in need.</u> Besides being a surgeon in his own practice, Gamble often volunteers in India and South Africa, going so far as to document his research on television and in books. A quick look at Gamble's website **⑩** <u>shows the skill with which Gamble is able to create a visually appealing introduction to his work.</u> Certainly, the glamour and excitement associated with Gamble's daily life in veterinary medicine and research is far from typical, but that doesn't make it any less **⑪** <u>enthralling</u>.

8. (A) NO CHANGE
(B) acceptance
(C) exception
(D) exceptance

9. (A) NO CHANGE
(B) that require the assistance of humankind.
(C) which demand help of the global community.
(D) that may live in different parts of the world and need our aid.

10. Which choice would most specifically elaborate on the range of Gamble's medical capabilities?

(A) NO CHANGE
(B) provides users with videos, links to articles, blog pieces, and helpful graphics.
(C) gives interesting insights on his multitudinous hobbies and passions.
(D) reveals a practice that expands from pet rabbits to wild lions.

11. Which of the following alternatives to the underlined word would NOT work?

(A) fascinating
(B) riveting
(C) impulsive
(D) captivating

Exercise B

Maslow's Hierarchy and Violence

[1]

There are many issues involved in trying to explain how the people who commit vicious crimes are created. Are they formed by society? Is violent behavior genetically encoded in ❶ his or her DNA? Or was there some sort of trauma in their lives that causes them to behave this way? One theory attempts to explain the evolution of murder ❷ to it's ancient origins through what we describe as the modern day serial killer by applying Maslow's Hierarchy of Needs to the psychology of a murderer.

[2]

Improvements in farming and taxes on alcohol eventually helped people gain enough money to feed themselves, ❸ and allowed them to focus on the next level of needs: safety needs. We usually have little awareness of this type of need, except for in times of emergency. ❹ Emergencies can come any place, any time, and people need to be prepared for them. Beginning around the mid-19th century, murders moved to a new stage of evolution. Throughout this period they dealt primarily with maintaining domestic security. People were frequently compelled to defend their homes by force, as the majority of the population ❺ hold only precarious ownership of their house and a meager income.

1. (A) NO CHANGE
   (B) its
   (C) one's
   (D) their

2. (A) NO CHANGE
   (B) to its
   (C) from it's
   (D) from its

3. (A) NO CHANGE
   (B) but
   (C) or
   (D) with

4. The writer is considering deleting the underlined portion. Should it be kept or deleted?

   (A) Kept, because it clarifies an important concept.
   (B) Kept, because it builds on the argument in the previous sentence.
   (C) Deleted, because it makes an unnecessary point.
   (D) Deleted, because it diverges from the theme of the previous sentence.

5. (A) NO CHANGE
   (B) held
   (C) holded
   (D) helded

[3]

The first level of Maslow's pyramid involves the basic biological needs. These include food, water, and oxygen, and are necessary to carry out the ❻ <u>fundamentally body</u> functions that keep us alive. In the 18th century, the majority of crimes and murders that were recorded involved obtaining food. Poverty and starvation ran rampant in this era of history, so it follows that this first level of physiological needs would be particularly emphasized and perhaps motivate someone to kill. ❼

[4]

In the late 19th century, laws were passed which allowed parishes to pave and clean streets and build suburbs. These communities were safer and more permanent than those at the beginning of the century, enabling people to move on to their third level of ❽ <u>needs, and—by extension—to</u> new motives for murder. This third level includes love, affection and sexual needs. In regards to the evolution of murder, no sexually motivated murders were recorded in Europe prior to the 19th-century, when "Jack the Ripper" emerged ❾ <u>between</u> many similarly violent deviants.

6. (A) NO CHANGE
   (B) fundamentally bodily
   (C) fundamental bodily
   (D) fundamental body

7. The writer is considering moving paragraph 3 to a different point in the essay. Where would it best be placed?

   (A) Where it currently is
   (B) Before paragraph 1
   (C) Before paragraph 2
   (D) After paragraph 4

8. (A) NO CHANGE
   (B) needs; by extension to
   (C) needs and by extension, to
   (D) needs: by extension to

9. (A) NO CHANGE
   (B) among
   (C) within
   (D) throughout

[5]

It took a while for the fourth level of Maslow's hierarchy—esteem needs—to come around as a murder motivation. Murder and serial killing motivated by this level began around the mid-20th century when the majority of Western society had more or less ❿ become a better place in which to reside. It's theorized that a killer's reason for committing this variety of murder often involves a desire to stand out, become famous, or to be recognized by society. ⓫

10. Which choice would be most closely and specifically tied to the points made previously in the essay?

(A) NO CHANGE
(B) found Maslow to be an insightful engineering mind.
(C) secured physiological, safety, and love needs.
(D) undergone wide-ranging poverty in the aftermath of World War II.

11. Which sentence, if inserted at this point, would provide the most logical conclusion to the paragraph and relevantly expand on the point made in the previous sentence?

(A) Society will one day come to understand the widespread influence of Maslow's psychological theories.
(B) Murderers use a variety of weapons to carry out their nefarious plans, including guns, knives, and ropes.
(C) If society did more to feed the hungry, then perhaps gruesome murders would be a thing of the past.
(D) This may explain why they frequently commit multiple murders, which they believe will distinguish them from other criminals.

Exercise C

Folklore

Think traditions. Think stories, dances, jokes, and old fairy tales. ❶ <u>Why is this the case?</u> Think about ways of living and expressing oneself—maybe through language, or cooking, or laughing, or rituals. The Center for Folklore Studies at Ohio State University defines it this way: "Folklore may be seen as the products of human work and thought that have developed within a limited community and that are communicated directly from generation to generation, usually orally, with the author or creator unknown." The University of North Carolina's Folklore program at Chapel Hill "focuses attention on those expressive realms that communities ❷ <u>inflame</u> with cultural meaning and through which they give voice to the issues and concerns that they see as central to their being."

1. Which of the following choices would most logically connect the introductory sentences to the sentences that follow?

   (A) NO CHANGE
   (B) But, don't stop there.
   (C) Life is what we make of it.
   (D) Think about the economy.

2. (A) NO CHANGE
   (B) infuse
   (C) imply
   (D) infer

❸ Technically only a discipline since the end of the 19th century, folklore is as old as humanity, and has as much to do with the present as it does with the past.

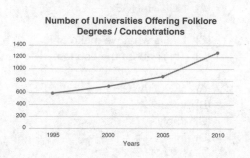

Number of Universities Offering Folklore Degrees / Concentrations

3. The author would like to insert a statement at this point in the essay to demonstrate the increasing interest in folklore scholarship. Which statement would be best supported by the information in the graph?

(A) In fact, if the number of universities offering folklore degrees and concentrations increases between 2010 and 2015 at the same rate as it did between 2000 and 2005, there will be approximately 2,000 schools in 2015 that offer such programs.

(B) In fact, if the number of universities offering folklore degrees and concentrations increases between 2010 and 2015 at the same rate as it did between 1995 and 2005, there will be approximately 1,800 schools in 2015 that offer such programs.

(C) In fact, if the number of universities offering folklore degrees and concentrations increases between 2010 and 2015 at the same rate as it did between 2005 and 2010, there will be approximately 1,700 schools in 2015 that offer such programs.

(D) In fact, if the number of universities offering folklore degrees and concentrations increases at the same rate between 2010 and 2015 as it did between 1995 and 2010, there will be approximately 1,400 schools in 2015 that offer such programs.

Folklorists—regardless of their focus within the wide, interdisciplinary field of Folklore—often ❹ uses a similar approach and methodology, called "ethnographic fieldwork." This means the folklorist's job is not confined to a desk, a university, ❺ or a museum; instead, the work is participatory and engaging, often in real-world settings in the expressive realms of festival, narrative, faith, art, architecture, and food, ❻ as such. Naturally, this work overlaps with that of anthropologists, sociologists, feminists, historians, and cultural studies, race, class, and literature scholars. Digging into the lifestyles ❼ atop a community, the study of folklore questions and imagines how artistic forms of expression may be used as spaces of reflection, resistance, autonomy, and identity.

Ruth Benedict, perhaps one of the best known women anthropologists and folklorists, studied under Franz Boas—the so-named "Father of Anthropology"—and is credited with helping to transition the study of folklore from the confinements of the historical and the vernacular, ❽ to the performance of expression as a means of interpreting culture and values. Another prominent folklorist, Richard Bauman, is widely celebrated in performance studies, linguistics, and folkloristics. His work on language ideology examines how people's ideas about ❾ their language affect their linguistic practices; and, along with other scholars of folklore, Bauman is part of the shift to verbal art and the moment of performance.

4. (A) NO CHANGE
   (B) uses a similarly
   (C) use a similar
   (D) use a similarly

5. (A) NO CHANGE
   (B) or a museum, instead, the
   (C) or a museum, instead the
   (D) or a museum instead: the

6. Which wording would best express the idea that there are further settings in which folklorists can conduct their work?

   (A) NO CHANGE
   (B) which comes as no surprise.
   (C) sparingly.
   (D) among others.

7. (A) NO CHANGE
   (B) within
   (C) from which
   (D) to

8. (A) NO CHANGE
   (B) with the performance of expression by means of interpreting cultural values.
   (C) for the interpretation of the culture and values instigated by the performance of meaningful expression.
   (D) by the cultural, valued interpretation that involves expressive performance.

9. (A) NO CHANGE
   (B) there
   (C) one's
   (D) ones'

By looking at the breadth of research of a couple folklorists, **⑩ <u>you will learn about the scholarly qualifications of these researchers.</u>** A folklorist may enter a city or village or subculture, and begin to participate in that population's day-to-day life. Possibly, **⑪ <u>he or she</u>** may end up studying a story, a joke, a dance, a dish, or even a child's game—an apparently trivial practice that, when looked at closely, turns out to be substantial in meaning.

10. Which choice gives the most logical and relevant conclusion to this sentence?

   (A) NO CHANGE
   (B) you will begin to understand the definition of folklore.
   (C) you can come to see the expanse of the field.
   (D) you will find contrasting, if not conflicting viewpoints.

11. (A) NO CHANGE
    (B) it
    (C) you
    (D) they

Exercise D

Age of the Drone

Could robots soon be delivering your mail? Allow me to set the scene: you're coming home from school, walking toward your front door, and ❶ bam a flying robot drops your oldest sister's just-ordered DVD collection on your head. It may not be as farfetched as it sounds. Today is the age of the drone, also known as the unmanned aerial vehicle (UAV), and it's only a matter of time before it becomes an everyday occurrence.

❷ Throughout the years of the past, drones have been controlled remotely and, most often, used for military services and special operations. In World War II, it became common practice ❸ to use drones to fly attack missions. By the early 2000s, more than 50 countries had operating military drones. In recent years, ❹ we've seen drones move into other fields such as photography, surveillance, search and rescue, security, and policing. And they aren't stopping there. ❺ In fact, researchers project that between 2015 and 2030, the economic impact of drones will roughly triple.

Projected Economic Impact of UAV Industry, U.S.

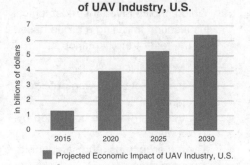

■ Projected Economic Impact of UAV Industry, U.S.

1. (A) NO CHANGE
   (B) bam—a flying robot drops your oldest sister's just-ordered DVD collection on your head.
   (C) bam, a flying robot drops, your oldest sisters just-ordered DVD collection on your head.
   (D) bam: a flying robot drops your oldest sisters' just-ordered DVD collection on your head.

2. (A) NO CHANGE
   (B) In the past years of history,
   (C) In the decades of the past,
   (D) Historically,

3. (A) NO CHANGE
   (B) in use
   (C) for the using
   (D) while use

4. (A) NO CHANGE
   (B) we've saw
   (C) we have sawed
   (D) we had saw

5. Which choice represents an accurate interpretation of the information in the graph?

   (A) NO CHANGE
   (B) In fact, researchers project that between 2015 and 2020, the economic impact of drones will roughly quintuple.
   (C) In fact, researchers project that between 2015 and 2030, the economic impact of drones will roughly double.
   (D) In fact, researchers project that between 2015 and 2025, the economic impact of drones will roughly quadruple.

As technology advances, an increasing number of autonomous drones are being designed for everyday services. Recently, Amazon announced its plan to use small, pilotless aircraft to deliver the majority of its packages. The end goal—although, still far off—is to be able to get goods to Amazon customers in approximately 30 minutes from the time they are ordered. ❻ <u>Unmanned aerial vehicles are clearly safe for the majority of uses for which they are intended.</u> To help with the more temporary obstacles—birds, strong winds, or you attempting to unlock your front door—will be on-the-ground human operators. Yet, ❼ <u>drone engineers and roboticists have their way,</u> these human operators won't be necessary for long.

Amazon isn't the only company replacing parts of its labor force with drones. Aurizon, Australia's largest rail company, uses drones to survey ❽ <u>its</u> entire transport infrastructure. When a job is too dirty, too dangerous, or too inaccessible, Aurizon utilizes a drone ❾ <u>in order to maximize its corporate bond valuation.</u> With more than 2,600 kilometers of railway to inspect, it is not just safer, but more cost-effective to send a drone. In fact, company leaders are so confident in the implementation of microdrones,

6. The writer wants to address the reader's potential objection that using UAVs will be unsafe. Which option would most clearly and specifically accomplish this goal?

(A) NO CHANGE
(B) With their multiyear track record of safe use in this way, consumers and safety advocates have little cause for alarm.
(C) These microdrones will be programmed with destinations before liftoff and use navigation systems to avoid permanent obstacles like buildings and trees.
(D) It is highly unlikely that drone usage will result in a gradual decline in societal norms for moral behavior.

7. (A) NO CHANGE
(B) if drone engineers and roboticists have their way,
(C) drone engineers and roboticists,
(D) if they have their way,

8. (A) NO CHANGE
(B) it's
(C) its'
(D) it is

9. Which choice gives the most logical justification for using a drone based on the rest of the sentence?

(A) NO CHANGE
(B) instead of employing outside janitorial services.
(C) that is a machine controlled by a man.
(D) rather than risk the safety of its employees.

they are predicting a 50% **❿** <u>extermination</u> in operational failures.

While all of this sounds promising, it's hard to take in from the currently droneless day to day we live in. **⓫** <u>And</u> NASA believes that is to change rather quickly; representatives have estimated that drones will be a billion dollar business in the United States within the next ten years. Ready or not, here they come.

10. (A) NO CHANGE
    (B) decrease
    (C) less
    (D) fewness

11. (A) NO CHANGE
    (B) To
    (C) But
    (D) With

Answer Key

Exercise A

1. D	4. C	7. D	10. D
2. A	5. A	8. C	11. C
3. B	6. A	9. A	

Exercise B

1. D	4. C	7. C	10. C
2. D	5. B	8. A	11. D
3. A	6. C	9. B	

Exercise C

1. B	4. C	7. B	10. C
2. B	5. A	8. A	11. A
3. C	6. D	9. A	

Exercise D

1. B	4. A	7. B	10. B
2. D	5. D	8. A	11. C
3. A	6. C	9. D	

Answer Explanations

Exercise A

1. **(D)**

Make sure the verb is consistent with the number of the subject. The subject is "pay," which is singular, making choice (A) incorrect. Also, the tense needs to be in the past because this refers to the pay in a past year, 2012. So, choice (D) is needed since "was" gives the past tense. Choice (B) is in the present perfect (e.g., *has/have been*—something that is continuing through the present or has recently been completed), and choice (C) is in the past perfect (e.g., *had been*—typically to indicate that the event took place prior to another past event).

2. **(A)**

Choice (A) logically completes the sentence because it gives specific ways that Doctors of Veterinary Medicine can better compete for limited jobs. Choice (B) is too vague, choice (C) is irrelevant, and choice (D) is illogical since veterinarians would most likely not be in direct competition for jobs with people in these fields.

3. **(B)**

Choice (B) is numerically consistent with the singular subject, "number," and uses the correct infinitive form of the verb, "to keep." Choice (C) uses the plural verb "continue," and choices (A) and (D) use incorrect forms of "keep."

4. **(C)**

The degree belongs to a single person, so put the apostrophe before the "s." Choice (A) would work if you were using "bachelors" as a subject, but it does not show possession. Choice (B) would be accurate for multiple bachelors, and choice (D) incorrectly uses the verb "is" in a way that changes the original meaning away from possession.

5. **(A)**

Since this refers to the physical locations of classes and labs and since the veterinary program would have a physical location, "where" would make sense. Choices (B), (C), and (D) use improper prepositions to make the needed connection. "In which" could work instead of "where," but this is not an option.

6. **(A)**

Choice (A) is the only option to give a needed break after the introductory word "Eventually" and also to clearly break up the different verbs that state what vets will do. Choice (B) does not have a needed comma between the separate actions "research" and "diagnose," and choices (C) and (D) lack a comma after the introductory word "Eventually."

7. **(D)**

Choice (D) uses the proper idiomatic expression, "regardless of." Choice (A) is not a word, choice (B) would need the word "to" immediately following it instead of "of" to be correct, and choice (C) could work if the "of" immediately following were deleted, but not in its current form. Choices (B) and (C) can work grammatically in other contexts, like "regarding the latest assignment" or "regardless of his intentions."

8. **(C)**

Choice (C) uses the correct word "exception" to indicate that this is an unusual case. Choice (A) is not a word, choice (B) does not fit the needed definition given the context, and choice (D) is also not a word.

9. **(A)**

Choice (A) expresses the necessary idea most concisely. Choices (B), (C), and (D) are too wordy.

10. **(D)**

Choice (D) best accomplishes this task because it shows that Gamble's veterinary practice ranges from being able to treat small rabbits to large lions. Choices (A) and (B) focus on his skill in website design, not on the range of his capabilities. Choice (C) is far too vague.

11. **(C)**

Be sure you picked up on the word NOT in the question. The current word, "enthralling," means extremely interesting. Choices (A), (B), and (D) all are synonymous with this word. Choice (C), "impulsive," is associated with unconscious desires rather than something that consciously interests people.

Exercise B

1. **(D)**

"Their" is consistent with the plural "they" and "the people" earlier in the paragraph. Choices (A), (B), and (C) all refer to things in a singular way.

2. **(D)**

The proper idiomatic phrase is "evolution from," making choices (A) and (B) incorrect. Also, "its" as in choice (D) is the possessive form of "it," while "it's" means "it is," making choice (C) incorrect.

3. **(A)**

"And" gives an appropriate transition between the first and second parts of this sentence, since the improvements in farming and taxes on alcohol both helped people gain money _and_ allowed them to focus on their safety. Choice (B) ("but") shows a contrast, choice (C) ("or") shows that only one of these consequences would happen, and choice (D) ("with") changes these two separate ways of helping people into a single item, thereby changing the original meaning to an improper phrase, "with allowed them."

4. **(C)**

The description of emergencies gives vague, irrelevant, and unneeded information about the broad characteristics of emergencies. This statement is unnecessary and should be removed, making choice (C) correct and choices (A) and (B) incorrect. Choice (D) is not correct because it continues with the same theme of "emergency" from the previous sentence, albeit giving irrelevant information about it.

5. **(B)**

"Held" is consistent with the past tense of this sentence. Choice (A) is in the present tense, and choices (C) and (D) use incorrect forms of "hold."

6. **(C)**

Even though "bodily" ends in "ly," it is an adjective describing the noun "functions." "Fundamental" is also describing "functions," so it too must be in the adjective form. Choices (A) and (B) incorrectly use the adverb form "fundamentally." Choice (D) incorrectly uses the noun "body" to describe another noun.

7. **(C)**

The overall structure of the essay is to first introduce the topic of Maslow's Hierarchy and then to chronologically and sequentially present the different levels of Maslow's pyramid as they relate to murder psychology. Paragraph 3 analyzes the first level of Maslow's pyramid, so it makes sense to insert it before Paragraph 2. If the paragraph were left where it currently is (choice (A)), it would make Paragraph 2's placement illogical, since Paragraph 2 refers to the "next level of needs"—it makes no sense to refer to the "next" level of needs without mentioning the first level of needs. Choice (B) would not work, because the general introduction of Paragraph 1 would not make sense following Paragraph 3. Choice (D) would illogically place paragraph 3, which describes the first level of Maslow's pyramid, well after the other levels in the pyramid have been sequentially discussed.

8. **(A)**

Choice (A) correctly sets off the parenthetical phrase "by extension" using dashes. Choice (B) doesn't work because there must be a complete sentence before and after a semicolon. Choices (C) and (D) do not set aside "by extension" using punctuation like dashes or commas.

9. **(B)**

"Among" correctly means "out of" as it is used in this context. Choice A, "between," is used when comparing things considered one at a time. Choices (C) and (D) do not work because it is illogical to state that a murderer could emerge "within" or "throughout" many similarly minded people.

10. **(C)**

Choice (C) gives specific examples of needs that have been analyzed previously in the passage. It is not choice (A) because the passage has not focused on the relative quality of living conditions. It is not choice (B) because Maslow did not have an engineering mind but rather a psychological mind. It is not choice (D) because the passage did not make claims about poverty in the years following World War II.

11. **(D)**

The point made in the previous sentence is that killers may want to commit murders in order to become famous. Choice (D) logically ties in to this theme by giving a possible justification as to why people commit serial murder—they want to be recognized for their uniqueness. Choice (A) is not correct because it is too vague. Choice (B) is not correct because it fails to tie in to the murderers' likely motivation. Choice (C) is not correct because this makes an irrelevant, off-topic point.

Exercise C

1. **(B)**

The sentences both before and immediately after the underlined portion hook the reader's interest on the topic of folklore. Choice (B) provides a good transition from talking about this theme in more general terms to talking about more specific themes. Choice (A) doesn't work because the sentence that follows does not explain why someone would have these thoughts. Choices (C) and (D) are irrelevant to the theme of the surrounding sentences.

2. **(B)**

"Infuse" captures the intended meaning of "fill"—these expressive activities fill communities with cultural meaning. Choice (A), "inflame," is too negative; choice (C), "imply," means to suggest; and choice (D), "infer," means to pick up on the implicit meaning of something.

3. **(C)**

Between 2005 and 2010, there is a rough increase of about 400 along the y-axis. So, if the number of universities offering folklore increases at the same rate as this between 2010 and 2015, there will be approximately 1,700 schools in 2015 that offer such programs. Choices (A), (B), and (D) do not make conclusions supported by the trends in the presented data.

4. **(C)**

"Use" is the needed plural form of the verb, matching the plural subject "Folklorists." This makes choices (A) and (B) incorrect, since they use the singular "uses." Choice (C) also correctly uses the adjective "similar" rather than the adverb "similarly," as in choice (D), to describe the noun "approach."

5. **(A)**

A semicolon provides a needed break between the two independent clauses, making choice (A) correct. Choices (B) and (C) are run-on sentences. Choice (D) is incorrect because a longer pause is needed before the transitional word "instead" rather than after it.

6. **(D)**

Stating "among others" implies that even though a variety of settings is mentioned—festival, narrative, faith, etc.—there would be even more that are not mentioned. "As such," choice (A), means in the exact sense of the word, which does not work. Choice (B) does nothing to convey that there are further settings, and choice (C) would, if anything, make it seem like there were fewer such settings.

7. **(B)**

"Within" is the proper word to use in this context, since people live within a community, not "atop" it (choice (A)), "from which" it (choice (C)), or "to" it (choice (D)).

8. **(A)**

Choice (A) uses the correct transitional word to start off the phrase, since the proper wording is "from" one thing "to" another. Also, choice (A) is parallel to the structure of the previous part of the sentence. Choices (B), (C), and (D) do not use the proper initial transitional word.

9. **(A)**

"Their" is the possessive plural word needed to describe how the language belonged to the plural people. Choice (B) uses the spelling of "there," which generally refers to places. Choice (C) is singular, and choice (D) is not a word.

10. **(C)**

Choice (C) gives the best conclusion to this sentence, not only because it connects to the mention of "breadth" in research by mentioning the "expanse" of the field but because it introduces the presentation of diverse research methodologies that folklorists use. Choice (A) focuses too narrowly on the qualifications of the folklorists rather than on what they would actually do. Choice (B) doesn't work because folklore was defined earlier in the passage, and what follows this sentence doesn't define folklore but identifies the different ways folklorists can conduct research. Choice (D) doesn't work because although folklorists surely have some differing views on important topics, that is not what is emphasized in this paragraph.

11. **(A)**

"He or she" functions as a singular, gender-neutral way to identify the subject and works because the writer is referring to "a folklorist" in the previous sentence and continues to do so in this sentence. Choice (B) refers to things, not people. Choice (C) is in the second person, and choice (D) is plural.

Exercise D

1. **(B)**

An interruption is needed after "bam" since this comes as an abrupt end to the sequence of events with the surprising drone delivery coming immediately after. A dash can provide the needed pause. Choice (A) does not have the necessary pauses after "bam," and choice (C) has an unnecessary comma after "drops" and lacks an apostrophe in "sisters." While choice (D) correctly uses a colon, it incorrectly places an apostrophe after "sisters," which would not work because if one refers to the oldest sister, it can only be a singular person.

2. **(D)**

"Historically" is the most concise option—choices (A), (B), and (C) express the same idea as choice (D), but do so using many more words.

3. **(A)**

The proper phrase is "common ... to use," making choice (A) correct. Choice (B) can work in other contexts, like "the bathroom is in use," but choices (C) and (D) are idiomatically incorrect.

4. **(A)**

The present perfect tense, "we've seen" as a substitute for "we have seen," works because this states that this shift has happened in recent years, which means it would likely continue up to the present day. Choices (B), (C), and (D) use the incorrect conjugation of "to see," as "saw" is used as the past tense form of the verb, not a present or past perfect form.

5. **(D)**

In 2015, the economic impact of drones is around 1.25 billion dollars, and in 2025, it is around 5 billion dollars. Choice (D) correctly states that between 2015 and 2025 the economic impact would roughly quadruple, since 1.25 × 4 = 5. Choices (A), (B), and (C) do not accurately reflect the quantitative information in the graph.

6. **(C)**

Choice (C) does the best job in giving *clear and specific* ways that the researcher can address the notion that UAV usage will be unsafe. Since they will have preprogrammed destinations and the capability to avoid obstacles, they will be quite safe to operate. Choices (A) and (B) are too vague, and choice (D) is off-topic.

7. **(B)**

Without using "if" to start the phrase, the sentence as a whole would be illogical, making choices (A) and (C) incorrect. Choice (D) is too vague with "they"—the pronoun needs to be clarified in this case since it is unclear precisely to what it is referring.

8. **(A)**

The "its" correctly refers to the singular company's ownership of an infrastructure. "It's," choice B, is the same as "it is." "Its'," choice (C), is never correct. "It is," choice (D), expresses action rather than ownership.

9. **(D)**

The previous part of the sentence emphasizes how many jobs could be unsafe or filthy for humans to do; therefore, "rather than risk the safety of its employees" would logically follow since a drone could provide clean and safe access to otherwise dangerous and dirty places. Choice (A) focuses on just the economic benefits. Choice (B) focuses only on cleanliness, ignoring the safety and inaccessibility concerns. Choice (C) simply defines what a drone is.

10. **(B)**

All of these choices mean "go down" or "less" in some way; however, "decrease" is most appropriately used in conjunction with concrete numbers and percentages. Choice (A), "extermination," is too violent; choice (C), "less," is generally used with noncountable items; and choice (D), "fewness," is not a word.

11. (C)

The previous sentence and the current sentence have a contrasting relationship with one another—the first sentence states that we are not used to drones, and the current sentence states that this could very well change in the near future. "But" is the only one of these words that expresses a contrast.

THE 50-MINUTE ESSAY

The SAT Essay is an optional part of the SAT that requires you to demonstrate understanding and analysis of an argument. You will not need to have any specific background knowledge—you only need to focus on what is given in the source text. The rubric and general question will remain identical from test to test, but the source text will change, although it will consistently be a high-quality argument on a general topic intended for a broad audience of readers. The essay comes at the end of the SAT.

Sample Prompt

Review the following sample prompt, directions, and format.

Directions: This assignment will allow you to demonstrate your ability to skillfully read and understand a source text and write a response analyzing the source. In your response, you should show that you have understood the source, give proficient analysis, and use the English language effectively. If your essay is off-topic, it will not be scored.

Only what you write on the lined paper in your answer document will be scored—avoid skipping lines, using unreasonably large handwriting, and using wide margins in order to have sufficient space to respond. You can also write on the planning sheet in the answer document, but this will not be evaluated—no other scrap paper will be given. Be sure to write clearly and legibly so your response can be scored.

You will be given 50 minutes to complete the assignment, including reading the source text and writing your response.

Read the following passage, and think about how the author uses:

• Evidence, such as applicable examples, to justify the argument
• Reasoning to show logical connections among thoughts and facts
• Rhetoric, like sensory language and emotional appeals, to give weight to the argument

Life: Pass It On

1   I have been called many things throughout the course of life—some fit for publication, and others a little less ... savory, we'll say. Yet, despite my host of titles, Saint is something with which I will never be confused. This is not to say that I'm unconcerned with being a good person. Rather, it's more an indictment of my laziness; when doing nothing is often so much easier than doing the right thing, inaction is an appealing choice.

2   So, when I stumble across one of those rare ways to make a difference that manages to coincide with my penchant for convenience, I'm anxious to oblige—especially if my sole obligation is to checkmark a box at the DMV once every five years when I renew my driver's license. Really, that's the extent of my hassle. Besides, I already have to go there, anyway.

3   If you have a driver's license, I expect that you are aware that this is the process by which one registers as an organ donor (at least in the majority of states). No monetary sacrifice, no extensive paperwork, and really no time at all are required on your part. Just a checkmark. ✔

4   Yet, it may surprise you that only 40% of American adults have registered; that's only two out of every five. This statistic is particularly jarring when it is contrasted with another: 95% of Americans strongly support organ donation (according to a 2005 Gallup poll). That is every 19 out of 20 people, which is a figure that positively dwarfs the number who have actually registered.

5   My question to you is a simple one: why? When such a vast majority is fervently in favor of the concept, and when the societal benefits absolutely eclipse the (lack of) personal costs involved, why is such a depressing minority willing to check that tiny box?

6   Two out of five. Now, if you are part of that 40%, I salute you. But, should you fall in that silent majority, my plea today is on your behalf. (And if you fall into neither group and don't have a driver's license in the first place, feel free to carry on at your pedestrian leisure.) You have the opportunity to save several lives and improve several more—just with a casual flick of the wrist. Convenience isn't the issue; check the box, then pat yourself on the back. Good deed for the day, just like that.

7   So if it's not a matter of convenience, then what? Is it fear? I was 18 when I first registered to be a donor. This was also the first time in my life that I was required to acknowledge my own mortality, and I recall it was quite surreal. When I die? When, not if?! But you don't understand, I can't die yet! I haven't even gone to senior prom! But I reflected on this decision

to be a donor, and it was really quite simple: I will die when I die, whether I admit my mortality on my driver's license or not; burying my head in the sand would not deter the inevitable.

8   Moreover, contrary to tabloid sensationalism, no organ donor has ever been declared dead prematurely; donors are actually subject to more post-mortem testing than non-donors just to ensure that this scenario never occurs. Thus, you are far more likely to be buried alive as a non-donor than to be declared dead as a donor. Roll that around in your head for a moment.

9   Ultimately, though, I expect that people are so reluctant to register primarily because of the anonymity of the people one would be saving. When dealing with strangers, the whole concept is more abstract and impersonal, because you haven't seen the suffering of those you would help. You haven't spoken to these people and listened to the infinite gratitude of those who have been saved, or to the despair of those who pass away before an organ can be procured. But, I have; I worked in transplant centers in my first job out of college, and, if there was one thing that I learned, it's that those in need are just like you and me. So, should the day come when I need an organ (and it could for all of us), I hope somebody would be willing to do something as simple as check a box to save my life.

Write a response that demonstrates how the author makes an argument to persuade an audience that it makes sense to become a registered organ donor. In your response, analyze how the author uses at least one of the features from the essay directions (or features of your own choosing) to develop a logical and persuasive argument. Be certain that your response cites relevant aspects of the source text.

Your response should not give your personal opinion on the merit of the source text but instead show how the author crafts an argument to persuade readers.

Sample Response

How will you be evaluated on the SAT Essay? Essay graders use a general rubric like this:

SAT Essay Rubric

Each of the two graders will use a similar rubric to this one, grading your essay from 1 to 4 for each category, and then the two graders' individual scores will be combined to give you category scores between 2 and 8. Your score on the Essay will be reported separately and will not affect your overall SAT composite score.

Score: 4	
Reading	Excellent: The essay shows excellent understanding of the source. The essay shows an understanding of the source's main argument and key details and a firm grasp of how they are interconnected, demonstrating clear comprehension of the source. The essay does not misinterpret or misrepresent the source. The essay skillfully uses source evidence, such as direct quotations and rephrasing, representing a thorough comprehension of the source.
Analysis	Excellent: The essay gives excellent analysis of the source and shows clear understanding of what the assignment requires. The essay gives a complete, highly thoughtful analysis of the author's use of reasoning, evidence, rhetoric, and/or other argumentative elements the student has chosen to highlight. The essay has appropriate, adequate, and skillfully chosen support for its analysis. The essay focuses on the most important parts of the source in responding to the prompt.
Writing	Excellent: The essay is focused and shows an excellent grasp of the English language. The essay has a clear thesis. The essay has a well-executed introduction and conclusion. The essay shows a clear and well-crafted progression of thoughts both within paragraphs and in the essay as a whole. The essay has a wide range of sentence structures. The essay consistently shows precise choice of words. The essay is formal and objective in its style and tone. The essay demonstrates a firm grasp of the rules of standard English and has very few to no errors.
Score: 3	
Reading	Skillful: The essay shows effective understanding of the source. The essay shows an understanding of the source's main argument and key details. The essay is free of major misinterpretations and/or misrepresentations of the source. The essay uses appropriate source evidence, such as direct quotations and rephrasing, representing comprehension of the source.
Analysis	Skillful: The essay gives effective analysis of the source and shows an understanding of what the assignment requires. The essay decently analyzes the author's use of reasoning, evidence, rhetoric, and/or other argumentative elements the student has chosen to highlight. The essay has appropriate and adequate support for its analysis. The essay focuses primarily on the most important parts of the source in responding to the prompt.

Writing	Skillful: The essay is mostly focused and shows an effective grasp of the English language. The essay has a thesis, either explicit or implicit. The essay has an effective introduction and conclusion. The essay has a clear progression of thoughts both within paragraphs and in the essay as a whole. The essay has an assortment of sentence structures. The essay shows some precise choice of words. The essay is formal and objective in its style and tone. The essay demonstrates a grasp of the rules of standard English and has very few significant errors that interfere with the writer's argument.
Score: 2	
Reading	Limited: The essay shows some understanding of the source. The essay shows an understanding of the source's main argument, but not of key details. The essay may have some misinterpretations and/or misrepresentations of the source. The essay gives only partial evidence from the source, showing limited comprehension of the source.
Analysis	Limited: The essay gives partial analysis of the source and shows only limited understanding of what the assignment requires. The essay tries to show how the author uses reasoning, evidence, rhetoric, and/or other argumentative elements the student has chosen to highlight, but only states rather than analyzes their importance, or at least one part of the essay's analysis is unsupported by the source. The essay has little or no justification for its argument. The essay may lack attention to those elements of the source that are most pertinent to responding to the prompt.
Writing	Limited: The essay is mostly not cohesive and shows an ineffective grasp of the English language. The essay may not have a thesis, or may diverge from the thesis at some point in the essay's development. The essay may have an unsuccessful introduction and/or conclusion. The essay may show progression of thoughts within the paragraphs, but not in the essay as a whole. The essay is relatively uniform in its sentence structures. The essay shows imprecise and possibly repetitive choice of words. The essay may be more casual and subjective in style and tone. The essay demonstrates a weaker grasp of the rules of standard English and does have errors that interfere with the writer's argument.

Score: 1	
Reading	Insufficient: The essay shows virtually no understanding of the source. The essay is unsuccessful in showing an understanding of the source's main argument. It may refer to some details from the text, but it does so without tying them to the source's main argument. The essay has many misinterpretations and/or misrepresentations of the source. The essay gives virtually no evidence from the source, showing very poor comprehension of the source.
Analysis	Insufficient: The essay gives little to no accurate analysis of the source and shows poor understanding of what the assignment requires. The essay may show how the author uses reasoning, evidence, rhetoric, and/or other argumentative elements that the student has chosen to highlight but does so without analysis. Or many parts of the essay's analysis are unsupported by the source. The support given for points in the essay's argument are largely unsupported or off-topic. The essay may not attend to the elements of the source that are pertinent to responding to the prompt. Or the essay gives no explicit analysis, perhaps only resorting to summary statements.
Writing	Insufficient: The essay is not cohesive and does not demonstrate skill in the English language. The essay may not have a thesis. The essay does not have a clear introduction and conclusion. The essay does not have a clear progression of thoughts. The essay is quite uniform and even repetitive in sentence structure. The essay shows poor and possibly inaccurate word choice. The essay is likely casual and subjective in style and tone. The essay shows a poor grasp of the rules of standard English and may have many errors that interfere with the writer's argument.

What does a good response look like? Here is an example of a top-scoring response to the sample prompt. As you read, think about how the student demonstrated his/her skill in Reading, Analysis, and Writing. When you finish, review the aspects of an essay that scored a 4 in all of these areas. What do you think? Did the writer do an exceptional job in each aspect?

Response with Scores Of 4/4 Reading, 4/4 Analysis, and 4/4 Writing

In a whimsical and intimate voice, the writer tackles a very sobering issue. "Life: Pass It On" forcefully contends for more organ donors by presenting its argument in a journal-like letter to those who have failed "to check that tiny box."

Although statistics are utilized, the writer relies more emphatically on a personal appeal to potential donors, alluding to the convenience, harmlessness, and morality in the decision to donate organs after death. The evidence, reasoning, and plea to the reader arise from the writer's own experience, and are accompanied by a chummy and likeable affectation. It is through this friendly writer-reader exchange that the piece drives home its ultimate goal: to bridge the gap between strangers and advocate for compassion toward others in a potentially life-or-death situation.

First, let us acknowledge the writer's relatability. The essay begins with a brutally honest self-reflection: the writer is no "Saint." And let's face it: laziness is something we can all relate to. Yet, despite the author's lack of philanthropy, he is amiable and even kindhearted. In the author's reflection on his mortality, the reader is able to stop and recall a similar moment—or perhaps, have that moment for the very first time. And suddenly, the reader is participating in a direct dialogue with the writer—a dialogue so cordial that it allows the writer to pose baffling questions to the reader him/herself. If the reader is one of the 60% who failed to check that box, he/she is instantly questioning his or her own motives. This very approachable style of writing proves effective in the buildup of the argument for organ donation.

Initially, the writer testifies—through his own usual passiveness—the utter convenience of becoming an organ donor; it boils down to "Just a checkmark." Since you need not enter sainthood to mark this box, it is free game for all, the writer argues. Next, the passage deals with the possibility of fear, alleviating it with a personal anecdote that is simultaneously dramatic, comical, and yet recognizable. Again, the reader is aligned with the writer in mortality, "I will die when I die." Though, this indication may seem trivial, it is the author's intent to leap nonchalantly over the irrelevant fear of death, safely bringing his reader along. Then, the writer appeals to the reader morally, insisting that if "you" had only seen the power behind that checkmark, you'd surely have signed up without a second thought. These techniques are exerted in an effort to unite reader and writer, while refuting any counterarguments—the author simply cannot find a good reason *not* to be an organ donor.

The dichotomy between registered donors and those who "*strongly support* organ donation" is equally effective in setting the foundation for the author's argument. The figures don't add up, and the writer appeals to the reader by asking for his opinion on such a wide contrast. Saving lives is easy, he argues; in fact, it takes just "a casual flick of the wrist." Once the writer enlists the readers to disregard inconvenience and fear in their interpretation of the stark statistics, it comes down to the author's opinion on the previously unanswered question.

Anonymity and impersonality are, for the writer, at the heart of the lagging organ donors. Here, the reasoning stands that author has experience with transplant survivors (and those corpses failed by the numerous unchecked boxes), and is, therefore, in a position of authority to declare that they are "just like you and me."

Now, who wouldn't want to help (especially when you could be on the other end of it)? The case for more organ donors is made via an intimate plea to the reader—the writer and reader, once strangers, are now companionable; it is this hospitable demeanor that encourages the uncertain to check the box and do a part in saving lives. Experts, in-depth statistics, and quotes are hardly needed because the writer allows the reader to make his own call while presenting a somewhat infallible argument: if Americans support it, it is time we show our support. By being relatable and divulging personal insight, the writer effectively asserts his position for increased organ donation.

TIPS TO HELP YOU COPE

1. **KEEP YOUR PERSONAL OPINIONS TO YOURSELF!** Unlike many essays you have written, this is not a persuasive opinion piece. One of the most significant errors students will make on the SAT Essay will be inserting their own views on a topic and criticizing the argument provided. The task is to analyze *how the author makes his or her argument*, not to make your own argument on the topic.

2. **LOOK FOR WHAT IS GOOD IN THE ARGUMENT—DON'T RIP IT APART.** The source text you will analyze will be a well-written argument for a general audience. There will likely be no major argumentative fallacies in the piece, and the assignment does not ask you to find problems in the source. So, instead of critiquing the source text as you read, carefully take it all in and look for the skillful ways in which the author uses evidence, reasoning, and rhetoric to make his or her argument.

3. **THE PROMPT WILL NOT CHANGE, WHILE THE SOURCE TEXT WILL. KNOW THE QUESTION, FORMAT, AND DIRECTIONS AHEAD OF TIME.** You will always need to read the source text carefully, looking for how the author builds an argument. You will always need to write a response that describes and analyzes how the author makes this argument. You will always have 50 minutes to do all of this. With the source text changing with each essay, prepare yourself by being completely familiar with what stays consistent with each SAT essay.

4. **ALLOW ENOUGH TIME TO READ THE PASSAGE WELL.** You will be tempted to rush through reading the passage, but don't—if you don't fully understand the argument, you will not be able to produce a good response. Time invested up front in the initial reading will pay major dividends when you write an essay that accurately and thoroughly analyzes the source text.

5. **READ *ACTIVELY*!** While reading the source text, ask yourself this two part question over and over: *What is the author saying and why?* "What" the author is saying aligns with the "Reading" component of the essay rubric, and "why" aligns with the "Analysis" component of the rubric. Here are some more specific things to focus on as you read:

   • **Paraphrase:** What is the author generally saying? What is the thesis?
   • **Intention:** Why might the author have argued this?
   • **Tone:** Is it informal or formal? Why?
   • **Perspective:** Is it first, second, or third person? Why?
   • **Structure:** Is the essay structured chronologically? Does it move general observations to specific illustrations? Does the essay illustrate the pros and cons of an idea? Does it gradually "discover" a general conclusion? Why has the author structured the essay in this way?
   • **Style:** What kind of wording does the author use? How about imagery and sensory appeal? Why was this done?
   • **Evidence:** How does the author support his or her claims? Are there examples, evidence, statistics, or anecdotes? Why was this evidence chosen?

6. **DETERMINE YOUR PREFERRED PREWRITING METHOD.** Figure out the best way to organize your thoughts for the essay, and do so before the actual test so you don't just "wing it." Here are three major ways you might want to prewrite:

   • **Outline:** Write a step-by-step outline of what you are going to argue in each body paragraph and what examples you will use. This is a good approach if you sometimes go on tangents when you write, and you appreciate having a clear plan before you begin.
   • **Plan your general points:** After reading the text, jot down the 3–4 major points you are going to make in the essay. As you write your body paragraphs, frequently go back to the text to find support for your claims.
   • **Get going:** If you have a difficult time determining the overall structure and thesis of your argument ahead of time, you may want to start by writing your body paragraphs, leaving a few lines blank at

the beginning of your essay for the introduction that you will write later. As you write the body paragraphs, be mindful of the general points you are arguing. With 5–10 minutes remaining, write your conclusion and go back to the beginning of your response and write your introductory paragraph. If you plan on doing this approach, be certain to practice it ahead of time so you allow adequate time to have a well-developed introduction and a clear thesis.

7. **STAY FOCUSED.** The graders will look to see whether you have a clear thesis and whether you are able to sustain your argument all the way through your essay. Be sure you have a well-constructed introduction and conclusion and that you are explicit in stating your claims. You don't have time for digressions. Make it as easy as possible for the graders to understand and follow your argument so that they can give you the best score.

8. **DETERMINE HOW YOU WANT TO PACE YOURSELF.** Review the following chart and fill in the last column with your personal plan for timing. You can make a solid determination without writing an entire essay simply by practicing the reading and prewriting steps and noting how long these two steps take.

Part of the Process	Range of Times	How to Decide	How Much Time Will I Take for Each Part?
Reading the Source	4–10 minutes	Are you are a faster or slower reader? Be sure you take the time to understand the source text fully. If you are going to spend more time prewriting, you may want to spend less time with the initial reading, and vice versa.	
Prewriting	1–5 minutes	If you need to have a clear outline to stay focused as you write, take the time to prewrite well. If you stay focused without a detailed outline, devote more time to writing your response.	
Writing the Essay	35–45 minutes	The response is handwritten, so be mindful of how quickly you are physically able to write. Factor in how much time you want to devote to reading and prewriting.	

Part of the Process	Range of Times	How to Decide	How Much Time Will I Take for Each Part?
Editing	0–5 minutes	Do you generally make quite a few spelling/grammar errors that need to be fixed? If so, allow enough time to proofread. If you are generally careful in your initial writing, devote less time to editing and focus on writing a more in-depth response.	

Be sure your total time adds up to 50 minutes!

As you practice writing SAT essays, you will learn what pacing plan works best for you.

9. **DON'T LET THE PERFECT BE THE ENEMY OF THE GOOD!** The SAT graders realize that you are a high school student writing a challenging essay along with doing hours of multiple-choice questions. They don't expect perfection. You will certainly want to minimize grammar and spelling errors, but you should not devote so much time to proofreading that you sacrifice the development of your argument.

10. **BUILD YOUR ARGUMENT ANALYSIS SKILLS OVER THE LONG TERM.** There is a great deal you can do besides working through practice SAT essays to improve your skills for test day. Here are some ideas:

- Read and analyze editorial and opinion articles from major newspapers and magazines:
  - *New York Times*
  - *Wall Street Journal*
  - *Washington Post*
  - *L. A. Times*
  - *The Atlantic*
  - *The Economist*
  - *Legal Affairs*
  - *The New Republic*
  - *Sports Illustrated Writers*
  - *Popular Science*
  - *Scientific American*
  - *Discover*

- Debate with your friends on current events and other issues. The more you practice argumentation, the more easily you will recognize its structure.

- Become an active reader and commenter on blog discussions.

- Make a habit of not taking things on face value. If you are watching the news, ask why the information is being presented as it is. If you are watching a commercial, question the use of evidence and make note of emotional appeals. Be an active, rather than passive, consumer of information.

Putting It All Together

Let's go step by step through everything you will need to do to write a successful essay.

First, let's actively read the prompt. Know the directions ahead of time so you can focus your energy on actively reading the source text. The types of thoughts/notes you could have while reading are given after the prompt.

Directions: This assignment will allow you to demonstrate your ability to skillfully read and understand a source text and write a response analyzing the source. In your response, you should show that you have understood the source, give proficient analysis, and use the English language effectively. If your essay is off-topic, it will not be scored.

Only what you write on the lined paper in your answer document will be scored—avoid skipping lines, using unreasonably large handwriting, and using wide margins in order to have sufficient space to respond. You can also write on the planning sheet in the answer document, but this will not be evaluated—no other scrap paper will be given. Be sure to write clearly and legibly so your response can be scored.

You will be given 50 minutes to complete the assignment, including reading the source text and writing your response.

Read the following passage, and think about how the author uses:

- Evidence, such as applicable examples, to justify the argument
- Reasoning to show logical connections among thoughts and facts
- Rhetoric, like sensory language and emotional appeals, to give weight to the argument

The History Major

1   I am sure you have heard by now—news trickles fast down the steep façade of the ivory tower. Perhaps, you've already packed up my room, taken my portrait off the mantel, and relayed my unfortunate accident to the intrusive Mr. and Mrs. Duta ("a rare condition," "such ill-fated tragedy," "nonetheless, Swanson's Home for the Irresponsibly Insane

provides the very best care"). Or, you've called the Dean, pleaded for immediate intervention (surely, the choice should belong to those whose pockets dwindle every semester), and sabotaged my class schedule so that I inadvertently end up at the College of Science and Technology once again. And so, it is with utmost austerity that I beg for your ear; fear not, I am no lost cause.

2   The Liberal Arts education is far from obsolete. Despite the rumors of late, you need not worry that your son will end up unemployed and homeless, pining over unheeded art in shadowy bars with rickety tabletops and flyer-covered walls. Nor must you relinquish hopes for a charming daughter-in-law and animated, curly-haired grandchildren. What I mean to say is that liberal arts graduates are well-suited—in some ways, even better suited—for success and happiness than their narrowed, specializing counterparts. Not only are our skills coveted in graduate school and the workforce, but we are also more adaptable and likely to move up rank in our careers. The breadth of study emphasized in a liberal arts education provides an exemplary foundation for a variety of professional fields and career paths, while molding open-minded, curious problem solvers. *Mom and Dad*, I implore you to reconsider my cosmopolitan ambitions and reinstate my place at the dinner table.

3   A third of all Fortune 500 CEOs possess liberal arts degrees. LEAP, or Liberal Education & America's Promise, is an initiative launched by the Association of American Colleges & Universities to emphasize the importance of a 21st Century liberal education for individuals and a nation "dependent on economic creativity and democratic vitality." According to LEAP's recent national survey, 93% of employers say that "a demonstrated capacity to think critically, communicate clearly, and solve complex problems is more important than undergraduate major." You've guessed it—these three skill sets are the unifying objective of liberal arts programs nationwide.

4   Furthermore, these skills are timelessly useful and valuable; in a quickly evolving world, they are the few ingenuities that will neither be replaced nor outdated. Whether students decide on graduate education, law or medical school, or dive right into the job hunt, a broad and diverse interdisciplinary education provides the analytical, research, and independent judgment training necessary to gain an edge on other applicants. Acquisition of self-understanding, accompanied by a respect for others and an aptitude for clear expression, shapes leaders in a variety of work

environments from government to business to education. The lucrative liberal arts education results in a life-long learner who asks difficult questions, presents information intelligibly, and makes coherent arguments across disciplines. *Is this not what you want for your baby boy?*

5   Even more intriguing is the evidence that a liberal arts education spawns happier individuals. With a capacity to understand and enjoy humanity's achievements, my artsy cohort and I will be more likely to spend time appreciating literature, music, art, and even witty conversation, and to participate in our communities and global politics. An active and engaged life is indeed something to be happy about. According to Robert Harris's *On the Purpose of a Liberal Education*, in addition to teaching students how to think, learn, and see things whole, a liberal education also enhances students' faith and wisdom, with their gained knowledge begetting increased pleasure.

6   Let us not forget Leonard da Vinci, Michelangelo, or America's own, Benjamin Franklin, who made their marks on society not with one expertise, but with a legion of talents—renaissance men of the highest degree. It is the cultivated mind of the multifarious and enlightened that I endeavor toward with my decision to declare a History major. If I manage to avoid the fate of the shaggy-haired drifter of your nightmares, I could turn out to be brilliant (or mediocre with a steady job and varied interests).

> Write a response that demonstrates how the author makes an argument to persuade an audience that a liberal arts education is valuable. In your response, analyze how the author uses at least one of the features from the essay directions (or features of your own choosing) to develop a logical and persuasive argument. Be certain that your response cites relevant aspects of the source text.
>
> Your response should not give your personal opinion on the merit of the source text but instead show how the author crafts an argument to persuade readers.

Active Reading Notes

This is a detailed paragraph-by-paragraph summary of the essay's argument. These are the types of things you can think about and make notes of while reading the source text:

1. Draws you in—at first you're not sure what the author is talking about
   a. Seems like something dramatic, like suicide
   b. The dramatization plays to your emotions and draws you in
   c. After the first paragraph dramatization, the author announces that he is talking about choosing to get a liberal arts education
2. The fact that it's written as a sort of letter to the parents causes you to put yourself in the author's shoes
   a. This is a particularly effective technique with this topic because this is a topic about which many students probably have argued, or will argue, with their parents
3. Considers possible objections to the liberal arts education
   a. Graduates end up unemployed
      i. Combats this with facts:
         1. 1/3 of Fortune 500 CEOs have liberal arts degrees
         2. 93% of employers say the very skills a liberal arts education strives to provide are more important than a major
4. Appeals to anxieties many students may have
   a. Not finding a job in the future
   b. Happiness in the future
      i. There is evidence that those with liberal arts educations may tend to be happier
      ii. Cites *On the Purpose of a Liberal Education*
         1. Enhances students' faith and wisdom
            a. Leads to increased pleasure
5. Compares getting a liberal arts education to being a renaissance man and references some of the greats—who wouldn't want to be like them?

Then, you can spend time prewriting your essay. The following is a rough prewrite for this essay; the author summarizes the theme of each of her body paragraphs.

- *Author uses persuasive techniques.*
- *We empathize with him as teenagers.*
- *Explain how he addresses objections.*
- *Analyze how he appeals to reader anxieties.*
- *Examine renaissance man argument.*

Now, review an excellent response to this essay that builds upon the above reading notes and prewrite.

Full Top-Scoring Essay Response

This author uses a wide variety of persuasive techniques in his essay to craft an extremely well thought-out argument for why liberal arts educations are useful. He considers possible objections to his argument, which he combats with facts. He very purposely evokes certain emotions in the reader, such as empathy and anxiety. He proceeds to alleviate these anxieties with facts that make the reader want to pursue a liberal arts education, before wrapping up the argument by comparing the liberal arts educated to renaissance men.

The author is mindfully persuasive from the very beginning, introducing the topic with a dramatization that draws the reader in. The description of the family cleaning out the author's room out and taking the author's picture off of the mantel makes the reader think that something tragic has happened. The author then shocks the reader by announcing that the "tragedy" that has taken place was simply his choice to pursue a liberal arts education. The author seems to have carefully chosen such an introduction to get the reader to think that such a "tragedy" is extremely trivial; this is the author's first step in his persuasion.

The author also seems to have carefully chosen to write this essay as a mock address to his parents. It seems as if the purpose for this choice was to put the reader in the author's shoes. This is a seamless transition for the reader, as many students have had, or will have, similar arguments with their parents. This forces the reader to feel empathy, making the author's attempt at persuasion more effective.

After the initial dramatization, the author goes on to consider some possible objections to a liberal arts education. For instance, the author alludes to the parents expressing concern that their child will end up unemployed after college. The author's rebuttal to such concerns is twofold. First, he uses tongue-in-cheek humor to brush off such concerns, by assuring his parents that he will not end up homeless. Second, and more effectively, he uses facts to the contrary. For instance, he states that 1/3 of Fortune 500 CEOs have liberal arts degrees.

Another technique used in the argument is appealing to the reader's own anxieties. Many students worry that they won't find jobs in today's competitive job market. The author eases this anxiety by assuring the reader that 93% of employers say that they care more that an employee possess the skills that a liberal arts education strives to foster than about the particular major the employee chose. Another thing that many young people worry about is whether or not they'll be happy in the future. The author assures the reader that many liberal arts degree recipients tend to be happier than their peers. He cites *On the Purpose of a Liberal Education* as saying that a liberal arts education can increase faith and wisdom, which leads to an increase in pleasure.

Finally, the author compares getting a liberal arts education to being a renaissance man. Both the liberal arts educated and the people we tend to think of as renaissance men are well-versed in a wide array of disciplines. He cites Leonardo da Vinci, Michelangelo, and Ben Franklin, forcing the reader to consider why someone wouldn't strive to be like these greats.

In conclusion, the author begins his argument by first hinting that something tragic has happened to him. When he reveals that this "tragedy" was choosing a liberal arts path, this forces the reader to think, "how disastrous can such a decision really be?" Once the reader is feeling fairly neutral on the subject matter, the author begins persuading. He uses a variety of techniques, such as appealing to the emotions of the reader and considering possible objections. He also backs up his argument with facts about how job and happiness prospects are very good for those with liberal arts educations. Finally, he allows the reader to compare what they could be with a liberal arts education to some of the great renaissance men. Overall, the argument was very well developed, owing much of its effectiveness to the success of evoking chosen emotions in the reader.

Scoring: Reading = 4, Analysis = 4, Writing = 4

EXPLANATION: The response demonstrates an excellent grasp of the source text's argument, primarily using paraphrase to show understanding. The writer's response is well structured and focused on analysis of the text's use of evocation of emotions. The essay has a well-developed introduction and conclusion. The author's word choice is precise, and there is a variety of sentence structure. Underneath the central umbrella of emotional evocation, the response analyzes how and why the author of the source does this, citing (among other things) how readers can relate to arguments with parents, how the author uses humor, and how the author hooks the audience in the introduction.

PRACTICE EXERCISES

How can you use these prompts? Here are some ideas:

- Practice your reading and analytical skills as you annotate the source texts.
- Work on your prewriting.
- Write full responses and have a teacher, parent, or friend review your work and give suggestions for improvement.

Directions: You will be given 50 minutes to complete the assignment, including reading the source text and writing your response.

Read the following passage, and think about how the author uses:

- Evidence, such as applicable examples, to justify the argument
- Reasoning to show logical connections among thoughts and facts
- Rhetoric, like sensory language and emotional appeals, to give weight to the argument

Education Reimagined

1 Since 2012—the year of Massive Open Online Courses (MOOCs)—the discourse on the success of open online education and its implications for traditional colleges has been mixed, and often conflicting. While some raved that e-learning platforms would dismantle and revolutionize the university overnight, others doubted their maturation and assimilation into the job market. In response to the influx of online learning platforms that offer free content, President Obama called upon online learning as a key ingredient in redefining higher education, stating colleges must, "embrace innovative new ways to prepare our students for a 21st-century economy and maintain a high level of quality without breaking the bank." Although open online courses have failed to transform higher education in the abrupt manner that many reformers predicted, the current push for discernible and accessible digital credentials from accredited institutions will be a turning point in education.

2 The open educational movement really took off in 2008; and, within just a few short years, providers like Coursera, Udacity, and edX emerged among hundreds of other self-paced, virtual education platforms, including the immensely popular Khan Academy, that offer quality learning at a great price, *free*. Now, students could enjoy learning outside of a formal education environment with asynchronous and unconstrained access to free content. And many took advantage. Coursera, associated with Stanford University, boasts that it currently offers more than 1,000 free courses. Udacity, similarly connected with Stanford, specializes in vocational courses for professionals who can choose to pay a fee for a certificate of completion to submit to employers. MIT and Harvard introduced edX, a nonprofit provider that now has more than three million users. Then, in November 2012, the University of Miami launched the first high school MOOC to assist students in preparing for the SAT.

3 As programs expanded and quality increased, many speculated that MOOCs would be the vanguard for a reduction in rising costs of higher

education that could potentially replace the business model of education. Others pointed to the meager 10% completion rate common among MOOCs and the unceasing admission rates and rising tuition costs in traditional universities, and chalked open online education up to a fleeting fad. Thus far, neither prediction has manifested, but the former is seemingly more indicative of current trends than the latter. Stanford celebrates several courses that have "graduated" over 20,000 students; and, as distance education moves toward reputable degree-granting, these numbers will soar. In collaborative e-platforms, more students than ever are watching video lectures, participating in discussion boards, engaging in peer-review exercises, and taking up interactive blogging. Imagine unlimited access to a college education for anyone who can get in front of a computer screen.

4   The prophesized revolution will come with the next step in open online courses: the reconception of education. Students are failing to turn to the cheaper, more convenient online platform because it is yet to lead to jobs. More than a broad, encompassing education for personal growth and intellectual stimulation, students are paying for degrees that get jobs. A lag with employers is expected and understandable; the conventional diploma is well-tested and time-honored, so naturally employers are skeptical of change. Moreover, ways to recognize and measure quality in online education had to be established. But now, as online education becomes accredited and archives make it easy for employers to see students' work and achievements, open online education is in position to overtake its predecessor. Digital credentials and reputable degrees and/or certificates mean that employers can not only rest assured that employees have extensive training and knowledge, but will also, for the first time, be able to effortlessly glimpse academic accomplishments, rather than try to decipher the meaningless acronyms on standardized transcripts.

5   While it is still unlikely to happen overnight, employer-friendly online platforms are already working to bridge the gap. Acknowledgement and recognition of accredited virtual education leaves a lot of questions for the traditional university model. If students are afforded quality education at unbeatable costs without having to move on campus *and* are competing for first-rate jobs, there will be little incentive to attend the expensive, corporeal universities where memories created are only outshone by debt accumulated. Higher education will soon become accessible for the masses and "college" will look very different, for students, instructors, and employers.

Write a response that demonstrates how the author makes an argument to persuade an audience that MOOCs represent a turning point in education. In your response, analyze how the author uses at least one of the features from the essay directions (or features of your own choosing) to develop a logical and persuasive argument. Be certain that your response cites relevant aspects of the source text.

Your response should not give your personal opinion on the merit of the source text, but instead show how the author crafts an argument to persuade readers.

Directions: You will be given 50 minutes to complete the assignment, including reading the source text and writing your response.

Read the following passage, and think about how the author uses:

- Evidence, such as applicable examples, to justify the argument
- Reasoning to show logical connections among thoughts and facts
- Rhetoric, like sensory language and emotional appeals, to give weight to the argument

Promoting Dignity: Freedom from Trafficking

1   "Congratulations!" we exclaim, after hearing of a baby's birth, a joyful time of celebration. Regardless of who people are, where they come from, or what stage of life they are in, human beings have great worth and dignity. From the beginning of the Universal Declaration of Human Rights, the international community recognizes this reality. The idea that people have inherent rights just in virtue of the fact that they are human beings is based in the inherent moral value of human beings. Human trafficking, however, which involves exploiting someone for financial gain, is a direct attack on human dignity. Therefore, we must work together to create a world free of such exploitation.

2   It is estimated that nearly 21 million people worldwide are victims of forced labor or sexual exploitation. Human trafficking is a modern day form of slavery, in which victims typically are kept in unsanitary conditions and endure physical, sexual, and psychological harms. The average age at which people are trafficked is about 13 years old, and they are sometimes brutally violated many times a day. Traffickers use force, fraud, deception, or coercion in order to use other people for the purpose of

making money for themselves. Victims' inability to escape leads to self-destructive behaviors, including attempted suicide.

3   Achieving freedom from trafficking first requires promoting awareness of the signs of it in order to help prevent becoming a victim. Experienced traffickers have subtle tactics to lure people by getting to know them gradually, happening to show up at the same places as the one being targeted, and making attractive offers of good jobs, marriage, or a "better life." One former perpetrator recounted how many times he heard young ladies say that "it can't happen to me," and yet they gradually became desensitized in environments where, despite earning money at first and receiving many compliments, they end up with shattered lives. Some signs that someone is being trafficked include working excessively long hours, having high security measures around the place of employment or living, being fearful or anxious, showing signs of abuse, and having a lack of control of possessions, money, and identification.

4   Creating a world free from trafficking also includes not contributing to it. The Super Bowl is said to be the single largest human trafficking incident in the United States, where traffickers take advantage of so many men being out of town at a hotel with a festive atmosphere and lowered inhibitions. There are, however, many ways to have a great time without using and abusing other people's sons and daughters. Bringing trafficking to an end does not just involve our behavior though; it also includes changing the attitudes and ideas that lead to such behaviors, stimulating the demand for it. Instead of viewing others as objects for one's own gratification, we must recognize them as whole persons with minds, wills, and emotions. Each person has intrinsic moral worth and so is deserving of respect and kindness, not degradation and humiliation. According to the U.S. Department of State Office to Monitor and Combat Trafficking in Persons, an end to human trafficking "can only be achieved by rejecting long-held notions that regard commercial sex as a 'boys will be boys' phenomenon, and instead sending the clear message that buying sex is wrong." Leaders, they argued, "must foster the belief that it is everyone's responsibility to reduce the demand for sex trafficking."

5   In addition to not becoming a victim or a perpetrator, protecting people from trafficking requires that we take positive steps to stop it from happening. At the governmental level, it is important to enact laws that carry with them penalties proportional to the seriousness of the crimes of human trafficking, the enforcement of which will bring people to justice

and actually deter them from committing such crimes in the first place. At the individual level, we need to be aware of our surroundings, notice the signs of trafficking, and report suspicious activities to the appropriate authorities. A final essential component involves groups of people forming organizations to educate the public, help identify victims and provide aftercare for those that are rescued from enslavement, and contribute toward the elimination of demand for trafficked victims.

6   It is commonly thought that slavery ended long ago. Let us work together so that one day we can hold that belief truly.

Write a response that demonstrates how the author makes an argument to persuade an audience that human trafficking must come to an end. In your response, analyze how the author uses at least one of the features from the essay directions (or features of your own choosing) to develop a logical and persuasive argument. Be certain that your response cites relevant aspects of the source text.

Your response should not give your personal opinion on the merit of the source text, but instead show how the author crafts an argument to persuade readers.

Directions: You will be given 50 minutes to complete the assignment, including reading the source text and writing your response.

Read the following passage, and think about how the author uses:

- Evidence, such as applicable examples, to justify the argument
- Reasoning to show logical connections among thoughts and facts
- Rhetoric, like sensory language and emotional appeals, to give weight to the argument

The Hunt for Success

1   Ask parents what they want most for their children and many will answer success. By "success," they may mean happiness, financial stability, good health, etc. Chances are, they mean a combination of these things and many more. Perhaps, success is not a concept that falls to easy measurement or simple understanding because of its tendency to particularity; it is different for every individual—there is no one recipe. So then, without

a clear definition of success let alone an apprehensible path toward its fulfillment, how is one to choose a field of study, a major, and eventually a career?

2   According to *Forbes* magazine, more than half of Americans are unhappy at work, with disconsolation hitting a record high in 2010. Fifty-two percent of people report feeling disengaged at work, while eighteen percent say they downright hate their jobs. *Business Insider* complicates the statistics further by asking the working public whether they chose a passion or a paycheck, and whether these two are incompatible. The argument only gains complexity when one considers how much fulfillment comes from the pay itself: would the unfulfilled be bigger fans of their current jobs if the salary was higher, or do they, regardless of pay, need to feel pride in what they spend forty hours a week or more doing? With so many falling short of self-realization, surely there needs to be more attention paid to what makes up a successful career.

3   The answer to choosing the right career lies in the nuances of success itself. Just as there is no one definition of success, there is no one path to it, and one will rarely find success by sitting around thinking about it. Furthermore, it can be equally futile to weigh everything in the name of one small part of the plethora that makes up success: there are plenty of wealthy men and women who do not consider their work fulfilling, just like there are many who don't consider themselves successful despite their contentment at work. The fact is, one does not know the best career path for them until they feel it, see it, hear it. This balance, particular to an individual's personal needs and priorities, is found most often through action.

4   In Lindsey Pollak's *Getting from College to Career*, she suggests that career-hunters "follow every rainbow," a tip that involves finding and exploring every opportunity that comes one's way. From job shadowing to career fairs to campus ads to online resumes, Pollak asserts that the potential paths to one's dream job are innumerable, so every angle and every avenue should be pursued. Her work as a career expert has allowed her to interview thousands of people who boast that they found success in a fulfilling and engaging career; their paths are as many as their number. Some cite a family friend, a coincidental conversation with a stranger, an employment agency, or a referral as the reason behind their success. Yet, all successful stories have this in common: action.

5 Many universities have caught on and are beginning to implement programs that encourage, or even mandate, action throughout a student's undergraduate study. These initiatives often include study abroad, research experiences, internships, community outreach, career fairs, and senior project fairs—all with the goal of bolstering one's exploration of opportunities and exposing one's talents to prospective employers. When students are able to expand their interests and experiences by trying new things and meeting new people, they are likewise expanding their career search. Not only are students more likely to find employment, they are more likely to be engaged, challenged, and enriched by their work. While universities are undeniably attempting to improve their career placement rates, they are simultaneously doing something much more important—changing the lives of their students.

6 With the evidence for action so overwhelming, one must ask if the university is really the best place to start. College applications indeed ask students for their intended majors, and with many undergraduate degrees taking five and even six years to complete, it would appear that students are expected to come into the university with some sort of direction. High schools—which are presumed to prepare students for the workforce, military, and/or college—must take on some of this responsibility in order to ensure the success of future generations. Seventeen-year-olds with an idea of where their interests lie and what makes them happy, albeit uncommon, undoubtedly have the advantage in exploring meaningful opportunities.

Write a response that demonstrates how the author makes an argument to persuade an audience that schools should do more to help students determine what they want to do for their careers. In your response, analyze how the author uses at least one of the features from the essay directions (or features of your own choosing) to develop a logical and persuasive argument. Be certain that your response cites relevant aspects of the source text.

Your response should not give your personal opinion on the merit of the source text, but instead show how the author crafts an argument to persuade readers.

Directions: You will be given 50 minutes to complete the assignment, including reading the source text and writing your response.

Read the following passage, and think about how the author uses:

- Evidence, such as applicable examples, to justify the argument
- Reasoning to show logical connections among thoughts and facts
- Rhetoric, like sensory language and emotional appeals, to give weight to the argument

The Customer Is Always Right

1   The dormitories are ten stories high, bounded by ovals of forest green lawn and narrow brick walkways. The recreation center is enclosed by six thousand square feet of unblemished glass and equipped with no less than thirteen pools, one hundred and fifty-seven treadmills, and a full time massage therapist. The football stadium is unmatched, sitting thrice the number of fans as enrolled students. Campus night life, with all its shining neon lights and immaculate dance floors, is a tropical haven for the lonesome and homesick. And the admission brochure brags aimlessly that university students are "making the impossible possible." So it goes. College is a business, eighteen-year-old students (and their preferably wealthy parents) the consumers. As appealing as it all sounds, the current university model is failing the student in arguably the most important ways.

2   Take Psychology 101, now offered on Thursdays at 1 P.M. because lethargic and fetid students stopped coming on Fridays, and the remaining sleepwalkers were hesitant to enroll in a course before 11 A.M. Next, consider Instructor Evaluation Day, the next-to-last class meeting where a semester's worth of interpretive intelligence and deliberation culminates in a 1 to 5 rating; 1 being "I wish I would have taken this course at the community college down the street and passed" and 5 being "the professor is such a hunk that I totally clicked the chili pepper on ratemyprofessor.com." Dare we mention exams, when 79% of the class failed so miserably that a curve was fabricated to soothe exasperated parents and riled department chairs? Failing, after all, leads to transfers and drop-outs, which of course means less money, and *can this shrinking department really afford any more cuts?*

3   So, where did it all go wrong? Long before admission offices began hiring the top marketing students and graphic designers to *sell* their respective universities, there was the idea of a college education being somewhat unsettling, something to push and challenge and stimulate and unearth the dissenter within. Prior to softened grades and political correctness, classrooms were marked by tough student-instructor exchange, passionate intellectual debates, and an eagerness to expand thinking. Today, the university model mass produces graduates who can unequivocally repeat facts, memorize definitions, and reference experts (at least for a semester at a time), but fails to truly engage, ripen, or educate its *customers*.

4   Currently, the government rewards universities for innovative research; so, it is hardly surprising that this is where professors direct their focus. Professors, busy with research and ceaseless publishing, have little time to teach. Frequently, teaching is left to inexperienced graduate students who are just as occupied with research and thesis or doctorate writing. And so, the students suffer. On the other end, students are less concerned with notable faculty and demanding curriculum, and more interested in impressing employers. Employers are most enthralled with rankings and selectivity. Meanwhile, colleges, in order to be desirable, must keep enrollment low (i.e., be selective) and, therefore, must charge students more to keep revenue high. And so the student-consumer cycle continues with its first-rate communal bathrooms and seventeen cafeterias, including a Chik-fil-A and, get this, a Starbucks.

5   Almost half of college graduates show no improvement in critical thinking, reasoning, and writing skills according to *Academically Adrift*, a recent book that explores the stagnant and, at times, utterly ineffective U.S. collegiate system. Critical thinking and deductive reasoning aren't the only areas in which the university is failing either: the *Wall Street Journal* asserts that four of every ten college graduates don't have the skills needed to manage white-collar work, with less than 2 out of 5 employers finding recent graduate interviewees ready for the workforce. Indeed, the high-points of the American university don't seem to include progression, preparedness, or professionalization.

6   Are we to give up hope and abandon college education? Not exactly. Yet the paradox of the current student-consumer university is something that cannot go on unaddressed. If U.S. students fail to compete, it won't be long before other job-seekers take advantage of our stupor. One proposal suggests that common tests be given upon admission and graduation to see

which colleges are doing their job and which are not. Acknowledging the complexity of testing graduates from a myriad of majors, others turn to the government to back programs that encourage quality graduates. Whichever alternatives we pursue, teaching must regain the foreground.

Write a response that demonstrates how the author makes an argument to persuade an audience that college is changing for the worst as it becomes increasingly consumerist. In your response, analyze how the author uses at least one of the features from the essay directions (or features of your own choosing) to develop a logical and persuasive argument. Be certain that your response cites relevant aspects of the source text.

Your response should not give your personal opinion on the merit of the source text, but instead show how the author crafts an argument to persuade readers.

Directions: You will be given 50 minutes to complete the assignment, including reading the source text and writing your response.

Read the following passage, and think about how the author uses:

- Evidence, such as applicable examples, to justify the argument
- Reasoning to show logical connections among thoughts and facts
- Rhetoric, like sensory language and emotional appeals, to give weight to the argument

Poor Potential

"Give me your tired, your poor,
Your huddled masses yearning to breathe free,
The wretched refuse of your teeming shore.
Send these, the homeless, tempest-tost to me,
I lift my lamp beside the golden door!"

—from "The New Colossus," the Statue of Liberty

1   Howard Schultz, billionaire CEO of Starbucks, grew up in a government housing complex before attending the University of Northern Michigan on a football scholarship. Oprah Winfrey was born into a poor Mississippi family, but worked tirelessly to gain a scholarship to Tennessee State

University, where she became the first African American TV correspondent in the state at age 19. Founder of Oracle—one of the largest technology companies in the world—Larry Ellison was born to a poor mother in Brooklyn, NY, and raised by an aunt who passed away during his sporadic college years, when he alternated classes with odd jobs. Ben Carson, the first surgeon to successfully separate conjoined twins at the head, grew up in Detroit under the care of a poor, single mother who had never finished the third grade but encouraged her sons to read. What all these public figures have in common is that the world, as we know it, would not exist without their contribution, and their contribution would be null and void without efforts to diversify the university.

2   For those without the resources, college may seem like an ambiguous dream floating dangerously out of reach on the words *scholarship*, *grant*, and *financial aid*. The battle to gain support from working class parents and time to study in a backdrop that demands all free hands is, for many, just the beginning to academic success and the chance for a brighter future. Then, there is admission, where these same underprivileged students are measured against more affluent peers who benefit from more time devoted to academics, superior school systems, costly tutoring, opportunities to job shadow and intern, and a myriad of networking contacts via their prosperous parents. While one of these advantages is sufficient to forge an insurmountable gap of inequality, the combination of them leaves students in tremendous discordance as they fill out applications. Hence, the very real need for consideration of socioeconomic diversity as a factor in college admissions.

3   The grounds for socioeconomic diversity within the university lie on the axiom of the American Dream itself, the ethos of freedom, opportunity, and prosperity for all who are willing to work for it in a nation devoid of substantial barriers. Where would the world be without the Winfreys and Ellisons, and those innumerable innovators, scholars, artists, and philanthropists who were left out of the spare list that begins this essay? The National Association for College Admissions Counseling failed to list class or economic-status in their 2011 article "Factors of Admission Decision." Yet, *The New York Times* found in 2014 that socioeconomic affirmative action not only opened doors for students from low-income and under-resourced high schools, but also effectively promoted racial, ethnic, and religious diversity.

4   Catherine B. Hill, the president of Vassar College in New York, calls for increased resources for financial aid, saying, "If higher education in America is to continue to contribute to equal opportunity and economic mobility, not only do its leaders need to make more places available across the entire system, the highly selective institutions need to do their fair share by educating a more socioeconomically diverse student body." It is not lack of talent, but finite resources that deter access. Hill's research found that the shortage of low-income students at the nation's most select universities wasn't based on scarcity of student competency, but scarcity of university funds and awareness. Opportunity and diversity within the U.S. post-secondary education system rely on the incorporation of socioeconomics into the admissions process.

5   Others argue that admissions should be blind to class, race, and gender; just as historical preference to white, wealthy males is wrong, so is the "reverse discrimination" implied in favoring another group. The argument allows that merit-based admissions will lead to the best quality of students and promote fairness. Yet, the danger in evaluating students by virtue of rigorous high school coursework and standardized testing is in its blindness to disadvantage—that life-long penal sentence of choosing the wrong parents; a debilitating condition which obscures the talent of even the most prodigious. Furthermore, in a merit-based model, even those highly-qualified, low-income students who gain admission are more likely to decline it without apt resources provided. It is time that our system does more to ensure outlook, or risk crippling the next Ben Carson.

Write a response that demonstrates how the author makes an argument to persuade an audience that socioeconomic diversity should have an impact on college admissions. In your response, analyze how the author uses at least one of the features from the essay directions (or features of your own choosing) to develop a logical and persuasive argument. Be certain that your response cites relevant aspects of the source text.

    Your response should not give your personal opinion on the merit of the source text, but instead show how the author crafts an argument to persuade readers.

The Mathematics Sections: Strategies, Tips, and Practice

6

The College Board considers the SAT to be a test of general reasoning abilities. It attempts to use basic concepts of arithmetic, algebra, geometry, and data analysis as a method of testing your ability to think logically. The Board is not testing whether you know how to calculate an average, find the area of a circle, use the Pythagorean theorem, or read a bar graph. *It assumes you can.* In fact, because the Board is not even interested in testing your memory, many of the formulas you will need are given to you at the beginning of each math section. In other words, the College Board's objective is to use your familiarity with basic mathematics as a way of testing your logical thinking skills.

Most of the arithmetic that you need to know for the SAT is taught in elementary school, and much of the other material is taught in middle school or junior high school. You do need to know some high school math, especially some elementary algebra, a little geometry, the basic definitions of trigonometry, and function notation. To do well on the SAT, you must know this basic material. But that's not enough. You have to be able to use these concepts in ways that may be unfamiliar to you. That's where the test-taking tactics come in.

THE USE OF CALCULATORS ON THE SAT

- You must bring a calculator to the test. Some, but not all, of the questions in the 55-minute section cannot be solved without using one.
- You should use a scientific calculator. A graphing calculator is acceptable but offers no real advantage.
- *Don't* buy a new calculator the night before the SAT. If you need one, *buy one now* and became familiar with it. Do all the practice exams in this book with the calculator you plan to take to the test—probably the same calculator you use in school.
- Use your calculator when you *need* to; ignore it when you don't. Most students use calculators more than they should. You can solve many problems without doing *any* calculations—mental, written, or calculator-assisted.

- The College Board's position is that a "calculator is a tool" and that knowing when to use one and when not to use one is an important skill. Therefore, they intentionally include some questions in the calculator section on which it is better not to use your calcuator.
- If you forget to bring a calculator to the actual test, you will not be able to use one, since none will be provided and you will not be allowed to share one with a friend. For the same reason, be sure that you have new batteries in your calculator or that you bring a spare, because if your calculator fails during the test, you will have to finish without one.

Throughout this book, the icon will be placed next to a problem where the use of a calculator is recommended. As you will see, this judgment is very subjective. Sometimes a question can be answered in a few seconds, with no calculations whatsoever, if you see the best approach. In that case, the use of a calculator is not recommended. If you don't see the easy way, however, and have to do some arithmetic, you may prefer to use a calculator.

Here are two sample questions on which some students would use calculators a lot, others a little, and still others not at all.

EXAMPLE 1

If $16 \times 25 \times 36 = (4a)^2$, what is the value of a?
(A) 6   (B) 15   (C) 30   (D) 36

 (i) **Heavy calculator use:** WITH A CALCULATOR multiply: $16 \times 25 \times 36$ = 14,400. Observe that $(4a)^2 = 16a^2$, and so $16a^2 = 14,400$. WITH A CALCULATOR divide:

$$a^2 = 14,400 \div 900$$

Finally, WITH A CALCULATOR take the square root:
$a = \sqrt{900} = 30$. The answer is **C.**

 (ii) **Light calculator use:** Immediately notice that you can "cancel" the 16 on the left-hand side with the 4^2 on the right-hand side. WITH A CALCULATOR multiply: $25 \times 36 = 900$, and WITH A CALCULATOR take the square root of 900: $\sqrt{900} = 30$.

(iii) **No calculator use:** "Cancel" the 16 and the 4^2. Notice that $25 = 5^2$ and $36 = 6^2$, so $a^2 = 5^2 \times 6^2 = 30^2$, and $a = 30$.

EXAMPLE 2 (GRID-IN)

If the length of a diagonal of a rectangle is 13, and if one of the sides is 5, what is the perimeter of the rectangle?

Whether you intend to use your calculator a lot, a little, or not at all, the first thing to do is to draw a diagram.

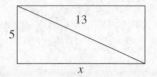

 (i) **Heavy calculator use:** By the Pythagorean theorem, $x^2 + 5^2 = 13^2$. Observe that $5^2 = 25$, and WITH A CALCULATOR evaluate: $13^2 = 169$. Then WITH A CALCULATOR subtract: $169 - 25 = 144$, so $x^2 = 144$. Hit the square-root key on your CALCULATOR to get $x = 12$. Finally, WITH A CALCULATOR add to find the perimeter: $5 + 12 + 5 + 12 = 34$.

 (ii) **Light calculator use:** The steps are the same as in (i) except that *some of the calculations* are done mentally: taking the square root of 144 and adding at the end.

(iii) **No calculator use:** *All calculations* are done mentally. Better yet, *no calculations are done at all*, because you immediately see that each half of the rectangle is a 5-12-13 right triangle, and you add the sides mentally.

MEMORIZE IMPORTANT FACTS AND DIRECTIONS

On the first page of every mathematics section of the SAT, there will be a box containing mathematical facts (see page 142).

Some guides to the SAT offer the following tip:

The test doesn't require you to memorize formulas. Commonly used formulas are provided in the test booklet at the beginning of each mathematical section.

If you interpret this to mean "Don't bother memorizing the formulas provided," this is terrible advice. It may be reassuring to know that, if you should forget a basic geometry fact, you can look it up in the box headed "Reference Information," but you should decide right now that you will never have to do that. During the test, you don't want to spend any precious time looking up facts that you can learn now. All of these "commonly used formulas" and other important facts are listed in this chapter. As you learn and review these facts, you should commit them to memory. Also in this chapter you will learn the instructions for the two types of mathematics questions on the SAT. *They will not change.* They will be exactly the same on the test you take.

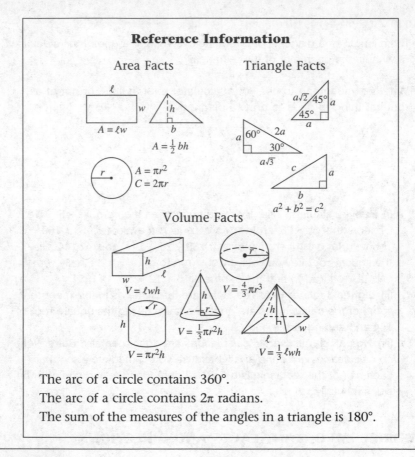

Reference Information

The arc of a circle contains 360°.

The arc of a circle contains 2π radians.

The sum of the measures of the angles in a triangle is 180°.

Helpful Hint

As you prepare for this test, memorize the directions for each section. *When you take the SAT, do not waste even one second reading directions.*

AN IMPORTANT SYMBOL

Throughout the book, the symbol "$\Rightarrow$" is used to indicate that one step in the solution of a problem follows *immediately from the preceding one, and that no explanation is necessary.* You should read:

$$2x = 12 \Rightarrow x = 6$$

as "$2x = 12$ *implies that* $x = 6$," or, "*since* $2x = 12$, *then* $x = 6$."

Here is a sample solution, using $\Rightarrow$, to the following problem:

What is the value of $3x^2 - 7$ when $x = -5$?

$$x = -5 \Rightarrow x^2 = (-5)^2 = 25 \Rightarrow 3x^2 = 3(25) = 75 \Rightarrow$$
$$3x^2 - 7 = 75 - 7 = \mathbf{68}$$

When the reason for a step is not obvious, $\Rightarrow$ is not used: rather, an explanation is given. In many solutions, some steps are explained, while others are linked by the $\Rightarrow$ symbol, as in the following example:

EXAMPLE

In the diagram at the right, if $w = 30$, what is z?

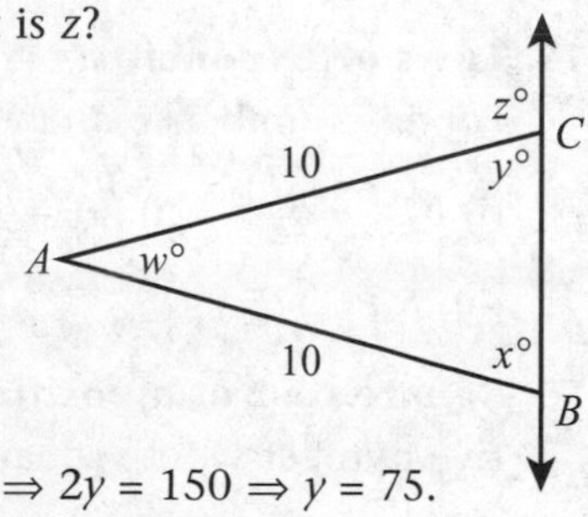

- $w + x + y = 180$.
- Since $\triangle ABC$ is isosceles, $x = y$.
- Therefore, $w + 2y = 180 \Rightarrow 30 + 2y = 180 \Rightarrow 2y = 150 \Rightarrow y = 75$.
- Finally, since $y + z = 180$, $75 + z = 180 \Rightarrow z = \mathbf{105}$.

IMPORTANT DEFINITIONS, FACTS, FORMULAS, AND STRATEGIES

1. **Sum:** the result of an addition: 8 is the sum of 6 and 2

2. **Difference:** the result of a subtraction: 4 is the difference of 6 and 2

3. **Product:** the result of a multiplication: 12 is the product of 6 and 2

4. **Quotient:** the result of a division: 3 is the quotient of 6 and 2

5. **Remainder:** when 15 is divided by 6, the quotient is 2 and the remainder is 3: $15 = 6 \times 2 + 3$

6. **Integers:** $\{..., -3, -2, -1, 0, 1, 2, 3, ...\}$

7. **Factor** or **Divisor:** any integer that leaves no remainder (i.e., a remainder of 0) when it is divided into another integer: 1, 2, 5, 10 are the factors (or divisors) of 10

8. **Multiple:** the product of one integer by a second integer:
   $-14, -7, 0, 7, 14, 21, 28, ...$ are multiples of 7
   ($-14 = -2 \times 7$, $0 = 0 \times 7$, $7 = 1 \times 7$, $14 = 2 \times 7$, and so on)

9. **Even integers:** the multiples of 2: $\{..., -4, -2, 0, 2, 4, ...\}$

10. **Odd integers:** the non-multiples of 2: $\{..., -3, -1, 1, 3, 5, ...\}$

11. **Consecutive integers:** two or more integers, written in sequence, each of which is 1 more than the preceding one. For example:
    $7, 8, 9 \qquad -2, -1, 0, 1, 2 \qquad n, n + 1, n + 2$

12. **Prime number:** a positive integer that has exactly two divisors. The first few primes are 2, 3, 5, 7, 11, 13, 17. (*not* 1)

13. **Exponent:** a number written as a superscript: the 3 in 7^3. On the SAT, the only exponents you need to know about are positive integers: $2^n = 2 \times 2 \times 2 \times \ldots \times 2$, where 2 appears as a factor n times.

14. **Laws of Exponents:**
    For any numbers b and c and positive integers m and n:

    (i) $b^m b^n = b^{m+n}$ (ii) $\dfrac{b^m}{b^n} = b^{m-n}$ (iii) $(b^m)^n = b^{mn}$

    (iv) $b^m c^m = (bc)^m$

15. **Square root of a positive number:** if a is positive, $\sqrt{a}$ is the only positive number whose square is a: $(\sqrt{a})^2 = \sqrt{a} - \sqrt{a} = a$

16. The product and the quotient of two positive numbers or two negative numbers are positive; the product and the quotient of a positive number and a negative number are negative.

17. • The product of an *even* number of negative factors is positive.
    • The product of an *odd* number of negative factors is negative.

18. For any positive numbers a and b:

$$\sqrt{ab} = \sqrt{a} - \sqrt{b} \quad \text{and} \quad \sqrt{\dfrac{a}{b}} = \dfrac{\sqrt{a}}{\sqrt{b}}$$

19. For any real numbers a, b, and c:

    • $a(b + c) = ab + ac$ • $a(b - c) = ab - ac$
    and, if $a \neq 0$,

    • $\dfrac{b+c}{a} = \dfrac{b}{a} + \dfrac{c}{a}$ • $\dfrac{b-c}{a} = \dfrac{b}{a} - \dfrac{c}{a}$

20. To compare two fractions, use your calculator to convert them to decimals.

21. To multiply two fractions, multiply their numerators and multiply their denominators:

$$\frac{3}{5} \times \frac{4}{7} = \frac{3 \times 4}{5 \times 7} = \frac{12}{35}$$

22. To divide any number by a fraction, multiply that number by the reciprocal of the fraction:

$$\frac{3}{5} \div \frac{2}{3} = \frac{3}{5} \times \frac{3}{2} = \frac{9}{10}$$

23. To add or subtract fractions with the same denominator, add or subtract the numerators and keep the denominator:

$$\frac{4}{9}+\frac{1}{9}=\frac{5}{9} \quad \text{and} \quad \frac{4}{9}-\frac{1}{9}=\frac{3}{9}=\frac{1}{3}$$

24. To add or subtract fractions with different denominators, first rewrite the fractions as equivalent fractions with the same denominator:

$$\frac{1}{6}+\frac{3}{4}=\frac{2}{12}+\frac{9}{12}=\frac{11}{12}$$

25. Percent: a fraction whose denominator is 100:

$$15\%=\frac{15}{100}=.15$$

26. The **percent increase** of a quantity is

$$\frac{\text{actual increase}}{\text{original amount}}\times100\%$$

The **percent decrease** of a quantity is

$$\frac{\text{actual decrease}}{\text{original amount}}\times100\%$$

27. Ratio: a fraction that compares two quantities that are measured in the same units. The ratio 2 to 3 can be written $\frac{2}{3}$ or $2:3$.

28. In any ratio problem, write the letter x after each number and use some given information to solve for x.

29. Proportion: an equation that states that two ratios (fractions) are equal. Solve proportions by cross-multiplying: if $\frac{a}{b}=\frac{c}{d}$, then $ad=bc$.

30. Average of a set of n numbers: the sum of those numbers divided by n:

$$\text{average}=\frac{\text{sum of the } n \text{ numbers}}{n} \quad \text{or simply}$$

$$A=\frac{\text{sum}}{n}$$

31. If you know the average, A, of a set of n numbers, multiply A by n to get their sum: $\text{sum}=nA$.

32. To multiply two binomials, use the **FOIL** method: multiply each term in the first parentheses by each term in the second parentheses and simplify by combining terms, if possible.

$$(2x - 7)(3x + 2) = (2x)(3x) + (2x)(2) + (-7)(3x) + (-7)(2) =$$

First terms   Outer terms   Inner terms   Last terms

$$6x^2 + 4x - 21x - 14 = 6x^2 - 17x - 14$$

33. The three most important binomial products on the SAT are these:

- $(x - y)(x + y) = x^2 - y^2$
- $(x - y)^2 = (x - y)(x - y) = x^2 - 2xy + y^2$
- $(x - y)^2 = (x + y)(x + y) = x^2 + 2xy + y^2$

34. Although some **quadratic equations** can be solved by factoring, all quadratic equations can be solved by using the **Quadratic Formula**:

If a, b, and c are real numbers with $a \neq 0$, and if $ax^2 + bx + c = 0$, then:

$$x = \frac{-b \pm \sqrt{b^2 - 4ac}}{2a}$$

35. All **distance problems** involve one of three variations of the same formula:

$$\text{distance} = \text{rate} \times \text{time} \qquad \text{rate} = \frac{\text{distance}}{\text{time}}$$

$$\text{time} = \frac{\text{distance}}{\text{rate}}$$

36.

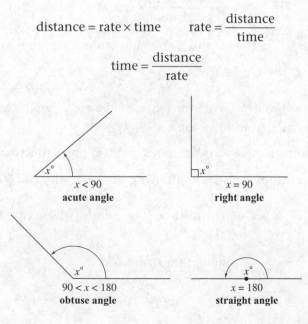

$x < 90$
acute angle

$x = 90$
right angle

$90 < x < 180$
obtuse angle

$x = 180$
straight angle

37. If two or more angles form a **straight angle**, the sum of their measures is 180°.

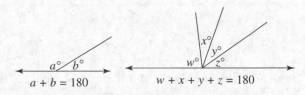

$a + b = 180$

$w + x + y + z = 180$

38. The sum of all the measures of all the angles around a point is 360°.

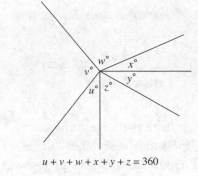

$u + v + w + x + y + z = 360$

39.

vertical angles

40. Vertical angles have equal measures.

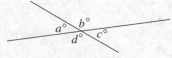

$a = c$ and $b = d$.

41. If a pair of parallel lines is cut by a transversal that is *not* perpendicular to the parallel lines:

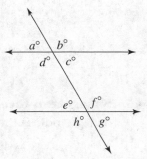

- Four of the angles are acute, and four are obtuse.
- All four acute angles have the same measure:
  $$a = c = e = g$$
- All four obtuse angles have the same measure:
  $$b = d = f = h$$
- The sum of any acute angle and any obtuse angle is 180°: for example, $d + e = 180$, $c + f = 180$, $b + g = 180$, ...

42. In any triangle, the sum of the measures of the three angles is 180°.

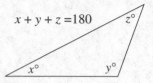

$x + y + z = 180$

43. The measure of an **exterior angle** of a triangle is equal to the sum of the measures of the two opposite interior angles.

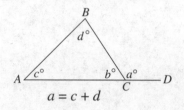

$a = c + d$

44. In any triangle:
- the longest side is opposite the largest angle;
- the shortest side is opposite the smallest angle;
- sides with the same length are opposite angles with the same measure.

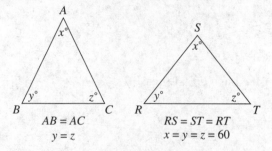

$AB = AC$
$y = z$

$RS = ST = RT$
$x = y = z = 60$

45. In any right triangle, the sum of the measures of the two acute angles is 90°.

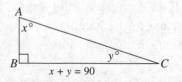

$x + y = 90$

46. Pythagorean theorem: In a right triangle, if a and b are the lengths of the legs and c is the length of the hypotenuse, then $a^2 + b^2 = c^2$.

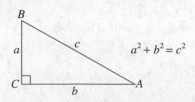

$a^2 + b^2 = c^2$

47. In a **45-45-90 right triangle**, if the length of each leg is x, then the length of the hypotenuse is $x\sqrt{2}$.

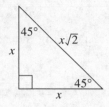

48. In a **30-60-90 right triangle**, if the length of the shorter leg is x, then the length of the longer leg is $x\sqrt{3}$, and the length of the hypotenuse is $2x$.

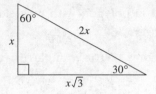

49. The Triangle Inequality: The sum of the lengths of any two sides of a triangle is greater than the length of the third side.
The difference between the lengths of any two sides of a triangle is less than the length of the third side.

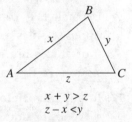

50. The **area of a triangle** is given by $A = \dfrac{1}{2}bh$, where b is the base and h is the height.

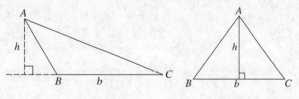

51. If A represents the area of an equilateral triangle with side s, then $A = \dfrac{s^2\sqrt{3}}{4}$.

52. Two triangles, such as ABC and DEF below,

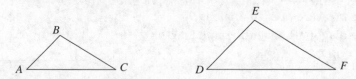

are **similar**, provided the following two conditions are satisfied:

- The three angles in the first triangle are congruent to the three angles in the second triangle:

$$m\angle A = m\angle D, \quad m\angle B = m\angle E, \quad m\angle C = m\angle F$$

- The lengths of the corresponding sides of the two triangles are in proportion:

$$\frac{AB}{DE} = \frac{BC}{EF} = \frac{AC}{DF}$$

53. If the measures of two angles of a triangle are equal to the measures of two angles of a second triangle, the triangles are similar.

54. In any **quadrilateral** (a polygon with four sides), the sum of the measures of the four angles is 360°.

55. The sum of the measures of the n angles in a polygon with n sides is $(n - 2) \times 180$.

56. A **trapezoid** is a quadrilateral in which exactly one pair of opposite sides is parallel. A **parallelogram** is a quadrilateral in which both pairs of opposite sides are parallel. A **rectangle** is a parallelogram in which all four angles are right angles. A **square** is a rectangle in which all four sides have the same length.

57. In any **parallelogram:**
- Opposite sides are congruent: $AB = CD$ and $AD = BC$.
- Opposite angles are congruent: $a = c$ and $b = d$.
- The sum of the measures of any two consecutive angles is 180°: $a + b = 180$, $b + c = 180$, and so on.
- The two diagonals bisect each other: $AE = EC$ and $BE = ED$.

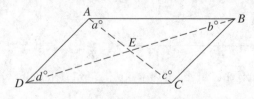

58. In any **rectangle:**
- The measure of each angle is 90°.
- The diagonals have the same length: $AC = BD$.

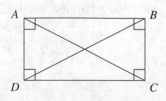

59. In any **square:**
- All four sides have the same length.
- Each diagonal divides the square into two 45-45-90 right triangles.
- The diagonals are perpendicular to each other: $AC \perp BD$.

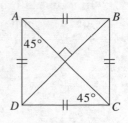

60. A trapezoid is ***isosceles*** if the non-parallel sides are congruent. In any **isosceles trapezoid:**
- The base angles (the angles opposite the congruent sides) are congruent: $a = b$ and $c = d$.
- The diagonals are congruent: $AC = BD$

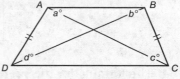

61. Formulas for perimeter and area:
- For a parallelogram: $A = bh$ and $P = 2(a + b)$.
- For a rectangle: $A = \ell w$ and $P = 2(\ell + w)$.
- For a square: $A = s^2$ or $A = \dfrac{1}{2}d^2$ and $P = 4s$.

- For a trapezoid: $A = \dfrac{1}{2}h(b_1 + b_2)$.

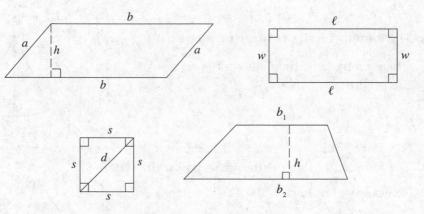

62. Let r be the radius, d the diameter, C the circumference, and A the area of a circle, then

$$d = 2r \qquad C = \pi d = 2\pi r \qquad A = \pi r^2$$

63. The formula for the **volume of a rectangular solid** is $V = \ell wh$, where ℓ, w, and h represent the length, width, and height, respectively.

In a cube, all the edges are equal. Therefore, if e is the edge, the formula for the volume is $V = e^3$.

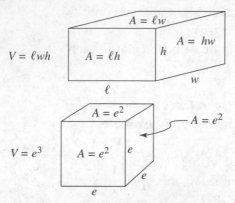

64. The formula for the **surface area of a rectangular solid** is

$A = 2(\ell w + \ell h + wh)$. The formula for the surface area of a cube is $A = 6e^2$.

65. The formula for the **volume of a cylinder** is $V = \pi r^2 h$, where r represents the radius of the circular top and h represents the height.

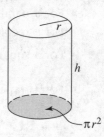

66. The formula for the **volume of a cone** is $V = \dfrac{1}{3}\pi r^2 h$, where r represents the radius and h represents the height.

$V = \frac{1}{3}\pi r^2 h$

67. The formula for the **volume of a pyramid with a rectangular base** is $V = \dfrac{1}{3}\ell w h$, where ℓ and w represent the length and width of the base, respectively, and h represents the height.

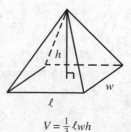

$V = \frac{1}{3}\ell w h$

68. The formula for the **volume of a sphere** of radius r is $V = \dfrac{4}{3}\pi r^3$.

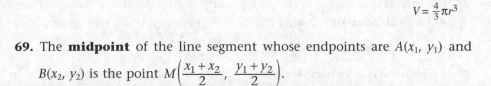

$V = \frac{4}{3}\pi r^3$

69. The **midpoint** of the line segment whose endpoints are $A(x_1, y_1)$ and $B(x_2, y_2)$ is the point $M\left(\dfrac{x_1 + x_2}{2}, \dfrac{y_1 + y_2}{2}\right)$.

70. The **distance, d, between two points**, $A(x_1, y_1)$ and $B(x_2, y_2)$, can be calculated using the distance formula:

$$d = \sqrt{(x_2 - x_1)^2 + (y_2 - y_1)^2}.$$

71. The formula for the **slope** of the line that passes through the points (x_1, y_1) and (x_2, y_2) is:

$$\text{slope} = \frac{y_2 - y_1}{x_2 - x_1}$$

72. • The slope of any horizontal line is 0.
   • The slope of any line that goes up as you move from left to right is positive.
   • The slope of any line that goes down as you move from left to right is negative.

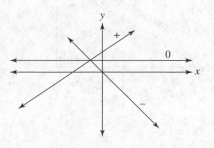

73. The **equation of a non-vertical line** is $y = mx + b$ where m is the slope of the line and $(0, b)$ is the point where the line crosses the y-axis.

74. The **equation of the circle** whose center is the point (h, k) and whose radius is r is $(x - h)^2 + (y - k)^2 = r^2$.

75. For any real numbers a, b, and c, with $a \neq 0$, $y = ax^2 + bx + c$ is the **equation of a parabola**, whose axis of symmetry is the vertical line whose equation is $x = \dfrac{-b}{2a}$.

76. The Counting Principle: If two jobs need to be completed and there are m ways to do the first job and n ways to do the second job, then there are $m \times n$ ways to do one job followed by the other. This principle can be extended to any number of jobs.

77. If E is any event, the **probability** that E will occur is given by

$$P(E) = \frac{\text{number of favorable outcomes}}{\text{total number of possible outcomes}},$$

assuming that all of the possible outcomes are equally likely.

78–81. Let E be an event, and let $P(E)$ be the probability that it will occur.

78. If it is **impossible** for E to occur, then **$P(E) = 0$**.

79. If it is **certain** that E will occur, then **$P(E) = 1$**.

80. In all other cases, **$0 < P(E) < 1$**.

81. The probability that event E will *not* occur is **$1 - P(E)$**.

82. If an experiment is repeated 2 (or more) times and if the outcome of any event does not depend on the outcome of any previous event, the probability that first one event will occur and then a second event will occur is the product of the probabilities.

83–86. Let θ be one of the acute angles in a right triangle.

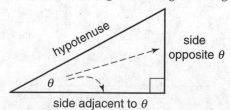

83. The formula for the **sine of** θ, denoted $\sin \theta$, is:

$$\sin \theta = \frac{\text{the length of the side opposite } \theta}{\text{the length of the hypotenuse}}$$

$$= \frac{\text{opposite}}{\text{hypotenuse}}$$

84. The formula for the **cosine of** θ, denoted $\cos \theta$, is:

$$\cos \theta = \frac{\text{the length of the side adjacent to } \theta}{\text{the length of the hypotenuse}}$$

$$= \frac{\text{adjacent}}{\text{hypotenuse}}$$

85. The formula for the **tangent of** θ, denoted $\tan \theta$, is:

$$\tan \theta = \frac{\text{the length of the side opposite } \theta}{\text{the length of the side adjacent to } \theta}$$

$$= \frac{\text{opposite}}{\text{adjacent}}$$

86. For any acute angle θ, $\tan \theta = \dfrac{\sin \theta}{\cos \theta}$.

87. The **imaginary unit, *i*,** has the property that $i^2 = -1$. We often refer to *i* as the square root of –1 and write $i = \sqrt{-1}$.

88. If x is a real number, then $x^2 \geq 0$, so *i is not a real number.*

89. The powers of *i* form a repeating sequence in which the four terms, i, -1, $-i$, 1 repeat in that order indefinitely.

90. A **complex number** is a number that can be written in the form $a + bi$, where a and b are real numbers.

91. The **conjugate** of the complex number $a + bi$ is the complex number $a - bi$.

92. To add complex numbers, add their real parts and add their imaginary parts. For example:

$$(3 + 5i) + (2 + 3i) = 5 + 8i$$

93. To subtract complex numbers, subtract their real parts and subtract their imaginary parts. For example:

$$(3 + 5i) - (2 + 3i) = 1 + 2i$$

94. To multiply complex numbers, "FOIL" them as if they were binomials and then replace i^2 by -1. For example:

$$(3 + 5i)(2 + 3i) = 6 + 9i + 10i + 15i^2$$
$$= 6 + 19i + 15(-1)$$
$$= 6 + 19i - 15$$
$$= -9 + 19i$$

95. The product of the complex number $(a + bi)$ and its conjugate $(a - bi)$ is the real number $a^2 + b^2$:

$$(a + bi)(a - bi) = a^2 - (bi)^2 = a^2 - b^2(-1) = a^2 + b^2$$

For example: $(2 + 3i)(2 - 3i) = 2^2 + 3^2 = 4 + 9 = 13$

96. To divide two complex numbers, write the quotient as a fraction, and multiply the numerator and the denominator by the conjugate of the demoninator. For example:

$$(3 + 5i) \div (2 + 3i) = \frac{3 + 5i}{2 + 3i} = \frac{3 + 5i}{2 + 3i} \cdot \frac{2 - 3i}{2 - 3i} = \frac{6 - 9i + 10i - 15i^2}{4 + 9} = \frac{21 + i}{13} = \frac{21}{13} + \frac{1}{13}i$$

⚷ GENERAL MATH STRATEGIES

Later in this chapter, you will learn tactics that will help you with the two types of math questions on the SAT: multiple-choice and grid-in. In this section you will learn several important strategies that can be used on either type of question. Mastering these tactics will improve your performance on all mathematics tests.

Tactic 1. Draw a Diagram

On any geometry question for which a figure is not provided, draw one (as accurately as possible) in your test booklet.

Let's consider some examples.

EXAMPLE 1

What is the area of a rectangle whose length is twice its width and whose perimeter is equal to that of a square whose area is 1?

Solution. Don't even think of answering this question until you have drawn a square and a rectangle and labeled each of them: each side of the square is 1; and if the width of the rectangle is *w*, its length is 2*w*.

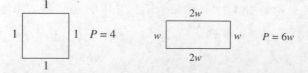

Now, write the required equation and solve it:

$$6w = 4 \Rightarrow w = \frac{4}{6} = \frac{2}{3} \Rightarrow 2w = \frac{4}{3}$$

The area of the rectangle = $lw = \left(\frac{4}{6}\right)\left(\frac{2}{3}\right) = \frac{8}{9}$.

Drawings should not be limited, however, to geometry questions; there are many other questions on which drawings will help.

EXAMPLE 2

A jar contains 10 red marbles and 30 green ones. How many red marbles must be added to the jar so that 60% of the marbles will be red?

Solution. Draw a diagram and label it. From the diagram it is clear that there are now 40 + x marbles in the jar, of which 10 + x are red. Since we want the fraction of red marbles to be 60% $\left(= \frac{3}{5}\right)$, we have

x	Red
30	Green
10	Red

$$\frac{10+x}{40+x} = \frac{3}{5}.$$

Cross-multiplying, we get:

$$50 + 5x = 120 + 3x \Rightarrow 2x = 70 \Rightarrow x = 35$$

Of course, you could have set up the equation and solved it without the diagram, but the drawing makes the solution easier and you are less likely to make a careless mistake.

Tactic 2. If a Diagram Is Drawn to Scale, Trust It, and Use Your Eyes

Remember that every diagram that appears on the SAT has been drawn as accurately as possible *unless* you see "Note: Figure not drawn to scale" written below it.

For figures that are drawn to scale: line segments that appear to be the same length *are* the same length; if an angle clearly looks obtuse, it *is* obtuse; and if one angle appears larger than another, you may assume that it *is* larger.

EXAMPLE 3

In the figure at the right, what is the sum of the measures of all of the marked angles?
     (A) 540°   (B) 720°   (C) 900°   (D) 1080°

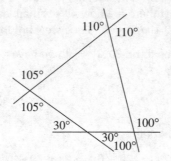

Solution. Make your best estimate of each angle, and add up the values. The five choices are so far apart that, even if you're off by 15° or more on some of the angles, you'll get the right answer. The sum of the estimates shown is 690°, so the correct answer *must* be 720° **(B).**

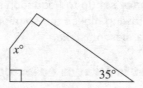

EXAMPLE 4

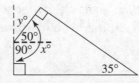

In the figure above, what is the value of *x*?
     (A) 95   (B) 125   (C) 135   (D) 145

Solution. Since the diagram is drawn to scale, trust it. Look at *x*: it appears to be *about* 90 + 50 = 140.

In this case, using TACTIC 2 does not get you the exact answer. It only enables you to narrow down the choices to (C) or (D). At this point you should guess—unless, of course, you know the correct solution. The correct answer is 145° **(D).**

Tactic 3. If a Diagram Is *Not* Drawn to Scale, Redraw It to Scale, and Then Use Your Eyes

For figures that have not been drawn to scale, you can make *no* assumptions. Lines that look parallel may not be; an angle that appears to be obtuse may, in fact, be acute; two line segments may have the same length even though one looks twice as long as the other.

EXAMPLE 5

In △*ACB*, what is the value of *x*?
(A) 75 (B) 60 (C) 45 (D) 30

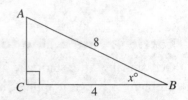

Note: Figure not drawn to scale

Solution. In what way is this figure not drawn to scale? *AB* = 8 and *BC* = 4, but in the figure $\overline{AB}$ is *not* twice as long as $\overline{BC}$. Redraw the triangle so that $\overline{AB}$ is twice as long as $\overline{BC}$. When you redraw the triangle, be sure to draw a right triangle. Even though the figure is not drawn to scale, the little square in angle *C* guarantees that *C* is a right angle.

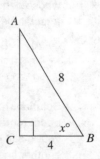

Now, just look: *x* is about **60 (B)**. In fact, *x* is exactly 60. If the hypotenuse of a right triangle is twice the length of one of the legs, you have a 30-60-90 triangle, and the angle formed by the hypotenuse and that leg is 60°.

EXAMPLE 6

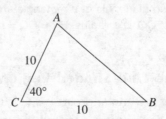

Note: Figure not drawn to scale

In the figure above, which of the following *must* be true?
(A) m∠*A* = 40 (B) m∠*B* = 40° (C) *AB* > 10 (D) *AB* < 10

Solution. In the given diagram, $\overline{AB}$ is longer than $\overline{AC}$, which is 10, but *we cannot trust the diagram*. Actually, there are two things wrong: $\angle C$ is labeled 40°, but looks much more like 60° or 70°, and $\overline{AC}$ and $\overline{BC}$ are each labeled 10, but $\overline{BC}$ is drawn much longer. Use TACTIC 3. Redraw the triangle with a 40° angle and two sides of the same length. Now, it's clear that $AB < 10$. Choose **D**.

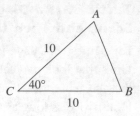

Tactic 4. Add a Line to a Diagram

Occasionally, after staring at a diagram, you still have no idea how to solve the problem to which it applies. It looks as though there isn't enough given information. When this happens, it often helps to draw another line in the diagram.

EXAMPLE 7

In the figure at the right, Q is a point on the circle whose center is O and whose radius is r, and $OPQR$ is a rectangle. What is the length of diagonal $\overline{PR}$?

(A) r (B) r^2 (C) $\dfrac{r^2}{\pi}$ (D) $\dfrac{r\sqrt{2}}{\pi}$

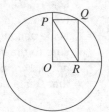

Solution. If, after staring at the diagram and thinking about rectangles, circles, and the Pythagorean theorem, you're still lost, don't give up. Ask yourself, "Can I add another line to this diagram?" As soon as you think to draw in $\overline{OQ}$, the other diagonal, the problem becomes easy: the two diagonals of a rectangle are congruent, and, since $\overline{OQ}$ is a radius, $PR = OQ = r$ **(A)**.

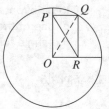

Tactic 5. Subtract to Find Shaded Regions

Whenever part of a figure is white and part is shaded, the straightforward way to find the area of the shaded portion is to find the area of the entire figure and then subtract from it the area of the white region. Of course, if you are asked for the area of the white region, you can, instead, subtract the shaded area from the total area. Occasionally, you may see an easy way to calculate the shaded area directly, but usually you should subtract.

EXAMPLE 8

In the figure below, $ABCD$ is a rectangle, and $\overarc{BE}$ and $\overarc{CF}$ are arcs of circles centered at A and D. What is the area of the shaded region?

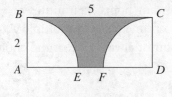

(A) $10 - \pi$ (B) $2(5 - \pi)$ (C) $2(5 - 2\pi)$ (D) $5(2 - \pi)$

Solution. The entire region is a 2×5 rectangle whose area is 10. Since each white region is a quarter-circle of radius 2, the combined area of these regions is that of a semicircle of radius 2:

$$\frac{1}{2}\pi(2)^2 = 2\pi$$

Therefore, the area of the shaded region is $10 - 2\pi = 2(5 - \pi)$ **(B)**.

Tactic 6. Don't Do More Than You Have To

Look for shortcuts. Since a problem can often be solved in more than one way, you should always look for the easiest method. Consider the following example.

EXAMPLE 9

If $5(3x - 7) = 20$, what is $3x - 8$?

It's not difficult to solve for x:

$$5(3x - 7) = 20 \Rightarrow 15x - 35 = 20 \Rightarrow 15x = 55 \Rightarrow$$
$$x = \frac{55}{15} = \frac{11}{3}$$

But it's too much work. Besides, once you find that $x = \frac{11}{3}$, you still have

to multiply to get $3x$: $3\left(\frac{11}{3}\right) = 11$, and then subtract to get $3x - 8$: $11 - 8 = 3$.

Solution. The key is to recognize that you don't need x. Finding $3x - 7$ is easy (just divide the original equation by 5), and $3x - 8$ is just 1 less:

$$5(3x - 7) = 20 \Rightarrow 3x - 7 = 4 \Rightarrow 3x - 8 = 3$$

Tactic 7. Pay Attention to Units

Often the answer to a question must be in units different from those used in the given data. As you read the question, <u>underline</u> exactly what you are being asked. Do the examiners want hours or minutes or seconds, dollars or cents, feet or inches, meters or centimeters? On multiple-choice questions an answer with the wrong units is almost always one of the choices.

EXAMPLE 10

At a speed of 48 miles per hour, how many minutes will be required to drive 32 miles?

(A) $\dfrac{2}{3}$ (B) $\dfrac{3}{2}$ (C) 40 (D) 45

Solution. This is a relatively easy question. Just be attentive. Since $\dfrac{32 \text{ miles}}{48 \text{ miles per hour}} = \dfrac{2}{3}$ hours. Choice A is $\dfrac{2}{3}$; but that is *not* the correct answer because the question asks how many *minutes* will be required. (Did you underline the word "minutes" in the question?) The correct answer is $\dfrac{2}{3}$ hour $= \dfrac{2}{3}$(60 minutes) = **40 minutes (C)**.

Tactic 8. Systematically Make Lists

When a question asks "how many," often the best strategy is to make a list of all the possibilities. It is important that you make the list in a *systematic* fashion so that you don't inadvertently leave something out. Often, shortly after starting the list, you can see a pattern developing and can figure out how many more entries there will be without writing them all down.

EXAMPLE 11

The product of three positive integers is 300. If one of them is 5, what is the least possible value of the sum of the other two?

Solution. Since one of the integers is 5, the product of the other two is 60 (5 × 60 = 300). Systematically, list all possible pairs, (a, b), of positive integers whose product is 60, and check their sums. First, let $a = 1$, then 2, and so on.

a	b	a + b
1	60	61
2	30	32
3	20	23
4	15	19
5	12	17
6	10	16

The answer is **16**.

EXAMPLE 12

A palindrome is a number, such as 93539, that reads the same forward and backward. How many palindromes are there between 100 and 1000?

Solution. First, write down the numbers 101, 111, 121, 131, 141, 151, in the 100's that end in 1:   161, 171, 181, 191

Now write the numbers beginning and   202, 212, 222, 232, 242, 252, ending in 2:   262, 272, 282, 292

By now you should see the pattern: there are 10 palindromes beginning with 1, and 10 beginning with 2, and there will be 10 beginning with 3, 4, ..., 9 for a total of 9 × 10 = **90** palindromes.

PRACTICE EXERCISES

Answers given on pages 167–169.

Multiple-Choice Questions

1. In the figure at the right, if the radius of circle O is 10, what is the length of diagonal AC of rectangle OABC?

   (A) $\sqrt{10}$ (B) $5\sqrt{2}$ (C) 10   (D) $10\sqrt{2}$

2. If $5x + 13 = 31$, what is the value of $\sqrt{5x + 31}$?

   (A) $\sqrt{13}$ (B) 7   (C) 13   (D) 169

3. At Nat's Nuts a $2\frac{1}{4}$-pound bag of pistachio nuts costs $6.00. At this rate, what is the cost, in cents, of a bag weighing 9 ounces?

   (A) 1.5   (B) 24   (C) 150   (D) 1350

4. In the figure at the right, three circles of radius 1 are tangent to one another. What is the area of the shaded region between the circles?

   (A) $\frac{\pi}{2} - \sqrt{3}$ (B) $\pi - \sqrt{3}$ (C) $\sqrt{3} - \frac{\pi}{2}$ (D) $2 - \frac{\pi}{2}$

Grid-in Questions

5. In writing all of the integers from 1 to 300, how many times is the digit 1 used?

6. If $a + 2b = 14$ and $5a + 4b = 16$, what is the average (arithmetic mean) of a and b?

7. A bag contains 4 marbles, 1 of each color: red, blue, yellow, and green. The marbles are removed at random, 1 at a time. If the first marble is red, what is the probability that the yellow marble is removed before the blue marble?

8. The area of circle O in the figure below is 12. What is the area of the shaded sector?

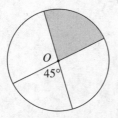

Note: Figure not drawn to scale

Answer Key

1. C   2. B   3. C   4. C

5.   6.

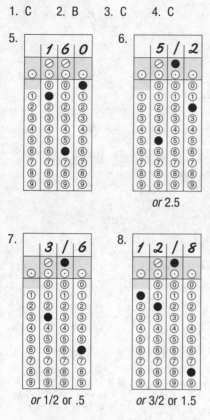

or 2.5

7.   8.

or 1/2 or .5   *or 3/2 or 1.5*

Answer Explanations

1. **(C)**

Even if you can't solve this problem, don't just take a wild guess. Use TACTIC 2: trust the diagram. $\overline{AC}$ is clearly longer than $\overline{OC}$, and very close to radius $\overline{OE}$.

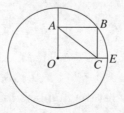

Therefore, $\overline{AC}$ must be about 10. Either by inspection or with your calculator, check the choices. They are approximately as follows:

(A) $\sqrt{10} \approx 3.1$;   (B) $5\sqrt{2} \approx 7$;   (C) 10;   (D) $10\sqrt{2} \approx 14$.

The answer must be **10**.

The answer *is* **10. The two diagonals are equal, and diagonal $\overline{OB}$ is a radius.

2. **(B)**

Use TACTIC 6: don't do more than you have to. In particular, don't solve for x. Here

$5x + 13 = 31 \Rightarrow 5x = 18 \Rightarrow 5x + 31 = 18 + 31 = 49$

So, $\sqrt{5x + 31} = \sqrt{49} = \mathbf{7}$.

3. **(C)**

This is a relatively simple ratio, but use TACTIC 7 and make sure you get the units right. You need to know that there are 100 cents in a dollar and 16 ounces in a pound.

$$\frac{\text{price}}{\text{weight}} : \frac{6 \text{ dollars}}{2.25 \text{ pounds}} = \frac{600 \text{ cents}}{36 \text{ ouncces}} = \frac{x \text{ cents}}{9 \text{ ouncces}}$$

Now cross-multiply and solve: $36x = 5400 \Rightarrow x = \mathbf{150}$.

4. **(C)**

Use TACTIC 4 and add some lines: connect the centers of the three circles to form an equilateral triangle whose sides are 2. Now use TACTIC 5 and find the shaded area by subtracting the area of the three sectors from the area of the triangle, which is $\dfrac{2^2\sqrt{3}}{4} = \sqrt{3}$ (Fact 50). Since the

measure of each angle in an equilateral triangle is 60°,

each sector is $\dfrac{60}{360} = \dfrac{1}{6}$ of a circle of radius 1. Together the three sectors form

$\dfrac{3}{6}$ or $\dfrac{1}{2}$ of such a circle, so their total area is $\dfrac{1}{2}\pi(1)^2 = \dfrac{\pi}{2}$. Finally, subtract:

the area of the shaded region is $\mathbf{\sqrt{3} - \dfrac{\pi}{2}}$.

5. **(160)**

Use TACTIC 8. Systematically list the numbers that contain the digit 1, writing as many as you need to see the pattern. Between 1 and 99 the digit 1 is used 10 times as the units digit (1, 11, 21, ... , 91) and 10 times as the tens digit (10, 11, 12, ... , 19) for a total of 20 times. From 200 to 299, there are 20 more times (the same 20 but preceded by 2). Finally, from 100 to 199 there are 20 more plus 100 numbers where the digit 1 is used in the hundreds place. The total is 20 + 20 + 20 + 100 = **160**.

6. $\left(\dfrac{5}{2} \text{ or } 2.5\right)$

Use TACTIC 6: don't do more than is necessary. You don't need to solve this system of equations; you don't need to know the values of a and b, only their average. Adding the two equations gives

$$6a + 6b = 30 \Rightarrow a + b = 5 \Rightarrow \frac{a+b}{2} = \frac{5}{2} \text{ or } \mathbf{2.5}$$

7. $\left(\dfrac{3}{6} \text{ or } \dfrac{1}{2} \text{ or } .5\right)$

Use TACTIC 8. Systematically list all of the orders in which the marbles could be drawn. With 4 colors, there would ordinarily have been 24 orders, but since the first marble drawn was red, there are only 6 arrangements for the other 3 colors: BYG, BGY, YGB, YBG, GYB, GBY. In 3 of these 6 the yellow comes before the blue, and in the other 3 the blue comes before the yellow. Therefore, the probability that the yellow marble will be removed before the blue marble is $\dfrac{3}{6}$ or $\dfrac{1}{2}$ or **.5**.

8. $\left(\dfrac{12}{8} \text{ or } \dfrac{3}{2} \text{ or } 1.5\right)$

The shaded sector is $\dfrac{45}{360} = \dfrac{1}{8}$ of the circle, so its area is $\dfrac{1}{8}$ of 12: $\dfrac{12}{8}$ or $\dfrac{3}{2}$ or **1.5**. If you didn't see that, use TACTIC 3 and redraw the figure to scale by making the angle as close as possible to 45°. It is now clear that the sector is $\dfrac{1}{8}$ of the circle (or very close to it).

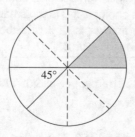

THE MULTIPLE-CHOICE QUESTION

Each math section on the SAT contains multiple-choice questions. On the first page of each section, you will see the following directions:

In this section *solve each problem*, using any available space on the page for scratchwork. *Then* decide which is the best of the choices given and fill in the corresponding circle on the answer sheet. (Emphasis added.)

The directions are very simple. Basically, they tell you to ignore, at first, the fact that these are multiple-choice questions. Just *solve each problem*, and *then* look at the four choices to see which one is best. As you will see, that is not always the best strategy.

In this section you will learn important strategies you need to help you answer multiple-choice questions on the SAT. However, as invaluable as these tactics are, use them only when you need them. *If you know how to solve a problem and are confident that you can do so accurately and reasonably quickly, JUST DO IT!*

Tactic 9. Test the Choices, Starting with B or C

TACTIC 9, often called *backsolving*, is useful when you are asked to solve for an unknown and you understand what needs to be done to answer the question, but you want to avoid doing the algebra. The idea is simple: test the various choices to see which one is correct.

Note

On the SAT the answers to virtually all numerical multiple-choice questions are listed in either increasing or decreasing order. Consequently B and C are the middle values; and in applying TACTIC 9, *you should always start with one of them.* For example, assume that choices A, B, C, and D are given in increasing order. Try C. If it works, you've found the answer. If C doesn't work, you should now know whether you need to test a larger number or a smaller one, and that information permits you to eliminate more choices. If C is too small, you need a larger numbers, so A and B are out, and the answer is D; if C is too large, you can eliminate D, which is even larger, and then test A or B.

Examples 13 and 14 illustrate the proper use of TACTIC 9.

EXAMPLE 13

If the average (arithmetic mean) of 2, 7, and x is 12, what is the value of x?
(A) 12 (B) 21 (C) 27 (D) 36

Solution. Use TACTIC 9. Test choice B: $x = 21$.
- Is the average of 2, 7, and 21 equal to 12?
- No: $\dfrac{2+7+21}{3} = \dfrac{30}{3} = 10$, which is *too small*.

- Eliminate B; also, since, for the average to be 12, x must be *greater* than 21, also eliminate A.
- Try choice C: $x = 27$. Is the average of 2, 7, and 27 equal to 12?
- Yes: $\dfrac{2+7+27}{3} = \dfrac{36}{3} = 12$. The answer is **C**.

Every problem that can be solved using TACTIC 9 can be solved directly, usually in less time. Therefore, we stress: *if you are confident that you can solve a problem quickly and accurately, just do so*.

EXAMPLE 14

If the sum of five consecutive odd integers is 735, what is the largest of these integers?
(A) 155   (B) 151   (C) 145   (D) 143

Solution. Use TACTIC 9. Test choice C: 145.
- If 145 is the largest of the five integers, the integers are 145, 143, 141, 139, and 137. Quickly add them on your calculator. The sum is 705.
- Since 705 is too small, eliminate C and D.
- If you noticed that the amount by which 705 is too small is 30, you should realize that each of the five numbers needs to be increased by 6; therefore, the largest is **151 (B)**.
- If you didn't notice that, just try 151, and see that it works.

This solution is easy, and it avoids having to set up and solve the required equation:

$$n + (n + 2) + (n + 4) + (n + 6) + (n + 8) = 735$$

Tactic 10. Replace Variables with Numbers

Mastery of TACTIC 10 is critical for anyone developing good test-taking skills. This tactic can be used whenever the five choices involve the variables in the question. There are three steps:

1. Replace each letter with an easy-to-use number.
2. Solve the problem using those numbers.
3. Evaluate each of the five choices with the numbers you picked to see which choice is equal to the answer you obtained.

Examples 15 and 16 illustrate the proper use of TACTIC 10.

EXAMPLE 15

If a is equal to b multiplied by c, which of the following is equal to b divided by c?

(A) $\dfrac{a}{bc}$ (B) $\dfrac{ab}{c}$ (C) $\dfrac{a}{c}$ (D) $\dfrac{a}{c^2}$

Solution.
- Pick three easy-to-use numbers that satisfy $a = bc$: for example, $a = 6, b = 2, c = 3$.
- Solve the problem with these numbers: $b - c = \dfrac{b}{c} = \dfrac{2}{3}$.
- Check each of the five choices to see which one is equal to $\dfrac{2}{3}$:
- (A) $\dfrac{a}{bc} = \dfrac{6}{(2)(3)} = 1$: NO.   (B) $\dfrac{ab}{c} = \dfrac{(6)(2)}{(3)} = 4$: NO.

  (C) $\dfrac{a}{c} = \dfrac{6}{3} = 2$: NO.   (D) $\dfrac{a}{c^2} = \dfrac{6}{3^2} = \dfrac{6}{9} = \dfrac{2}{3}$: YES!
- The answer is **D**.

EXAMPLE 16

If the sum of four consecutive odd integers is s, then, in terms of s, what is the greatest of these integers?

(A) $\dfrac{s-12}{4}$ (B) $\dfrac{s-6}{4}$ (C) $\dfrac{s+6}{4}$ (D) $\dfrac{s+12}{4}$

Solution.
- Pick four easy-to-use consecutive odd integers: say, 1, 3, 5, 7. Then s, their sum, is 16.
- Solve the problem with these numbers: the greatest of these integers is 7.
- When $s = 16$, the four choices are $\dfrac{s-12}{4} = \dfrac{4}{4}$, $\dfrac{s-6}{4} = \dfrac{10}{4}$, $\dfrac{s+6}{4} = \dfrac{22}{4}$, $\dfrac{s+12}{4} = \dfrac{28}{4}$.
- Only $\dfrac{28}{4}$, choice **D**, is equal to 7.

Of course, Examples 15 and 16 can be solved without using TACTIC 10 *if your algebra skills are good.*

The important point is that, if you are uncomfortable with the correct algebraic solution, you don't have to omit these questions. You can use TACTIC 10 and *always* get the right answer.

Example 17 is somewhat different. You are asked to reason through a word problem involving only variables. Most students find problems like these mind-boggling. Here, the use of TACTIC 10 is essential.

> **Helpful Hint**
>
> Replace the letters with numbers that are easy to use, not necessarily ones that make sense. *It is perfectly OK to ignore reality.* A school can have five students, apples can cost $10 each, trains can go 5 miles per hour or 1000 miles per hour—it doesn't matter.

EXAMPLE 17

If a school cafeteria needs c cans of soup each week for each student, and if there are s students in the school, for how many weeks will x cans of soup last?

(A) $\dfrac{cx}{s}$ (B) $\dfrac{xs}{c}$ (C) $\dfrac{s}{cx}$ (D) $\dfrac{x}{cs}$

Solution.

- Replace c, s, and x with three easy-to-use numbers. If a school cafeteria needs 2 cans of soup each week for each student, and if there are 5 students in the school, for how many weeks will 20 cans of soup last?
- Since the cafeteria needs $2 \times 5 = 10$ cans of soup per week, 20 cans will last for 2 weeks.
- Which of the choices equals 2 when $c = 2$, $s = 5$, and $x = 20$?
- The four choices become: $\dfrac{cx}{s} = 8$, $\dfrac{xs}{c} = 50$, $\dfrac{s}{cx} = \dfrac{1}{8}$, $\dfrac{x}{cs} = 2$.

The answer is **D**.

Tactic 11. Choose an Appropriate Number

TACTIC 11 is similar to TACTIC 10 in that we pick convenient numbers. However, here no variable is given in the problem. TACTIC 11 is especially useful in problems involving fractions, ratios, and percents.

> **Helpful Hint**
>
> In problems involving fractions, the best number to use is the least common denominator of all the fractions. In problems involving percents, the easiest number to use is 100.

EXAMPLE 18

At Central High School each student studies exactly one foreign language. Three-fifths of the students take Spanish, and one-fourth of the remaining students take Italian. If all of the others take French, what <u>percent</u> of the students take French?

(A) 15   (B) 20   (C) 25   (D) 30

Solution. The least common denominator of $\frac{3}{5}$ and $\frac{1}{4}$ is 20, so assume that there are 20 students at Central High. (Remember that the numbers you choose don't have to be realistic.) Then the number of students taking Spanish is $12\left(\frac{3}{5}\text{ of }20\right)$. Of the remaining 8 students, $2\left(\frac{1}{4}\text{ of }8\right)$ take Italian. The other 6 take French. Finally, 6 is **30%** of 20. The answer is **D**.

EXAMPLE 19

From 2010 to 2011 the sales of a book decreased by 80%. If the sales in 2012 were the same as in 2010, by what percent did they increase from 2011 to 2012?

(A) 100% (B) 120% (C) 400% (D) 500%

Solution. Use TACTIC 11, and assume that 100 copies were sold in 2010 (and 2012). Sales dropped by 80 (80% of 100) to 20 in 1995 and then increased by 80, from 20 back to 100, in 2012. The percent increase was

$$\frac{\text{actual increase}}{\text{original amount}} \times 100\% = \frac{80}{20} \times 100\% = 400\% \text{ (C)}$$

Tactic 12. Add Equations

When a question involves two equations, either add them or subtract them. If there are three or more equations, add them.

Helpful Hint

Very often, answering a question does *not* require you to solve the equations. Remember TACTIC 6: *Do not do any more than is necessary.*

EXAMPLE 20

If $3x + 5y = 14$ and $x - y = 6$, what is the average of x and y?

(A) 2.5 (B) 3 (C) 3.5 (D) 5

Solution. Add the equations:

$$\begin{array}{r} 3x+5y=14 \\ +\quad x-y=\ \ 6 \\ \hline 4x+4y=20 \end{array}$$

Divide each side by 4: $\quad x + y = 5$

The average of x and y is their sum divided by 2: $\dfrac{x+y}{2} = \dfrac{5}{2} = 2.5$

The answer is **A**.

EXAMPLE 21

If $a - b = 1$, $b - c = 2$, and $c - a = d$, what is the value of d?
(A) –3 (B) –1 (C) 1 (D) 3

Solution. Add the three equations:

$$a - b = 1$$
$$b - c = 2$$
$$\underline{+\ c - a = d}$$
$$0 = 3 + d \Rightarrow d = -3$$

The answer is **A**.

Tactic 13. Eliminate Absurd Choices, and Guess

When you have no idea how to solve a problem, eliminate all the absurd choices and *guess* from among the remaining ones.

EXAMPLE 22

The average of 5, 10, 15, and x is 20. What is x?
(A) 20 (B) 25 (C) 45 (D) 50

Solution. If the average of four numbers is 20, and three of them are less than 20, the other one must be greater than 20. Eliminate A and guess. But, you realize that, since 5 and 10 are *a lot* less than 20, x will probably be *a lot* more than 20, you should eliminate B, as well. Then guess either C or D.

EXAMPLE 23

If 25% of 220 equals 5.5% of w, what is w?
(A) 55 (B) 100 (C) 110 (D) 1000

Solution. Since 5.5% of w equals 25% of 220, which is surely greater than 5.5% of 220, w must be *greater* than 220. Eliminate A, B, and C. The answer *must* be **D**!

PRACTICE EXERCISES

Answers given on pages 176–178.

1. Judy is now twice as old as Adam but 6 years ago she was 5 times as old as he was. How old is Judy now?

(A) 10 (B) 16 (C) 20 (D) 24

2. If $a < b$ and c is the sum of a and b, which of the following is the positive difference between a and b?

   (A) $2a - c$ (B) $2b - c$ (C) $c - a + b$ (D) $c - a - b$

3. If w widgets cost c cents, how many widgets can you get for d dollars?

   (A) $\dfrac{100dw}{c}$ (B) $\dfrac{dw}{100c}$ (C) $\dfrac{dw}{c}$ (D) cdw

4. What is a divided by $a\%$ of a?

   (A) $\dfrac{a}{100}$ (B) $\dfrac{100}{a}$ (C) $\dfrac{a^2}{100}$ (D) $\dfrac{100}{a^2}$

5. On a certain Russian-American committee, $\dfrac{2}{3}$ of the members are men, and $\dfrac{3}{8}$ of the men are Americans. If $\dfrac{3}{5}$ of the committee members are Russian, what fraction of the members are American women?

   (A) $\dfrac{3}{20}$ (B) $\dfrac{11}{60}$ (C) $\dfrac{1}{4}$ (D) $\dfrac{2}{5}$

6. Nadia will be x years old y years from now. How old was she z years ago?

   (A) $x + y + z$ (B) $x + y - z$ (C) $x - y - z$ (D) $y - x - z$

7. If $12a + 3b = 1$ and $7b - 2a = 9$, what is the average (arithmetic mean) of a and b?

   (A) 0.1   (B) 0.5   (C) 1   (D) 2.5

8. If $x\%$ of y is 10, what is y?

   (A) $\dfrac{100}{x}$ (B) $\dfrac{1000}{x}$ (C) $\dfrac{x}{100}$ (D) $\dfrac{x}{10}$

Answer Key

1. B   3. A   5. A   7. B
2. B   4. B   6. C   8. B

Answer Explanations

1. **(B)**

Use TACTIC 9: backsolve, starting with C. If Judy is now 20, Adam is 10; 6 years ago, they would have been 14 and 4, which is less than 5 times as much. Eliminate C and D, and try a smaller value. If Judy is now **16**, Adam is 8; 6 years ago, they would have been 10 and 2. That's it; 10 is 5 times 2.

2. **(B)**

Use TACTIC 10. Pick simple values for a, b, and c. Let $a = 1$, $b = 2$, and $c = 3$. Then $b - a = 1$. Only $2b - c$ is equal to 1.

3. **(A)**

Use TACTIC 10: replace variables with numbers. If 2 widgets cost 10 cents, then widgets cost 5 cents each; and for 3 dollars, you can get 60 widgets. Which of the choices equals 60 when $w = 2$, $c = 10$, and $d = 3$?

Only $\dfrac{100dw}{c}$.

4. **(B)**

Use TACTICS 10 and 11: replace a by a number, and use 100 since the problem involves percents.

$$100 \div (100\% \text{ of } 100) = 100 \div 100 = 1$$

Test each choice; which one equals 1 when $a = 100$? Both A and B are equal to $\dfrac{100}{100}$, which is 1, but you can eliminate C and D. Now test A and B with another value for a, such as 50:

$$50 \div (50\% \text{ of } 50) = 50 \div (25) = 2$$

Now, only choice B, $\dfrac{100}{a}$, works: $\dfrac{100}{50} = 2$.

5. **(A)**

Use TACTIC 11: choose appropriate numbers. The LCM of all the denominators is 120, so assume that the committee has 120 members. Then there are $\dfrac{2}{3} \times 120 = 80$ men and 40 women. Of the 80 men, $30 \left(\dfrac{3}{8} \times 80 \right)$ are American.

Since there are $72\left(\frac{3}{5}\times120\right)$ Russians, there are $120 - 72 = 48$ Americans, of whom 30 are men, so the other 18 are women. Finally, the fraction of American women is $\frac{18}{120}=\frac{\textbf{3}}{\textbf{20}}$.

6. **(C)**

Use TACTIC 10: replace x, y, and z with easy-to-use numbers.

Assume Nadia will be 10 in 2 years. How old was she 3 years ago? If she will be 10 in 2 years, she is 8 now and 3 years ago was 5. Which of the choices equals 5 when $x = 10$, $y = 2$, and $z = 3$? Only $\textbf{\textit{x}} - \textbf{\textit{y}} - \textbf{\textit{z}}$.

7. **(B)**

Use TACTIC 12: The sum of the two equations is

$$10a + 10b = 10 \Rightarrow a + b = 1 \Rightarrow \frac{a+b}{2} = \frac{1}{2} \text{ or } \textbf{0.5}$$

8. **(B)**

Use TACTICS 10 and 11. Since 100% of 10 is 10, let $x = 100$ and $y = 10$. When $x = 100$, choices B and D are each 10. Eliminate A and C, and try some other numbers: 50% of 20 is 10. Of B and D, only $\dfrac{\textbf{1000}}{\textbf{\textit{x}}} = 20$ when $x = 50$.

THE GRID-IN QUESTION

On the SAT, both math sections contain questions for which no choices are given. These are the grid-in problems, which represent the type of question with which you are most familiar—you solve a problem and then write the answer on your answer sheet. The only difference is that, on the SAT, you must enter the answer on a special grid that can be read by a computer.

Your answer sheet will have a blank grid for each such question. Each one will look like the grid on the left below. After solving a problem, the first step is to write the answer in the four boxes at the top of the grid. You then blacken the appropriate circle under each box. For example, if your answer to a question is 2450, you write 2450 at the top of the grid, one digit in each box, and then in each column blacken the circle that contains the number you wrote at the top of the column, as shown in the grid below on the right. This is not difficult; but there are some special rules concerning grid-in questions, so let's go over them before you practice gridding in some numbers.

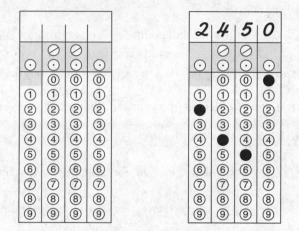

1. The only symbols that appear in the grid are the digits 0 to 9, a decimal point, and a slash (/), used to write fractions. Keep in mind that, since there is no negative sign, **the answer to every grid-in question is a positive number or zero.**

2. You will receive credit for a correct answer no matter where you grid it. For example, the answer 17 could be gridded in any of three positions:

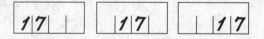

Neverthelesss, we suggest that you consistently **write all your answers** the way numbers are usually displayed—**to the right, with blank spaces at the left.**

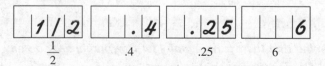

$$\frac{1}{2} \qquad .4 \qquad .25 \qquad 6$$

3. **Never round off your answers.** If a decimal answer will fit in the grid and you round it off, your answer will be marked wrong. For example, if the answer is .148 and you correctly round it off to the nearest hundredth and enter .15, you will receive *no credit*. If a decimal answer will not fit in the grid, enter a decimal point in the first column, followed by the first three digits. For example, if your answer is 0.454545..., enter it as .454. You would receive credit if you rounded it to .455, but don't. You might occasionally make a mistake in rounding, whereas you'll *never*

make a mistake if you just copy the first three digits. *Note:* If the correct answer has more than two decimal digits, *you must use all four columns of the grid.* You will receive *no credit* for .4 or .5 or .45. (These answers are not accurate enough.)

4. ***Never write a 0 before the decimal point.*** The first column of the grid doesn't even have a 0 in it. If the correct answer is 0.3333..., you must grid it as .333. You can't grid 0.33, and 0.3 is not accurate enough.

5. ***Be aware that you can never enter a mixed number.*** If your answer is $2\frac{1}{2}$, you *cannot* leave a space and enter your answer as 2 1/2, and if you enter $\boxed{2\,1\,/\,2}$, it will be read as $\frac{21}{2}$ and marked wrong. You must enter $2\frac{1}{2}$ as the improper fraction $\frac{5}{2}$ or as the decimal 2.5.

6. Since full credit is given for any equivalent answer, use these guidelines to ***enter your answer in the simplest way.*** If your answer is $\frac{6}{9}$, you should enter 6/9. (However, credit would be given for any of the following: 2/3, 4/6, 8/12, .666, .667.)

7. Sometimes grid-in questions have more than one correct answer. On these questions, ***grid in only one of the acceptable answers***. For example, if a question asked for a positive number less than 100 that was divisible by both 5 and 7, you could enter *either* 35 *or* 70, but not both. Similarly, if a question asked for a number between $\frac{3}{7}$ and $\frac{5}{9}$, you could enter any *one of* hundreds of possibilities: fractions such as $\frac{1}{2}$ and $\frac{4}{9}$ or *any* decimal between .429 and .554. For example, .43 or .499 or .52.

8. ***Keep in mind that there is no penalty for a wrong answer on any question*** *on the SAT*. Therefore, you should guess, even if you have no idea what to do. As you will see shortly, there are some strategies for making intelligent guesses.

9. Be sure to ***grid every answer very carefully***. The computer does not read what you have written in the boxes; it reads only the answer in the grid. If the correct answer to a question is 100 and you write 100 in the boxes, but accidentally grid in 200, you get *no* credit.

10. If you know that the answer to a question is 100, can you just grid it in and not bother writing it on top? Yes, you will get full credit, and so some SAT guides recommend that you don't waste time writing the answer. This is terrible advice. Instead, **write each answer in the boxes.** It takes less than 2 seconds per answer to do this, and it definitely cuts down on careless errors in gridding. More important, if you go back to check your work, it is much easier to read what's in the boxes on top than what's in the grid.

TESTING TACTICS

Tactic 14. Backsolve

If you think of a grid-in problem as a multiple-choice question in which the choices accidentally got erased, you can still use TACTIC 9: test the choices. You just have to make up the choices as you go.

EXAMPLE 24

If the average (arithmetic mean) of 2, 7, and x is 12, what is the value of x?

Solution. You could start with 10; but if you immediately realize that the average of 2, 7, and 10 is less than 10 (so it can't be 12), you'll try a larger number, say 20. The average of 2, 7, and 20 is

$$\frac{2+7+20}{3} = \frac{29}{3} = 9\frac{2}{3}$$

which is too small. Try $x = 30$:

$$\frac{2+7+30}{3} = \frac{39}{3} = 13$$

just a bit too big. Since 12 is closer to 13 than it is to $9\frac{2}{3}$, your next choice should be closer to 30 than 20, surely more than 25. Your third try might well be 27, which works.

Tactic 15. Choose an Appropriate Number

This is exactly the same as TACTIC 12. The most appropriate numbers to choose are 100 for percent problems, the LCD (least common denominator) for fraction problems, and the LCM (least common multiple) of the coefficients for problems involving equations. Each of the problems discussed under TACTIC 11 could have been a grid-in, because we didn't even look at the choices until we had the correct answer.

EXAMPLE 25

During an Election Day sale, the price of every television set in a store was reduced by $33\frac{1}{3}$%. By what percent must these sale prices be raised so that the TVs now sell for their original prices? (Do not grid the % sign.)

Solution. Since this problem involves percents, you should think about using 100. But the fraction $\frac{1}{3}$ is also involved, so 300 is an even better choice. Assume the original price was $300. Since $33\frac{1}{3}$% of 300 is $\frac{1}{3}$ of 300 or 100, the sale price was $200. To restore the price to $300, it must now be raised by $100. The percent increase is

$$\frac{\text{actual increase}}{\text{original amount}} \times 100\% = \frac{100}{200} \times 100\% = \mathbf{50\%}$$

PRACTICE EXERCISES

Answers given on pages 184–186.

Directions: Enter your response to these problems on the grids on page 183.

1. For what number $b > 0$ is it true that b divided by b% of b equals b?

2. Patty has 150 coins, each of which is a dime or a quarter. If she has $27.90, how many quarters does she have?

3. A fair coin is flipped repeatedly. Each time it lands "heads," Ali gets a point, and whenever it lands "tails," Jason gets a point. The game continues until someone gets 5 points. If the score is now 4 to 3 in Ali's favor, and the probability that Ali will win the game is k times the probability that Jason will win the game, what is the value of k?

4. At a certain university, $\frac{1}{4}$ of the applicants failed to meet minimum standards and were rejected immediately. Of those who met the standards, $\frac{2}{5}$ were accepted. If 1200 applicants were accepted, how many applied?

5. More than half of the members of the Key Club are girls. If $\frac{4}{7}$ of the girls and $\frac{7}{11}$ of the boys in the Key Club attended the April meeting, what is the smallest number of members the club could have?

6. Jessica copied a column of numbers and added them. The only mistake she made was that she copied one number as 5095 instead of 5.95. If the sum she got was 8545.05, what should the answer have been?

7. Jerry spent $105 for a tool kit and a box of nails. If the tool kit cost $100 more than the nails, how many boxes of nails could be purchased for the price of the tool kit?

8. Ken is now 3 times as old as his younger sister, but in 7 years he will be only twice as old as she will be then. How old is Ken now?

9. The value of an investment increased 50% in 2012 and again in 2013. In each of 2014 and 2015 the value of the investment decreased by 50%. At the end of 2015 the value of the investment was how many times the value at the beginning of 2012?

10. How many integers between 1 and 1000 are the product of two consecutive integers?

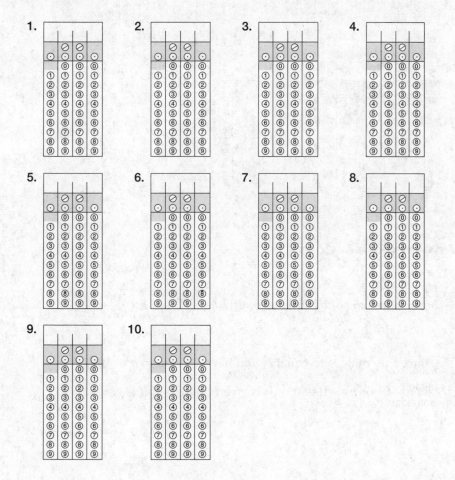

Answer Key

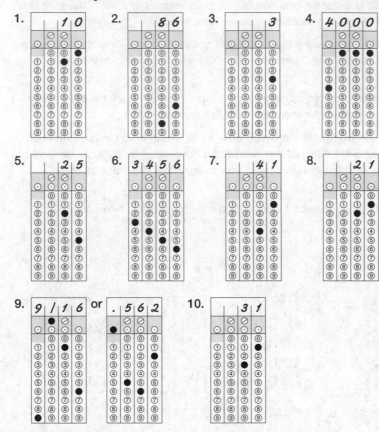

Answer Explanations

1. **(10)**

$$b \div (b\% \text{ of } b) = b \div \left(\frac{b}{100} \times b\right) = b \div \left(\frac{b^2}{100}\right) = b \times \frac{100}{b^2} = \frac{100}{b}$$

Since this value is to equal b, you have $\frac{100}{b} = b \Rightarrow b^2 = 100$.

So $b = 10$ or $b = -10$. Since it is given that $b > 0$, it is equal to 10.

2. **(86)**

Use TACTIC 14: backsolve. Pick an easy starting value, say $q = 100$. If this gives a value greater than \$27.90, decrease q; if it gives a value less than \$27.90, increase q.

Number of Quarters	Number of Dimes	Value
100	50	\$25.00 + \$5.00 = \$30.00
80	70	\$20.00 + \$7.00 = \$27.00
85	65	\$21.25 + \$6.50 = \$27.75
86	64	\$21.50 + \$6.40 = \$27.90

3. **(3)**

Jason can win only if the next two flips are both tails. The probability of that happening is $\frac{1}{2} \times \frac{1}{2} = \frac{1}{4}$. Therefore, the probability that Ali wins is $1 \times \frac{1}{4} = \frac{3}{4}$. Since $\frac{3}{4} = 3\left(\frac{1}{4}\right)$, $k = $ **3**.

4. **(4000)**

Use TACTIC 15: choose an appropriate number. The LCD of $\frac{1}{4}$ and $\frac{2}{5}$ is 20, so *assume* that there were 20 applicants. Then $\frac{1}{4}(20) = 5$ failed to meet the minimum standards. Of the remaining 15 applicants, $\frac{2}{5}$, or 6, were accepted, so 6 of every 20 applicants were accepted. Set up a proportion:

$$\frac{6}{20} = \frac{1200}{x} \Rightarrow 6x = 24{,}000 \Rightarrow x = \mathbf{4000}$$

5. **(25)**

Since $\frac{4}{7}$ of the girls attended the meeting, the number of girls in the club must be a multiple of 7: 7, 14, 21, ... Similarly, the number of boys in the club must be a multiple of 11: 11, 22, ... Since there are at least 11 boys and there are more girls than boys, there must be at least 14 girls. The smallest possible total is $14 + 11 = $ **25**.

6. **(3456)**

To get the correct sum, subtract the number Jessica added in error and add the number she left out:

$$8545.05 - 5095 + 5.95 = \mathbf{3456}$$

7. **(41)**

The first thing to do is to calculate the prices of the tool kit and the nails. *Be careful*—they are *not* $100 and $5. You can get the answer algebraically or by trial and error. If you let x = cost of the nails, then $100 + x$ = cost of the tool kit, and

$$x + (100 + x) = 105 \Rightarrow 2x + 100 = 105 \Rightarrow$$
$$2x = 5 \Rightarrow x = 2.5$$

Then the nails cost $2.50, and the tool kit $102.50. Finally, $102.50 \div 2.50 = \mathbf{41}$.

8. **(21)**

Use TACTIC 15. Pick a value for the sister's age—say, 2. Then Ken is 6. In 7 years, sister and brother will be 9 and 13, respectively. No good; 13 is less than twice 9. Try a bigger number—5. Then Ken is 15, and in 7 years the two will be 12 and 22. That's closer, but still too small. Try 7. Then Ken is **21**, and in 7 years his sister and he will be 14 and 28, respectively. That's it!

9. $\left(\mathbf{.562\ or\ \dfrac{9}{16}} \right)$

Use TACTIC 15. Pick an easy-to-use starting value—$100, say. Then the value of the investment at the end of each of the 4 years 2012, 2013, 2014, 2015 was $150, $225, $112.50, $56.25, so the final value was .5625 times the initial value. Note that some initial values would lead to an answer more easily expressed as a fraction. For example, if you start with $16, the yearly values would be $24, $36, $18, and $9, and the answer would be $\dfrac{9}{16}$.

10. **(31)**

Use TACTIC 8. List the integers systematically: 1×2, 2×3, ..., 24×25, ... You don't have to multiply and list the products (2, 6, 12, ..., 600, ...); you just have to know when to stop. The largest product less than 1000 is 31 $\times$ 32 = 992, so there are **31** numbers.

SUMMARY OF IMPORTANT TIPS AND TACTICS

1. Whenever you know how to answer a question directly, just do it. The tactics given in this chapter should be used only when you need them.

2. Memorize all the formulas you need to know. Even though some of them are printed on the first page of each math section, during the test you do not want to waste any time referring back to that reference material.

3. Be sure to bring a calculator, but use it only when you need it. Don't use it for simple arithmetic that you can easily do in your head.

4. Remember that no problem requires lengthy or difficult computations. If you find yourself doing a lot of arithmetic, stop and reread the question. You are probably not answering the question asked.

5. Answer every question you attempt. Even if you can't solve it, you can almost always eliminate one or two choices. Often you know that an answer must be negative, but two or three of the choices are positive, or an answer must be even, and some of the choices are odd.

6. Unless a diagram is labeled "<u>Note</u>: Figure not drawn to scale," it is perfectly accurate, and you can trust it in making an estimate.

7. When a diagram has not been provided, draw one, especially on any geometry problem.

8. If a diagram has been provided, feel free to label it, mark it up in any way, including adding line segments, if necessary.

9. Answer any question for which you can estimate the answer, even if you are not sure you are correct.

10. When a question involves two equations, either add them or subtract them. If there are three or more, just add them.

11. Never make unwarranted assumptions. Do not assume numbers are positive or integers. If a question refers to two numbers, do not assume that they have to be different. If you know a figure has four sides, do not assume that it is a rectangle.

12. Be sure to work in consistent units. If the width and length of a rectangle are 8 inches and 2 feet, respectively, either convert the 2 feet to 24 inches or the 8 inches to two-thirds of a foot before calculating the area or perimeter.

Standard Multiple-Choice Questions

1. Whenever you backsolve, start with Choice B or C.

2. When you replace variables with numbers, choose easy-to-use numbers, whether or not they are realistic.

3. Choose appropriate numbers. The best number to use in percent problems is 100. In problems involving fractions, the best number to use is the least common denominator.

4. When you have no idea how to solve a problem, first eliminate all of the absurd choices before you guess.

Student-Produced Response (Grid-in) Questions

1. Write your answer in the four spaces at the top of the grid, and *carefully* grid in your answer below. No credit is given for a correct answer if it has been gridded improperly.

2. Remember that the answer to a grid-in question can never be negative.

3. You can never grid in a mixed number—you must convert it to an improper fraction or a decimal.

4. If a fraction can fit in the four spaces of the grid, enter it. If not, use your calculator to convert it to a decimal (by dividing) and enter a decimal point followed by the first three decimal digits.

5. When gridding a decimal, do not write a 0 before the decimal point.

6. If a question has more than one possible answer, only grid in one of them.

7. When you are truly stuck you should grid in anything that seems reasonable, rather than just take a wild guess.

Practice SAT Exams | 7

You are now about to take a major step in preparing yourself to handle an actual SAT. Before you are two practice tests patterned after the released SAT practice exam. Up to now, you've concentrated on specific areas and on general testing techniques. You've mastered testing tips and worked on practice exercises. Now you have a chance to test yourself before you walk in that test center door.

These practice tests resemble the SAT in format, in difficulty, and in content. When you take one, take it as if it *were* the actual SAT.

Build Your Stamina

Don't start and stop and take time out for a soda or for a phone call. To do well on the SAT, you have to focus on the test, the test, and nothing but the test for hours at a time. Most high school students have never had to sit through a three- or four-hour examination before they take their first SAT. To survive such a long exam takes stamina, and, as marathon runners know, the only way to build stamina is to put in the necessary time.

Refine Your Skills

You know how to maximize your score by tackling easy questions first and by eliminating wrong answers whenever you can. Put these skills into practice. If you find yourself spending too much time on any one question, take a guess and move on. Remember to check frequently to make sure you are answering the questions in the right spots. This is a great chance for you to get these skills down pat.

Take a Deep Breath—and Smile!

It's hard to stay calm when those around you are tense, and you're bound to run into some pretty tense people when you take the SAT. So you may experience a slight case of "exam nerves" on the big day. Don't worry about it.

1. Being keyed up for an examination isn't always bad: you may outdo yourself because you are so worked up.
2. Total panic is unlikely to set in: you know too much.

3. You know you can handle a test this long.

4. You know you can handle the sorts of questions you'll find on the SAT.

5. You know that you can get a really good score even if you don't attempt all of the questions. Pace yourself and don't worry about finishing any section. Just be sure to quickly guess at every question you don't have time to work on.

Make Your Practice Pay—Approximate the Test

1. Complete an entire Practice Exam at one sitting.

2. Use a clock or timer.

3. Allow precisely 65 minutes for section 1, 35 minutes for section 2, 25 minutes for section 3, and 55 minuters for section 4. (If you have time left over, review your answers in that section.)

4. Between sections 2 and 3, give yourself a five- or ten-minute break.

5. After section 4, take another break and then allow 50 minutes to write the essay.

6. Allow no talking in the test room.

7. Work rapidly without wasting time.

ANSWER SHEET—TEST 1

Section 1: Reading

1. Ⓐ Ⓑ Ⓒ Ⓓ
2. Ⓐ Ⓑ Ⓒ Ⓓ
3. Ⓐ Ⓑ Ⓒ Ⓓ
4. Ⓐ Ⓑ Ⓒ Ⓓ
5. Ⓐ Ⓑ Ⓒ Ⓓ
6. Ⓐ Ⓑ Ⓒ Ⓓ
7. Ⓐ Ⓑ Ⓒ Ⓓ
8. Ⓐ Ⓑ Ⓒ Ⓓ
9. Ⓐ Ⓑ Ⓒ Ⓓ
10. Ⓐ Ⓑ Ⓒ Ⓓ
11. Ⓐ Ⓑ Ⓒ Ⓓ
12. Ⓐ Ⓑ Ⓒ Ⓓ
13. Ⓐ Ⓑ Ⓒ Ⓓ
14. Ⓐ Ⓑ Ⓒ Ⓓ
15. Ⓐ Ⓑ Ⓒ Ⓓ
16. Ⓐ Ⓑ Ⓒ Ⓓ
17. Ⓐ Ⓑ Ⓒ Ⓓ
18. Ⓐ Ⓑ Ⓒ Ⓓ

19. Ⓐ Ⓑ Ⓒ Ⓓ
20. Ⓐ Ⓑ Ⓒ Ⓓ
21. Ⓐ Ⓑ Ⓒ Ⓓ
22. Ⓐ Ⓑ Ⓒ Ⓓ
23. Ⓐ Ⓑ Ⓒ Ⓓ
24. Ⓐ Ⓑ Ⓒ Ⓓ
25. Ⓐ Ⓑ Ⓒ Ⓓ
26. Ⓐ Ⓑ Ⓒ Ⓓ
27. Ⓐ Ⓑ Ⓒ Ⓓ
28. Ⓐ Ⓑ Ⓒ Ⓓ
29. Ⓐ Ⓑ Ⓒ Ⓓ
30. Ⓐ Ⓑ Ⓒ Ⓓ
31. Ⓐ Ⓑ Ⓒ Ⓓ
32. Ⓐ Ⓑ Ⓒ Ⓓ
33. Ⓐ Ⓑ Ⓒ Ⓓ
34. Ⓐ Ⓑ Ⓒ Ⓓ
35. Ⓐ Ⓑ Ⓒ Ⓓ
36. Ⓐ Ⓑ Ⓒ Ⓓ

37. Ⓐ Ⓑ Ⓒ Ⓓ
38. Ⓐ Ⓑ Ⓒ Ⓓ
39. Ⓐ Ⓑ Ⓒ Ⓓ
40. Ⓐ Ⓑ Ⓒ Ⓓ
41. Ⓐ Ⓑ Ⓒ Ⓓ
42. Ⓐ Ⓑ Ⓒ Ⓓ
43. Ⓐ Ⓑ Ⓒ Ⓓ
44. Ⓐ Ⓑ Ⓒ Ⓓ
45. Ⓐ Ⓑ Ⓒ Ⓓ
46. Ⓐ Ⓑ Ⓒ Ⓓ
47. Ⓐ Ⓑ Ⓒ Ⓓ
48. Ⓐ Ⓑ Ⓒ Ⓓ
49. Ⓐ Ⓑ Ⓒ Ⓓ
50. Ⓐ Ⓑ Ⓒ Ⓓ
51. Ⓐ Ⓑ Ⓒ Ⓓ
52. Ⓐ Ⓑ Ⓒ Ⓓ

Section 2: Writing and Language

1. Ⓐ Ⓑ Ⓒ Ⓓ
2. Ⓐ Ⓑ Ⓒ Ⓓ
3. Ⓐ Ⓑ Ⓒ Ⓓ
4. Ⓐ Ⓑ Ⓒ Ⓓ
5. Ⓐ Ⓑ Ⓒ Ⓓ
6. Ⓐ Ⓑ Ⓒ Ⓓ
7. Ⓐ Ⓑ Ⓒ Ⓓ
8. Ⓐ Ⓑ Ⓒ Ⓓ
9. Ⓐ Ⓑ Ⓒ Ⓓ
10. Ⓐ Ⓑ Ⓒ Ⓓ
11. Ⓐ Ⓑ Ⓒ Ⓓ
12. Ⓐ Ⓑ Ⓒ Ⓓ
13. Ⓐ Ⓑ Ⓒ Ⓓ
14. Ⓐ Ⓑ Ⓒ Ⓓ
15. Ⓐ Ⓑ Ⓒ Ⓓ

16. Ⓐ Ⓑ Ⓒ Ⓓ
17. Ⓐ Ⓑ Ⓒ Ⓓ
18. Ⓐ Ⓑ Ⓒ Ⓓ
19. Ⓐ Ⓑ Ⓒ Ⓓ
20. Ⓐ Ⓑ Ⓒ Ⓓ
21. Ⓐ Ⓑ Ⓒ Ⓓ
22. Ⓐ Ⓑ Ⓒ Ⓓ
23. Ⓐ Ⓑ Ⓒ Ⓓ
24. Ⓐ Ⓑ Ⓒ Ⓓ
25. Ⓐ Ⓑ Ⓒ Ⓓ
26. Ⓐ Ⓑ Ⓒ Ⓓ
27. Ⓐ Ⓑ Ⓒ Ⓓ
28. Ⓐ Ⓑ Ⓒ Ⓓ
29. Ⓐ Ⓑ Ⓒ Ⓓ
30. Ⓐ Ⓑ Ⓒ Ⓓ

31. Ⓐ Ⓑ Ⓒ Ⓓ
32. Ⓐ Ⓑ Ⓒ Ⓓ
33. Ⓐ Ⓑ Ⓒ Ⓓ
34. Ⓐ Ⓑ Ⓒ Ⓓ
35. Ⓐ Ⓑ Ⓒ Ⓓ
36. Ⓐ Ⓑ Ⓒ Ⓓ
37. Ⓐ Ⓑ Ⓒ Ⓓ
38. Ⓐ Ⓑ Ⓒ Ⓓ
39. Ⓐ Ⓑ Ⓒ Ⓓ
40. Ⓐ Ⓑ Ⓒ Ⓓ
41. Ⓐ Ⓑ Ⓒ Ⓓ
42. Ⓐ Ⓑ Ⓒ Ⓓ
43. Ⓐ Ⓑ Ⓒ Ⓓ
44. Ⓐ Ⓑ Ⓒ Ⓓ

Section 3: Math (No Calculator)

1. Ⓐ Ⓑ Ⓒ Ⓓ
2. Ⓐ Ⓑ Ⓒ Ⓓ
3. Ⓐ Ⓑ Ⓒ Ⓓ
4. Ⓐ Ⓑ Ⓒ Ⓓ
5. Ⓐ Ⓑ Ⓒ Ⓓ

6. Ⓐ Ⓑ Ⓒ Ⓓ
7. Ⓐ Ⓑ Ⓒ Ⓓ
8. Ⓐ Ⓑ Ⓒ Ⓓ
9. Ⓐ Ⓑ Ⓒ Ⓓ
10. Ⓐ Ⓑ Ⓒ Ⓓ

11. Ⓐ Ⓑ Ⓒ Ⓓ
12. Ⓐ Ⓑ Ⓒ Ⓓ
13. Ⓐ Ⓑ Ⓒ Ⓓ
14. Ⓐ Ⓑ Ⓒ Ⓓ
15. Ⓐ Ⓑ Ⓒ Ⓓ

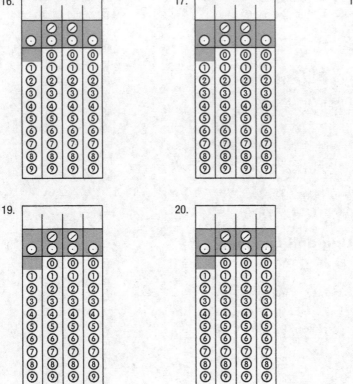

Section 4: Math (Calculator)

1. Ⓐ Ⓑ Ⓒ Ⓓ
2. Ⓐ Ⓑ Ⓒ Ⓓ
3. Ⓐ Ⓑ Ⓒ Ⓓ
4. Ⓐ Ⓑ Ⓒ Ⓓ
5. Ⓐ Ⓑ Ⓒ Ⓓ
6. Ⓐ Ⓑ Ⓒ Ⓓ
7. Ⓐ Ⓑ Ⓒ Ⓓ
8. Ⓐ Ⓑ Ⓒ Ⓓ
9. Ⓐ Ⓑ Ⓒ Ⓓ
10. Ⓐ Ⓑ Ⓒ Ⓓ

11. Ⓐ Ⓑ Ⓒ Ⓓ
12. Ⓐ Ⓑ Ⓒ Ⓓ
13. Ⓐ Ⓑ Ⓒ Ⓓ
14. Ⓐ Ⓑ Ⓒ Ⓓ
15. Ⓐ Ⓑ Ⓒ Ⓓ
16. Ⓐ Ⓑ Ⓒ Ⓓ
17. Ⓐ Ⓑ Ⓒ Ⓓ
18. Ⓐ Ⓑ Ⓒ Ⓓ
19. Ⓐ Ⓑ Ⓒ Ⓓ
20. Ⓐ Ⓑ Ⓒ Ⓓ

21. Ⓐ Ⓑ Ⓒ Ⓓ
22. Ⓐ Ⓑ Ⓒ Ⓓ
23. Ⓐ Ⓑ Ⓒ Ⓓ
24. Ⓐ Ⓑ Ⓒ Ⓓ
25. Ⓐ Ⓑ Ⓒ Ⓓ
26. Ⓐ Ⓑ Ⓒ Ⓓ
27. Ⓐ Ⓑ Ⓒ Ⓓ
28. Ⓐ Ⓑ Ⓒ Ⓓ
29. Ⓐ Ⓑ Ⓒ Ⓓ
30. Ⓐ Ⓑ Ⓒ Ⓓ

31. 32. 33. 34.

35. 36. 37. 38.

Essay

PLANNING PAGE

START YOUR ESSAY HERE

READING TEST

65 Minutes, 52 Questions

Turn to Section 1 of your answer sheet to answer the questions in this section.

Directions: Following each of the passages (or pairs of passages) below are questions about the passage (or passages). Read each passage carefully. Then, select the best answer for each question based on what is stated in the passage (or passages) and in any graphics that may accompany the passage.

Questions 1–11 are based on the following passage.

In this adaptation of an excerpt from An Occurrence at Owl Creek Bridge, *a short story set in Civil War times, a man is about to be hanged. The first two paragraphs set the scene; the remainder of the passage presents a flashback to an earlier, critical encounter.*

A man stood upon a railroad bridge in Northern Alabama, looking down into the swift waters twenty feet below. The man's hands were behind his back, the wrists bound with a cord. A rope loosely encircled his neck. It was
Line
attached to a stout cross-timber above his head, and the slack fell to the level
(5)
of his knees. Some loose boards laid upon the sleepers supporting the metals of the railway supplied a footing for him and his executioners—two private soldiers of the Federal army, directed by a sergeant, who in civil life may have been a deputy sheriff. At a short remove upon the same temporary platform was an officer in the uniform of his rank, armed. He was a captain. A sentinel
(10)
at each end of the bridge stood with his rifle in the position known as "support"—a formal and unnatural position, enforcing an erect carriage of the body. It did not appear to be the duty of these two men to know what was occurring at the center of the bridge; they merely blockaded the two ends of the foot plank which traversed it.
(15)
The man who was engaged in being hanged was apparently about thirty-five years of age. He was a civilian, if one might judge from his dress, which was that of a planter. His features were good—a straight nose, firm mouth, broad forehead, from which his long, dark hair was combed straight back, falling behind his ears to the collar of his well-fitting frock coat. He wore a
(20)
moustache and pointed beard, but no whiskers; his eyes were large and dark grey and had a kindly expression that one would hardly have expected in one whose neck was in the hemp. Evidently this was no vulgar assassin. The liberal military code makes provision for hanging many kinds of people, and gentlemen are not excluded.

(25) Peyton Farquhar was a well-to-do planter, of an old and highly respected Alabama family. Being a slave-owner, and, like other slave-owners, a politician, he was naturally an original secessionist and ardently devoted to the Southern cause. Circumstances had prevented him from taking service with the gallant army that had fought the disastrous campaigns ending with (30) the fall of Corinth, and he chafed under the inglorious restraint, longing for the release of his energies, the larger life of the soldier, the opportunity for distinction. That opportunity, he felt, would come, as it comes to all in war time. Meanwhile, he did what he could. No service was too humble for him to perform in aid of the South, no adventure too perilous for him to undertake if (35) consistent with the character of a civilian who was at heart a soldier, and who in good faith and without too much qualification assented to at least a part of the frankly villainous dictum that all is fair in love and war.

 One evening while Farquhar and his wife were sitting near the entrance to his grounds, a grey-clad soldier rode up to the gate and asked for a drink of (40) water. Mrs. Farquhar was only too happy to serve him with her own white hands. While she was gone to fetch the water, her husband approached the dusty horseman and inquired eagerly for news from the front.

 "The Yanks are repairing the railroads," said the man, "and are getting ready for another advance. They have reached the Owl Creek bridge, put it in (45) order, and built a stockade on the other bank. The commandant has issued an order, which is posted everywhere, declaring that any civilian caught interfering with the railroad, its bridges, tunnels, or trains, will be summarily hanged. I saw the order."

 "How far is it to the Owl Creek bridge?" Farquhar asked.

(50) "About thirty miles."

 "Is there no force on this side of the creek?"

 "Only a picket post half a mile out, on the railroad, and a single sentinel at this end of the bridge."

 "Suppose a man—a civilian and a student of hanging—should elude the (55) picket post and perhaps get the better of the sentinel," said Farquhar, smiling, "what could he accomplish?"

 The soldier reflected. "I was there a month ago," he replied. "I observed that the flood of last winter had lodged a great quantity of driftwood against the wooden pier at the end of the bridge. It is now dry and would burn like tow."

(60) The lady had now brought the water, which the soldier drank. He thanked her ceremoniously, bowed to her husband, and rode away. An hour later, after nightfall, he repassed the plantation, going northward in the direction from which he had come. He was a Yankee scout.

1. As used in line 7, "civil" most nearly means

 (A) polite.
 (B) noncriminal.
 (C) nonmilitary.
 (D) individual.

2. In cinematic terms, the first two paragraphs most nearly resemble

   (A) a wide-angle shot followed by a close-up.
   (B) a sequence of cameo appearances.
   (C) a trailer advertising a feature film.
   (D) two episodes of an ongoing serial.

3. It can most reasonably be inferred from the passage that the man awaiting hanging was

   (A) innocent of any criminal intent.
   (B) an unlikely candidate for execution.
   (C) a victim of mistaken identity.
   (D) purposely assuming a harmless demeanor.

4. Which choice provides the best evidence for the answer to the previous question?

   (A) Lines 15–16 ("The man . . . age")
   (B) Lines 16–17 ("He was . . . planter")
   (C) Lines 19–22 ("He wore . . . hemp")
   (D) Lines 26–28 ("Being . . . cause")

5. The author's tone in discussing "the liberal military code" (lines 22–23) can best be described as

   (A) approving.
   (B) ironic.
   (C) irked.
   (D) regretful.

6. It can most reasonably be inferred from the passage that Peyton Farquhar would consider which of the following a good example of how a citizen should behave in wartime?

   (A) He should use even underhanded methods to support his cause.
   (B) He should enlist in the army without delay.
   (C) He should turn to politics as a means of enforcing his will.
   (D) He should avoid involving himself in disastrous campaigns.

7. As used in line 35, "consistent" most nearly means

   (A) unchanging.
   (B) compatible.
   (C) logically sound.
   (D) steady and predictable.

8. It can most reasonably be inferred from the passage that Mrs. Farquhar is

    (A) sympathetic to the Confederate cause.

    (B) too proud to perform menial tasks.

    (C) uninterested in news of the war.

    (D) reluctant to ask her slaves to fetch water.

9. Which choice provides the best evidence for the answer to the previous question?

    (A) Lines 33–37 ("No service . . . war")

    (B) Lines 40–41 ("Mrs. Farquhar . . . hands")

    (C) Lines 41–42 ("While she . . . front")

    (D) Lines 60–61 ("He thanked . . . away")

10. From Farquhar's exchange with the soldier (lines 41–59), it can most reasonably be inferred that Farquhar is going to

    (A) sneak across the bridge to join the Confederate forces.

    (B) attempt to burn down the bridge to halt the Yankee advance.

    (C) remove the driftwood blocking the Confederates' access to the bridge.

    (D) undermine the pillars that support the railroad bridge.

11. The main purpose of the concluding sentence of the passage is to

    (A) offer an excuse for Farquhar's failure to destroy the bridge.

    (B) provide context useful in understanding Farquhar's emotional reactions.

    (C) establish that Farquhar has been entrapped into taking an unwise action.

    (D) contrast Farquhar's patriotic behavior with the scout's treachery.

Questions 12–21 are based on the following passage.

The following passage is taken from Franklin Delano Roosevelt's Third Inaugural Address, made on January 20, 1941, nearly a year before the bombing of Pearl Harbor triggered America's entry into the Second World War.

A nation, like a person, has something deeper, something more permanent, something larger than the sum of all its parts. It is that something which matters most to its future—which calls forth the most sacred guarding
Line of its present.
(5)   It is a thing for which we find it difficult—even impossible—to hit upon a single, simple word.
And yet we all understand what it is—the spirit—the faith of America. It is the product of centuries. It was born in the multitudes of those who came from many lands—some of high degree, but mostly plain people, who sought
(10) here, early and late, to find freedom more freely.
The democratic aspiration is no mere recent phase in human history. It is human history. It permeated the ancient life of early peoples. It blazed anew in the middle ages. It was written in the Magna Carta.
In the Americas its impact has been irresistible. America has been the
(15) New World in all tongues, to all peoples, not because this continent was a new-found land, but because all those who came here believed they could create upon this continent a new life—a life that should be new in freedom.
Its vitality was written into our own Mayflower Compact, into the Declaration of Independence, into the Constitution of the United States, into
(20) the Gettysburg Address.
Those who first came here to carry out the longings of their spirit, and the millions who followed, and the stock that sprang from them—all have moved forward constantly and consistently toward an ideal which in itself has gained stature and clarity with each generation.
(25)   The hopes of the Republic cannot forever tolerate either undeserved poverty or self-serving wealth.
We know that we still have far to go; that we must more greatly build the security and the opportunity and the knowledge of every citizen, in the measure justified by the resources and the capacity of the land.
(30)   But it is not enough to achieve these purposes alone. It is not enough to clothe and feed the body of this Nation, and instruct and inform its mind. For there is also the spirit. And of the three, the greatest is the spirit.
Without the body and the mind, as all men know, the Nation could not live. But if the spirit of America were killed, even though the Nation's body
(35) and mind, constricted in an alien world, lived on, the America we know would have perished.
That spirit—that faith—speaks to us in our daily lives in ways often unnoticed, because they seem so obvious. It speaks to us here in the Capital of the Nation. It speaks to us through the processes of governing in the
(40) sovereignties of 48 States. It speaks to us in our counties, in our cities, in our towns, and in our villages. It speaks to us from the other nations of the

hemisphere, and from those across the seas—the enslaved, as well as the free. Sometimes we fail to hear or heed these voices of freedom because to us the privilege of our freedom is such an old, old story.

(45)   The destiny of America was proclaimed in words of prophecy spoken by our first President in his first inaugural in 1789—words almost directed, it would seem, to this year of 1941: *"The preservation of the sacred fire of liberty and the destiny of the republican model of government are justly considered . . . deeply, ... finally, staked on the experiment intrusted to the*

(50) *hands of the American people."*

If we lose that sacred fire—if we let it be smothered with doubt and fear—then we shall reject the destiny which Washington strove so valiantly and so triumphantly to establish. The preservation of the spirit and faith of the Nation does, and will, furnish the highest justification for every sacrifice that

(55) we may make in the cause of national defense.

In the face of great perils never before encountered, our strong purpose is to protect and to perpetuate the integrity of democracy.

For this we muster the spirit of America, and the faith of America.

We do not retreat. We are not content to stand still. As Americans, we go

(60) forward, in the service of our country, by the will of God.

12. As used in line 9, "plain" most nearly means

(A) candid.
(B) ordinary.
(C) homely.
(D) intelligible.

13. The author indicates which of the following about the American belief in freedom?

(A) It lacked any supporters who belonged to the upper classes.
(B) It had its origins at the time of the American Revolution.
(C) It is an ideal that has lost its hold on the public.
(D) It has deep-seated historical roots.

14. Which choice provides the best evidence for the answer to the previous question?

(A) Lines 1–2 ("A nation . . . parts")
(B) Lines 11–13 ("The democratic . . . Carta")
(C) Lines 14–17 ("America has been . . . freedom")
(D) Lines 21–24 ("Those who first . . . generation")

15. The author uses the Mayflower Compact, Declaration of Independence, Constitution, and Gettysburg Address as examples of

    (A) subjects of previous inaugural addresses.
    (B) expressions of the democratic aspiration.
    (C) documents of historical interest.
    (D) writings with ongoing legal implications.

16. The author recognizes counterarguments to the position he takes in lines 21–24 ("Those who first . . . generation") by

    (A) acknowledging that economic injustices must be addressed before democracy can prevail.
    (B) admitting that the native-born descendents of our immigrant forebears have lost faith in democracy.
    (C) conceding the lack of resources and capacity that hinder the fulfillment of the American dream.
    (D) likening the Nation to a human body with physical, mental, and spiritual needs.

17. As used in line 46, "directed" most nearly means

    (A) addressed.
    (B) ordered.
    (C) supervised.
    (D) guided.

18. What main effect does the repetition of the phrase "It speaks to us" in lines 37–43 have on the tone of the passage?

    (A) It creates a whimsical tone, endowing an abstract quality with a physical voice.
    (B) It creates a colloquial tone, describing commonplace activities in ordinary words.
    (C) It creates a dramatic tone, emphasizing the point being made and adding to its emotional impact.
    (D) It creates a menacing tone, reminding us of our failure to heed the voices of freedom crying for our aid.

19. It can most reasonably be inferred that the experiment to which Washington refers in line 49 is

    (A) a scientific investigation.
    (B) a presidential inauguration.
    (C) democratic government.
    (D) national defense.

20. Which choice provides the best evidence for the answer to the previous question?

(A) Lines 34–36 ("But . . . perished")
(B) Lines 37–38 ("That spirit . . . obvious")
(C) Lines 51–53 ("If we . . . establish")
(D) Lines 56–57 ("In the face . . . democracy")

21. It is reasonable to conclude that a major goal of Roosevelt in making this speech was to

(A) inform American citizens of changes of policy in the new administration.
(B) impress his European counterparts with the soundness of America's foreign policy.
(C) encourage American voters to avoid the divisiveness inherent in partisan politics.
(D) inspire the American people to defend the cause of freedom in dangerous times.

<u>Questions 22–31</u> are based on the following passage.

This passage is from Mortal Lessons: Notes on the Art of Surgery, *a classic book written by a contemporary American surgeon about his art.*

One holds the knife as one holds the bow of a cello or a tulip—by the stem. Not palmed nor gripped nor grasped, but lightly, with the tips of the fingers. The knife is not for pressing. It is for drawing across the field of skin.
Line Like a slender fish, it waits, at the ready, then, go! It darts, followed by a fine
(5) wake of red. The flesh parts, falling away to yellow globules of fat. Even now, after so many times, I still marvel at its power—cold, gleaming, silent. More, I am still struck with dread that it is I in whose hand the blade travels, that my hand is its vehicle, that yet again this terrible steel-bellied thing and I have conspired for a most unnatural purpose, the laying open of the body of a
(10) human being.

A stillness settles in my heart and is carried to my hand. It is the quietude of resolve layered over fear. And it is this resolve that lowers us, my knife and me, deeper and deeper into the person beneath. It is an entry into the body that is nothing like a caress; still, it is among the gentlest of acts. Then stroke
(15) and stroke again, and we are joined by other instruments, hemostats and forceps, until the wound blooms with strange flowers whose looped handles fall to the sides in steely array.

There is a sound, the tight click of clamps fixing teeth into severed blood vessels, the snuffle and gargle of the suction machine clearing the field of
(20) blood for the next stroke, the litany of monosyllables with which one prays his way down and in: *clamp, sponge, suture, tie, cut.* And there is color. The green of the cloth, the white of the sponges, the red and yellow of the body. Beneath the fat lies the fascia, the tough fibrous sheet encasing the muscles. It must be sliced and the red beef of the muscles separated. Now there are
(25) retractors to hold apart the wound. Hands move together, part, weave. We are fully engaged, like children absorbed in a game or the craftsmen of some place like Damascus.

Deeper still. The peritoneum, pink and gleaming and membranous, bulges into the wound. It is grasped with forceps, and opened. For the first time we
(30) can see into the cavity of the abdomen. Such a primitive place. One expects to find drawings of buffalo on the walls. The sense of trespassing is keener now, heightened by the world's light illuminating the organs, their secret colors revealed—maroon and salmon and yellow. The vista is sweetly vulnerable at this moment, a kind of welcoming. An arc of the liver shines
(35) high and on the right, like a dark sun. It laps over the pink sweep of the stomach, from whose lower border the gauzy omentum is draped, and through which veil one sees, sinuous, slow as just-fed snakes, the indolent coils of the intestine.

You turn aside to wash your gloves. It is a ritual cleansing. One enters
(40) this temple doubly washed. Here is man as microcosm, representing in all his parts the Earth, perhaps the universe.

I must confess that the priestliness of my profession has ever been impressed on me. In the beginning there are vows, taken with all solemnity. Then there is the endless harsh novitiate of training, much fatigue, much sacrifice. At last one emerges as a celebrant, standing close to the truth lying curtained in the ark of the body. Not surplice and cassock but mask and gown are your regalia. You hold no chalice, but a knife. There is no wine, no wafer. There are only the facts of blood and flesh.

(45)

22. The passage is best described as

    (A) a definition of a concept.
    (B) an example of a particular method.
    (C) a lesson on a technique.
    (D) a description of a process.

23. It can most reasonably be inferred from the passage that the "wake of red" to which the author refers (line 5) is

    (A) a sign of embarrassment.
    (B) an infectious rash.
    (C) a line of blood.
    (D) the blade of the knife.

24. Which choice provides the best evidence for the answer to the previous question?

    (A) Lines 1–2 ("One . . . stem")
    (B) Lines 2–3 ("Not . . . fingers")
    (C) Line 5 ("The flesh . . . fat")
    (D) Line 11 ("A stillness . . . hand")

25. As used in line 5, "parts" most nearly means

    (A) leaves.
    (B) splits.
    (C) surrenders.
    (D) distributes.

26. As used in line 26, "engaged" most nearly means

    (A) betrothed.
    (B) engrossed.
    (C) hired.
    (D) embattled.

27. In lines 30–31, the comment "One expects to find drawings of buffalo on the walls" metaphorically compares the abdominal cavity to

   (A) an art gallery.
   (B) a zoological display.
   (C) a Western film.
   (D) a prehistoric cave.

28. The author most likely describes the colors of the internal organs as "secret" (line 32) because

   (A) they are beyond ordinary human understanding.
   (B) they normally are hidden from sight.
   (C) their access is limited to authorized personnel.
   (D) they are darker in color than the external organs are.

29. In creating an impression of abdominal surgery for the reader, the author primarily makes use of

   (A) comparison with imaginary landscapes.
   (B) contrast to other types of surgery.
   (C) references to religious imagery.
   (D) evocation of the patient's emotions.

30. Which choice provides the best evidence for the answer to the previous question?

   (A) Lines 23–25 ("Beneath the fat . . . wound")
   (B) Lines 28–30 ("The peritoneum . . . abdomen")
   (C) Lines 33–35 ("The vista . . . sun")
   (D) Lines 39–40 ("It is a . . . washed")

31. One aspect of the passage that may make it difficult to appreciate is the author's apparent assumption throughout that readers will

   (A) have qualms about reading descriptions of major surgery.
   (B) be already adept at handling surgical tools.
   (C) be familiar with the organs and tissues that are named.
   (D) relate accounts of specific surgical acts to their own experience of undergoing surgery.

Questions 32–42 are based on the following passages.

Passage 1 is taken from a historical study, done in the 1980s, of the relationship between the press and each American president from George Washington to Ronald Reagan. Passage 2 is taken from a 2006 master's thesis on the relationship between the president and the press during the first term of President George W. Bush.

Passage 1

In the shifting relationship between the press and the presidency over nearly two centuries, there has remained one primary constant—the dissatisfaction of one with the other. No president has escaped press criticism, and no president has considered himself fairly treated. The record of every administration has been the same, beginning with mutual protestations of goodwill, ending with recriminations and mistrust.

This is the best proof we could have that the American concept of a free press in a free society is a viable idea, whatever defects the media may have. While the Founding Fathers and their constituencies did not always agree on the role the press should play, there was a basic consensus that the newspaper (the only medium of consequence at the time) should be the buffer state between the rulers and the ruled. The press could be expected to behave like a watchdog, and government at every level, dependent for its existence on the opinions of those it governed, could expect to resent being watched and having its shortcomings, real or imaginary, exposed to the public view.

Reduced to such simple terms, the relationship of the presidents to the press since George Washington's first term is understandable only as an underlying principle. But this basic concept has been increasingly complicated by the changing nature of the presidency, by the individual nature of presidents, by the rise of other media, especially television, and by the growing complexity of beliefs about the function of both press and government.

In surveying nearly two centuries of this relationship, it is wise to keep in mind an axiom of professional historians—that we should be careful not to view the past in terms of our own times, and make judgments accordingly. Certain parallels often become obvious, to be sure, but to assert what an individual president should or should not have done, by present standards, is to violate historical context. Historians occasionally castigate each other for this failing, and in the case of press and government, the danger becomes particularly great because the words themselves—"press" and "government," even "presidency"—have changed in meaning so much during the past two hundred years.

It is part of American mythology that the nation was "cradled in liberty" and that the colonists, seeking religious freedom, immediately established a free society, but the facts are quite different. The danger of an uncontrolled press to those in power was well expressed by Sir William Berkeley, governor of Virginia, when he wrote home to his superiors in 1671: "I thank God there

Line (5)

(10)

(15)

(20)

(25)

(30)

(35)

(40) are no free schools nor printing, and I hope we shall not have these hundred years; for learning has brought disobedience, and heresy, and sects into the world, and printing has divulged them, and libels against the best government, God keep us from both." There are those in twentieth-century America who would say "Amen" to Berkeley's view of printing and "libels against the best government."

Passage 2

(45)   In their analysis of aggressive journalist behavior in a comparative study of press conferences held by Presidents Eisenhower and Reagan, Clayman and Heritage (2002) developed an original encoding system according to ten different features of question design. Their findings showed significantly greater levels of aggression and adversarial behavior by the press in dealings (50) with the more recent president. Clayman, Elliot, Heritage & McDonald's updated study (2004) refined the coding process and used a more continuous sample to test the validity and reliability of the original study. Their comparison of journalistic adversarialness covered each president from Eisenhower to Clinton and supported original results that show a long-term (55) decline in deference to the president. The continuous sample revealed more volatility than the simpler work on which it was based but is a further testament to the increased aggressiveness, sometimes adversarial treatment prevalent in press conferences regardless of partisanship or personal idiosyncrasy.

(60)   These findings would suggest that the increasingly contentious, adversarial relationship between the press and the highest ranking executive official has created a modern press conference where the president must relinquish more agenda-setting control than in other communicative processes. In each session, he subjects himself to open questioning that is (65) shown to be significantly less deferential, more direct and often more aggressive and hostile than ever before. This would seem an appropriate justification for the dwindling numbers of traditional solo press conferences in recent administrations (Kumar, 2003b).

Table 1
Solo and Joint Press Conferences by President 1981–2004

President	Total	Solo	Joint	Joint Sessions as Percent of Total
Reagan*	46	46	0	00.0%
George H. W. Bush*	142	83	59	41.5%
Clinton*	193	62	131	67.9%
George W. Bush**	88	20	68	77.3%

*Cited in Kumar, 2003b
**Compiled from Weekly Compilation of Presidential Documents

32. The main purpose of Passage 1 is to

    (A) examine methods of evaluating the relationship between the press and the president.
    (B) argue that the adversarial relationship between the press and the presidency has proven deleterious to both.
    (C) present an overview of an inherently conflicted relationship that faces new challenges.
    (D) consider a political dilemma created by the mutual antagonism between two major institutions.

33. According to the opening paragraph of Passage 1, all American presidents have experienced

    (A) defects in the quality of their press coverage.
    (B) goodwill from some reporters in the press corps.
    (C) alternating periods of antagonism and harmony with the press.
    (D) mutual animosity involving themselves and the press.

34. Which choice provides the best evidence for the answer to the previous question?

    (A) Lines 4–6 ("The record . . . mistrust")
    (B) Lines 7–8 ("This . . . may have")
    (C) Lines 9–12 ("While . . . ruled")
    (D) Lines 17–19 ("Reduced . . . principle")

35. As used in line 17, "reduced" most nearly means

    (A) decreased.
    (B) boiled down.
    (C) marked down.
    (D) demoted.

36. The authors of Passage 1 caution the reader about judging the actions of long-dead presidents because

    (A) historical accounts, when investigated, have proven to be untrustworthy.
    (B) contemporary authors have rewritten history to reflect current academic opinions.
    (C) readers today cannot fully grasp the significance these actions had in their own time.
    (D) history, at best, is an imprecise science.

37. Which choice provides the best evidence for the answer to the previous question?

    (A) Lines 1–4 ("In the shifting . . . treated")
    (B) Lines 12–16 ("The press . . . public view")
    (C) Lines 17–23 ("Reduced . . . government")
    (D) Lines 27–33 ("Certain parallels . . . years")

38. In the opening sentence of the final paragraph (lines 34–36) of Passage 1, the authors seek primarily to

   (A) define a term.
   (B) defend a widely held belief.
   (C) correct a misconception.
   (D) champion a cause.

39. As used in line 64, "open" most nearly means

   (A) receptive.
   (B) unrestricted.
   (C) unconcealed.
   (D) vulnerable.

40. Data in the graph about presidential solo and joint press conferences from 1981–2004 most strongly support which of the following statements?

   (A) President Clinton held more solo press conferences than President George H. W. Bush did.
   (B) Presidents Clinton and George W. Bush held a far higher percentage of joint press conferences than either of their predecessors did.
   (C) President Reagan's failure to hold joint press conferences resulted from a reluctance to share the spotlight with other members of his administration.
   (D) While President George H. W. Bush held far more press conferences than his son President George W. Bush did, both Presidents Bush held more joint sessions than solo sessions.

41. Which choice best describes the relationship between the two passages?

   (A) Passage 2 denies the static nature of the phenomenon described in Passage 1.
   (B) Passage 2 evaluates the conclusions drawn from assertions made in Passage 1.
   (C) Passage 2 predicts the eventual healing of a breach reported in Passage 1.
   (D) Passage 2 critiques the hypotheses proposed by researchers cited in Passage 1.

42. On which of the following points would the authors of both passages most likely agree?

   (A) Those who criticize the press for its treatment of the president fail to understand the press's watchdog function.
   (B) Members of the press corps are unlikely to prefer joint press conferences to solo sessions.
   (C) The relationship between the press and the presidency is inherently adversarial, and likely to remain so.
   (D) The president needs to regain agenda-setting control of traditional solo press conferences.

Questions 43–52 are based on the following passage.

The following passage is abridged from Rachel Ehrenberg's "The facts behind the frack" (Science News), an article on the controversies surrounding the hydraulic fracturing method of recovering natural gas from below the Earth's surface.

To call it a fractious debate is an understatement.

Hydraulic fracturing, or fracking, wrenches open rock deep beneath the Earth's surface, freeing the natural gas that's trapped inside. Proponents
Line argue that fracking-related gas recovery is a game changer, a bridge to the
(5) renewable energy landscape of the future. The gas, primarily methane, is cheap and relatively clean. Because America is brimful of the stuff, harvesting the fuel via fracking could provide the country with jobs and reduce its dependence on foreign sources of energy.

But along with these promises have come alarming local incidents and
(10) national reports of blowouts, contamination and earthquakes. Fracking opponents contend that the process poisons air and drinking water and may make people sick. What's more, they argue, fracking leaks methane, a potent greenhouse gas that can blow up homes, worries highlighted in the controversial 2010 documentary *Gasland*.

(15) Fears that fracking companies are operating in a Wild West environment with little regulation have prompted political action. In June, the group Don't Frack Ohio led thousands of protesters on a march to the statehouse, where they declared their commitment to halting hydraulic fracturing in the state. Legislation banning the process has been considered but is now on hold in
(20) California. New York—which sits atop a giant natural gas reserve—has a statewide fracking moratorium; pending policies would allow the process only where local officials support it.

Despite all this activity, not much of the fracking debate has brought scientific evidence into the fold. Yet scientists have been studying the risks
(25) posed by fracking operations. Research suggests methane leaks do happen. The millions of gallons of chemical-laden water used to fracture shale deep in the ground has spoiled land and waterways. There's also evidence linking natural gas recovery to earthquakes, but this problem seems to stem primarily from wastewater disposal rather than the fracturing process itself. While the
(30) dangers are real, most problems linked to fracking so far are not specific to the technology but come with many large-scale energy operations employing poor practices with little oversight, scientists contend. Whether the energy payoff can come with an acceptable level of risk remains an open question.

Hydraulic fracturing operations have been linked to some small
(35) earthquakes, including a magnitude 2.3 quake near Blackpool, England, last year. But scientists agree such earthquakes are extremely rare, occurring when a well hits a seismic sweet spot, and are avoidable with monitoring. Of greater concern are earthquakes associated with the disposal of fracking fluid into wastewater wells. Injected fluid essentially greases the fault, a long-
(40) known effect. In the 1960s, a series of Denver earthquakes were linked to wastewater disposal at the Rocky Mountain arsenal, an Army site nearby.

Wastewater disposal was also blamed for a magnitude 4.0 quake in Youngstown, Ohio, last New Year's Eve.

(45) A study headed by William Ellsworth of the U.S. Geological Survey in Menlo Park, Calif., documents a dramatic increase in earthquakes in the Midwest coinciding with the start of the fracking boom. From 1970 to 2000, the region experienced about 20 quakes per year measuring at or above magnitude 3.0. Between 2001 and 2008, there were 29 such quakes per year. Then there were 50 in 2009, 87 in 2010 and 134 in 2011. "The change was

(50) really quite pronounced," says Ellsworth. "We do not think it's a purely natural phenomenon." However, the earthquakes weren't happening near active drilling—they seemed to be clustered around wastewater wells.

It's hard to look back without pre-quake data and figure out what triggers a single earthquake, notes Ellsworth. There are several pieces of the geology

(55) equation that, if toggled, can tip a fault from stable to unstable. A recent study examining seismic activity at wastewater injection wells in Texas linked earthquakes with injections of more than 150,000 barrels of water per month. But not every case fits the pattern, suggesting the orientation of deep faults is important. Ellsworth advises that injection at active faults be avoided. Drill

(60) sites should be considered for their geological stability, and seismic information should be collected. (Only about 3 percent of the 75,000-odd hydraulic fracturing setups in the United States in 2009 were seismically monitored.) "There are many things we don't understand," says Ellsworth. "We're in ambulance-chasing mode where we're coming in after the fact."

Human-Induced Earthquakes

After decades of a steady earthquake rate (dotted line) in the central and eastern United States, activity began to rise in about 2009 and jumped to five times the normal rate by 2013, probably due to human activity.

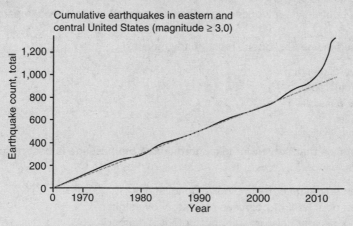

Cumulative earthquakes in eastern and central United States (magnitude ≥ 3.0)

Source: *W. L. Ellsworth*/Science *2013*

43. In line 1, the author chooses the word "fractious" (contentious; heated) to create

    (A) a metaphor.
    (B) a play on words.
    (C) an exaggeration.
    (D) a counterargument.

44. To call fracking-related gas recovery "a game changer" (line 4) is to assert that fracking

    (A) has no foreseeable negative consequences.
    (B) will radically alter natural gas production.
    (C) is not taken seriously by its proponents.
    (D) will require active federal regulation.

45. Which choice provides the best evidence for the answer to the previous question?

    (A) Lines 5–8 ("The gas . . . energy")
    (B) Lines 9–12 ("But . . . sick")
    (C) Lines 12–14 ("What's more . . . *Gasland*")
    (D) Lines 29–33 ("While . . . question")

46. What function does the discussion of fracking legislation in lines 19–22 serve in the passage?

    (A) It describes specific responses to concerns raised in the previous paragraph.
    (B) It analyzes theoretical objections to a claim made in the previous paragraph.
    (C) It provides an unanticipated reaction to an explicit demand made in the previous paragraph.
    (D) It contradicts a working hypothesis proposed in the previous paragraph.

47. As used in line 33, "open" most nearly means

    (A) unresolved.
    (B) vulnerable.
    (C) accessible.
    (D) ajar.

48. The stance that the author takes throughout the passage is best described as that of

    (A) an advocate of technological innovations.
    (B) an opponent of pointless regulatory oversight.
    (C) a legislator concerned about potential danger.
    (D) an observer striving to present a balanced account.

49. Which choice provides the best evidence for the answer to the previous question?

(A) Lines 15–16 ("Fears . . . political action")
(B) Lines 19–22 ("Legislation . . . support it")
(C) Lines 29–33 ("While . . . question")
(D) Lines 53–54 ("It's hard . . . Ellsworth")

50. The graph based on Ellsworth's figures accentuates the

(A) validity of his research team's methodology.
(B) increased magnitude of each individual earthquake.
(C) increasing frequency of earthquakes in the region.
(D) amount of fracking fluid injected into wastewater wells.

51. As used in line 50, "pronounced" most nearly means

(A) noticeable.
(B) declared.
(C) decided on.
(D) articulated.

52. It can be most reasonably inferred from the concluding paragraph that Ellsworth looks on current hypotheses about connections between the recent increases in earthquakes and the start of the fracking boom as

(A) corroborated by pre-quake data.
(B) based on insufficient knowledge.
(C) evidence of seismic activity.
(D) contradicted by his research findings.

IF THERE IS STILL TIME REMAINING, YOU MAY REVIEW YOUR ANSWERS.

WRITING AND LANGUAGE TEST

35 Minutes, 44 Questions

Turn to Section 2 of your answer sheet to answer the questions in this section.

Directions: Questions follow each of the passages below. Some questions ask you how the passage might be changed to improve the expression of ideas. Other questions ask you how the passage might be altered to correct errors in grammar, usage, and punctuation. One or more graphics accompany some passages. You will be required to consider these graphics as you answer questions about editing the passage.

There are three types of questions. In the first type, a part of the passage is underlined. The second type is based on a certain part of the passage. The third type is based on the entire passage.

Read each passage. Then, choose the answer to each question that changes the passage so that it is consistent with the conventions of standard written English. One of the answer choices for many questions is "NO CHANGE." Choosing this answer means that you believe the best answer is to make no change in the passage.

Questions 1–11 are based on the following passage.

Out with the Old and the New

Modernism can be characterized by its complete rejection of 19th-century traditions and values of prudish and proper etiquette. F. Scott Fitzgerald's "Bernice Bobs Her Hair" was written in 1920 and reflects this ❶ embrace of conventional morality most effectively through the character of Marjorie Harvey. Marjorie, an immensely popular and desirable young woman, is plagued by Bernice, her dull cousin who fails to entertain ❷ or be entertained by Marjorie's many social environments. In a desperate attempt to make Bernice

1. Which wording is most consistent with the paragraph as a whole?

(A) NO CHANGE
(B) ignorance
(C) rebuff
(D) significance

2. (A) NO CHANGE
(B) and entertainment
(C) with the entertaining of
(D) of the entertaining for

more popular and therefore, more bearable, Marjorie teaches Bernice to appear beautifully at ease with ❸ itself in order to gain social favor. Fitzgerald uses Bernice's transformation to embody Modernist ideals of moral relativism and ❹ the implementation of mockery of former Victorian standards of custom.

Marjorie, a quintessential modern girl, represents the destruction of conventional norms and former ideas of femininity. Young and beautiful, she is interested only in having a good time and being good company to the many suitors ❺ whom flock to her. Despite her good looks and family wealth, Bernice is disliked for her stifling and overly formal Victorian propriety. ❻ On the other hand, Bernice is old-fashioned, outdated, and unpopular.

The "new," modern woman is best denoted by her wit, carelessness, and lack of emotion. Where the dignified nature of Bernice is seen as snobbish and out of style, Marjorie's sardonic and indifferent manner is fresh and exciting. The stark contrast ❼ between the Victorian and Modernist eras is even depicted in the girls' taste in literature: Marjorie casts off Bernice's reference to *Little Women* in exchange for the more recent Oscar Wilde.

Still, Modernism isn't let off easy in Fitzgerald's well-liked short story. ❽ When Marjorie is preferred socially, she is flagrantly rude and always needing to be entertained. She instructs Bernice in social protocol in a ❾ few short sentences, causing the reader to question the frivolous hedonism that dominates the early 20th century. Once Bernice adopts her cousin's apathy, she easily falls into the world of dancing, dating, and

3. (A) NO CHANGE
   (B) oneself
   (C) themselves
   (D) herself

4. (A) NO CHANGE
   (B) for the mocking of
   (C) to mock
   (D) mocking

5. (A) NO CHANGE
   (B) who
   (C) whose
   (D) who's

6. Where in this paragraph should the underlined sentence be placed?

   (A) where it is now
   (B) before the first sentence
   (C) before the second sentence
   (D) before the third sentence

7. (A) NO CHANGE
   (B) among
   (C) for
   (D) on

8. (A) NO CHANGE
   (B) While
   (C) Because
   (D) Since

9. (A) NO CHANGE
   (B) short few
   (C) few, short
   (D) short, few

laughing. In fact, never being serious happens to come quite easy.

The equally ❿ <u>kind-hearted natures</u> of both of Fitzgerald's characters come crashing down when Marjorie tricks Bernice into getting her hair bobbed—a style so rebellious that it causes Bernice to faint. Bernice finds revenge in severing off a golden lock of Marjorie's hair while she sleeps. While using Bernice and Marjorie to model both eras, Fitzgerald finds flaws in ⓫ <u>both: the old manner is a lifeless forgery, while</u> the new approach is only relaxed on the surface.

10. Which choice would best be logically placed here to represent the characterizations of Marjorie and Bernice in the paragraph?

(A) NO CHANGE
(B) revolutionary dogmatism
(C) false facades
(D) frivolous piety

11. (A) NO CHANGE
(B) both, the old manner is a lifeless forgery while
(C) both—the old manner is a lifeless, forgery, while
(D) both; the old manner, is a lifeless forgery while

Questions 12–22 are based on the following passage and supplementary material.

Extra, Extra (Written in 2015)

If any field has drastically changed in the last two decades, it is journalism. Journalism includes the gathering and distribution of news through a variety of mediums, ⑫ <u>building upon the long-standing professional excellence with which journalism is associated.</u> Whether via print, broadcast, or digital, journalists are responsible for keeping the public informed, and often play a vital role in allowing the general population to participate in the political process. Although the digital age has understandably discouraged popularity in some traditional forms of ⑬ <u>news media the field itself is optimistic, not only</u> is the digital platform more than making up for the moderate declines in traditional news sources, ⑭ <u>but</u> also research shows that Americans are spending more time consuming news than they have since the early 1990s. ⑮ <u>The traditional dominance of newspapers has continued unabated.</u>

Quite simply, the days of print-only newsrooms are past. Now, one doesn't wait until the 6 P.M. broadcast to hear what's happening around the

12. Which choice most specifically elaborates on the first part of this sentence?

(A) NO CHANGE
(B) growing its reach to include urban, suburban, and rural population centers.
(C) which have recently expanded to incorporate smartphones, tablets, and blogs.
(D) demonstrating that seeking the average public opinion is most objective.

13. (A) NO CHANGE
(B) news media, the field itself is optimistic, not only
(C) news media, the field itself is optimistic: not only
(D) news media the field itself; is optimistic not only

14. (A) NO CHANGE
(B) and
(C) for
(D) since

15. Which choice best concludes this paragraph and transitions to the topic of the next paragraph?

(A) NO CHANGE
(B) Journalism isn't dying; the way reporters do their job is changing.
(C) Journalism is no longer the sort of career that globally minded people would chose.
(D) With the steady demise of public interest in quality journalism, it is only a matter of time before journalism falls by the wayside.

world, **⑯ nor** does one grab the
newspaper on Sunday morning for
breaking news. The public expects
minute-by-minute updates, and media
companies meet this demand with
24-7 online newsreels. Journalists can
no longer limit themselves to gathering
stories or writing articles or speaking
publicly—they must be able to do it all
and then some. Even entry-level
positions require candidates who have
had media training and internship
experience in addition to a formal
education. Internships at most media
outlets include everything from copy
editing to blogging.

The tough competition and
demanding prerequisites for the job
market need not be deterrents.
Leading journalism **⑰ department's
are reassuring that their** students leave
undergraduate with all the tools
necessary for success. For instance,
the University of Missouri at Columbia
**⑱ —boasting the number one
journalism department in the nation
according to *The Huffington Post*—**
offers more than 30 interest areas,
incorporating an intensive liberal arts
education along with hands-on
experience in media labs and
internships for academic credit. Ohio
**⑲ University also having, a journalism
department ranked in the top ten
nationwide offers** three campus
publications plus a broadcasting outlet
for students to gain professional
experience before graduation, not to
mention OU's Institute for International
Journalism, which offers opportunities
for reporting abroad.

Technology and its **⑳ endless
affects** on all areas of the job market
are tedious subjects for the student
and young professional. One cannot
consider a career field without hearing

16. (A) NO CHANGE
    (B) because
    (C) for
    (D) while

17. (A) NO CHANGE
    (B) departments' are insuring that
        they're
    (C) departments are assuring there
    (D) departments are ensuring that
        their

18. Which choice best connects this
    sentence to the previous sentence?

    (A) NO CHANGE
    (B) —located in the geographic
        near-middle of the United
        States—
    (C) —a university that offers a
        variety of possible
        undergraduate majors and
        minors—
    (D) —ranked among the best
        universities for average starting
        salary among its graduates—

19. (A) NO CHANGE
    (B) University also having a
        journalism department ranked
        in the top ten nationwide offers
    (C) University, also having a
        journalism department, ranked
        in the top ten, nationwide,
        offers
    (D) University, also having a
        journalism department ranked
        in the top ten nationwide,
        offers

20. (A) NO CHANGE
    (B) endless effects
    (C) endlessly affects
    (D) endlessly effects

how formidable its outlook is and how quickly one could fail in an uncertain economy. Indeed, journalism students have been well informed ㉑ <u>about the steadily increasing demand for journalists in the recent past,</u> but the truth stands that there will always be a demand for the news, and therefore, a need for journalists. The field ㉒ <u>is adapting</u> and so are its constituents.

21. Which choice offers the most accurate interpretation of the data in the chart?

(A) NO CHANGE
(B) about the gradual decline in jobs for journalists in the past decade,
(C) about the constant level of employment for journalists these past few years,
(D) about the job market fluctuations in recent years,

22. (A) NO CHANGE
(B) was adapting
(C) is adopting
(D) was adopting

Journalism-Related Job Openings

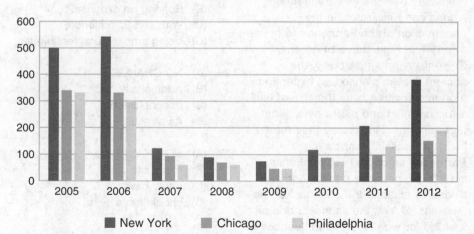

New York · Chicago · Philadelphia

Questions 23–33 are based on the following passage.

Parthenon

Of all the ancient, sacred, and truly splendid buildings to visit, the Parthenon may just be the most treasured of all. ❷❸ A long time past, the Greeks built their apotheosis over a span of nine years atop the Acropolis of Athens as a tribute to Athena, the city's beloved patron goddess of war and reason. The temple itself was completed in 438 B.C., although decorative sculpting and engraving within the structure went on for several more years. Since then, the structure has served as ❷❹ temple, treasury, church, and most recently, tourist attraction.

Pericles—leading politician in 5th century B.C.—recruited the sculptor Phidias to oversee two architects, Iktinos and Kallikrates, in the construction of the Parthenon to house a forty-foot high statue of Athena. ❷❺ Honestly and judiciously, the ancient Greeks planned an exceptional monument with a base the size of half a football field and pillars over thirty feet tall. Athenians stored their most lavish possessions inside the Parthenon among a host of statues, sculptures, precious metals, and treasures taken in the conquest of the Persians. ❷❻ Yet, the endeavor and all it stood for were short-lived: just seven years after the Parthenon was constructed, war broke out with Sparta. Sometime after the reign of Athens, in 5th century A.D., the statue of Athena was plundered and later destroyed.

Perhaps, even with Athena—the very core of Parthenon—missing, the temple ❷❼ could of still served as a

23. Which choice would most specifically describe how long ago the Parthenon was constructed?

(A) NO CHANGE
(B) More than 2,500 years ago,
(C) Many decades of ages past,
(D) In days gone by,

24. (A) NO CHANGE
(B) temple, treasury church, and most recently, tourist attraction.
(C) temple treasury, church and most recently tourist attraction.
(D) temple treasury church, and most recently tourist attraction.

25. What could best be used for the underlined portion to convey the high priority the Greeks placed on completing the Parthenon in a glorious fashion?

(A) NO CHANGE
(B) Sparing no expense,
(C) With artistic patience,
(D) Using architectural techniques,

26. (A) NO CHANGE
(B) Additionally,
(C) In conclusion,
(D) As a result,

27. (A) NO CHANGE
(B) might of
(C) could have
(D) should have been

great, inclusive museum of Greek history, tracing the founding of Ancient Greece, Athenian democracy, and early western civilization; yet, the Parthenon would endure many other foes. The Parthenon was first converted to a Christian church, which led to the removal of ㉘ its' "pagan gods." With the rise of the Ottoman Empire, the monument was used as a mosque until a Venetian attack on Athens destroyed large parts of the building and left its ㉙ archaeology deserted. By the 18th century, little was left of the Parthenon after decades of European pillaging.

㉚ In the contemporary world in which we reside, the Parthenon is one of the most popular tourist attractions in the world, enticing millions of people each year and warranting an ongoing restoration project currently in its third decade. Even in its antiquity, its subtle beauty and architectural refinement ㉛ is uncontested. Its miracle comes not from its magnitude, but from the curvatures between its platform and columns that offer an illusion of symmetry that exceeds its true dimensions, and in the elaborate engravings within its marble surfaces ㉜ that having to outlast centuries of calamity. Now, architects, engineers, and artists work to recreate the surprisingly balanced and unbelievably precise work of the Athenians. ㉝ How is it that today's architects are taking forty years to do what they did in less than ten?

28. (A) NO CHANGE
    (B) it's
    (C) it is
    (D) its

29. (A) NO CHANGE
    (B) components
    (C) particles
    (D) remnants

30. (A) NO CHANGE
    (B) In the world of today,
    (C) Contemptuously,
    (D) Today,

31. (A) NO CHANGE
    (B) are
    (C) was
    (D) were

32. (A) NO CHANGE
    (B) which has to outlast
    (C) that have outlasted
    (D) which had outlasted

33. Which of the following would be the most effective conclusion to the essay?

    (A) NO CHANGE
    (B) It is vital that we learn from the past in order to not repeat the mistakes of history.
    (C) Tourism is a growing business worldwide, as people seek out memorable experiences rather than to accumulate possessions.
    (D) The world continues to be haunted by the Venetian attack on the Parthenon, turning a brilliant accomplishment into utter ruins.

Questions 34–44 are based on the following passage.

Where Have all the Cavemen Gone?

㉞ All humans have their ultimate genetic roots in Africa. While our own ancestors were battling drought on the coasts of the African sub-continent, ㉟ the icebound north of modern Eurasia experienced the spread of the evolutionarily distinct species *Homo neanderthalensis,* where the Neanderthals developed the tools of flint and bone that have today come to characterize the so-called Mousterian culture of the early Stone Age.

(1) Early hypotheses for their extinction centered, predictably, around the ㊱ climate extreme change of the last Ice Age. (2) However, more recent studies of Neanderthal anatomy and artifacts suggest that they were remarkably well-equipped to deal with the fiercely cold and barren conditions, ㊲ and even thrived within them for nearly 200,000 years. (3) To cope with the glacial conditions, Neanderthals became short in stature—no more than a meter and half tall—and developed short, broad extremities

34. Which choice would best function as the introductory thesis of the essay?
    (A) NO CHANGE
    (B) The defeat of the Neanderthal invaders can only be considered a triumph of human ingenuity.
    (C) The disappearance of the Neanderthals is one of the great mysteries in the evolutionary success of modern humans.
    (D) In order to cope with the repercussions of possible global climate change, we should look to the example of Neanderthal adaptation.

35. (A) NO CHANGE
    (B) the evolutionarily distinct species *Homo neanderthalensis* had spread to the icebound north of modern Eurasia,
    (C) the species *Homo neanderthalensis*, being evolutionarily distinct, found itself spread to modern Eurasia in the north icebound,
    (D) the north icebound of modern Eurasia experience evolutionarily distinct species spread of the *Homo neanderthalensis,*

36. (A) NO CHANGE
    (B) climate, extreme
    (C) extreme climate
    (D) extreme, climate

37. (A) NO CHANGE
    (B) but
    (C) for it was the case that they
    (D) OMIT the underlined portion.

that would have increased the efficiency of circulation, and helped to preserve body heat. **㊳**

Another popular theory posits that Neanderthals met their extinction through absorption. That is— supposing Neanderthals were *not* a distinct species, but rather a subspecies of *Homo sapiens*—some researchers believe that they disappeared after **㊴** conflicts with humans when they arrived in Eurasia roughly 80,000 years ago. However, a sample of mitochondrial DNA surviving in the remains of a Neanderthal discovered in the Caucus Mountains demonstrates 3.5 percent genetic divergence from **㊵** contemporary *Homo sapiens*. While it is possible that some Neanderthals may have become culturally assimilated with our ancestors, it is highly unlikely that their DNA contributed to that of modern humans.

Currently, the most widely held theory to explain the extinction of the Neanderthals boils down quite simply to the processes of natural selection. While Neanderthals appear to have maintained a stable population during the Ice Age, **㊶** a drastic genetic bottleneck was experienced by our African ancestors, leaving only the strongest and most intelligent to survive and carry on the species. When *Homo neanderthalensis* at last met *Homo sapiens*, it is probable that

38. The writer would like to insert this sentence to provide further support to his argument in this paragraph.

"Further, there is strong evidence to suggest that later Neanderthals were capable of creating sophisticated and versatile garments from animal pelts designed to maintain core warmth without inducing perspiration."

Where would it best be placed?

(A) Before sentence 1
(B) Before sentence 2
(C) Before sentence 3
(D) After sentence 3

39. Which choice is the most consistent elaboration on the first sentence of this paragraph?

(A) NO CHANGE
(B) interbreeding
(C) discoveries
(D) commerce

40. Which wording best conveys that the Neanderthals only have a slight genetic divergence from present-day humans?

(A) NO CHANGE
(B) punctual
(C) unique
(D) scientific

41. (A) NO CHANGE
(B) a drastic genetic bottleneck by our African ancestors was experienced,
(C) our African ancestors drastically experienced a bottleneck that was genetic,
(D) our African ancestors experienced a drastic genetic bottleneck,

㊷ they was outmatched, at the very least, in technology, creativity, and social efficacy. In the several thousand years that followed, competition for resources would have pushed Neanderthals farther and farther to the **㊸** oceans of Europe and Asia. The last known remnants of Neanderthal culture issue from the remote location of Gorham's Cave on the Gibraltar coast. By this time—roughly 27,000 years ago—*Homo neanderthalensis* had been displaced by its evolutionary cousin **㊹** to the very edge of the land nearly back into Africa itself where our common ancestors, first emerged millions of years prior.

42. (A) NO CHANGE
    (B) they were
    (C) the Neanderthals are
    (D) the Neanderthals were

43. (A) NO CHANGE
    (B) margins
    (C) debris
    (D) remains

44. (A) NO CHANGE
    (B) to the very edge, of the land nearly back into Africa itself, where our common ancestors
    (C) to the very edge of the land, nearly back into Africa itself, where our common ancestors
    (D) to the very edge of the land nearly, back into Africa itself where our common, ancestors

STOP

IF THERE IS STILL TIME REMAINING, YOU MAY REVIEW YOUR ANSWERS.

MATH TEST (NO CALCULATOR)

25 Minutes, 20 Questions

Turn to Section 3 of your answer sheet to answer the questions in this section.

Directions: For questions 1–15, solve each problem and choose the best answer from the given options. Fill in the corresponding circle on your answer document. For questions 16–20, solve the problem and fill in the answer on the answer sheet grid.

Notes:
- Calculators are **NOT PERMITTED** in this section.
- All variables and expressions represent real numbers unless indicated otherwise.
- All figures are drawn to scale unless indicated otherwise.
- All figures are in a plane unless indicated otherwise.
- Unless indicated otherwise, the domain of a given function is the set of all real numbers x for which the function has real values.

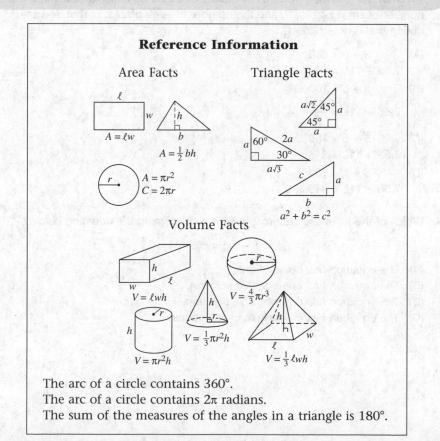

Reference Information

Area Facts

$A = \ell w$

$A = \frac{1}{2} bh$

$A = \pi r^2$
$C = 2\pi r$

Triangle Facts

$a\sqrt{2}$, $45°$, a, $45°$, a

a, $60°$, $2a$, $30°$, $a\sqrt{3}$

c, a, b

$a^2 + b^2 = c^2$

Volume Facts

$V = \ell wh$

$V = \frac{4}{3}\pi r^3$

$V = \frac{1}{3}\pi r^2 h$

$V = \pi r^2 h$

$V = \frac{1}{3}\ell wh$

The arc of a circle contains 360°.
The arc of a circle contains 2π radians.
The sum of the measures of the angles in a triangle is 180°.

1. At the beginning of January, John deposits A dollars into a non-interest-bearing bank account. If John withdraws d dollars from the account every month and makes no additional deposits, how much money, in dollars, will be in the account after m months?

(A) $A - md$

(B) $(A - m)d$

(C) $A - \dfrac{m}{d}$

(D) $A - \dfrac{d}{m}$

2. If $f(x) = x^2 - 11$, for what values of x is $f(x) < 25$?

(A) $-6 < x$

(B) $x < 6$

(C) $x \le -6$ or $x \ge 6$

(D) $-6 < x < 6$

3. At Joe's Pizzeria, small pizzas cost $7.50 and large pizzas cost $11.00. One day from 3:00 P.M. to 9:00 P.M., Joe sold 100 pizzas and took in $848. Solving which of the following systems of equations could be used to determine the number of small pizzas, S, and the number of large pizzas, L, that Joe sold during that 6-hour period?

(A) $\quad S + L = 848$
$\quad 7.5S + 11L = 100$

(B) $\quad S + L = 100$
$\quad 7.5S + 11L = \dfrac{848}{6}$

(C) $\quad S + L = 100$
$\quad 7.5S + 11L = 848$

(D) $\quad S + L = 100$
$\quad 7.5S + 11L = 848 \times 6$

4. Which of the following statements is true concerning the equation below?

$$3(5 - 2x) = 6(2 - x) + 3$$

(A) The equation has no solutions.

(B) The equation has one positive solution.

(C) The equation has one negative solution.

(D) The equation has infinitely many solutions.

5. The chart below shows the value of an investment on January 1 of each year from 2005 to 2010. During which year was the percent increase in the value of the investment the greatest?

Year	Value
2005	$150
2006	$250
2007	$450
2008	$750
2009	$1,200
2010	$1,800

(A) 2005
(B) 2006
(C) 2008
(D) 2009

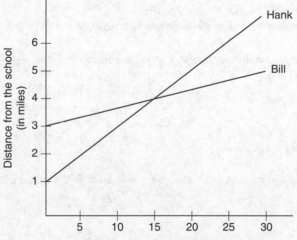

Minutes from the time the boys set out

6. Hank's and Bill's houses are 1 and 3 miles from their school, respectively. Each boy left his house on a bicycle at the same time and rode for 30 minutes. The graph above shows the distance, in miles, each boy was from the school during their rides. Based on this information, which of the following statements, if any, is *not* necessarily true?

(A) Hank is riding faster than Bill for the entire 30 minutes.
(B) The distance that Hank rode is greater than the distance that Bill rode.
(C) Hank and Bill's paths cross exactly once during their 30-minute rides.
(D) Each of the above statements must be true.

7. Which of the following is equivalent to $\dfrac{2x^2 - 8}{x^2 - 4x + 4}$?

    (A) $\dfrac{2(x + 2)}{x - 2}$

    (B) $\dfrac{2(x + 4)}{x - 4}$

    (C) $\dfrac{2x + 2}{x - 2}$

    (D) $\dfrac{6}{4x - 4}$

8. If $m \neq 0$, $m \neq 1$, and $f(x) = mx + b$, then which of the following statements concerning the graphs whose equations are $y = f(x) + 3$ and $y = f(x + 3)$ must be true?

    (A) The graphs don't intersect.
    (B) The graphs intersect in one point.
    (C) The graphs intersect in two points.
    (D) The graphs intersect in more than two points.

9. For how many positive integers, x, does the function $f(x) = \dfrac{\sqrt{x - 3}}{x^2 - 8x - 20}$ have no real values?

    (A) 2
    (B) 3
    (C) 4
    (D) Infinitely many

10. If for all real numbers x, $h(5 - x) = x^2 + x + 1$, what is the value of $h(9)$?

    (A) 13
    (B) 21
    (C) 28
    (D) 91

11. A white cube has a volume of 27. If a red circle of radius 1 is painted on each face of the cube, what is the total area of the surface of the cube that is *not* red?

    (A) $27 - 3\pi$
    (B) $27 - 6\pi$
    (C) $54 - 6\pi$
    (D) $54 - 12\pi$

12. Tim's Tennis Camp is open only to teenagers—all campers must be between 13 and 19 years old, inclusive. Which of the following inequalities can be used to determine if a person who is y years old is eligible to attend the camp?

(A) $|y - 13| \leq 6$
(B) $|y - 13| \leq 19$
(C) $|y - 19| \leq 13$
(D) $|y - 16| \leq 3$

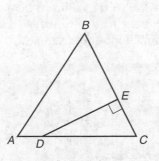

13. In the figure above, line segment $\overline{DE}$ is perpendicular to side $\overline{BC}$ of equilateral triangle ABC. If $AB = 12$ and $BE = 8$, what is the area of quadrilateral $ABED$?

(A) $14\sqrt{3}$
(B) $28\sqrt{3}$
(C) $36\sqrt{3}$
(D) $72\sqrt{3}$

14. The list price of a certain book is d dollars. Anne bought a copy of the book from an online dealer that offers a discount of 10% off the list price of all books and doesn't collect sales tax. Beth bought the same book at a bookstore, where the book was on sale for 15% off the list price. However, she had to pay 5% sales tax on his purchase. Which of the following statements is true?

(A) Anne and Beth paid the same price for their books.
(B) Anne paid more than Beth for the book.
(C) Anne paid less than Beth for the book.
(D) Who paid more for her book depends on d, the list price.

15. If the lines whose equations are $y = ax + b$ and $x = cy + d$ are parallel, which statement is true?

(A) $a = -\dfrac{1}{c}$

(B) $a = \dfrac{1}{c}$

(C) $c = a$
(D) $c = -a$

Grid-in Response Directions

In questions 16–20, first solve the problem, and then enter your answer on the grid provided on the answer sheet. The instructions for entering your answers follow.

- First, write your answer in the boxes at the top of the grid.
- Second, grid your answer in the columns below the boxes.
- Use the fraction bar in the first row or the decimal point in the second row to enter fractions and decimals.

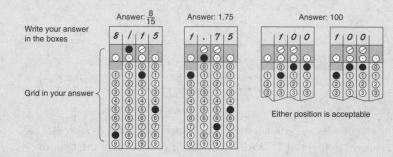

- Grid only one space in each column.
- Entering the answer in the boxes is recommended as an aid in gridding but is not required.
- The machine scoring your exam can read only what you grid, so you **must grid-in your answers correctly to get credit**.
- If a question has more than one correct answer, grid-in only one of them.
- The grid does not have a minus sign; so no answer can be negative.
- A mixed number *must* be converted to an improper fraction or a decimal before it is gridded. Enter $1\frac{1}{4}$ as 5/4 or 1.25; the machine will interpret 11/4 as $\frac{11}{4}$ and mark it wrong.

- **All decimals must be entered as accurately as possible.** Here are three acceptable ways of gridding

$$\frac{3}{11} = 0.272727\ldots$$

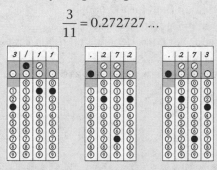

- Note that rounding to .273 is acceptable because you are using the full grid, but you would receive **no credit** for .3 or .27, because they are less accurate.

16. $A(1, 1)$, $B(5, 3)$, and $C(5, 9)$ are three points in the xy-plane. If $\overline{AB}$ is a diameter of Circle 1 and $\overline{BC}$ is a diameter of Circle 2, what is the slope of the line that goes through the centers of the two circles?

17. If a and b are positive constants and if $a(x - y) = b(y - x)$, what is the value of the ratio $\dfrac{x}{y}$?

18. If c is a real number and if $1 + i$ is a solution of the equation $x^2 - 2x + c = 0$, what is the value of c?

19. If (a, b) and (c, d) are the two points of intersection of the line whose equation is $y = x$ and the parabola whose equation is $y = x^2 - 6x + 12$, what is the value of $a + b + c + d$?

20. If $h(5 - 2x) = \sqrt{x^2 + 3x + 5}$ for all real numbers x, what is the value of $h(3)$?

STOP

IF THERE IS STILL TIME REMAINING, YOU MAY REVIEW YOUR ANSWERS.

MATH TEST (CALCULATOR)

55 Minutes, 38 Questions

Turn to Section 4 of your answer sheet to answer the questions in this section.

Directions: For questions 1–30, solve each problem and choose the best answer from the given options. Fill in the corresponding circle on your answer document. For questions 31–38, solve the problem and fill in the answer on the answer sheet grid.

Notes:
- Calculators **ARE PERMITTED** in this section.
- All variables and expressions represent real numbers unless indicated otherwise.
- All figures are drawn to scale unless indicated otherwise.
- All figures are in a plane unless indicated otherwise.
- Unless indicated otherwise, the domain of a given function is the set of all real numbers x for which the function has real values.

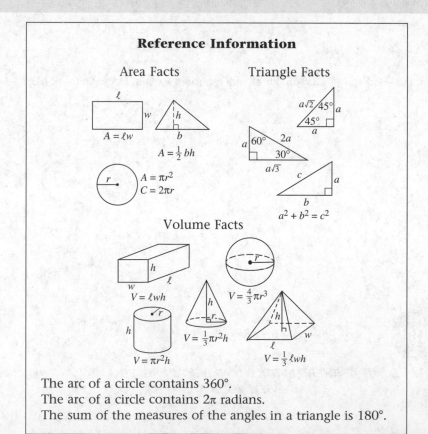

Reference Information

Area Facts

$A = \ell w$

$A = \frac{1}{2} bh$

$A = \pi r^2$
$C = 2\pi r$

Triangle Facts

$a^2 + b^2 = c^2$

Volume Facts

$V = \ell wh$

$V = \frac{4}{3}\pi r^3$

$V = \frac{1}{3}\pi r^2 h$

$V = \pi r^2 h$

$V = \frac{1}{3}\ell wh$

The arc of a circle contains 360°.
The arc of a circle contains 2π radians.
The sum of the measures of the angles in a triangle is 180°.

1. If Wally's Widget Works is open exactly 20 days each month and produces 80 widgets each day it is open, how many years will it take to produce 96,000 widgets?

   (A) fewer than 5
   (B) 5
   (C) more than 5 but fewer than 10
   (D) 10

2. What is the volume, in cubic inches, of a cube whose total surface area is 216 square inches?

   (A) 18
   (B) 36
   (C) 216
   (D) 1,296

3. If $2 - 3n \geq 5$, what is the greatest possible value of $2 + 3n$?

   (A) −1
   (B) 1
   (C) 4
   (D) 5

4. Which of the following statements concerning the equation $\dfrac{2x^2 - 3}{5 - x^2} = -2$ is true?

   (A) The equation has no solutions.
   (B) The equation has exactly one solution.
   (C) The equation has exactly two solutions.
   (D) The equation has infinitely many solutions.

5. If $f(x) = x^2 - 3x$ and $g(x) = f(3x)$, what is $g(-10)$?

   (A) 390
   (B) 490
   (C) 810
   (D) 990

Questions 6 and 7 refer to the following table.

Class	Number of Students	Number in Band
A	20	5
B	30	7
C	23	5
D	27	6
E	25	6

6. What is the average (arithmetic mean) number of students per class?

   (A) 24
   (B) 24.5
   (C) 25
   (D) 25.5

7. Which class has the highest percent of students in the band?

   (A) A
   (B) B
   (C) D
   (D) E

---

8. In a class, 20 children were sharing equally the cost of a present for their teacher. When 4 of the children decided not to contribute, each of the other children had to pay $1.50 more. How much, in dollars, did the present cost?

   (A) 50
   (B) 80
   (C) 100
   (D) 120

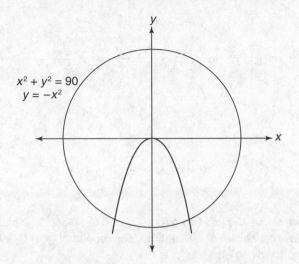

9. A system of two equations and their graphs are shown above. If (a, b) and (c, d) are the points of intersection of the circle and the parabola, what is the value of $a + b + c + d$?

(A) −18
(B) −6
(C) 6
(D) 18

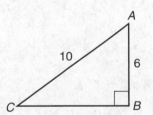

10. In the figure above, what is the value of the cosine of angle C?

(A) 0.4
(B) 0.5
(C) 0.6
(D) 0.8

11. For Jen's birthday, Wes bought her a ring, a bouquet of flowers, and a box of candy, for which he spent a total of $528. If the flowers cost three times as much as the candy, and the ring cost ten times as much as the flowers and candy combined, how much did he pay for the flowers?

(A) $12
(B) $24
(C) $30
(D) $36

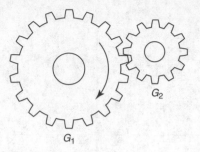

Note: Figure not drawn to scale.

12. The diagram above depicts two gears, G_1 and G_2. Gear G_1, which has 48 teeth, turns clockwise at a rate of 60 rotations per second. If gear G_2 has 36 teeth, which of the following statements is true?

(A) Gear G_2 turns clockwise at a rate of 45 rotations per second.
(B) Gear G_2 turns clockwise at a rate of 80 rotations per second.
(C) Gear G_2 turns counterclockwise at a rate of 45 rotations per second.
(D) Gear G_2 turns counterclockwise at a rate of 80 rotations per second.

Questions 13–15 are based on the information in the following graphs.

Lottery Ticket Sales – Type of Game and Use of Proceeds: 2009

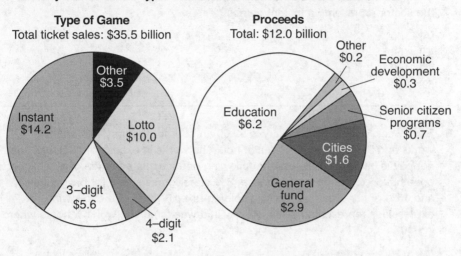

All figures are in billions of dollars.

13. The revenue from lottery ticket sales is divided between prize money and the various uses shown in the graph labeled "Proceeds." In 2009, approximately what percent of the money spent on tickets was returned to the purchasers in the form of prize money?

    (A) 23.5%
    (B) 50%
    (C) 66%
    (D) 74%

14. Approximately what percent of the proceeds that went to the states' General fund would have to be given to the Senior citizen program so that the proceeds for the Senior citizen program and the Cities would be equal?

    (A) 0.9%
    (B) 9%
    (C) 31%
    (D) 48%

15. Assume that in 2010 the sales of Lotto were discontinued, and the dollar value of the sales of all other games increased by 10% compared to 2009. If a new circle graph was created to reflect the Lottery Ticket Sales in 2010, which of the following would be closest to the degree measure of the central angle of the sector representing Instant games?

(A) 100°
(B) 150°
(C) 180°
(D) 200°

---

16. Each week, Alice's gross salary is $9.00 an hour for the first 40 hours she works and $15.00 an hour for each hour she works in excess of 40 hours. Her net pay is her gross pay less the following deductions: a flat fee of $20 for her contribution to her health insurance; 8% of her gross salary for payroll taxes, and 15% of her gross pay for withholding taxes. Which of the following expressions represents Alice's net pay in a week that she works x hours where $x > 40$?

(A) $0.23(15x - 240) - 20$
(B) $0.23(15x - 220)$
(C) $0.77(15x - 240) - 20$
(D) $0.77(15x - 220)$

17. If $i = \sqrt{-1}$, which of the following is equal to $(1 + i)^3$?

(A) $-2 + 2i$
(B) $2 - 2i$
(C) 4
(D) $4 + 4i$

18. If the x-intercepts of the graph of $y = 4x^2 - 8x + 3$ are a and b, what is the value of $a + b$?

(A) 0.5
(B) 1
(C) 1.5
(D) 2

Questions 19–20 are based on the information in the following graph.

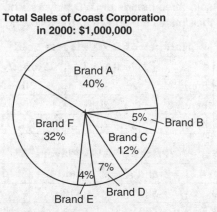

Total Sales of Coast Corporation
in 2000: $1,000,000

19. If the above circle graph were drawn to scale, then which of the following is closest to the difference in the degree measurements of the central angle of the sector representing Brand C and the central angle of the sector representing Brand D?

(A) 5°
(B) 12°
(C) 18°
(D) 25°

20. The total sales of Coast Corporation in 2005 were 50% higher than in 2000. If the dollar value of the sales of Brand A was 25% higher in 2005 than in 2000, then the sales of Brand A accounted for what percentage of total sales in 2005?

(A) 20%
(B) 25%
(C) $33\frac{1}{3}\%$
(D) 50%

21. Store 1 is a full-service retail store that charges regular prices. Store 2 is a self-service factory-outlet store that sells all items at a reduced price. In January 2014, each store sold three brands of DVD players. The number of DVD players sold and their prices are shown in the following tables.

Number of DVD Players Sold

	Store 1	Store 2
Brand A	10	30
Brand B	20	40
Brand C	20	20

Prices of DVD Players

	Brand A	Brand B	Brand C
Store 1	$80	$100	$150
Store 2	$50	$80	$120

What was the difference between Store 1 and Store 2 in the dollar values of the total sales of the three brands of DVD players?

(A) 80

(B) 140

(C) 330

(D) 1,300

Questions 22 and 23 refer to the figure below, which represents a solid piece of wood being used in the construction of a house. All of the dimensions are in feet.

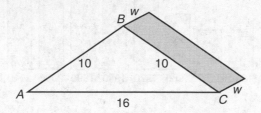

22. What is the area, in square feet, of the triangular face of the solid?

   (A) 24
   (B) 48
   (C) 50
   (D) 80

23. If the density of the wood is 3 pounds per cubic foot and if the weight of the solid is 360 pounds, what is the width, w, in feet, of the solid?

   (A) 5.0
   (B) 2.5
   (C) 2.4
   (D) 1.5

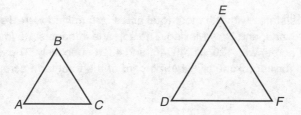

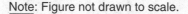

Note: Figure not drawn to scale.

24. In the figure above, both triangles are equilateral. If the area of $\triangle ABC$ is 6 and the area of $\triangle DEF$ is 10, to the nearest hundredth what is the ratio of AB to DE?

   (A) 0.36
   (B) 0.60
   (C) 0.75
   (D) 0.77

25. If $g(x) = (\sin x + \cos x)^2$, what is $g\left(\dfrac{\pi}{3}\right)$?

   (A) 1
   (B) 1.366
   (C) 1.866
   (D) 2

Questions 26–28 are based on the two graphs below.

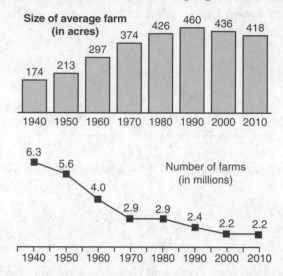

26. In which year was the total acreage of farmland in the United States the smallest?

(A) 1940
(B) 1970
(C) 2000
(D) 2010

27. In 2010, the states with the most total acres of farmland were Texas, Montana, Kansas, Nevada, and New Mexico. The acreage in each state (measured in millions of acres) was 130, 61, 46, 46, and 43, respectively. Those five states accounted for approximately what percent of the total farm acreage in the country?

(A) 15%
(B) 25%
(C) 35%
(D) 45%

28. If future projections are that the number of farms in the United States will decrease by 5% from 2010 to 2030 and that the average size of farms will decrease from 2010 to 2030 by the same percent as the decrease from 1990 to 2010, which of the following is closest to the total number of acres of farmland, in millions of acres, in the United States in 2030?

(A) 750
(B) 800
(C) 850
(D) 900

29. Let (h, k) be the center and r the radius of the circle whose equation is $x^2 + 2x + y^2 - 4y + 1 = 0$. What is the value of $h + k + r$?

    (A) 1
    (B) 2
    (C) 3
    (D) 4

30. In parallelogram $ABCD$, each side measures 10. If $m\angle A = 45°$, what is the area of the parallelogram?

    (A) 50
    (B) 64.6
    (C) 70.7
    (D) 78.2

Grid-in Response Directions

In questions 31–38, first solve the problem, and then enter your answer on the grid provided on the answer sheet. The instructions for entering your answers follow.

- First, write your answer in the boxes at the top of the grid.
- Second, grid your answer in the columns below the boxes.
- Use the fraction bar in the first row or the decimal point in the second row to enter fractions and decimals.

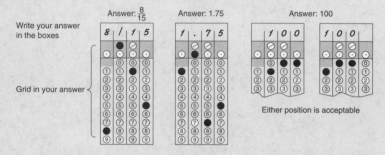

- Grid only one space in each column.
- Entering the answer in the boxes is recommended as an aid in gridding but is not required.
- The machine scoring your exam can read only what you grid, so you **must grid-in your answers correctly to get credit**.
- If a question has more than one correct answer, grid-in only one of them.
- The grid does not have a minus sign; so no answer can be negative.
- A mixed number *must* be converted to an improper fraction or a decimal before it is gridded. Enter $1\frac{1}{4}$ as 5/4 or 1.25; the machine will interpret 11/4 as $\frac{11}{4}$ and mark it wrong.

- **All decimals must be entered as accurately as possible.** Here are three acceptable ways of gridding

$$\frac{3}{11} = 0.272727\ldots$$

- Note that rounding to .273 is acceptable because you are using the full grid, but you would receive **no credit** for .3 or .27, because they are less accurate.

31. On a particular map of Long Island, one inch represents a distance of 20 miles. One day, Maurice drove from Hauppauge to Riverhead, which are 1.25 inches apart on that map, at an average speed of 40 miles per hour. How many minutes did his drive take?

32. Michelle participated in a 26-mile marathon that proceeded along a straight road. For the first 20 miles, she ran at a constant pace. At some point she passed a friend who was standing on the side of the road and who was cheering her on. Exactly 54 minutes and 36 seconds later, Michelle passed the 12-mile marker, and 31 minutes and 30 seconds after that, she passed the 15-mile marker. How far, in miles, was it from the starting line to the point where her friend was standing?

Base your answer to <u>Question 33</u> on the information in the following chart that shows the number of employees at Acme Air-Conditioning in three age groups and the average monthly salary of the workers in each group.

Age Group	Number of Employees	Average Monthly Salary
Under 35	12	$3,100
35–50	24	$3,800
Over 50	14	$4,200

33. What is the average (arithmetic mean) monthly salary, in dollars for all the employees?

---

34. To use a certain cash machine, you need a Personal Identification Code (PIC). If each PIC consists of two letters followed by one of the digits from 1 to 9 (such as AQ7 or BB3) or one letter followed by two digits (such as Q37 or J88), how many different PICSs can be assigned?

35. The base of pyramid 1 is a rectangle whose length is 3 and whose width is 2. The base of pyramid 2 is a square whose sides are 3. If the volumes of the pyramids are equal, what is the ratio of the height of pyramid 1 to the height of pyramid 2?

36. On October 20, 2015, one United States dollar was worth 0.88 euros and one Canadian dollar was worth 0.68 euros. On that date, to the nearest whole number, what is the number of Canadian dollars that could be purchased for 100 United States dollars?

Use the following information in answering <u>Questions 37 and 38</u>.

Every day to go to work, Ed drives the 6.3 miles between Exits 17 and 18 on Route 91, always at a constant rate of 60 miles per hour. At 60 miles per hour, Ed's car can go 24.3 miles per gallon of gasoline; at 70 miles per hour, Ed's car can only go 20.8 miles per gallon of gasoline.

37. How much less time, in seconds, would it take Ed to drive those 6.3 miles at 70 miles per hour instead of 60 miles per hour?

38. Last year, Ed drove the 6.3 miles from Exit 17 to Exit 18 a total of 240 times (always at 60 miles per hour). If during the year he paid an average of $3.50 per gallon for gasoline, how much more would it have cost him if he had driven at 70 miles per hour each day? (Express your answer to the nearest dollar, and grid it in without the dollar sign.)

IF THERE IS STILL TIME REMAINING, YOU MAY REVIEW YOUR ANSWERS.

ESSAY (OPTIONAL)

Directions: This assignment will allow you to demonstrate your ability to skillfully read and understand a source text and write a response analyzing the source. In your response, you should show that you have understood the source, give proficient analysis, and use the English language effectively. If your essay is off-topic, it will not be scored.

Only what you write on the lined paper in your answer document will be scored—avoid skipping lines, using unreasonably large handwriting, and using wide margins in order to have sufficient space to respond. You can also write on the planning sheet in the answer document, but this will not be evaluated—no other scrap paper will be given. Be sure to write clearly and legibly so your response can be scored.

You will be given 50 minutes to complete the assignment, including reading the source text and writing your response.

Read the following passage, and think about how the author uses:

- Evidence, such as applicable examples, to justify the argument
- Reasoning to show logical connections among thoughts and facts
- Rhetoric, like sensory language and emotional appeals, to give weight to the argument

A Lesson on Commas

> *"Think left and think right and think low and think high. Oh, the thinks you can think up if only you try."*
>
> —*Dr. Seuss*

1   It was my third year teaching English at Rosinburgh High when the freckled, garrulous Emily of the second row interrupted my comma lesson with an abrupt question, "Mrs. Jensen, why do you write?" I considered telling Emily to stay after class if she wished to converse off-topic. Yet, the abridged somnolence in the farthest row and my romantic inclinations to a teaching career somewhat like that of Julia Roberts in *Mona Lisa Smile*—both sparked by the most recent inquisition—conspired my actual response: "Why does one listen to music? Or dance? Or look to

the stars?" Amusement, surely. Communication and complex stimulation, absolutely. But mostly, I write in the name of indomitable creativity. I am of the distinct opinion that creativity is the most essential ingredient of erudition, expression, and future success, and being so, must be encouraged inside the classroom.

2   Creativity, contrary to popular belief, is not limited to the milieu of the elite, pedantic, or particularly adept; it is not reserved for the Picassos, the Bachs, or the Austens. Rather it is a gift bestowed to each and every one of us that should be maintained and even bolstered. The failure to include it in the public curriculum is a failure to society it in its entirety, as it indisputably dissuades curiosity, exploration, and activism. Emily, what if I told you that creativity is behind every piece of art, every new electronic, and every scientific discovery? What if I told you progress would be simply unfeasible without it? If you question its innateness, a moment's reflection on the sublime imagination of any child you have ever come into the briefest contact with will assure you otherwise.

3   As for its consequence, let us first consider personal fulfillment. Where would you suppose yourself most happy: in a desultory, routine job or an engaging, challenging career? While the question may seem puerile, its implications are far from trivial. The number one reason for unhappiness in adults is hating their jobs, and *LinkedIn* places "not being challenged" and "not feeling valued" at the top of the list for workplace dissatisfaction. If we can generalize creativity to the extent Google does, i.e., to the generation and contemplation of new ideas to create something perceived as valuable, then we can arrive at the need for it in our workplaces and domestic spheres. Simply put, humans need creativity to feel gratification. You may venture that the heretic without imagination is yet to be born, but I would add that the contented without imagination is just as uncommon.

4   Shall we move on to its effluence in a broader sense? Higher creativity preludes greater innovation and, thus, success and progress. In fact, a 2010 IBM survey ranked creativity as the single most important factor in corporate success. Let us ruminate for a moment on medical cures, energy alternatives, and space exploration—the need for creativity extends far beyond the recluse artist indeed. Perhaps your aspirations fall short of those of Steve Jobs or Shinya Yamanaka; still, you need to bring problem-solving and critical thinking into your career for the sake of efficiency, diversification, and job security. It is what allows you to see the world as

it is, exercise your interest in all that surrounds you, and bring fresh thinking to your circumstance. After all, it was Albert Einstein who said, "Imagination is more important than knowledge."

5   I have convinced you of creativity's import, but my rambling will seem only didactic if I neglect to address the ways that creativity can be nourished within the education system. You'll be surprised to learn how easily it can be incorporated into everyday scholarship. Schools, and teachers more specifically, can cultivate creativity by encouraging questioning and debate. The *why's* and the *how's* are a good place to start. Similarly, classrooms can make a habit of identifying problems and brainstorming solutions: the *what's good*, *what's bad*, and *how could it be improved*. A next step is in inspiring alternative problem solving—these are the beloved *what if's*. Promoting creativity begins with the generating of new knowledge, in lieu of the passing on of existing knowledge solely. It may be unclear to Emily why I write, particularly when I have so little success at it, but it is apparent to me how valuable her curiosity is, and how paramount that it be nurtured rather than dulled.

Write a response that demonstrates how the author makes an argument to persuade an audience that creativity should be taught in schools. In your response, analyze how the author uses at least one of the features from the essay directions (or features of your own choosing) to develop a logical and persuasive argument. Be certain that your response cites relevant aspects of the source text.

Your response should not give your personal opinion on the merit of the source text, but instead show how the author crafts an argument to persuade readers.

ANSWER KEY

Test 1

Section 1: Reading

1. C	14. B	27. D	40. B
2. A	15. B	28. B	41. A
3. B	16. A	29. C	42. C
4. C	17. A	30. D	43. B
5. B	18. C	31. C	44. B
6. A	19. C	32. C	45. A
7. B	20. D	33. D	46. A
8. A	21. D	34. A	47. A
9. B	22. D	35. B	48. D
10. B	23. C	36. C	49. C
11. C	24. C	37. D	50. C
12. B	25. B	38. C	51. A
13. D	26. B	39. B	52. C

Number Correct _____

Number Incorrect _____

Section 2: Writing and Language

1. C	12. C	23. B	34. C
2. A	13. C	24. A	35. B
3. D	14. A	25. B	36. C
4. C	15. B	26. A	37. A
5. B	16. A	27. C	38. D
6. D	17. D	28. D	39. B
7. A	18. A	29. D	40. A
8. B	19. D	30. D	41. D
9. A	20. B	31. B	42. D
10. C	21. D	32. C	43. B
11. A	22. A	33. A	44. C

Number Correct _____

Number Incorrect _____

Section 3: Math (No Calculator)

1. A	5. B	9. B	13. B
2. D	6. C	10. A	14. B
3. C	7. A	11. C	15. B
4. D	8. A	12. D	

16. 2

17. 1

18. 2

19. 14

20. 3

Number Correct _____

Number Incorrect _____

Section 4: Math (Calculator)

1. B	9. A	17. A	25. C
2. C	10. D	18. D	26. D
3. A	11. D	19. C	27. C
4. A	12. D	20. C	28. B
5. D	13. C	21. D	29. C
6. C	14. C	22. B	30. C
7. A	15. D	23. B	
8. D	16. C	24. D	

31. 37.5   32. 6.8   33. 3744   34. 8190

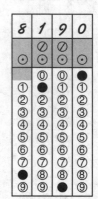

35. 3/2 or 1.5   36. 129   37. 54

38. 37

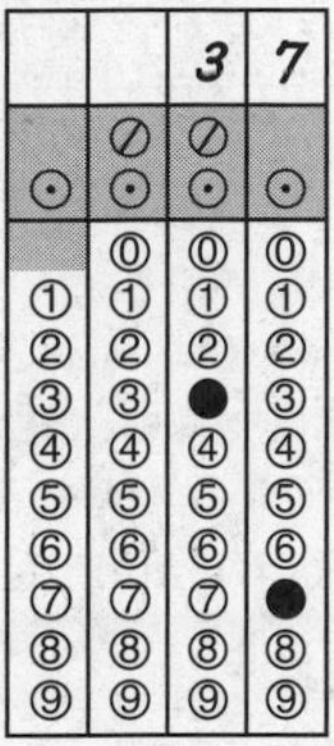

		3	7
	⊘	⊘	
⊙	⊙	⊙	⊙
	⓪	⓪	⓪
①	①	①	①
②	②	②	②
③	③	●	③
④	④	④	④
⑤	⑤	⑤	⑤
⑥	⑥	⑥	⑥
⑦	⑦	⑦	●
⑧	⑧	⑧	⑧
⑨	⑨	⑨	⑨

Number Correct _____

Number Incorrect _____

SCORE ANALYSIS

Reading and Writing Test

Section 1: Reading _____ = _____ (A)
                # correct   raw score

Section 2: Writing _____ = _____ (B)
                # correct   raw score

To find your Reading and Writing test scores, consult the chart below: find the ranges in which your raw scores lie and read across to find the ranges of your test scores.

$$\frac{}{\substack{\text{range of reading}\\\text{test scores}}} + \frac{}{\substack{\text{range of writing}\\\text{test scores}}} = \frac{}{\substack{\text{range of reading} + \text{writing}\\\text{test scores}}} \text{(C)}$$

To find the range of your Reading and Writing Scaled Score, multiply (C) by 10.

Test Scores for the Reading and Writing Sections

Reading Raw Score	Writing Raw Score	Test Score
44–52	39–44	35–40
36–43	33–38	31–34
30–35	28–32	28–30
24–29	22–27	24–27
19–23	17–21	21–23
14–18	13–16	19–20
9–13	9–12	16–18
5–8	5–8	13–15
less than 5	less than 5	10–12

Math Test

Section 3: _____ = _____ (C)
          # correct   raw score

Section 4: _____ = _____ (E)
          # correct   raw score

Total Math raw score: (D) + (E) = _____

To find your Math Scaled Score, consult the chart below: find the range in which your raw score lies and read across to find the range for your scaled score.

Scaled Scores for the Math Test

Raw Score	Scaled Score		Raw Score	Scaled Score
50–58	700–800		20–25	450–490
44–49	650–690		15–19	400–440
38–43	600–640		11–14	350–390
32–37	550–590		7–10	300–340
26–32	500–540		less than 7	200–290

ANSWERS EXPLAINED

Section 1: Reading Test

1. **(C)**

Substitute the answer choices in the original sentence. The sergeant is a person who might have been a deputy sheriff before he joined the army—that is, in his civil or *nonmilitary* life.

2. **(A)**

Paragraph 1 presents a general picture of the man on the bridge, the executioners and the officer standing nearby, the sentinels at the far ends of the bridge. Cinematically, it is like *a wide-angle shot* of the whole panorama. Paragraph 2 takes a closer look at the man, examining his clothes, his face, his expression. It is as if the camera has moved in for *a close-up* shot.

3. **(B)**

You can use the process of elimination to answer this question. Was the man awaiting hanging *innocent of any criminal intent*? No. He was willing to go along with the idea that all was fair in love and war, and would willingly perform a criminal act (assaulting a sentinel and burning down a bridge). Choice (A) is incorrect. Was the man awaiting hanging an *unlikely candidate for execution*? Possibly. Keep choice (B) in mind as you consider the other choices. Was the man awaiting hanging *a victim of mistaken identity*? No. He was caught in the act of attempting to burn down the bridge. Choice (C) is incorrect. Was the man awaiting hanging *purposely assuming a harmless demeanor*? Nothing in the passage suggests that he was putting on the appearance of being harmless. Choice (D) is incorrect. Only choice (B) is left. It is the correct answer.

4. **(C)**

To have one's neck "in the hemp" is to have one's neck in a noose, a rope made out of hemp. The author's comment that the man "had a kindly expression that one would hardly have expected in one whose neck was in the hemp" suggests that he is *an unlikely candidate for execution* and that some unusual circumstances must have brought him to this fate.

5. **(B)**

In calling the military code "liberal" because it doesn't exclude members of the upper classes from being executed, the author is being highly *ironic*. Generally, people would like regulations to be interpreted liberally to permit them to do the things they want. Here, the liberal military code is permitting the man to be hanged. Clearly, the gentleman facing execution would have preferred the code to be less liberal in this case.

6. **(A)**

Farquhar agrees readily with the saying that all is fair in love and war. This implies he is willing to use *underhanded* or unfair *methods to support his* [the Southern] *cause*.

7. **(B)**

Look at the context in which the word *consistent* occurs. "(N)o adventure [was] too perilous for him to undertake if [it was] *consistent* with the character of a civilian who was at heart a soldier." Farquhar has no objection to performing humble errands or undertaking dangerous tasks as long as these tasks are appropriate to someone who sees himself as a sort of "undercover soldier," a secret agent of the Confederacy. Anything he does must be consistent or *compatible* with his image of himself in this role.

8. **(A)**

The fact that Mrs. Farquhar is married to a man "ardently devoted to the Southern cause," together with her readiness to fetch water for a Confederate soldier, suggests some degree of sympathy on her part for the Confederate cause. Choice (B) is incorrect. Mrs. Farquhar's action, in hospitably fetching water "with her own white hands," contradicts the idea that she is too proud to perform menial tasks. Choices (C) and (D) are also incorrect. There is nothing in the passage to suggest either of them.

9. **(B)**

The assertion that Mrs. Farquhar "was only too happy" to fetch water for a soldier wearing the grey uniform of the Confederate army provides strong evidence that she is *sympathetic to the Confederate cause*.

10. **(B)**

Farquhar wishes to prevent the Yankee advance. To do so, he must somehow damage the railroad, its bridges, its tunnels, or its trains. The soldier tells him that some highly flammable driftwood is piled up at the base of the wooden railroad bridge. Clearly, it would make sense for Farquhar to try to set fire to the driftwood in *an attempt to burn down* the bridge.

11. **(C)**

The scout is a Yankee soldier disguised as a member of the enemy. By coming to the Farquhars' plantation in Confederate disguise, he is able to learn they are sympathetic to the enemy. By telling Farquhar of the work on the bridge, stressing both the lack of guards and the abundance of fuel, he is tempting Farquhar into an attack on the bridge (and into an ambush). The scout's job is to locate potential enemies and draw them out from cover. The concluding sentence thus establishes *that Farquhar has been entrapped into taking an unwise action*, an action that will lead to his execution at Owl Creek bridge.

12. **(B)**

President Roosevelt mentions two types of people who came to America seeking freedom: "some of high degree, but mostly plain people." The people of high degree were members of the upper classes, those set apart by aristocratic birth or social position; the others were plain, *ordinary* people.

13. **(D)**

Roosevelt describes the American spirit as "the product of centuries." In other words, the hope of freedom and the love of liberty go back for centuries; America's democratic ideal *has deep-seated* (firmly established) *historical roots*.

14. **(B)**

Choice (B) clearly supports the contention that the American belief in freedom "has deep-seated historical roots." It pointedly asserts that the "democratic aspiration is no mere recent phase in human history" and goes on to mention the Magna Carta or Great Charter of 1215 as a specific example of a historic document that embodies the spirit of democracy.

15. **(B)**

Look at the context in which these documents are mentioned. "Its vitality was written into our own Mayflower Compact, into the Declaration of

Independence, into the Constitution of the United States, into the Gettysburg Address." To what does the phrase "Its vitality" refer? The answer appears two paragraphs earlier, in the opening sentence "The democratic aspiration is no mere recent phase in human history." The democratic aspiration is Roosevelt's theme, the subject he is discussing. According to Roosevelt, the vitality and strength of democratic aspiration were written into America's founding documents. Thus, he clearly is citing these documents as examples of *expressions of the democratic aspiration*.

16. **(A)**

In lines 22–24, Roosevelt asserts that Americans "have moved forward constantly and consistently toward an ideal which in itself has gained stature and clarity with each generation." It is his optimistic contention that we have been coming closer and closer to reaching that ideal and that the democratic spirit has grown stronger. However, he acknowledges that "we still have far to go" before we reach that ideal: the existence of both "undeserved poverty" and "self-serving wealth" stands in the way of democracy. In other words, *economic injustices must be addressed before democracy can prevail*.

17. **(A)**

In his 1789 First Inaugural Address, Washington was directing his words to his contemporaries. In other words, he was *addressing* his words to them, speaking to them in a formal way. To Roosevelt, Washington's words sounded prophetic, as if he *addressed* his words to the people of 1941.

18. **(C)**

Repetition is a common, yet effective literary device that strengthens the power of the point being made. One website of popular literary terms describes the effect of repetition as follows: "The aura that is created by the usage of repetition cannot be achieved through any other device. It has the ability of making a simple sentence sound like a dramatic one. It enhances the beauty of a sentence and stresses on the point of main significance." Thus, the main effect of the repetition of the phrase "It speaks to us" is to create a *dramatic tone, emphasizing the point being made and adding to its emotional impact*.

19. **(C)**

What experiment was "intrusted to the hands of the American people"? Consider the context. Washington was writing an address that he was to deliver on his inauguration as president of the United States, a new nation founded upon democratic principles. The experiment entrusted to the American people was the radical experiment of *democratic government*.

20. **(D)**

Washington's "experiment intrusted to the hands of the American people" is the republican model of government, whose preservation he urges. It is this same model of government that Roosevelt urges Americans to defend when he asserts that "our strong purpose is to protect and to perpetuate the integrity of democracy."

21. **(D)**

As we know from the introduction to the passage, Roosevelt delivered his Third Inaugural Address in January of 1941, at a time when Britain and its allies were hard pressed by Hitler's forces but the United States had not yet gone to war. Nonetheless, it was clear that democracy was under attack and that America was facing "great perils never before encountered." The passage's final paragraphs emphasize the need to preserve the sacred fire of liberty. The president exhorts his listeners "to protect and to perpetuate the integrity of democracy." Thus, it is reasonable to conclude that a major goal of Roosevelt in making this speech was to *inspire the American people to defend the cause of freedom in dangerous times.*

22. **(D)**

Step by step, the author traces the course of a surgical procedure, from the initial grasping of the scalpel through the opening incision to the eventual sensory exploration of the internal organs. In doing so, he is *describing a process.* Choice (A) is incorrect. Although in the course of the passage the author occasionally defines a term (for example, the term *fascia*), the passage, taken as a whole, describes the process of surgery; it does not define a term. Choice (B) is incorrect. The passage does not provide an example of a particular method of surgery; instead, it describes the process of surgery. Choice (C) is incorrect. This is not a lesson, instructing novice surgeons in the steps they should take to perform a successful abdominal surgery; it is a vivid description of the process of surgery.

23. **(C)**

As the surgeon draws the knife across the skin, it leaves a thin *line of blood* in its wake (path or track passed over by a moving object). Choices (A) and (B) are incorrect; nothing in the opening paragraph supports either choice. Choice (D) is incorrect. The darting knife is *followed* by the fine wake of red; the knife blade is not the wake of red.

24. **(C)**

The darting knife is followed by a wake of red. If the meaning of the simile is still unclear at this point, the subsequent sentence, in which the parted flesh reveals yellow blobs of fat below, is a clue that the "fine wake of red" is a bloody incision made by the knife. Choices (A) and (B) are incorrect. They describe the way to hold the knife, not the effect of the knife as it cuts its way through the patient's skin. Choice (D) is incorrect. It has nothing to do with the knife's wake or trail of red.

25. **(B)**

To part the flesh is to *split* apart or separate the skin, cutting it apart with the knife. Choice (A) is incorrect. Although in some contexts "parts" means *leaves*, as in "parting from someone at the train station," that is not how it's used here. Choice (C) is incorrect. Although in some contexts "parts" means *surrenders* ("parting with hard-earned cash"), that is not how it is used here. Choice (D) is incorrect. Although in some contexts "parts" means *distributes* ("parting an estate into shares"), that is not how it's used here.

26. **(B)**

The simile "like children absorbed in a game" indicates that, in this context, "engaged" means *engrossed* or deeply involved. Choice (A) is incorrect. Although in some contexts "engaged" means *betrothed* or pledged to marry, that is not how it is used here. Choice (C) is incorrect. Although in some contexts "engaged" means *hired* ("engaged as a contractor"), that is not how it is used here. Choice (D) is incorrect. Although in some contexts "engaged" means *embattled* ("engaged forces"), that is not how it is used here.

27. **(D)**

Primitive drawings of buffalo and other wild beasts still exist in *caves* in which *prehistoric* humans dwelled. Thus, one might expect to find them in a cavity described as "a primitive place." Choice (A) is incorrect. In "a primitive place," one might expect to find primitive drawings; one wouldn't necessarily expect to find them in an art gallery. Choices (B) and (C) are incorrect. Nothing in the passage suggests that one might expect to find *drawings* of buffalo in either a zoological display or a Western film.

28. **(B)**

The colors of the internal organs are secret because, until the peritoneum is opened and the world's light illuminates the abdominal cavity, the internal organs cannot be seen. In other words, the colors of the internal organs *normally are hidden from sight.*

29. **(C)**

The author looks on his work as a surgeon as if it were a priestly vocation. The first hint of this comes in lines 20–21: "the litany of monosyllables with which one prays his way down and in: *clamp, sponge, suture, tie, cut.*" The one-word requests that the surgeon makes for a clamp or a sponge are like a litany, a form of prayer made up of a series of invocations or petitions that are usually led by the clergy. The surgeon "prays his way down and in." Clearly, the author is making use of priestly or *religious imagery*. Choice (A) is incorrect. Although the author likens the abdominal cavity to a cavern, he primarily describes the surgery in religious terms. Choice (B) is incorrect. The author never contrasts abdominal surgery with other types of surgery. Choice (D) is incorrect. The author never evokes or suggests the patient's emotions; if anything, he evokes the surgeon's emotions.

30. **(D)**

In these two sentences, the author makes explicit his sense of surgery as a religious rite, an impression he continues to develop in the subsequent paragraph ("the priestliness of my profession has ever been impressed on me").

31. **(C)**

Consider the various descriptive passages in which the author explores the formerly hidden organs and tissues now exposed to view through surgical intervention. "The peritoneum, pink and gleaming and membranous, bulges into the wound." "An arc of the liver shines high and on the right, like a dark sun. It laps over the pink sweep of the stomach, from whose lower border the gauzy omentum is draped, and through which veil one sees, sinuous, slow as just-fed snakes, the indolent coils of the intestine." Peritoneum, liver, stomach, omentum, intestine: the author names them, evokes their appearance in a brief descriptive phrase ("peritoneum, pink and gleaming and membranous," "gauzy omentum," "indolent coils of the intestine"). However, he does not bother to define these anatomical terms. Instead, he apparently assumes that his readers will *be familiar with the organs and tissues* to which he refers. Choice (A) is incorrect. The author freely goes into vivid detail about surgical procedures. He would be unlikely to be as free in his imagery if he assumed that his readers had qualms about reading descriptions of surgery. Choice (B) is incorrect. The author carefully describes how to hold a scalpel; he would not do so if he assumed his readers were already adept at handling surgical tools. Choice (D) is incorrect. Nothing in the passage suggests that the author assumes his readers have undergone surgery.

32. **(C)**

Throughout Passage 1, the author constantly emphasizes the lengthy time period his book will cover. In the passage's opening sentence he refers to "the shifting relationship between the press and the presidency *over nearly two centuries*"; later he refers to "the relationship of the presidents to the press *since George Washington's first term.*" The author is "surveying nearly two centuries of this relationship." In other words, he is presenting *an overview* of a relationship. What sort of relationship is it? It is one of "mutual . . . recriminations and mistrust." There has been one main constant in it, "the dissatisfaction of one with the other." In other words, it is *an inherently conflicted relationship.* Not only that, but this relationship "has been increasingly complicated by the changing nature of the presidency, by the individual nature of presidents, by the rise of other media, especially television, and by the growing complexity of beliefs about the function of both press and government." The inherently conflicted relationship clearly *faces new challenges* and will continue to do so as our institutions and technology continue to change. The correct answer is choice (C).

33. **(D)**

The first paragraph of the passage says that the administration of every president has ended with "recriminations and mistrust." Presidents, like everyone else, hate to be criticized in public. Therefore, they all have experienced *animosity involving themselves and the press.* Choice (C) is incorrect. The first paragraph states that, while the initial stage of the relationship between the press and the president may seem harmonious ("beginning with mutual protestations of good will"), the relationship ends in antagonism. The paragraph never suggests that periods of antagonism and harmony alternate.

34. **(A)**

If the record of *every* administration has begun with the press and the presidency claiming to feel goodwill toward one another and has ended with them blaming and mistrusting one another, then clearly *all* American presidents have experienced *mutual animosity* (ill will) *involving themselves and the press.*

35. **(B)**

To be reduced to simple terms is to be simplified or *boiled down* to its essential, basic nature. Choices (A), (C), and (D) are incorrect. Although reduced can mean *decreased* ("reduced speed"), *marked down* ("reduced prices"), or *demoted* ("reduced in rank"), it is not how the word is used here.

36. **(C)**

The author advises the reader to (lines 25–26) "be careful not to view the past in terms of our own times." This advice is an axiom (a statement or proposition regarded as being established, accepted, or self-evidently true) of professional historians. As a professional historian, he gives the reader this advice because *readers today cannot fully grasp the significance these actions had in their own time.*

37. **(D)**

To use present standards to judge the actions of past presidents "is to violate historical context." *Because* the words "press," "government," and "presidency" have changed in meaning, because our lives today differ so greatly from the lives of people in earlier times, we cannot fully understand the significance of presidential actions two centuries ago.

38. **(C)**

The opening sentence of the final paragraph concludes with the clause "but the facts are quite different." Many Americans believe that the colonists immediately established a free society. The author says that this belief is incorrect. Thus, he is trying to *correct a misconception* or mistaken idea.

39. **(B)**

The open questioning to which the author refers (line 64) is the *unrestricted*, no holds barred questioning that the president faces in modern solo press conferences. Choices (A), (C), and (D) are incorrect. Although "open" can mean *receptive* ("open to suggestions"), *unconcealed* ("open carry"), or *vulnerable* ("open to abuse"), that is not how it is used here.

40. **(B)**

Use the process of elimination to answer this question. Did President Clinton hold more solo press conferences than President George H. W. Bush did? No. President Clinton held 62 solo press conferences; President George H. W. Bush held 83 solo press conferences. Choice (A) is incorrect. Did Presidents Clinton and George W. Bush hold a far higher percentage of joint press conferences than either of their predecessors did? This seems to be correct. President Clinton's percentage of joint press conferences was 67.9%; President George W. Bush's percentage of joint press conferences was 77.3%. Neither of their predecessors came even close. Choice (B) is most likely the correct answer. Quickly scan the remaining choices to see whether you can find a better answer than choice (B). Choice (C) asks you to draw a conclusion that is unsupported by the data in the graph. True, the graph provides data showing President Reagan held no joint press conferences; however, it provides no information to indicate why he did this. Choice (C) is incorrect. Choice (D) is also incorrect. Unlike his son, President George H. W. Bush held fewer joint press conferences than solo sessions.

41. **(A)**

Passage 1 *describes a phenomenon*. This phenomenon is the dissatisfaction of the press and the president with each other. Passage 1 describes it as a constant, that is, an unchanging factor. Passage 2, however, focuses on changes in this relationship. It does not describe the situation as *static*. Instead, it emphasizes the "increasingly contentious, adversarial" nature of the relationship and suggests that this increased aggressiveness from the press may have brought about the shift from solo press conferences, during which the president is more open to direct hostility, to joint press conferences, in which he has more control of the situation. Thus, in focusing on the increases in press aggressiveness and on the changes in the structure of presidential press conferences, *Passage 2 denies the static nature of the phenomenon described in Passage 1.*

42. **(C)**

Both authors make a point of the adversarial nature of the relationship between the press and the president. This inherent antagonism is at the heart of the relationship and is likely to influence the actions of both the press and the president for years to come.

43. **(B)**

Choice (B) is correct. To describe the debate over fracking or hydraulic fracturing as "fractious" is to make *a play on* the words "fractious" and "fracturing." The author chooses the adjective "fractious" because it begins like "fracturing." The similarity in sound between the two words strengthens the sentence's effect. In contrast, consider the effect of this slight change on the opening sentence: "To call it a heated debate is an understatement." Lacking the word play, the revised sentence feels a bit flat. Choice (A) is incorrect. A metaphor is a figure of speech in which a term or phrase is applied to something to which it is not literally applicable in order to suggest a resemblance, as in "My boss is such a bear today." Choice (C) is incorrect. It is no exaggeration to say that the debate over fracking has become heated or *fractious*. Hydraulic fracturing is a controversial subject, and the discussion about it is contentious. Choice (D) is incorrect. A counterargument is an argument put forward to oppose an idea or theory developed in another argument. It has nothing to do with the author's word choice here.

44. **(B)**

Choice (B) is correct. A game changer is an event, idea, or procedure that brings about a significant shift in the current way of doing something. By calling fracking-related gas recovery a game changer, fracking's supporters are asserting that fracking is going to *radically alter natural gas production*. Choice (A) is incorrect. In calling fracking a game changer, its proponents do not assert that fracking has no foreseeable negative consequences. Instead, they assert that its positive benefits (reduced dependence on foreign sources of energy, new jobs, relatively clean energy, etc.) strongly outweigh its possible drawbacks. Choice (C) is incorrect. In calling fracking a game changer, its proponents are not asserting that they fail to take it seriously. Choice (D) is incorrect. Although later portions of the passage mention a need for regulation, fracking's proponents say nothing about any need for *active federal regulation*.

45. **(A)**

Choice (A) is correct. In lines 5–8, the author lists the following points made by fracking's supporters:

1. Compared to natural gas recovered by drilling oil wells, natural gas recovered through fracking is inexpensive (it "is cheap").
2. Compared to natural gas recovered by drilling oil wells, natural gas recovered through fracking is relatively free from pollutants or unpleasant substances (it is "relatively clean").
3. The United States contains an abundance of natural gas that can be recovered through fracking. ("America is brimful of the stuff.")

To have access through fracking to an abundant supply of inexpensive, relatively clean natural gas would *change* our methods of *natural gas production radically*. It would change the entire oil industry. Indeed, it is doing so. None of the remaining choices provide evidence in support of the assertion that fracking is a game changer.

46. **(A)**

In lines 9–22, the author relates the public's fears about the dangers of fracking. Media reports of fracking-triggered earthquakes and fracking-caused environmental contamination fuel these fears. In the paragraph immediately following, the author depicts the reaction these fears have produced in the political arena. She mentions protests and legislative attempts to halt or ban fracking in several states. Her discussion of fracking legislation thus *describes specific responses* (marches, moratoriums, policy changes) *to concerns raised in the previous paragraph.*

47. **(A)**

Choice (A) is correct. An open question is a matter that has not yet been decided, an issue that remains *unresolved*. Choice (B) is incorrect. Although "open" can mean *vulnerable*, as in the welfare system's being "open to abuse," that is not the sense in which it is used here. Choice (C) is incorrect. Although "open" can mean *accessible*, as in a school program's being "open to all students," that is not the sense in which it is used here. Choice (D) is incorrect. Although "open" can mean *ajar*, as in a door's being "left open," that is not the sense in which it is used here.

48. **(D)**

Use the process of elimination to answer this question. Choice (A) is incorrect. Nothing in the passage suggests that its author advocates or supports technological innovations such as fracking; she merely reports the opinions of fracking's advocates. Choice (B) is incorrect. Nothing in the passage suggests that its author either opposes or supports regulatory oversight, whether pointless or not; she merely describes legislative attempts to regulate fracking. Choice (C) is incorrect. Nothing in the passage suggests that its author is a concerned legislator; she merely recounts the actions taken by legislators regarding fracking. Only choice (D) is left. It is the correct answer. The author is *an observer striving* to be objective and *to present a balanced account*.

Remember to read the italicized introduction. Often it contains useful information. Here, the italicized introduction indicates that the passage comes from a popular science magazine, *Science News*. Such magazines have the task of presenting current research findings in an objective, unbiased manner, weighing both sides of an argument rather than arguing the merits of a particular claim.

49. **(C)**

The author acknowledges that the dangers of fracking are real. She also acknowledges that the potential energy payoff is real as well. She is striving to present both sides of the argument objectively.

50. **(C)**

The solid line on the graph vividly depicts a sudden, marked jump in the number and frequency of earthquakes from about 2009. This accentuates or emphasizes the *increasing frequency of earthquakes in the region*. Choice (B) is incorrect. The graph plots the increased frequency of earthquakes, not their increased magnitude. Choices (A) and (D) are incorrect. Nothing in the passage supports either answer.

51. **(A)**

In stating that the change in the frequency and number of earthquakes was pronounced, Ellsworth is asserting that it was marked or particularly *noticeable*. Choices (B), (C), and (D) are incorrect. Although "pronounced" can mean *declared* ("pronounced dead"), *decided on* ("pronounced on innocence or guilt"), or *articulated* ("correctly pronounced words"), that is not how it is used here.

52. **(C)**

Ellsworth indicates that researchers lack pre-quake data (lines 53–54). He advises researchers to collect seismic information about current and potential drilling sites. He concludes the paragraph by stating explicitly that "(t)here are many things we don't understand." All these comments in the passage's concluding paragraph suggest that Ellsworth looks on current hypotheses about connections between the recent increases in earthquakes and the start of the fracking boom as *based on insufficient knowledge*. Geologists simply don't know enough about what actually occurs during fracking to be able to properly test their hypotheses about fracking's possible effects on the increasing frequency of earthquakes.

Section 2: Writing and Language

1. **(C)**

The first sentence of the paragraph states that Modernism is characterized by the "complete rejection" of traditions and values, which is consistent with a "rebuff" of conventional morality. Moreover, the remainder of the paragraph mentions moral relativism, which further solidifies the notion of a "rebuff" of mainstream values. Choice (A) is not correct because it is the opposite of an embrace. Choice (B) is not right because it can be reasonably inferred that Fitzgerald must have understood conventional morality since he skillfully wrote about matters concerning it. Choice (D) is incorrect because its connotation is too positive.

2. **(A)**

The writer uses an interesting turn of phrase to state that Bernice does not listen to (entertain) or find amusing (be entertained by) Marjorie's social activities. Choice (B) does not work because a transitional word would be needed after "entertainment." Choices (C) and (D) result in nonsensical meanings.

3. **(D)**

The underlined portion refers to the female Bernice, so "herself" is appropriate. The other options are not consistent with a third-person singular female.

4. **(C)**

"To mock" is parallel with the earlier "to embody" in the sentence and concisely expresses the intended idea. Choices (A) and (B) are too wordy. Choice (D) is not parallel to the earlier phrasing.

5. **(B)**

"Who" is correct since it stands for a subject that is human. Choice (A) is used in reference to objects. Choice (C) shows possession. Choice (D) means "who is."

6. **(D)**

This sentence needs to come before the third sentence, which starts with "Despite her good looks. . . ." This sentence provides a transition between a description of Marjorie and a contrasting description of Bernice. The other placements are illogical as they would not allow for a clear transition between the descriptions of the two characters.

7. **(A)**

Two eras are being compared, so "between" is the best choice. Choice (B) is wrong because "among" is used for a comparison of three or more things. "Contrast for," which is choice (C), and "Contrast on," which is choice (D), are not idiomatically correct.

8. **(B)**

"While" is the only option that provides a contrast within the sentence between how Marjorie is preferred socially and her rudeness.

9. **(A)**

When adjectives have to be ordered a certain way to provide a logical meaning, there should be no commas separating them. In this case, it only makes sense to say "few short sentences," not "short few sentences," making choice (A) the only viable option. Choices (B) and (D) change the meaning, and choice (C) has an unnecessary comma.

10. **(C)**

The last sentence of the paragraph makes this choice the most clear, stating that both Bernice and Marjorie are quite superficial. So characterizing them as having "false facades" is most logical. With their vengeful dramatics, they are far from being "kind-hearted" as in choice (A). Choice (B) is incorrect since they are not revolutionary ideologues but, instead, more decadent. Choice (D) is not the right answer because being frivolous and pious is contradictory.

11. **(A)**

In choice (A), the colon comes after a complete sentence right before the flaws are clarified and the comma comes before the transitional "while." Choice (B) results in a run-on sentence. Choice (C) has an unnecessary comma after "lifeless." Choice (D) has an unnecessary comma after "manner."

12. **(C)**

The first part of the sentence states that journalism gathers and distributes news in a wide variety of ways, and choice (C) gives specific examples of the technology that does this. Choices (A), (B), and (D) are irrelevant to the first part of the sentence.

13. **(C)**

This choice places a comma after the introductory dependent clause ending in "media" and puts a colon before a clarification of how the field is optimistic. Choice (A) lacks a necessary comma after "media" and leads to a run-on sentence. Choice (B) leads to a run-on. Choice (D) puts a semicolon between a subject and a verb, which should not be separated.

14. **(A)**

"But also" follows "not only" when making a statement like "not only this but also that." None of the other options works with this idiomatic phrasing.

15. **(B)**

The current paragraph emphasizes that journalism has undergone major changes, while the following paragraph delves more deeply into concrete explanations of these changes. So choice (B) makes the most sense because it provides both a conclusion to the current paragraph and a transition into the topic of the next. Choices (A) and (C) contradict the information presented in the next paragraph. Choice (D) speaks more to the quality of journalism than to its overall popularity.

16. **(A)**

The sentence is stating two things that *do not* happen, so saying "doesn't" in conjunction with "nor" makes sense. Choice (B) shows cause and effect. Choice (C) shows a direct connection between two ideas. Choice (D) shows contrast.

17. **(D)**

This choice correctly does not have an apostrophe after "departments" because this word is functioning as the subject, not as a possessive adjective. Choices (A) and (B) incorrectly have apostrophes after "departments." Choice (D) is also correct because "ensuring" means to "make sure," which fits the context. "Assure" means to "reassure," and "insure" has to do with financial transactions.

18. **(A)**

The previous sentence refers to "leading journalism departments," so a sentence about the number one journalism department in the country is a logical connection. The other choices may very well give interesting and factual information about this school, but they are not directly connected to the previous sentence.

19. **(D)**

This choice correctly places commas around the parenthetical phrase. Choice (A) has a comma at an awkward point, choice (B) lacks the necessary pauses, and choice (C) is too choppy.

20. **(B)**

The adjective "endless" is needed to modify the noun "effects." Also, "affect" is generally a verb, and "effect" is generally a noun. The incorrect options either use the adverb "endlessly" and/or use the verb "affect."

21. **(D)**

According to the graph, the number of journalism-related job openings has gone up, then down, and then up again in recent years. This variation is best described as a "fluctuation." Choice (A) is incorrect because since the passage was written in 2015, there has not been a steady increase in demand for journalists in recent years, given the big drop from 2006 to 2009. Choice (B) is not right because in recent years, the number of jobs available increased. Choice (C) is not correct because the level of employment has gone up and down, not remained steady.

22. **(A)**

To "adapt" is to make something suitable, and to "adopt" is to make something one's own. In this case, the field of journalism is making gradual changes in order to adjust to technological advances, so "adapt" makes sense. Choices (C) and (D) are therefore incorrect. The paragraph is in the present tense, so "is adapting" works (choice (A)) and "was adapting" (choice (B)) does not.

23. **(B)**

Giving an approximation of the years is the most precise option. Choices (A), (C), and (D) are too vague.

24. **(A)**

This choice gives necessary breaks between all of the listed items and also has a break after the clarifying phrase "most recently." Choices (B), (C), and (D) all change the original meaning because of their comma placements or lack thereof.

25. **(B)**

To convey giving a high priority to making the Parthenon glorious, the phrase "sparing no expense" is the best choice. It indicates that the Greeks were willing to put as many economic resources as needed into finishing the Parthenon in a beautiful manner. Honesty and judiciousness, choice (A), do not necessarily relate to making the Parthenon glorious. Although "artistic patience" and the use of "architectural techniques" (choices (C) and (D)) could be loosely related to completing the Parthenon in the glorious fashion, these do not convey that finishing it was a high priority.

26. **(A)**

This is the only option that expresses the needed contrast between the previous sentence and the current one since there is a contrast between the glorious construction of the Parthenon and the fact that the glory was very short-lived. The other options do not express the needed contrast.

27. **(C)**

"Could've" sounds like "could of," but it is short for "could have." The use of the word "of" in this context is therefore incorrect, making choices (A) and (B) wrong. Choice (C) correctly expresses the verb "have." Choice (D) makes the sentence say "should have been still served," which is nonsensical.

28. **(D)**

"Its" correctly refers to the singular Parthenon's possession of "pagan gods." The word "Its'" is always incorrect (choice (A)). Both choice (B) and choice (C) mean "it is."

29. **(D)**

"Remnants" means "surviving pieces or traces of something," so logically these refer to the parts of the Parthenon that remained after its destruction.

Choice (A) refers to the study of such remains, not the remains themselves. Choices (B) and (C) do not give a precise description of what these are.

30. **(D)**

This choice concisely expresses the intended idea. Choices (A) and (B) are too wordy. Choice (C) likely wants to say something along the lines of "contemporary," but the word given actually means "with contempt."

31. **(B)**

"Beauty" and "refinement" create a compound subject, which requires the plural "are." In addition, the paragraph is in the present tense, so the verb must be in the present tense. Choices (C) and (D) are in the past tense, and choice (A) is singular.

32. **(C)**

The fact that these engravings have lasted for a long time is an essential part of their description, so "that" is needed instead of "which." Choice (C) also uses the proper tense. Choice (A) uses the incorrect verb tense. Choices (B) and (D) use "which," which works for nonessential characteristics of described objects.

33. **(A)**

The essay focuses throughout on the impressive feat of the Parthenon's construction, so choice (A) gives a direct connection to this general theme. Choices (B) and (C) are too vague. Choice (D) focuses on only a small part of the passage.

34. **(C)**

By examining the topic sentences of the paragraphs, you can see that the essay is presenting various theories about what happened to the Neanderthals. Choice (C) is therefore the most fitting option to introduce the essay's argument. Choice (A) is vague, and choice (B) is disconnected from the essay's argument. Choice (D) contradicts the essay's argument since the Neanderthals were not ultimately successful in adapting.

35. **(B)**

Mention of the Neanderthals at the beginning of the underlined portion is necessary to make a logical comparison with "our own ancestors." Choices (A) and (D) make illogical comparisons since they compare geographic regions to ancestors. Choice (C) has confusing word order at the end, placing "icebound" such that it literally means that the Neanderthals were icebound. Choice (B) puts things in a logical order and makes a logical comparison of people to Neanderthals.

36. **(C)**

It is necessary to have the words in the order "extreme climate" to express the correct meaning. Since the words must be in this order, no comma is needed to separate them. If the adjectives can be reversed, then a comma between them is necessary (e.g., "the big, tall mountain").

37. **(A)**

The last part of this sentence gives more support to the claim in the first part of the sentence, making "and" appropriate. Choice (B) shows contrast, choice (C) is too wordy, and choice (D) removes a needed transition.

38. **(D)**

This sentence is best placed at the end of the paragraph since it has the initial transition "further," which indicates that it is building on the previous argument. Moreover, it is logical to have this after sentence 3 since this sentence gives information in support of the idea that Neanderthals had excellent body heat-generating ability. The clothing cited in the sentence builds on this genetic advantage. Choice (A) makes no sense because this sentence cannot function as an introduction. Choice (B) interrupts a logical transition between sentences 1 and 2. Choice (C) inverts the logical sequence of the inserted sentence building upon sentence 3.

39. **(B)**

The first sentence of the paragraph states "absorption" may have been the cause of Neanderthal extinction. Therefore, "interbreeding" most logically expresses how this absorption could have taken place. Choice (A) would have resulted in Neanderthal extermination. Choices (C) and (D) do not give the strong explanation that "interbreeding" would.

40. **(A)**

"Contemporary" is the only option that clarifies that these are present-day humans to whom the Neanderthals are compared.

41. **(D)**

This choice concisely expresses the idea using logical word order. Choices (A) and (B) use passive voice. Choice (C) jumbles the word order such that the meaning is confused.

42. **(D)**

Without a clarification of the pronoun, it could be referring to *Homo neanderthalensis* or to *Homo sapiens*. Therefore, choices (A) and (B) are too vague. This took place in the past, so choice (D) is correct. The present tense in choice (C) is wrong.

43. **(B)**

"Margins" is the most logical wording, since Neanderthals would have been pushed to the outer reaches of these geographic areas. Choice (A) does not make sense since there are not oceans in Europe and Asia. Choices (C) and (D) do not make sense since human-like species could not live on "debris" or "remains."

44. **(C)**

This choice correctly places the clarifying phrase, "nearly back into Africa itself," out of the way using commas. Choice (A) breaks up the phrase "ancestors first emerged." Choice (B) breaks up the phrase "edge of the land." Choice (D) breaks up the phrase "nearly back to Africa."

Section 3: Math Test (No Calculator)

For some of the problems, an alternative solution, indicated by two asterisks (**) follows the first solution. When this occurs, one of the solutions is the direct mathematical one and the other is based on one of the strategies discussed in Chapter 6.

1. **(A)**

If John withdraws d dollars every month, the total amount he withdraws in m months is md dollars, and the amount remaining in the account is **$A - md$** dollars.

**Plug in easy-to-use numbers. Assume John's initial deposit is $100 and that he withdraws $10 a month. After 6 months, he will have withdrawn $60 and still have $40 in the account. Which answer choice is equal to 40 when $A = 100$, $d = 10$, and $m = 6$? Only choice (A) works.

2. **(D)**

$f(x) < 25 \Rightarrow x^2 - 11 < 25 \Rightarrow x^2 < 36 \Rightarrow \mathbf{-6 < x < 6}$

3. **(C)**

Since S represents the number of small pizzas sold during that 6-hour period and L represents the number of large pizzas sold during that same period, $S + L$ is the total number of pizzas sold. So $S + L$ must equal 100.

Since each small pizza costs 7.5 dollars and each large pizza costs 11 dollars, $7.5S + 11L$ is the total number of dollars Joe took in. So this expression must equal 848. The two equations are **$S + L = 100$** and **$7.5S + 11L = 848$**.

4. **(D)**

Note that the left side and the right side of the given equation are equivalent:

$$3(5 - 2x) = 15 - 6x \quad \text{and} \quad 6(2 - x) + 3 = 12 - 6x + 3 = 15 - 6x$$

Since every real number is a solution of the equation $15 - 6x = 15 - 6x$, **the equation has infinitely many solutions**.

**A solution to the equation $3(5 - 2x) = 6(2 - x) + 3$ would be the x-coordinate of the point of intersection of the straight lines $y = 3(5 - 2x)$ and $y = 6(2 - x) + 3$. Since these lines are the same line (they both have the equation $y = 15 - 6x$), *every* point on one line is a point on the other.

5. **(B)**

The percent increase in a quantity is $\dfrac{\text{actual increase}}{\text{original}} \times 100\%$ (KEY FACT C5). For *each* year calculate the actual increase and divide. For example, in 2005 the increase was $100 (from $150 to $250), so the percent increase was $\dfrac{100}{150} \times 100\% = 66.66\%$. In **2006** the increase was $\dfrac{200}{250} \times 100\% = 80\%$. Check the other choices; this is the greatest.

6. **(C)**

- The slope of each line represents each boy's speed. Since the slope of Hank's line is greater than the slope of Bill's line, Hank is always riding faster than Bill. Choice (A) must be true.
- Since Hank and Bill rode for the same amount of time and since Hank was riding faster, Hank covered a greater distance than Bill. Choice (B) is true.
- After 15 minutes, each boy is the same distance (4 miles) from the school. However, they are not necessarily anywhere near each other. It is possible that Hank's house is 1 mile south of the school and that Hank rode for 30 minutes due south, whereas Bill's house might be 3 miles north of the school and Bill rode due north. After 15 minutes, they could each be 4 miles from the school but be several miles apart from one another. Choice (C) is not necessarily true.

7. **(A)**

$$\frac{2x^2 - 8}{x^2 - 4x + 4} = \frac{2(x^2 - 4)}{(x-2)(x-2)} = \frac{2\,\cancel{(x-2)}(x+2)}{\cancel{(x-2)}(x-2)} = \frac{2(x+2)}{(x-2)}$$

**Use TACTIC 6: Plug in a number for x. For example, if $x = 3$:

$$\frac{2x^2 - 8}{x^2 - 4x + 4} \text{ is } \frac{2(3^2) - 8}{3^2 - 4(3) + 4} = \frac{18 - 8}{9 - 12 + 4} = \frac{10}{1} = 10$$

Only choice (A) is 10 when $x = 3$: $\dfrac{2(3+2)}{3-2} = \dfrac{2(5)}{1} = 10$.

8. **(A)**

$y = f(x) + 3 = mx + b + 3$ and $y = f(x + 3) = m(x + 3) + b = mx + 3m + b$. So both graphs are straight lines whose slopes are m. Therefore, the graphs are either a pair of parallel lines (if their y-intercepts are different) or the same line (if their y-intercepts are equal). The y-intercepts are $b + 3$ and $3m + b$, which are equal only if $3m = 3$. However, it is given that $m \neq 1$, so the intercepts are not equal. The lines are parallel, so **the graphs do not intersect**.

9. **(B)**

The function $f(x) = \dfrac{\sqrt{x - 3}}{x^2 - 8x - 20}$ is undefined whenever the expression under the square root sign is negative and whenever the denominator is equal to 0.

- $x - 3 < 0$ whenever $x < 3$. There are 2 positive integers that satisfy this inequality: 1 and 2.
- Since $x^2 - 8x - 20 = (x - 10)(x + 2)$, this expression is equal to 0 only when $x = 10$ and $x = -2$. So there is only 1 positive integer that makes the denominator 0.

In total, there are **3** positive integers for which $f(x)$ has no real values.

10. **(A)**

If $9 = 5 - x$, then $x = -4$. So $h(9) = h(5 - (-4)) = (-4)^2 + (-4) + 1 = 16 - 4 + 1 = \mathbf{13}$.

11. **(C)**

Since the volume of the white cube is 27 cubic inches, each edge is 3 inches. Then the area of each face is 9, and the total surface of the cube is $6 \times 9 = 54$. Each face has a red circle whose radius is 1, so the area of each circle is $\pi(1^2) = \pi$. Finally, the total red area is 6π, and the total surface area that is NOT red is **$54 - 6\pi$**.

12. **(D)**

In questions such as these, first find the midpoint of the eligible values. Here, a value for y is acceptable only if $13 \le y \le 19$; the midpoint of this interval is 16. All of the acceptable ages are within 3 years of 16—anywhere from 3 years less than 16 to 3 years greater than 16. The inequality that expresses this is $|y - 16| \le 3$.

13. **(B)**

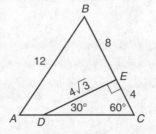

- Since triangle ABC is equilateral, $BC = AB = 12$, and so $EC = 12 - 8 = 4$.
- Since $\overline{DE}$ is perpendicular to $\overline{BC}$, $m\angle E = 90°$. Since triangle ABC is equilateral, $m\angle C = 60°$. So triangle DEC is a 30-60-90 triangle and $DE = 4\sqrt{3}$.
- Since the formula for the area of an equilateral triangle is $A = \dfrac{S^2 - \sqrt{3}}{4}$, the area of triangle ABC is $\dfrac{12^2\sqrt{3}}{4} = \dfrac{144\sqrt{3}}{4} = 36\sqrt{3}$.
- The area of triangle DEC is $\dfrac{1}{2}(4)(4\sqrt{3}) = 8\sqrt{3}$.
- So the area of quadrilateral $ABED = 36\sqrt{3} - 8\sqrt{3} = \mathbf{28\sqrt{3}}$.

14. **(B)**

It should be clear that the answer does *not* depend on d. So the easiest thing to do, as in all problems involving percents, is to assume that the list price of the book is $100. Then Anne paid $90 after receiving a $10 discount ($10 being 10% of $100). Beth, on the other hand, received a $15 discount. So she paid $85 for her copy of the book plus a sales tax of 5% of $85, which is $0.05 \times \$85 = \$4.25$. So Beth's total cost was $89.25. Anne paid 75 cents more than Beth.

15. **(B)**

The slope of the line whose equation is $y = ax + b$ is a. To find the slope of the line whose equation is $x = cy + d$, first solve for y:

$$x = cy + d \Rightarrow cy = x - d \Rightarrow y = \frac{1}{c}x - \frac{d}{c}$$

Since the slope of the line is the coefficient of x, the slope is $\dfrac{1}{c}$. Since parallel lines have equal slopes, $\mathbf{a = \dfrac{1}{c}}$.

16. **2**

The centers of the two circles are the midpoints of the two diameters.

- The midpoint of $\overline{AB}$ is $\left(\dfrac{1+5}{2}, \dfrac{1+3}{2}\right) = (3, 2)$.
- The midpoint of $\overline{BC}$ is $\left(\dfrac{5+5}{2}, \dfrac{3+9}{2}\right) = (5, 6)$.
- The slope of the line that passes through (3, 2) and (5, 6) is
  $= \dfrac{6-2}{5-3} = \dfrac{4}{2} = \mathbf{2}$.

17. **1**

$a(x - y) = b(y - x) \Rightarrow ax - ay = by - bx \Rightarrow ax + bx = by + ay \Rightarrow x(a + b) = y(a + b) \Rightarrow x = y$. So the ratio $\dfrac{x}{y} = \mathbf{1}$.

18. **2**

If $1 + i$ is a solution of the equation $x^2 - 2x + c = 0$, then

$\quad (1 + i)^2 - 2(1 + i) + c = 0 \Rightarrow (1 + 2i + i^2) - (2 + 2i) + c = 0 \Rightarrow$
$\quad 1 + 2i - 1 - 2 - 2i + c = 0$

So $-2 + c = 0$, and $c = \mathbf{2}$.

19. **14**

Replacing y by x in the equation $y = x^2 - 6x + 12$ gives:

$\quad x = x^2 - 6x + 12 \Rightarrow x^2 - 7x + 12 = 0 \Rightarrow$
$\quad (x - 3)(x - 4) = 0 \Rightarrow x = 3$ or $x = 4$

Since $y = x$, $(a, b) = (3, 3)$ and $(c, d) = (4, 4)$. So $a + b + c + d = \mathbf{14}$.

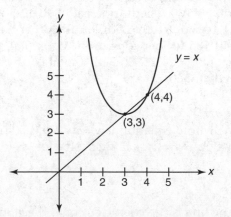

20. **3**

If $3 = 5 - 2x$, then $2x = 2$ and $x = 1$.

So $h(3) = h(5 - 2(1)) = \sqrt{(1)^2 + 3(1) + 5} = \sqrt{9} = \mathbf{3}$.

Section 4: Math Test (Calculator)

For some of the problems, an alternative solution, indicated by two asterisks (**) follows the first solution. When this occurs, one of the solutions is the direct mathematical one and the other is based on one of the strategies discussed in Chapter 6.

1. **(B)**

Wally produces 80 widgets per day × 20 days per month × 12 months per year = 19,200 widgets per year; $96{,}000 \div 19{,}200 = \mathbf{5}$.

2. **(C)**

If the total surface area of the cube is 216, then the area of each of the 6 faces is $216 \div 6 = 36$. Since each face is a square of area 36, each edge is 6. Finally, the volume of the cube is $6^3 = \mathbf{216}$.

3. **(A)**

$2 - 3n \geq 5 \Rightarrow -3n \geq 3$. Dividing both sides of this inequality by -3, and remembering to reverse the direction of the inequality gives $n \leq -1$. Therefore, $3n \leq -3$, and $2 + 3n \leq 2 + (-3) = \mathbf{-1}$.

4. **(A)**

If $\dfrac{2x^2 - 3}{5 - x^2} = -2$, then $2x^2 - 3 = -2(5 - x^2) = -10 + 2x^2$. Subtracting $2x^2$ from both sides of this equation gives $-3 = -10$, which of course is false. So the **equation has no solutions**.

5. **(D)**

$g(-10) = f(3(-10)) = f(-30) = (-30)^2 - 3(-30) = 900 - (-90) = 900 + 90 = \mathbf{990}$

**$g(x) = f(3x) = (3x)^2 - 3(3x) = 9x^2 - 9x$

Then $g(-10) = 9(-10)^2 - 9(-10) = 900 + 90 = \mathbf{990}$.

6. **(C)**

The average is just the sum of the number of students in the five classes (125) divided by 5: $125 \div 5 = \mathbf{25}$.

7. **(A)**

In class **A**, one-fourth, or 25% (5 of 20), of the students are in the band. In each of the other classes, the number in the band is *less than* one-fourth of the class.

8. **(D)**

Let x be the amount, in dollars, that each of the 20 children was going to contribute, then $20x$ represents the cost of the present. When 4 children dropped out, the remaining 16 each had to pay $(x + 1.50)$ dollars, so

$$16(x + 1.5) = 20x \Rightarrow 16x + 24 = 20x \Rightarrow 24 = 4x \Rightarrow x = 6$$

So the cost of the present was $20 \times 6 = $ **120** dollars.

**Use TACTIC 5: backsolve. Try choice (C), 100. If the present cost $100, then each of the 20 children would have to pay $5. When 4 dropped out, the remaining 16 would have to pay $100 ÷ 16 = $6.25 apiece, an increase of $1.25. Since the actual increase was $1.50, the gift was more expensive. Eliminate (A), (B), and (C). The answer must be (D).

9. **(A)**

Since $y = -x^2$, $x^2 = -y$. Replacing x^2 by $-y$ in the equation of the circle, we get:

$$-y + y^2 = 90 \Rightarrow y^2 - y - 90 = 0 \Rightarrow (y - 10)(y + 9) = 0 \Rightarrow y = 10 \text{ or } y = -9$$

A quick glance at the graphs shows that y cannot possibly be equal to 10, so y must equal –9. If you didn't think to check the graphs, plugging in 10 for y into either equation leads to a contradiction. Since x^2 can't be negative, $-x^2$ can't be positive. Also if $x^2 + 10^2 = 90$, then x^2 would be negative.
Then $x^2 + (-9)^2 = 90 \Rightarrow x^2 + 81 = 90 \Rightarrow x^2 = 9 \Rightarrow x = 3$ or $x = -3$.
So $(a, b) = (-3, -9)$ and $(c, d) = (3, -9)$.
Finally, $a + b + c + d = -3 + -9 + 3 + -9 = $ **–18**.

10. **(D)**

Since triangle ABC is a right triangle, we can use the Pythagorean theorem to find BC: $6^2 + (BC)^2 = 10^2 \Rightarrow (BC)^2 = 100 - 36 = 64 \Rightarrow BC = 8$.
(Of course, if you immediately realize that triangle ABC is a 6-8-10 right triangle, then you don't have to use the Pythagorean theorem.)

So $\cos C = \dfrac{\text{adjacent}}{\text{hypotenuse}} = \dfrac{8}{10} = 0.8$.

11. **(D)**

Let c represent the cost, in dollars, of the candy. Then $3c$ is the cost of the flowers, and $10(c + 3c) = 10(4c) = 40c$ is the cost of the ring. So,

$$528 = 40c + 3c + c = 44c \Rightarrow c = 528 \div 44 = 12$$

Therefore, the candy cost $12, the flowers cost **$36**, and the ring cost $480.

12. **(D)**

It should be clear from the diagram that gear G_2 turns in a **counterclockwise** direction. As tooth A pushes against tooth C followed by tooth B pushing against tooth D, the teeth on gear G_2 are turning in the opposite direction as those on gear G_1.

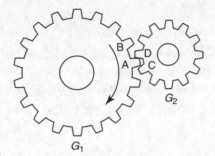

It should also be clear that the fewer the teeth on a gear, the faster it goes. In fact, the number of teeth is inversely proportional to the number of rotations per second:

number of teeth on G_1 × number of rotations per second of G_1 =
number of teeth on G_2 × number of rotations per second of G_2

So if r represents the number of rotations per second of G_2, we have

$$48 \times 60 = 36r \Rightarrow 2{,}880 = 36r \Rightarrow r = 2{,}880 \div 36 = \mathbf{80}$$

13. **(C)**

The difference between the total ticket sales ($35.5 billion) and the total distribution of the proceeds $12.0 billion) was the amount returned to the purchasers of lottery tickets in the form of prize money: $35.5 billion – $12.0 billion = $23.5 billion. Divide 23.5 by 35.5 to see that approximately **66%** of the ticket sales was allocated to prize money.

14. **(C)**

In order for the amount received by Senior citizens programs to be the same as the amount received by the Cities, an additional $0.9 billion would have to be allocated to the Senior citizen programs: $0.9 billion is approximately **31%** of the $2.9 billion currently going to the General fund.

15. **(D)**

in 2009, the total sales for all games other than Lotto in billions of dollars was 35.5 − 10.0 = 25.5. In 2010, each of the remaining games experienced a 10% increase in sales, so the total sales in 2010 was 25.5 + 10%(25.5) = 25.5 + 2.55 = 28.05. In 2010, the sales of the Instant games was 10% higher than in 2009: 14.2 + 1.42 = 15.62. So in 2010, the percent of the total sales attributed to Instant games was $\frac{15.62}{28.05} = .557 = 55.7\%$. Finally, the measure of the central angle for the sector representing Instant games is 55.7% of 360° = **200°**.

16. **(C)**

Alice's gross pay in dollars is:

$$40 \times 9 + (x - 40) \times 15 = 360 + 15x - 600 = 15x - 240$$

23% of her gross pay (8% for payroll taxes and 15% for withholding taxes) is deducted from her gross pay. So her net pay is 77% of her gross pay (100% − 23%) minus a $20 contribution for her health insurance premium:

$$\mathbf{0.77(15x - 240) - 20}$$

17. **(A)**

$(1 + i)^3 = [(1 + i)(1 + i)](1 + i) = [1 + 2i + i^2](1 + i) = [1 + 2i - 1](1 + i) = [2i](1 + i) = 2i + 2i^2 = 2i - 2 = \mathbf{-2 + 2i}$

18. **(D)**

If the graph of a function crosses the x-axis at n, then $(n, 0)$ is a point on the graph. So $(a, 0)$ and $(b, 0)$ are points on the graph. Therefore, a and b are the solutions of the equation $4x^2 - 8x + 3 = 0$. There are a few ways to solve this equation.

- First solution: Factor $4x^2 - 8x + 3 = (2x - 3)(2x - 1)$. So,

$$2x - 3 = 0 \text{ or } 2x - 1 = 0 \Rightarrow x = \frac{3}{2} \text{ or } x = \frac{1}{2}$$

So a and b are $\frac{3}{2}$ and $\frac{1}{2}$, respectively, and $a + b = \frac{3}{2} + \frac{1}{2} = \mathbf{2}$.

- Second solution: Use the quadratic formula on the equation $4x^2 - 8x + 3 = 0$.

$$x = \frac{8 \pm \sqrt{(-8)^2 - 4(4)(3)}}{2(4)} = \frac{8 \pm \sqrt{64 - 48}}{8} - \frac{8 \pm \sqrt{16}}{8} = \frac{8 \pm 4}{8}$$

So $x = \frac{12}{8} = \frac{3}{2}$ or $x = \frac{4}{8} = \frac{1}{2}$.

- Third solution: Use a graphing calculator. Graph $y = 4x^2 - 8x + 3$, and see where the graph crosses the x-axis.

19. **(C)**

The central angle of the sector representing Brand C is 12% of 360°:

$$(0.12) \times 360° = 43.2°$$

The central angle of the sector representing Brand D is 7% of 360°:

$$(0.7) \times 360° = 25.2°$$

Finally, 43.2° − 25.2° = **18°**.

**Note this can be done in one step by noticing that the percentage difference between Brands C and D is 5%, and 5% of 360 is $(0.05) \times 360 = 18$.

20. **(C)**

Since total sales in 2000 were $1,000,000, in 2005 sales were $1,500,000 (a 50% increase).

In 2000, sales of Brand A were $400,000 (40% of $1,000,000).

In 2005, sales of Brand A were $500,000 (25% or $\frac{1}{4}$ more than in 2000).

Finally, $500,000 is $\frac{1}{3}$ or $\mathbf{33\frac{1}{3}}$**%** of $1,500,000.

21. **(D)**

Store 2 sold 30 DVDs at $50, 40 DVDs at $80, and 20 DVDs at $120.

Store 2: $(30 \times \$50) + (40 \times \$80) + (20 \times \$120) = \$7,100$

Store 1 sold 10 DVDs at $80, 20 DVDs at $100, and 20 DVDs at $150.

Store 1: $(10 \times \$80) + (20 \times \$100) + (20 \times \$150) = \$5,800$

Finally, $7,100 − $5,800 = **$1,300**.

22. **(B)**

The face of the solid is an isosceles triangle whose base is 16. To find its area, draw in altitude $\overline{BD}$ in the diagram below.

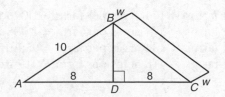

Since the altitude to the base of an isosceles triangle is also a median, $AD = DC = 8$. So triangle ABD is a 6-8-10 right triangle. (If you don't immediately recognize that, use the Pythagorean theorem: $10^2 = 8^2 + (BD)^2 \Rightarrow (BD)^2 = 100 - 64 = 36 \Rightarrow BD = 6$.) The area of triangle ABC is

$$\frac{1}{2}bh = \frac{1}{2}(16)(6) = \mathbf{48}$$

23. **(B)**

The solid is a prism whose triangular face has an area of 48 square feet (see the solution to question 22) and whose width is w. So the volume of the solid is $48w$ cubic feet, and its weight is

$$(48w \text{ cubic feet}) \times (3 \text{ pounds per cubic foot}) = 144w \text{ pounds}$$

Then $144w = 360 \Rightarrow w = 360 \div 144 = \mathbf{2.5}$.

24. **(D)**

Since they have the same angles, by KEY FACT J16 all equilateral triangles are similar. If k is the ratio of the sides of two similar triangles, then by KEY FACT J18 the ratio of their areas is k^2. Here the ratio of the areas is 6:10, or 0.6, so $k^2 = 0.6$ and $k = \sqrt{0.6} = \mathbf{0.77}$.

25. **(C)**

Here are two ways to answer this question.

- You can just put your calculator into radian mode and evaluate:

$$\left(\sin\frac{\pi}{3} + \cos\frac{\pi}{3}\right)^2 = (0.866 + 0.5)^2 = 1.366^2 = \mathbf{1.866}$$

- Leave your calculator in degree mode and convert $\frac{\pi}{3}$ radians to degrees:

$$\frac{\pi}{3} \text{ radians} = \frac{180}{3} = 60 \text{ degrees}$$

$$(\sin 60° + \cos 60°)^2 = (0.866 + 0.5)^2 = 1.366^2 = \mathbf{1.866}$$

26. **(D)**

For each of the given years, the total acreage of farmland can be calculated by multiplying the number of farms by the average size of a farm. There is no way to answer this question, without doing the calculation for each year.

- 1940: 6.3 million farms × 174 acres per farm = 1,096 million acres
- 1970: 2.9 million farms × 374 acres per farm = 1,085 million acres
- 2000: 2.2 million farms × 436 acres per farm = 959 million acres
- 2010: 2.2 million farms × 418 acres per farm = 919 million acres

27. **(C)**

Find the sum: 130 + 61 + 46 + 46 + 43 = 326. The sum of the farm acreages for the five states is 326 million acres. In the solution to the previous question, we saw that the total farm acreage in the country in 2010 was 919 million acres, and 326 ÷ 919 = 0.3547 or approximately **35%**.

28. **(B)**

It is projected that from 2010 to 2030, the number of farms will decrease by 5%. Since 5% of 2.2 million is 110,000, the number of farms in 2030 will be approximately 2,200,000 – 110,000 = 2,090,000 = 2.09 million. From 1990 to 2010, the average size of a farm decreased by 42 acres from 460 acres to 418 acres, and 42 ÷ 460 = 0.091 = 9.1%. If from 2010 to 2030 the average size of a farm again decreases by 9.1%, there will be a decrease of 0.091 × 418 = 38 acres, bringing the average size to 418 – 38 = 380 acres. Finally, the total farm acreage in 2030 in millions of acres is projected to be about 2.09 × 380 = 794 ≈ **800**.

29. **(C)**

The method we use to convert the given equation, $x^2 + 2x + y^2 - 4y + 1 = 0$, into the standard form for a circle, $(x - h)^2 + (y - k)^2 = r^2$, is completing the square.

$$x^2 + 2x + y^2 - 4y + 1 = 0$$
$$(x^2 + 2x) + (y^2 - 4y) = -1$$
$$(x^2 + 2x + \underline{1}) + (y^2 - 4y + \underline{4}) = -1 + \underline{1} + \underline{4} = 4$$
$$(x^2 + \underline{1})^2 + (y^2 - 2)^2 = 2^2$$

So the center of the circle, (h, k), is the point $(-1, 2)$ and the radius, r, is 2. Finally, $h + k + r = -1 + 2 + 2 = 3$.

30. **(C)**

The formula for the area of a parallelogram is $A = bh$. Sketch the parallelogram and draw the height.

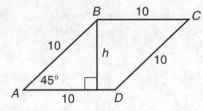

To find h, use the sine ratio:

$$\sin 45° = \frac{h}{10} \Rightarrow h = 10\sin 45° = 10(0.707) = 7.07$$

An alternative method of finding h is to use the fact that in a 45-45-90 right triangle, the length of each leg is equal to the length of the hypotenuse divided by $\sqrt{2}$: $h = \frac{10}{\sqrt{2}} = 7.07$.

Either way, $h = 7.07$ and the area of the parallelogram is:

$$A = bh = 10(7.07) = \mathbf{70.7}$$

31. **37.5**

First set up a proportion to determine the distance between Hauppauge and Riverhead:

$$\frac{1 \text{ inch}}{20 \text{ miles}} = \frac{1.25 \text{ inches}}{x \text{ miles}}$$

So $x = (1.25)(20) = 25$. Traveling at 40 miles per hour, it takes $\frac{25}{40} = \frac{5}{8}$ of an hour to drive 25 miles. Finally, $\frac{5}{8}$ of an hour is equal to $\frac{5}{8}(60 \text{ minutes})$ = **37.5** minutes.

32. **6.8**

Since Michelle took 31.5 minutes to run the 3 miles from the 12-mile marker to the 15-mile marker, she was running at the constant rate of 1 mile every 10.5 minutes ($31.5 \div 3 = 10.5$). Michelle took 54.6 minutes (36 seconds = $36 \div 60 = 0.6$ minutes) to run from where her friend was standing to the 12-mile marker. So that distance was 54.6 minutes ÷ 10.5 minutes per mile = 5.2 miles.

Her friend was 5.2 miles from the 12-mile marker, and so was $12 - 5.2 = $ **6.8** miles from the starting line.

33. **3744**

Use a weighted average:

$$\frac{12(3,100) + 24(3,800) + 14(4,200)}{(12 + 24 + 14)} = \frac{187,200}{50} = \textbf{3,744}$$

34. **8190**

There are $26 \times 26 \times 9 = 6,084$ PICs with two letters and one digit, and there are $26 \times 9 \times 9 = 2,106$ PICs with one letter and two digits, for a total of $6,084 + 2,106 = \textbf{8,190}$.

35. $\dfrac{3}{2}$ **or 1.5**

The formula for the volume of a pyramid with a rectangular base is $V = \frac{1}{3}lwh$, where l and w are the length and width of the rectangle, respectively, and where h is the height of the pyramid. (Remember that this fact is given to you on the first page of each math section.)

The base of pyramid 1 is a 2 by 3 rectangle whose area is $(2)(3) = 6$.

The base of pyramid 2 is a square of side 3 whose area is $3^2 = 9$. If h_1 and h_2 represent the two heights, then:

$$\frac{1}{3}(6)h_1 = \frac{1}{3}(9)h_2 \Rightarrow 2h_1 = 3h_2 \Rightarrow \frac{h_1}{h_2} = \frac{3}{2}$$

36. **129**

Let c, d, and e represent the value of one Canadian dollar, one U.S. dollar, and one euro, respectively. Since $c = .68e$, we have that $e = \dfrac{c}{.68}$. Then we have:

$$d = .88e = .88\left(\frac{c}{.68}\right) \Rightarrow d = \left(\frac{.88}{.68}\right)c = 1.294c$$

So, one U.S. dollar could have purchased 1.294 Canadian dollars, and 100 U.S. dollars could have purchased 129.40, or approximately **129** Canadian dollars.

37. **54**

- 60 miles per hour = 60 miles per 60 minutes = 1 mile per 1 minute. Driving at 60 miles per hour, Ed takes 6.3 minutes to drive those 6.3 miles.

- 70 miles per hour = 70 miles per 60 minutes = $\dfrac{7}{6}$ mile per 1 minute.

  Driving at 70 miles per hour, Ed would take
  $6.3 \div \dfrac{7}{6} = 6.3 \times \dfrac{6}{7} = 0.9 \times 6 = 5.4$ minutes to drive those 6.3 miles.

- So Ed would take 6.3 – 5.4 = 0.9 minutes less to drive those 6.3 miles at 70 miles per hour.

- Finally, 0.9 minutes = 0.9 × 60 seconds = **54** seconds.

38. **37**

- 6.3 miles per day × 240 days = 1,512 miles.
- At 60 miles per hour, Ed used 1,512 ÷ 24.3 = 62.222 gallons of gasoline, which cost 62.222 × \$3.50 = \$217.78.
- At 70 miles per hour, Ed would have used 1,512 ÷ 20.8 = 72.692 gallons of gasoline, which would have cost 72.692 × \$3.50 = \$254.42.
- So traveling at 70 miles per hour instead of 60 miles per hour would have cost Ed \$254.42 – \$217.78 = \$36.64 more, which to the nearest dollar is **\$37**.

SAT Essay Scoring

SAT Essay Scoring Rubric

	Score: 4
Reading	Excellent: The essay shows excellent understanding of the source. The essay shows an understanding of the source's main argument and key details and a firm grasp of how they are interconnected, demonstrating clear comprehension of the source. The essay does not misinterpret or misrepresent the source. The essay skillfully uses source evidence, such as direct quotations and rephrasing, representing a thorough comprehension of the source.
Analysis	Excellent: The essay gives excellent analysis of the source and shows clear understanding of what the assignment requires. The essay gives a complete, highly thoughtful analysis of the author's use of reasoning, evidence, rhetoric, and/or other argumentative elements the student has chosen to highlight. The essay has appropriate, adequate, and skillfully chosen support for its analysis. The essay focuses on the most important parts of the source in responding to the prompt.
Writing	Excellent: The essay is focused and shows an excellent grasp of the English language. The essay has a clear thesis. The essay has a well-executed introduction and conclusion. The essay shows a clear and well-crafted progression of thoughts both within paragraphs and in the essay as a whole. The essay has a wide range of sentence structures. The essay consistently shows precise choice of words. The essay is formal and objective in its style and tone. The essay demonstrates a firm grasp of the rules of standard English and has very few to no errors.
	Score: 3
Reading	Skillful: The essay shows effective understanding of the source. The essay shows an understanding of the source's main argument and key details. The essay is free of major misinterpretations and/or misrepresentations of the source. The essay uses appropriate source evidence, such as direct quotations and rephrasing, representing comprehension of the source.
Analysis	Skillful: The essay gives effective analysis of the source and shows an understanding of what the assignment requires. The essay decently analyzes the author's use of reasoning, evidence, rhetoric, and/or other argumentative elements the student has chosen to highlight. The essay has appropriate and adequate support for its analysis. The essay focuses primarily on the most important parts of the source in responding to the prompt.

Score: 3	
Writing	Skillful: The essay is mostly focused and shows an effective grasp of the English language. The essay has a thesis, either explicit or implicit. The essay has an effective introduction and conclusion. The essay has a clear progression of thoughts both within paragraphs and in the essay as a whole. The essay has an assortment of sentence structures. The essay shows some precise choice of words. The essay is formal and objective in its style and tone. The essay demonstrates a grasp of the rules of standard English and has very few significant errors that interfere with the writer's argument.

Score: 2	
Reading	Limited: The essay shows some understanding of the source. The essay shows an understanding of the source's main argument, but not of key details. The essay may have some misinterpretations and/or misrepresentations of the source. The essay gives only partial evidence from the source, showing limited comprehension of the source.
Analysis	Limited: The essay gives partial analysis of the source and shows only limited understanding of what the assignment requires. The essay tries to show how the author uses reasoning, evidence, rhetoric, and/or other argumentative elements the student has chosen to highlight, but only states rather than analyzes their importance, or at least one part of the essay's analysis is unsupported by the source. The essay has little or no justification for its argument. The essay may lack attention to those elements of the source that are most pertinent to responding to the prompt.
Writing	Limited: The essay is mostly not cohesive and shows an ineffective grasp of the English language. The essay may not have a thesis, or may diverge from the thesis at some point in the essay's development. The essay may have an unsuccessful introduction and/or conclusion. The essay may show progression of thoughts within the paragraphs, but not in the essay as a whole. The essay is relatively uniform in its sentence structures. The essay shows imprecise and possibly repetitive choice of words. The essay may be more casual and subjective in style and tone. The essay demonstrates a weaker grasp of the rules of standard English and does have errors that interfere with the writer's argument.

Score: 1	
Reading	Insufficient: The essay shows virtually no understanding of the source. The essay is unsuccessful in showing an understanding of the source's main argument. It may refer to some details from the text, but it does so without tying them to the source's main argument. The essay has many misinterpretations and/or misrepresentations of the source. The essay gives virtually no evidence from the source, showing very poor comprehension of the source.
Analysis	Insufficient: The essay gives little to no accurate analysis of the source and shows poor understanding of what the assignment requires. The essay may show how the author uses reasoning, evidence, rhetoric, and/or other argumentative elements that the student has chosen to highlight but does so without analysis. Or many parts of the essay's analysis are unsupported by the source. The support given for points in the essay's argument are largely unsupported or off-topic. The essay may not attend to the elements of the source that are pertinent to responding to the prompt. Or the essay gives no explicit analysis, perhaps only resorting to summary statements.
Writing	Insufficient: The essay is not cohesive and does not demonstrate skill in the English language. The essay may not have a thesis. The essay does not have a clear introduction and conclusion. The essay does not have a clear progression of thoughts. The essay is quite uniform and even repetitive in sentence structure. The essay shows poor and possibly inaccurate word choice. The essay is likely casual and subjective in style and tone. The essay shows a poor grasp of the rules of standard English and may have many errors that interfere with the writer's argument.

Top-Scoring Sample Student Response

In the passage, "A Lesson on Commas," the author is presented with an off-topic question from one of her students in regards to why she chooses to write. When faced with a crossroads on whether to continue on with her planned lesson, or go off on a tangent and respond to the student's question, the teacher uses the opportunity to explain why creativity must be taught in the classroom.

As the author looks around the room and notices that her own lesson may be lacking in creativity, specifically in regards to "the abridged somnolence" of the students "in the farthest row," she realizes that she has an opportunity to seize the moment and further explain why this is so important. She first looks to begin her argument by engaging the students with a creative response—Why does one listen to music? Or dance? Or look to the stars? And then goes on to state her belief in regards to the importance of creativity in that it is "the most essential ingredient of erudition, expression, and future success," in order to make an impactful statement to catch her students' attention.

Her next focus is to debunk the concept that the term "creativity" is only applicable to art. To support her belief that creativity "is not reserved for the Picassos, the Bachs, or the Austens," she identifies that it is something that is rooted within all of us, which she bolsters by asking the class to think about the "sublime imagination" of any child that they have ever met. Furthermore, she identifies that creativity is used in every walk of life, as it is the primary driver behind not just art, but also "every new electronic, and every scientific discovery." Statements such as these help to connect students that might not see themselves as "artistic" to the fact that "creativity" is still relevant to them.

Mrs. Jenson then explains the significance that creativity holds, which she does by asking her students a simple question about their future. While alluding to the idea that everyone would prefer a "challenging" job over a "routine" one, she quotes a well-known source, LinkedIn, on the fact that "not being challenged . . . is at the top of the list for workplace dissatisfaction" in order to add validity to her argument. When tied together with the fact that "hating their jobs" is the "number one reason for unhappiness in adults," she is able to make the greater connection between how one's work-life impacts their overall well being.

However, this alone does not explain how creativity directly ties in with feeling challenged at the workplace. While acknowledging that it is easier to see how creativity is used by some of the world's top minds, in fields such as medicine and engineering, she uses a two-step process in order to bring this together for those that may end up in less notable areas. The first is by referencing creativity in a "Google" sense, undoubtedly a concept that students are familiar with. By breaking down the meaning of creativity to its most general terms, "generation and contemplation of new ideas to create something perceived as valuable," we can think of it as something that can be used in almost any setting. And when applied in the context of a working environment, creativity can therefore be thought of in terms of our "problem-solving and critical thinking" abilities, which in turn helps with our "efficiency, diversification, and job security." In this sense, she is explaining how one must use creativity in order to help make their job more challenging, which will in turn help improve their overall happiness in their adult life.

Having stated her belief in the importance of creativity, providing support for how it is relevant for everyone to practice, and making the connection between it, work, and a healthy sense of self-worth, the author then addresses how this can be taught in school. Whether it be by "encouraging questioning and debate" to get students to think about "the why's and how's," "identifying problems and brainstorming solutions" to help students determine "what's good, what's bad and what can be improved," or by "inspiring alternative problem-solving" to enable students to consider the "what-ifs," she identifies many ways to help foster creativity. And because of her aforementioned statements regarding the importance of creative thinking, her conclusion serves to make a sound argument for the importance of actively teaching creativity in schools.

ANSWER SHEET—TEST 2

Section 1: Reading

1. Ⓐ Ⓑ Ⓒ Ⓓ
2. Ⓐ Ⓑ Ⓒ Ⓓ
3. Ⓐ Ⓑ Ⓒ Ⓓ
4. Ⓐ Ⓑ Ⓒ Ⓓ
5. Ⓐ Ⓑ Ⓒ Ⓓ
6. Ⓐ Ⓑ Ⓒ Ⓓ
7. Ⓐ Ⓑ Ⓒ Ⓓ
8. Ⓐ Ⓑ Ⓒ Ⓓ
9. Ⓐ Ⓑ Ⓒ Ⓓ
10. Ⓐ Ⓑ Ⓒ Ⓓ
11. Ⓐ Ⓑ Ⓒ Ⓓ
12. Ⓐ Ⓑ Ⓒ Ⓓ
13. Ⓐ Ⓑ Ⓒ Ⓓ
14. Ⓐ Ⓑ Ⓒ Ⓓ
15. Ⓐ Ⓑ Ⓒ Ⓓ
16. Ⓐ Ⓑ Ⓒ Ⓓ
17. Ⓐ Ⓑ Ⓒ Ⓓ
18. Ⓐ Ⓑ Ⓒ Ⓓ

19. Ⓐ Ⓑ Ⓒ Ⓓ
20. Ⓐ Ⓑ Ⓒ Ⓓ
21. Ⓐ Ⓑ Ⓒ Ⓓ
22. Ⓐ Ⓑ Ⓒ Ⓓ
23. Ⓐ Ⓑ Ⓒ Ⓓ
24. Ⓐ Ⓑ Ⓒ Ⓓ
25. Ⓐ Ⓑ Ⓒ Ⓓ
26. Ⓐ Ⓑ Ⓒ Ⓓ
27. Ⓐ Ⓑ Ⓒ Ⓓ
28. Ⓐ Ⓑ Ⓒ Ⓓ
29. Ⓐ Ⓑ Ⓒ Ⓓ
30. Ⓐ Ⓑ Ⓒ Ⓓ
31. Ⓐ Ⓑ Ⓒ Ⓓ
32. Ⓐ Ⓑ Ⓒ Ⓓ
33. Ⓐ Ⓑ Ⓒ Ⓓ
34. Ⓐ Ⓑ Ⓒ Ⓓ
35. Ⓐ Ⓑ Ⓒ Ⓓ
36. Ⓐ Ⓑ Ⓒ Ⓓ

37. Ⓐ Ⓑ Ⓒ Ⓓ
38. Ⓐ Ⓑ Ⓒ Ⓓ
39. Ⓐ Ⓑ Ⓒ Ⓓ
40. Ⓐ Ⓑ Ⓒ Ⓓ
41. Ⓐ Ⓑ Ⓒ Ⓓ
42. Ⓐ Ⓑ Ⓒ Ⓓ
43. Ⓐ Ⓑ Ⓒ Ⓓ
44. Ⓐ Ⓑ Ⓒ Ⓓ
45. Ⓐ Ⓑ Ⓒ Ⓓ
46. Ⓐ Ⓑ Ⓒ Ⓓ
47. Ⓐ Ⓑ Ⓒ Ⓓ
48. Ⓐ Ⓑ Ⓒ Ⓓ
49. Ⓐ Ⓑ Ⓒ Ⓓ
50. Ⓐ Ⓑ Ⓒ Ⓓ
51. Ⓐ Ⓑ Ⓒ Ⓓ
52. Ⓐ Ⓑ Ⓒ Ⓓ

Section 2: Writing and Language

1. Ⓐ Ⓑ Ⓒ Ⓓ
2. Ⓐ Ⓑ Ⓒ Ⓓ
3. Ⓐ Ⓑ Ⓒ Ⓓ
4. Ⓐ Ⓑ Ⓒ Ⓓ
5. Ⓐ Ⓑ Ⓒ Ⓓ
6. Ⓐ Ⓑ Ⓒ Ⓓ
7. Ⓐ Ⓑ Ⓒ Ⓓ
8. Ⓐ Ⓑ Ⓒ Ⓓ
9. Ⓐ Ⓑ Ⓒ Ⓓ
10. Ⓐ Ⓑ Ⓒ Ⓓ
11. Ⓐ Ⓑ Ⓒ Ⓓ
12. Ⓐ Ⓑ Ⓒ Ⓓ
13. Ⓐ Ⓑ Ⓒ Ⓓ
14. Ⓐ Ⓑ Ⓒ Ⓓ
15. Ⓐ Ⓑ Ⓒ Ⓓ

16. Ⓐ Ⓑ Ⓒ Ⓓ
17. Ⓐ Ⓑ Ⓒ Ⓓ
18. Ⓐ Ⓑ Ⓒ Ⓓ
19. Ⓐ Ⓑ Ⓒ Ⓓ
20. Ⓐ Ⓑ Ⓒ Ⓓ
21. Ⓐ Ⓑ Ⓒ Ⓓ
22. Ⓐ Ⓑ Ⓒ Ⓓ
23. Ⓐ Ⓑ Ⓒ Ⓓ
24. Ⓐ Ⓑ Ⓒ Ⓓ
25. Ⓐ Ⓑ Ⓒ Ⓓ
26. Ⓐ Ⓑ Ⓒ Ⓓ
27. Ⓐ Ⓑ Ⓒ Ⓓ
28. Ⓐ Ⓑ Ⓒ Ⓓ
29. Ⓐ Ⓑ Ⓒ Ⓓ
30. Ⓐ Ⓑ Ⓒ Ⓓ

31. Ⓐ Ⓑ Ⓒ Ⓓ
32. Ⓐ Ⓑ Ⓒ Ⓓ
33. Ⓐ Ⓑ Ⓒ Ⓓ
34. Ⓐ Ⓑ Ⓒ Ⓓ
35. Ⓐ Ⓑ Ⓒ Ⓓ
36. Ⓐ Ⓑ Ⓒ Ⓓ
37. Ⓐ Ⓑ Ⓒ Ⓓ
38. Ⓐ Ⓑ Ⓒ Ⓓ
39. Ⓐ Ⓑ Ⓒ Ⓓ
40. Ⓐ Ⓑ Ⓒ Ⓓ
41. Ⓐ Ⓑ Ⓒ Ⓓ
42. Ⓐ Ⓑ Ⓒ Ⓓ
43. Ⓐ Ⓑ Ⓒ Ⓓ
44. Ⓐ Ⓑ Ⓒ Ⓓ

Section 3: Math (No Calculator)

1. Ⓐ Ⓑ Ⓒ Ⓓ
2. Ⓐ Ⓑ Ⓒ Ⓓ
3. Ⓐ Ⓑ Ⓒ Ⓓ
4. Ⓐ Ⓑ Ⓒ Ⓓ
5. Ⓐ Ⓑ Ⓒ Ⓓ

6. Ⓐ Ⓑ Ⓒ Ⓓ
7. Ⓐ Ⓑ Ⓒ Ⓓ
8. Ⓐ Ⓑ Ⓒ Ⓓ
9. Ⓐ Ⓑ Ⓒ Ⓓ
10. Ⓐ Ⓑ Ⓒ Ⓓ

11. Ⓐ Ⓑ Ⓒ Ⓓ
12. Ⓐ Ⓑ Ⓒ Ⓓ
13. Ⓐ Ⓑ Ⓒ Ⓓ
14. Ⓐ Ⓑ Ⓒ Ⓓ
15. Ⓐ Ⓑ Ⓒ Ⓓ

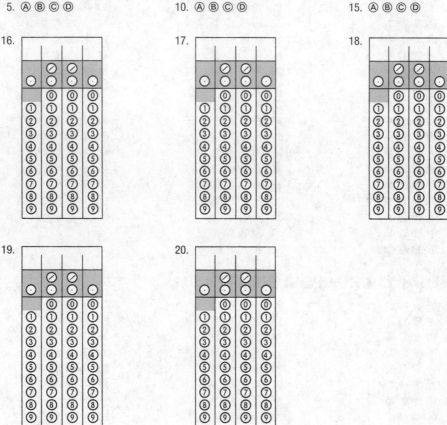

16.   17.   18.

19.   20.

Section 4: Math (Calculator)

1. Ⓐ Ⓑ Ⓒ Ⓓ
2. Ⓐ Ⓑ Ⓒ Ⓓ
3. Ⓐ Ⓑ Ⓒ Ⓓ
4. Ⓐ Ⓑ Ⓒ Ⓓ
5. Ⓐ Ⓑ Ⓒ Ⓓ
6. Ⓐ Ⓑ Ⓒ Ⓓ
7. Ⓐ Ⓑ Ⓒ Ⓓ
8. Ⓐ Ⓑ Ⓒ Ⓓ
9. Ⓐ Ⓑ Ⓒ Ⓓ
10. Ⓐ Ⓑ Ⓒ Ⓓ

11. Ⓐ Ⓑ Ⓒ Ⓓ
12. Ⓐ Ⓑ Ⓒ Ⓓ
13. Ⓐ Ⓑ Ⓒ Ⓓ
14. Ⓐ Ⓑ Ⓒ Ⓓ
15. Ⓐ Ⓑ Ⓒ Ⓓ
16. Ⓐ Ⓑ Ⓒ Ⓓ
17. Ⓐ Ⓑ Ⓒ Ⓓ
18. Ⓐ Ⓑ Ⓒ Ⓓ
19. Ⓐ Ⓑ Ⓒ Ⓓ
20. Ⓐ Ⓑ Ⓒ Ⓓ

21. Ⓐ Ⓑ Ⓒ Ⓓ
22. Ⓐ Ⓑ Ⓒ Ⓓ
23. Ⓐ Ⓑ Ⓒ Ⓓ
24. Ⓐ Ⓑ Ⓒ Ⓓ
25. Ⓐ Ⓑ Ⓒ Ⓓ
26. Ⓐ Ⓑ Ⓒ Ⓓ
27. Ⓐ Ⓑ Ⓒ Ⓓ
28. Ⓐ Ⓑ Ⓒ Ⓓ
29. Ⓐ Ⓑ Ⓒ Ⓓ
30. Ⓐ Ⓑ Ⓒ Ⓓ

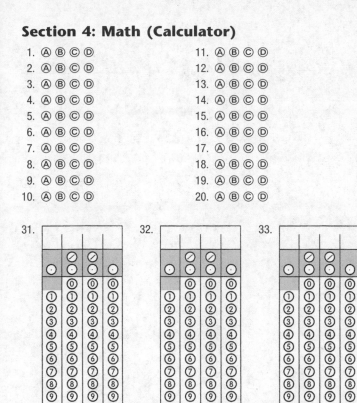

31. 32. 33. 34.

35. 36. 37. 38.

Essay

PLANNING PAGE

START YOUR ESSAY HERE

READING TEST

65 Minutes, 52 Questions

Turn to Section 1 of your answer sheet to answer the questions in this section.

> **Directions:** Following each of the passages (or pairs of passages) below are questions about the passage (or passages). Read each passage carefully. Then, select the best answer for each question based on what is stated in the passage (or passages) and in any graphics that may accompany the passage.

Questions 1–11 are based on the following passage.

The following passage is taken from Jane Austen's novel Persuasion. *In this excerpt we meet Sir Walter Elliot, father of the heroine.*

Vanity was the beginning and end of Sir Walter Elliot's character: vanity of person and of situation. He had been remarkably handsome in his youth, and at fifty-four was still a very fine man. Few women could think more of
Line their personal appearance than he did, nor could the valet of any new-made
(5) lord be more delighted with the place he held in society. He considered the blessing of beauty as inferior only to the blessing of a baronetcy; and the Sir Walter Elliot, who united these gifts, was the constant object of his warmest respect and devotion.

His good looks and his rank had one fair claim on his attachment, since
(10) to them he must have owed a wife of very superior character to anything deserved by his own. Lady Elliot had been an excellent woman, sensible and amiable, whose judgment and conduct, if they might be pardoned the youthful infatuation which made her Lady Elliot, had never required indulgence afterwards. She had humored, or softened, or concealed his
(15) failings, and promoted his real respectability for seventeen years; and though not the very happiest being in the world herself, had found enough in her duties, her friends, and her children, to attach her to life, and make it no matter of indifference to her when she was called on to quit them. Three girls, the two eldest sixteen and fourteen, was an awful legacy for a mother to
(20) bequeath, an awful charge rather, to confide to the authority and guidance of a conceited, silly father. She had, however, one very intimate friend, a sensible, deserving woman, who had been brought, by strong attachment to herself, to settle close by her, in the village of Kellynch; and on her kindness and advice Lady Elliot mainly relied for the best help and maintenance of the
(25) good principles and instruction which she had been anxiously giving her daughters.

This friend and Sir Walter did not marry, whatever might have been anticipated on that head by their acquaintance. Thirteen years had passed away since Lady Elliot's death, and they were still near neighbors and
(30)   intimate friends, and one remained a widower, the other a widow.

That Lady Russell, of steady age and character, and extremely well provided for, should have no thought of a second marriage, needs no apology to the public, which is rather apt to be unreasonably discontented when a woman *does* marry again, than when she does *not;* but Sir Walter's continuing
(35)   in singleness requires explanation. Be it known, then, that Sir Walter, like a good father (having met with one or two disappointments in very unreasonable applications), prided himself on remaining single for his dear daughters' sake. For one daughter, his eldest, he would really have given up anything which he had not been very much tempted to do. Elizabeth had
(40)   succeeded at sixteen to all that was possible of her mother's rights and consequence; and being very handsome, and very like himself, her influence had always been great, and they had gone on together most happily. His two other children were of very inferior value. Mary had acquired a little artificial importance by becoming Mrs. Charles Musgrove; but Anne, with an elegance
(45)   of mind and sweetness of character, which must have placed her high with any people of real understanding, was nobody with either father or sister; her word had no weight, her convenience was always to give way—she was only Anne.

1. The main purpose of the passage is to

   (A) provide an overview of the interrelationships of the members of a family.
   (B) point out some unfortunate personality defects in a main character.
   (C) explain the relationship between a main character and his amiable wife.
   (D) describe a main character and a major change in his life.

2. As used in line 2, "situation" most nearly means

   (A) position of employment.
   (B) physical surroundings.
   (C) state of affairs.
   (D) social standing.

3. Which choice best summarizes the first two paragraphs of the passage (lines 1–26)?

   (A) Even though the loss of his admirable wife devastates a character, he perseveres in caring for their young children.
   (B) A vain and foolish character is left to care for three daughters after the death of his sensible wife.
   (C) After seventeen years, a character who can no longer endure being married to a conceited fool abandons her family.
   (D) Largely prompted by a character's good looks, an otherwise intelligent woman enters into a misalliance.

4. Which action of Lady Elliot does the narrator view most critically?

   (A) Her concealment of Sir Walter's shortcomings
   (B) Her choice of an intimate friend
   (C) Her guidance of her three daughters
   (D) Her decision to marry Sir Walter

5. Which choice provides the best evidence for the answer to the previous question?

   (A) Lines 3–5 ("Few women . . . society")
   (B) Lines 11–14 ("Lady . . . afterwards")
   (C) Lines 14–18 ("She had . . . them")
   (D) Lines 18–21 ("Three . . . father")

6. It can most reasonably be inferred that over the years Lady Elliot was less than happy because of

   (A) her lack of personal beauty.
   (B) her separation from her most intimate friend.
   (C) the disparity between her character and that of her husband.
   (D) her inability to teach good principles to her young daughters.

7. As used in line 20, "charge" most nearly means

   (A) accusation.
   (B) responsibility.
   (C) official instruction.
   (D) headlong rush.

8. The narrator indicates that Lady Elliot's emotions regarding her approaching death were complicated by her

   (A) pious submissiveness to her fate.
   (B) anxieties over her daughters' prospects.
   (C) resentment of her husband's potential remarriage.
   (D) reluctance to face the realities of her situation.

9. Which choice provides the best evidence for the answer to the previous question?

   (A) Lines 14–18 ("She . . . quit them")
   (B) Lines 18–21 ("Three . . . father")
   (C) Lines 21–26 ("She . . . daughters")
   (D) Lines 27–30 ("This friend . . . widow")

10. The phrase "make it no matter of indifference to her when she was called on to quit them" (lines 17–18) is an example of

   (A) ironic understatement.
   (B) effusive sentiment.
   (C) metaphorical expression.
   (D) personification.

11. The "applications" made by Sir Walter (line 37) were most likely

   (A) professional.
   (B) insincere.
   (C) marital.
   (D) paternal.

Questions 12–22 are based on the following passage.

The following passage is taken from a book of popular history written in 1991.

The advantage of associating the birth of democracy with the Mayflower Compact is that it is easy to do so. The public loves a simple explanation, and none is simpler than the belief that on November 11, 1620—the day the *Line* compact was approved—a cornerstone of American democracy was laid.
(5) Certainly it makes it easier on schoolchildren. Marking the start of democracy in 1620 relieves students of the responsibility of knowing what happened in the hundred some years before, from the arrival of the Santa Maria to the landing of the Mayflower.

The compact, to be sure, demonstrated the Englishman's striking
(10) capacity for self-government. And in affirming the principle of majority rule, the Pilgrims showed how far they had come from the days when the king's whim was law, and nobody dared say otherwise.

But the emphasis on the compact is misplaced. Scholarly research in the last half-century indicates that the compact had nothing to do with the
(15) development of self-government in America. In truth, the Mayflower Compact was no more a cornerstone of American democracy than the Pilgrim hut was the foundation of American architecture. As Samuel Eliot Morrison so emphatically put it, American democracy "was not born in the cabin of the Mayflower."
(20) The Pilgrims indeed are miscast as the heroes of American democracy. They spurned democracy and would have been shocked to see themselves held up as its defenders. George Willison, regarded as one of the most careful students of the Pilgrims, states that "the merest glance at the history of Plymouth" shows that they were not democrats.
(25) The mythmakers would have us believe that even if the Pilgrims themselves weren't democratic, the Mayflower Compact itself was. But in fact the compact was expressly designed to curb freedom, not promote it. The Pilgrim governor and historian, William Bradford, from whom we have gotten nearly all of the information there is about the Pilgrims, frankly conceded as
(30) much. Bradford wrote that the purpose of the compact was to control renegades aboard the Mayflower who were threatening to go their own way when the ship reached land. Because the Pilgrims had decided to settle in an area outside the jurisdiction of their royal patent, some aboard the Mayflower had hinted that upon landing they would "use their owne libertie, for none had
(35) power to command them." Under the terms of the compact, they couldn't; the compact required all who lived in the colony to "promise all due submission and obedience" to it.

Furthermore, despite the compact's mention of majority rule, the Pilgrim fathers had no intention of turning over the colony's government to the
(40) people. Plymouth was to be ruled by the elite. And the elite wasn't bashful in the least about advancing its claims to superiority. When the Mayflower Compact was signed, the elite signed first. The second rank consisted of the

"goodmen." At the bottom of the list came four servants' names. No women or children signed.

(45)   Whether the compact was or was not actually hostile to the democratic spirit, it was deemed sufficiently hostile that during the Revolution, the Tories put it to use as "propaganda for the crown." The monarchists made much of the fact that the Pilgrims had chosen to establish an English-style government that placed power in the hands of a governor, not a cleric, and a governor

(50) who owed his allegiance not to the people or to a church but to "our dread Sovereign Lord King James." No one thought it significant that the authorities had adopted the principle of majority rule. Tory historian George Chalmers, in a work published in 1780, claimed the central meaning of the compact was the Pilgrims' recognition of the necessity of royal authority. This may have

(55) been not only a convenient argument, but a true one. It is at least as plausible as the belief that the compact stood for democracy.

Mayflower Passengers

■ First Rank ("The Elite") — Landed/Professional

■ Second Rank ("Goodmen") — Farmers

■ Servants

Male Adult

Male Minor

Female Adult

Female Minor

5   10   15   20   25   30   35   40

12. The author's attitude toward the general public can best be described as

(A) sympathetic.
(B) condescending.
(C) perplexed.
(D) hostile.

13. The purpose of the first paragraph (lines 1–8) is to

(A) present an elaborate speculation.
(B) develop a chronological summary.
(C) capture the reader's attention.
(D) provide a working hypothesis.

14. As used in line 5, "Marking" most nearly means

    (A) assessing.
    (B) forming.
    (C) designating.
    (D) manifesting.

15. In stating that "[t]he compact, to be sure, demonstrated the Englishman's striking capacity for self-government," the author

    (A) concedes a point.
    (B) invokes an expert.
    (C) offers a rationale.
    (D) rejects an assumption.

16. The Pilgrims' attitude toward the concept of democracy can best be described as

    (A) complete rejection.
    (B) qualified endorsement.
    (C) marked approbation.
    (D) objective neutrality.

17. As used in line 22, "held up" most nearly means

    (A) delayed.
    (B) cited.
    (C) waylaid.
    (D) carried.

18. According to the passage, the compact's primary purpose was to

    (A) establish legal authority within the colony.
    (B) banish non-Pilgrims from the settlement.
    (C) eradicate heretical thinking among the settlers.
    (D) protect each individual's civil rights.

19. Which choice provides the best evidence for the answer to the previous question?

    (A) Lines 25–26 ("The mythmakers . . . itself was")
    (B) Lines 26–30 ("But in fact . . . as much")
    (C) Lines 32–37 ("Because the Pilgrims . . . to it")
    (D) Lines 38–40 ("Furthermore . . . elite")

20. In the passage, the details about the signers of the Mayflower Compact are used to emphasize

    (A) the Pilgrims' respect for the social hierarchy.
    (B) the inclusion of servants among those signing.
    (C) the great variety of social classes aboard.
    (D) the lack of any provision for minority rule.

21. Which choice provides the best evidence for the answer to the previous question?

    (A) Lines 27–30 ("The Pilgrim . . . much")
    (B) Lines 35–37 ("Under . . . it")
    (C) Lines 38–40 ("Furthermore . . . people")
    (D) Lines 41–44 ("When . . . signed")

22. Which category of passenger is least represented on the accompanying graph?

    (A) Male adult servants
    (B) Female adult servants
    (C) Male minor farmers
    (D) Female minor farmers

Questions 23–32 are based on the following passage.

The following passage is based on Emily Underwood's "Sleep: The Brain's House-keeper?", published in Science magazine in 2013.

Every night since we first evolved, humans have made what might be considered a baffling, dangerous mistake. Despite the once-prevalent threat of being eaten by predators and the loss of valuable time for gathering food,
Line accumulating wealth, or reproducing, we go to sleep. Scientists have long
(5) speculated and argued about why we devote roughly a third of our lives to sleep, but with little concrete data to support any particular theory. Now, new evidence has refreshed a long-held hypothesis: During sleep, the brain cleans itself.

Most physiologists agree that sleep serves many different purposes,
(10) ranging from memory consolidation to the regulation of metabolism and the immune system. While the purposes of biological functions such as breathing and eating are easy to understand, scientists have never agreed on any such original purpose for sleeping. A new study by Maiken Nedergaard provides what sleep researcher Charles Czeisler calls the "first direct experimental
(15) evidence at the molecular level" for what could be sleep's basic purpose: It clears the brain of toxic metabolic byproducts. The new work confirms a long-standing hypothesis that sleep promotes recovery—something is paid back or cleaned out. It builds on Nedergaard's recent discovery of a network of microscopic, fluid-filled channels that clear toxins from the brain, much as
(20) the lymphatic system clears out metabolic waste products from the rest of the body. Instead of carrying lymph, this system transports waste-laden cerebrospinal fluid (CSF). Before the discovery of this "glymphatic" system, as Nedergaard has dubbed it, the brain's only known method for disposing of cellular waste was breaking it down and recycling it within individual cells,
(25) she says.

The earlier study showed that glia, the brain's non-neuronal cells, control the flow of CSF through channels in their cell membranes. "If we delete the channels in glial cells, the flow almost stops," Nedergaard says. Because the transport of fluid across cell membranes requires a lot of energy, Nedergaard
(30) and her team had a hunch that the brain would not be able both to clean the brain and to process sensory information at the same time. Therefore, they decided to test whether the activity of the glymphatic system changed during sleep. Lulu Xie, the new study's first author, spent the next two years training mice to relax and fall asleep on a two-photon microscope, which can image
(35) the movement of dye through living tissue.

Once Xie was sure the mice were asleep by checking their EEG (electroencephalogram) brain activity, she injected a green dye into their CSF through a catheter-like device in their necks. After half an hour, she awakened them by touching their tails and injected a red dye that the two-photon
(40) microscope could easily distinguish from the green. By tracking the movements of red and green dye throughout the brain, the team found that

large amounts of CSF flowed into the brain during sleep, but not during the
waking state, Nedergaard reports.

A comparison of the volume of space between nerve cells while the mice
(45) were awake and asleep revealed that the glial channels carrying CSF
expanded by 60% when the mice were asleep. The team also injected labeled
β amyloid proteins into the brains of sleeping mice and wakeful mice and
found that during sleep, CSF cleared away this "dirt" outside of the cells
twice as quickly—"like a dishwasher," Nedergaard says. Such proteins can
(50) aggregate as pathogenic plaques outside cells and are associated with
Alzheimer's disease, she says.

Many neurological diseases—from Alzheimer's disease to stroke and
dementia—are associated with sleep disturbances. The study suggests that
lack of sleep could have a causal role, by allowing the byproducts to build up
(55) and cause brain damage.

New scientific results often raise new questions, and this study of sleep
is no exception to the rule. Does the need to remove waste products actively
regulate sleep? In other words, does the buildup of metabolic byproducts
make us sleepy? Is this cleaning function of sleep shared across species? No
(60) one role of sleep rules out all others, and sleep presumably has many
functions, just as the weekend is variously for shopping, socializing, and
cleaning the house. It is possible that different species have evolved different
functions of sleep to suit their different habitats.

23. The main purpose of the passage is to

(A) explain why humans sleep more than other mammals.
(B) prove that sleep is in fact beneficial to human beings.
(C) discuss recent experiments regarding brain activity during sleep.
(D) clarify the workings of the lymphatic system.

24. It may most reasonably be inferred from the passage that one function of the
lymphatic system is the

(A) relay of sensory information.
(B) regulation of temperature.
(C) transport of cerebrospinal fluid.
(D) drainage of waste.

25. Which choice provides the best evidence for the answer to the previous
question?

(A) Lines 13–16 ("A new . . . byproducts")
(B) Lines 16–18 ("The new . . . cleaned out")
(C) Lines 18–21 ("It builds . . . body")
(D) Lines 22–25 ("Before . . . says")

26. The new experiment described indicates that the purpose of sleep is to

    (A) build up pathogenic plaques outside cells.
    (B) replenish the body's energy stores.
    (C) clean the brain and provide other unknown benefits.
    (D) reduce the buildup of electrical signals.

27. As used in line 17, "promotes" most nearly means

    (A) exchanges a pawn.
    (B) raises in rank.
    (C) fosters.
    (D) publicizes.

28. Why did the scientists consider the fact that glial channels expanded by 60 percent a significant result?

    (A) It suggested that the brain expanded during sleep.
    (B) It suggested that the flow of cerebrospinal fluid increased during sleep.
    (C) It suggested that other organs expanded simultaneously in similar fashion.
    (D) It suggested a peak in the processing of sensory information.

29. As used in line 40, "distinguish" most nearly means

    (A) characterize.
    (B) tell apart.
    (C) make prominent.
    (D) discern.

30. Which statement about the function of Xie's injection of two different colored dyes into the mice's cerebrospinal fluid is best supported by the passage?

    (A) It enabled the researchers to differentiate between different types of molecules in the cerebrospinal fluid.
    (B) It enabled the researchers to differentiate cerebrospinal fluid that entered the brain during a sleeping state from cerebrospinal fluid that entered the brain during a wakeful state.
    (C) It enabled the researchers to differentiate between cerebrospinal fluid and lymph.
    (D) It enabled the researchers to differentiate between fluids that cleared out waste products from the lymphatic system and fluids that cleared out waste products from the glymphatic system.

31. Which choice provides the best evidence for the answer to the previous question?

    (A) Lines 33–35 ("Lulu Xie . . . living tissue")
    (B) Lines 38–40 ("After half an hour . . . green")
    (C) Lines 40–43 ("By tracking . . . reports")
    (D) Lines 44–46 ("A comparison . . . asleep")

32. The reference to common weekend activities in lines 61–62 ("the weekend . . . cleaning the house") primarily serves to

    (A) emphasize the importance of leisure time for mental and physical health.
    (B) determine which activities provide the most benefits.
    (C) illustrate by analogy the likely diversity of the roles played by sleep.
    (D) demonstrate the fundamental similarity between recreation and sleep.

Questions 33–42 are based on the following passages.

The first passage is taken from Sojourner Truth's 1851 speech before the Women's Convention in Akron, Ohio. The second passage is adapted from a speech made by Frederick Douglass in 1888, some 23 years after the end of the Civil War.

Passage 1

Well, children, where there is so much racket there must be something out of kilter. I think that 'twixt the negroes of the South and the women at the North, all talking about rights, the white men will be in a fix pretty soon. But *Line* what's all this here talking about?
(5) That man over there says that women need to be helped into carriages, and lifted over ditches, and to have the best place everywhere. Nobody ever helps me into carriages, or over mud-puddles, or gives me any best place! And ain't I a woman? Look at me! Look at my arm! I have ploughed and planted, and gathered into barns, and no man could head me! And ain't I a
(10) woman? I could work as much and eat as much as a man—when I could get it—and bear the lash as well! And ain't I a woman? I have borne thirteen children, and seen most all sold off to slavery, and when I cried out with my mother's grief, none but Jesus heard me! And ain't I a woman?
Then they talk about this thing in the head; what's this they call it?
(15) [Member of audience whispers, "intellect."] That's it, honey. What's that got to do with women's rights or negroes' rights? If my cup won't hold but a pint, and yours holds a quart, wouldn't you be mean not to let me have my little half measure full?
Then that little man in black there, he says women can't have as much
(20) rights as men, 'cause Christ wasn't a woman! Where did your Christ come from? Where did your Christ come from? From God and a woman! Man had nothing to do with Him.
If the first woman God ever made was strong enough to turn the world upside down all alone, these women together ought to be able to turn it back,
(25) and get it right side up again! And now they is asking to do it, the men better let them.
Obliged to you for hearing me, and now old Sojourner ain't got nothing more to say.

Passage 2

Long years ago Henry Clay said, on the floor of the American Senate, "I
(30) know there is a visionary dogma that man cannot hold property in man," and, with a brow of defiance, he said, "That is property which the law makes property. Two hundred years of legislation has sanctioned and sanctified Negro slaves as property." But neither the power of time nor the might of legislation has been able to keep life in that stupendous barbarism. The
(35) universality of man's rule over woman is another factor in the resistance to

the woman-suffrage movement. We are pointed to the fact that men have not only always ruled over women, but that they do so rule everywhere, and they easily think that a thing that is done everywhere must be right. Though the fallacy of this reasoning is too transparent to need refutation, it still exerts a
(40) powerful influence. Even our good Brother Jasper yet believes, with the ancient Church, that the sun "do move," notwithstanding all the astronomers of the world are against him. One year ago I stood on the Pincio in Rome and witnessed the unveiling of the statue of Galileo. . . . One or two priests passed the statue with averted eyes, but the great truths of the solar system
(45) were not angry at the sight, and the same will be true when woman shall be clothed, as she will yet be, with all the rights of American citizenship. . . . [W]hatever the future may have in store for us, one thing is certain—this new revolution in human thought will never go backward. When a great truth once gets abroad in the world, no power on earth can imprison it, or prescribe its
(50) limits, or suppress it. It is bound to go on till it becomes the thought of the world. Such a truth is woman's right to equal liberty with man.

33. The author of Passage 1 demonstrates that women are not frail and in need of protection by

(A) using the example of Northern women who have fought for the right to vote.
(B) emphasizing the importance of their role as mothers.
(C) pointing out that women undergo the rigors of childbearing.
(D) describing her work and treatment as a slave.

34. Which choice provides the best evidence for the answer to the previous question?

(A) Lines 2–3 ("I think . . . pretty soon")
(B) Lines 8–11 ("Look at . . . as well")
(C) Lines 16–18 ("If my cup . . . measure full")
(D) Lines 23–25 ("If the first . . . up again")

35. As used in line 3, "fix" most nearly means

(A) repair.
(B) rut.
(C) battle.
(D) predicament.

36. The author of Passage 2 predicts that women will ultimately achieve equal rights because

(A) the truth cannot be held back.
(B) the Church supports it.
(C) they are American citizens.
(D) people adapt to revolutionary ideas.

37. Which choice provides the best evidence for the answer to the previous question?

    (A) Lines 34–36 ("The universality . . . movement")
    (B) Lines 38–40 ("Though the . . . influence")
    (C) Lines 43–46 ("One or two . . . citizenship")
    (D) Lines 48–50 ("When a great . . . suppress it")

38. As used in line 32, "sanctioned" most nearly means

    (A) authorized.
    (B) penalized.
    (C) prohibited.
    (D) praised.

39. The reference to "the unveiling of the statue of Galileo" in Rome (line 43) serves mainly to

    (A) introduce the scientific basis for the equality of women.
    (B) demonstrate that truth always triumphs despite powerful opposition.
    (C) argue that women's rights are an important issue around the world.
    (D) prove that the teachings of the Church are not always correct.

40. Which choice best states the relationship between the two passages?

    (A) Passage 2 attacks the political position that Passage 1 strongly advocates.
    (B) Passage 2 argues that the political position advocated in Passage 1 will inevitably succeed.
    (C) Passage 2 supports the political position that Passage 1 strongly advocates but cautions against moving too quickly.
    (D) Passage 2 demonstrates that the political position advocated in Passage 1 has gained increased support.

41. How would the author of Passage 2 most likely react to the arguments of "that man over there," referred to in line 5, Passage 1?

    (A) He would agree with the man's arguments about women's need for support and protection.
    (B) He would disagree with the man, but also not fully agree with the author of Passage 1.
    (C) He would disagree with and be angered by the man's arguments.
    (D) He would liken the man's arguments to those of the Church when it rejected Galileo's observation that the Earth revolves around the sun.

42. Where does Passage 2 answer what happened as a result of "the negroes of the South . . . talking about rights" (lines 2–3)?

    (A) Lines 32–33 ("Two hundred . . . property")
    (B) Lines 33–34 ("But neither . . . barbarism")
    (C) Lines 38–40 ("Though the . . . influence")
    (D) Lines 47–48 ("[W]hatever . . . backward")

Questions 43–52 are based on the following passage.

The following passage is taken from "Dinosaur metabolism neither hot nor cold, but just right," *an article by Michael Balter that appeared in the 13 June 2014 issue of* Science.

Call it the Goldilocks solution. Paleontologists have struggled for 50 years to determine whether dinosaurs were cold-blooded ectotherms like today's reptiles, making little effort to control their body temperatures, or warm-

Line blooded endotherms, like most modern mammals and birds, which keep their
(5) body temperatures at a constant, relatively high set point. The answer greatly influences our view of dinosaurs, as endotherms tend to be more active and faster growing.

A recent study concludes that dinosaur blood ran neither cold nor hot but something in between. Examining growth and metabolic rates of nearly 400
(10) living and extinct animals, the researchers conclude that dinosaurs, like a handful of modern creatures including tuna and the echidna, belonged to an intermediate group that can raise their body temperature but don't keep it at a specific level. The researchers christen these creatures mesotherms.

Establishing a new metabolic category is "audacious," admits lead author
(15) John Grady, an evolutionary biologist at the University of New Mexico, Albuquerque. And some still think dinosaurs were "just fast-growing ectotherms," as vertebrate physiologist Frank Paladino of Indiana University–Purdue University Fort Wayne insists. But paleobiologist Gregory Erickson of Florida State University in Tallahassee calls the paper "a remarkably
(20) integrative, landmark study" that transforms our view of the great beasts.

Metabolic Middle Ground
Dinosaurs and some living animals are mesotherms, raising but not maintaining their body temperature.

Ectotherms

Endotherms

Metabolic rate

For the first 150 years after their discovery, dinosaurs were considered ectotherms like today's reptiles. Ectothermy makes some sense: "It requires much less energy from the environment," explains Roger Seymour, a zoologist at the University of Adelaide in Australia. But it has drawbacks, too:
(25) "The animal cannot feed in cold conditions and has a much more limited capacity for sustained, powerful activity, even if warmed by the sun," he says.

Beginning in the late 1960s, researchers put forward the then-heretical idea of dinosaurs as endotherms, and evidence for this has accumulated. Annual growth rings in dinosaur bones suggest fast, energy-hungry
(30) developmental rates. Birdlike air sacs may have boosted their respiratory efficiency, suggesting rapid movements. And isotopic data from fossils suggest higher body temperatures (*Science*, 22 July 2011, p. 443).

Giant endotherms pose their own puzzles, however, such as the huge quantities of food needed to sustain them. An endothermic Tyrannosaurus rex
(35) "would probably have starved to death," Grady says.

He and his colleagues tackled the problem by examining the relationship between an animal's growth rate—how fast it becomes a full-sized adult—and its resting metabolic rate (RMR), a measure of energy expenditure. Earlier studies, based on limited data, had suggested that growth rates scale with
(40) metabolic rates. That is, the more energy an animal can expend, the faster it can grow and the bigger it can get. The team pulled together updated data on 381 living and extinct vertebrates, including 21 species of dinosaurs, and developed mathematical equations that predict the relationship between metabolic rate, growth rate, and body size in living animals.
(45) These equations show that ectotherms and endotherms fall into distinct clusters when growth rate is plotted against metabolic rate. High-energy endotherms grow fast and have high metabolic rates, whereas ectotherms have low values of both. Those two categories include most living species, but the team found that a handful, such as fast-swimming sharks, tuna,
(50) reptiles such as large sea turtles, and a few odd mammals like the echidna, fall into an in-between state: mesothermy. These animals use their metabolism to raise their body temperatures, but do not "defend" a set temperature.

Using their equations, the team calculated dinosaur RMRs, plugging in
(55) reliable published data on these extinct animals. Dino growth rates can be estimated because rings of bone, which give a measure of age, were laid down annually, and body size can be estimated from bone size. The results placed dinosaurs squarely among the mesotherms. The earliest birds—direct descendants of dinosaurs—plotted as mesotherms, too.
(60) Grady and colleagues think mesothermy may have allowed dinosaurs to grow large and active with lower energy costs. Geochemist Robert Eagle of the California Institute of Technology in Pasadena agrees: "In a world that was generally hotter than today, it wasn't really necessary to be a full endotherm." Previous studies have suggested that during the Mesozoic, even
(65) mammalian endotherms kept their bodies at a lower set point than they do today, he says.

Grady suggests that mesothermy might even help explain why dinosaurs ruled the Earth: They could easily outcompete other reptiles, which were lethargic ectotherms. And by getting big quickly, they occupied the large-
(70) animal niches, and prevented the small, energy-hungry endothermic mammals from getting bigger themselves. Until, of course, the fateful asteroid struck, and dinosaurs vanished.

43. The primary purpose of the chart accompanying the passage is to illustrate that

   (A) tyrannosaurs were carnivores that preyed on mammals and birds.
   (B) ostriches are birds that have lost the ability to fly.
   (C) alligators have a lower metabolic rate than sharks.
   (D) in metabolic rate dinosaurs are most akin to sharks.

44. The passage is written from the perspective of someone who is

   (A) an active participant in evolutionary biology research.
   (B) a supporter of the long-held theory that dinosaurs were ectotherms.
   (C) well-informed about competing theories regarding dinosaur metabolism.
   (D) skilled at developing mathematical equations.

45. In the opening sentence, the author makes

   (A) an allusion to a familiar tale.
   (B) a contrast with a literary archetype.
   (C) an exaggeration about a theory's significance.
   (D) an exception to a rule.

46. By admitting that the action of establishing a new metabolic category is "audacious," study author Grady is

   (A) denying the action's validity.
   (B) acknowledging its radical nature.
   (C) confessing an error in methodology.
   (D) refuting a hypothesis.

47. What function do the fourth and fifth paragraphs (lines 21–32) serve in the passage as a whole?

   (A) They acknowledge that a theory described by the author of the passage has some limitations.
   (B) They give an overview of previous theories about the body temperature and activity level of dinosaurs.
   (C) They advocate the abandonment of a long-established assumption about the nature of dinosaur metabolism.
   (D) They illustrate the difficulty of reaching any conclusions about the physiology of prehistoric reptiles.

48. It is reasonable to conclude that the main goal of the scientists conducting the research described in the passage is to

    (A) learn the history of classifying dinosaurs as cold-blooded or warm-blooded.
    (B) explore possible ways to predict the body temperatures of mammals and birds.
    (C) characterize dinosaurs according to their metabolic and growth rates.
    (D) determine the role that dinosaur metabolism played in their extinction.

49. Which choice provides the best evidence for the answer to the previous question?

    (A) Lines 8–13 ("A recent . . . level")
    (B) Lines 14–16 ("Establishing . . . Albuquerque")
    (C) Lines 21–22 ("For the first . . . reptiles")
    (D) Lines 61–64 ("Geochemist . . . endotherm'")

50. As used in line 39, "scale" most nearly means

    (A) flake.
    (B) reduce.
    (C) ascend.
    (D) correlate.

51. As used in lines 56–57, "laid down" most nearly means

    (A) rested.
    (B) deposited.
    (C) sacrificed.
    (D) formulated.

52. In line 52, the quotes around the word "defend" indicate that

    (A) the word is being used for ironic effect.
    (B) it has been quoted from an authoritative source.
    (C) the author would prefer a different word in its place.
    (D) the word is being used in an unusual sense.

IF THERE IS STILL TIME REMAINING, YOU MAY
REVIEW YOUR ANSWERS.

WRITING AND LANGUAGE TEST

35 Minutes, 44 Questions

Turn to Section 2 of your answer sheet to answer the questions in this section.

Directions: Questions follow each of the passages below. Some questions ask you how the passage might be changed to improve the expression of ideas. Other questions ask you how the passage might be altered to correct errors in grammar, usage, and punctuation. One or more graphics accompany some passages. You will be required to consider these graphics as you answer questions about editing the passage.

There are three types of questions. In the first type, a part of the passage is underlined. The second type is based on a certain part of the passage. The third type is based on the entire passage.

Read each passage. Then, choose the answer to each question that changes the passage so that it is consistent with the conventions of standard written English. One of the answer choices for many questions is "NO CHANGE." Choosing this answer means that you believe the best answer is to make no change in the passage.

Questions 1–11 are based on the following passage and supplementary material.

Chiroptera

❶ <u>As insignificant animals,</u> bats make up a quarter of mammal species worldwide. They are the only mammals capable of true flight; their webbed forelimbs— which anatomically resemble the human hand—can sustain flight unlike the "gliding" of squirrels and opossums. ❷ <u>Although</u> often considered pests themselves, most bats feed on insects and share a large part of natural pest control. The remaining percentage of bat species, whose diet doesn't consist of insects, are frugivores,

1. Which choice best expresses that bats are not quite the most widespread mammalian species?
   (A) NO CHANGE
   (B) Representing 12 percent of mammals,
   (C) Second only to rodents,
   (D) Far more populous than humans,

2. (A) NO CHANGE
   (B) Because they are
   (C) However
   (D) For this very reason, they are

carnivores, or hematophagous. It is the latter bloodsuckers who attract the most attention. The ecological roles of bats ❸ <u>do</u> not end with pest control. They are also responsible for pollinating and dispersing fruit seeds. In fact, some tropical plants rely solely on bats for reproduction.

Bats are of the order Chiroptera and divided into two suborders: Microchiroptera and Megachiroptera. ❹ <u>The smallest bats are known to have bodies approximately one inch long.</u> And some are known to live up to 30 years. Echolocation is the highly sophisticated sense of hearing in which sound waves bounce off objects and emit echoes that microbats use to detect obstacles. It is this ❺ <u>object</u> that allows the nocturnal microbat to sense where an object is, how big or small that object may be, and even how fast that object is moving. In contrast, megabats have well-developed eyesight and more advanced characteristics in their brains. They often inhabit warm climates and live socially in colonies.

Recently, bat populations have been threatened by the deadly white-nose syndrome. Since the winter of 2007–2008, millions of bats have died as a result of this white fungus that spreads into the ears, muzzle, and wings of hibernating bats. Some estimates show a ❻ <u>10 percent increase</u> in the brown bat population in United States since the initial spread of the disease through the end of 2010. While the full consequences of such a large population reduction are yet unknown, ❼ <u>and</u> it is clear that farmers will feel the ❽ <u>affect</u> with

3. (A) NO CHANGE
   (B) does
   (C) don't
   (D) do's

4. (A) NO CHANGE
   (B) The smallest bats are known, to have bodies approximately one inch long.
   (C) The smallest bats are known, to have bodies, approximately one inch long.
   (D) The smallest, bats are known to have bodies approximately one inch long.

5. (A) NO CHANGE
   (B) material
   (C) phenomenon
   (D) thing

6. Which choice is best supported by the information in the accompanying graph?

   (A) NO CHANGE
   (B) 15 percent decline
   (C) 40 percent decline
   (D) 65 percent decline

7. (A) NO CHANGE
   (B) but
   (C) or
   (D) OMIT the underlined portion.

8. (A) NO CHANGE
   (B) effect
   (C) affectedness
   (D) effectively

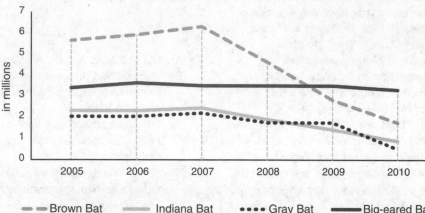

Bat Population in Pennsylvania

Note: The population numbers are tallied at the *end* of each year.

their best pest controllers now all but absent. Scientists at Michigan Technological University are working hard to prevent further spread of the disease. Using chemical fingerprinting, these scientists are tracing the **❾** <u>bats</u> hibernation sites and movements to detect what areas are infected and how the syndrome is being transmitted. Their research is particularly significant with the disease spreading to the **❿** <u>brown</u> bats of Tennessee—a species that is already on the endangered list. Interestingly, some species have altered their mating and living habits to help protect themselves, and it is through observation of these adaptations that researchers **⓫** so preservationists can make the necessary interventions.

9. (A) NO CHANGE
   (B) bat's
   (C) bat is
   (D) bats'

10. Based on the latter part of the sentence and the information in the graph, which bats most likely fit this description?

   (A) NO CHANGE
   (B) Indiana
   (C) gray
   (D) big-eared

11. Which choice is most logically inserted at this point in the sentence?

   (A) have decided how the species are thriving
   (B) are learning which species are in the most danger
   (C) are finding the preferred cultural associations of bats
   (D) may locate major bat predators

Questions 12–22 are based on the following passage.

The Tyrannical and the Taciturn

The so-called "marriage group" from Geoffrey Chaucer's *The Canterbury Tales* consists of five stories, in each of which marriage is ⑫ <u>not—as tradition would dictate, the resolution, but</u> instead functions as a central narrative conflict. Generally, the dysfunctional aspects of each married pair ⑬ <u>are supported by specific textual quotations:</u> an unbalanced distribution of power and ineffective communication between the espoused.

Perhaps nowhere ⑭ <u>is this</u> timeless marital troubles better illustrated than in the second narrative of the suite, "The Clerk's Tale." ⑮ <u>In the story of "The Clerk's Tale,"</u> we find the greatest power imbalance of any of Chaucer's unhappy couples. A Marquis of Lombardy, Lord Walter, fears that marriage will mean the surrender of

12. (A) NO CHANGE
    (B) not—as tradition would dictate—the resolution, but
    (C) not as tradition would dictate, the resolution, but
    (D) not, as tradition would dictate—the resolution, but

13. Which of the following would most logically connect to what comes next in the sentence?

    (A) NO CHANGE
    (B) could be said to derive from two critical failings:
    (C) are ironic given the dominant themes in the work:
    (D) contribute to a resolution between the protagonist and antagonist:

14. (A) NO CHANGE
    (B) is these
    (C) are those
    (D) are them

15. (A) NO CHANGE
    (B) In this medieval narrative found in *The Canterbury Tales*,
    (C) Here
    (D) Therefore

his personal freedom, stating ⓰ <u>"I me rejoysed of my</u> <u>liberte / That seelde tyme is founde in marriage."</u> To ensure that his "liberte" is uncompromised by wedlock, he does not choose for his bride a noblewoman of equal birth but, instead, the daughter of his poorest subject, Griselda.

The disparity of partnership in the marriage inevitably leads Walter to abuse his power. Soon after the couple's first child is born, Walter begins "testing" his wife's devotion through a series of truly mean-spirited pranks, including a false order for the execution of their two children and ⓱ <u>a renouncement of their marriage.</u> Griselda consents to each demand precisely as she promised on their wedding day, and one begins to imagine that the Marquis is not so much testing his wife's devotion ⓲ <u>so they are</u> exploring the extent to which his power reaches.

Conversely, Griselda contributes to the complications ⓳ <u>through</u> her unwillingness to communicate openly with Walter. In Griselda's final test, wherein she is cast out of the castle and replaced by a younger woman of higher birthright, Griselda asks ⓴ <u>that</u> Walter not send her away naked, once again emphasizing her intent to preserve the dignity of the bodies that fall victim to his wishes. This exchange is notable in that it is the first time Griselda directly asserts her desires to Walter, and although she desists as soon as he raises an objection, she allows herself, finally,

16. The author is considering removing the quotation marks in the underlined portion. Should she do so?

(A) Yes. The underlined portion represents the internal monologue of the narrator.
(B) Yes. The underlined portion is written in the medieval style, which is consistent with the style of the rest of the essay.
(C) No. The quotation marks serve to demonstrate the narrator's possession of specific thoughts.
(D) No. The quotation marks serve to set aside a statement by a character.

17. (A) NO CHANGE
(B) a marriage of their renouncing.
(C) of their marriage, a renouncing.
(D) with the renouncement of their marital vows.

18. (A) NO CHANGE
(B) when they were
(C) so he was
(D) as he is

19. (A) NO CHANGE
(B) as
(C) since
(D) to

20. Which choice best communicates Griselda's limited request?

(A) NO CHANGE
(B) so that
(C) only that
(D) from that

at ㉑ <u>what she believes, to be the end of their marriage, to communicate to him what</u> she feels to be right and honorable.

In any case, Griselda's concern for the physical body ㉒ <u>becomes</u> somewhat ironic given the tale's conclusion, particularly its invocation of the myth of Echo and Narcissus. Just as Echo could not speak of her own accord but only reflect the words of others, Griselda's inability to communicate with Walter beyond reflection of his immediate will causes her, in some sense, to lose even her physical body as a character, reduced to merely the echo of his desires.

21. (A) NO CHANGE
    (B) what she believes to be the end of their marriage to communicate to him what
    (C) what she believes—to be the end of their marriage, to communicate to him what
    (D) what she believes to be the end of their marriage, to communicate to him what

22. (A) NO CHANGE
    (B) became
    (C) had become
    (D) have become

Questions 23–33 are based on the following passage and supplementary material.

A, B, C—1, 2, 3

Few jobs are as important as that of teachers. A society's quality of life often depends on its economic growth, which is directly affected by its ㉓ <u>workforce, which, of course, is educated by its</u> school teachers. Take a moment to imagine the ten most influential people in your life—chances are, at least one of them is a teacher or an instructor you have presently or have had in the past. ㉔ <u>From English class during first period to mathematics as the final period,</u> teachers are those constant guardians molding you into the person you will become, pushing you to do ㉕ <u>your best and critiquing you when you're</u> falling short of your potential. Many students realize too late that relationships with their teachers, and later with their professors, should be fostered into life-long connections.

㉖ <u>However,</u> what is it that's so special about being a teacher? It begins with the decision to devote your life to the education of others. Most teachers have, at some point, entertained the idea of a career that requires less personal investment and pays better than ㉗ <u>an average of approximately $45,000 per year</u> in many cities; yet, when asked, few would take back their decision. The most probable explanation is that despite the negatives, the field of

23. (A) NO CHANGE
(B) workforce which, of course, are educated by its
(C) workforce, which, of course is educated by its'
(D) workforce, which of course is educated by it's

24. Which choice would most logically emphasize the wide span of time during which teachers have a direct influence over students?

(A) NO CHANGE
(B) From the opening of the school doors to their closing at day's end,
(C) From schools in the United States to schools located in faraway countries,
(D) From elementary to middle to high school and beyond,

25. (A) NO CHANGE
(B) you're best and criticizing you when your
(C) your best and criticizing one when one's
(D) you're best and critiquing you when you're

26. (A) NO CHANGE
(B) So,
(C) But,
(D) Further,

27. Which choice offers the most accurate interpretation of the data in the chart that accompanies this passage?

(A) NO CHANGE
(B) an average of approximately $50,000 per year
(C) an average of approximately $55,000 per year
(D) an average of approximately $60,000 per year

teaching is uniquely rewarding and exceptionally worthwhile. A **㉘** <u>teachers'</u> workday starts and ends with the training and shaping of the next generation; and for many, there's no better way to invest their own training **㉙** <u>compared</u> in the opening of young minds.

Nonetheless, becoming a teacher takes much more than a kind heart and a good dose of patience. All school teachers need to have a bachelor's degree—most commonly in education, but sometimes in the subject that the teacher wishes to teach—and it is increasingly common for teachers to obtain a master's degree. **㉚** <u>Obscuringly,</u> after degree completion, teachers need to acquire a teaching certificate, or a license to teach—most often, this licensing is achieved via teacher-education programs where **㉛** <u>perspective</u> teachers student-teach under more experienced instructors. Many schools prefer that their teachers continue to learn, train, and attend field-related events throughout their employment.

28. (A) NO CHANGE
    (B) teacher's
    (C) teachers
    (D) teacher has a

29. (A) NO CHANGE
    (B) than
    (C) then
    (D) related

30. (A) NO CHANGE
    (B) Given,
    (C) Furthermore,
    (D) Professionally,

31. (A) NO CHANGE
    (B) prospective
    (C) prospecting
    (D) previewing

Public School Teacher Salary

■ Median Annual Income in U.S. Dollars

San Diego, CA	$56,287
New York, NY	$62,382
Philadelphia, PA	$55,694
Dallas, TX	$53,208
Cleveland, OH	$52,732

$46,000 $48,000 $50,000 $52,000 $54,000 $56,000 $58,000 $60,000 $62,000 $64,000

Even then, the job is far from cookie-cutter. Most teachers are expected to be knowledgeable in psychology and counseling in order to provide other support for students. Licensure requirements and salaries can vary based on geography; ㉜ salaries in many urban school districts can vary by as much as approximately $4,000 based on the city's location. Additionally, if you choose to teach at the secondary level, it is best to be ready to answer questions about college, career planning, and young adult issues. One thing is ㉝ for sure, a good teacher is there because he or she wants to be.

32. Which choice offers the most accurate interpretation of the data in the chart?

(A) NO CHANGE
(B) salaries in many urban school districts can vary by as much as approximately $7,000 based on the city's location.
(C) salaries in many urban school districts can vary by as much as approximately $10,000 based on the city's location.
(D) salaries in many urban school districts can vary by as much as approximately $13,000 based on the city's location.

33. (A) NO CHANGE
(B) for sure: a good
(C) for sure a good
(D) for a

Questions 34–44 are based on the following passage.

Murder Most Fowl

Al Capone, speakeasies, the Saint Valentine's Day Massacre—most of us have at least heard of Chicago's **㉞** <u>transparent</u> affairs throughout the United States' thirteen-year "noble experiment" with prohibition. But while prohibition was repealed in 1933, another, less renowned noble experiment was inaugurated in Chicago in 2006—a citywide ban on the sale of foie gras, or fatty duck liver. Like veal, foie gras has often been a target of animal rights groups such as PETA **㉟** <u>because</u> ducks traditionally undergo a technique called "gavage" in order to fatten the liver artificially. **㊱** <u>Gavage involves, the force-feeding of corn, to ducks through a funnel.</u> Sponsors of the ban cited the raising of foie gras as a particularly heinous act of commercialized animal cruelty—one that overshadows the treatment of chickens, pigs, cows, and other animals raised for slaughter. The ban was passed by **㊲** <u>Chicago's City Council</u> in an omnibus bill despite the opposition of the city's mayor.

Foie gras is considered a very traditional and desirable ingredient in **㊳** <u>French cooking, not surprisingly, Chicago's many</u> respected French-style chefs were outraged by the council's decision.

34. Which word is most applicable to the types of "affairs" listed at the beginning of the sentence?

(A) NO CHANGE
(B) ancient
(C) alcoholic
(D) dubious

35. (A) NO CHANGE
(B) while
(C) although
(D) and

36. (A) NO CHANGE
(B) Gavage involves the, force-feeding of corn to ducks through a funnel.
(C) Gavage involves the force-feeding of corn to ducks through a funnel.
(D) Gavage involves the force-feeding, of corn to ducks through a funnel.

37. (A) NO CHANGE
(B) Chicagos City Council
(C) Chicagos' Cities Council
(D) Chicagos Cities Council

38. (A) NO CHANGE
(B) French cooking; not surprisingly, Chicago's many
(C) French cooking: not surprisingly Chicagos many
(D) French cooking not surprisingly, Chicago's many

Other chefs throughout the city expressed similar dismay at what they perceived as everything from artistic censorship to the Orwellian tyranny of an authoritarian state. Restaurant patrons, for the most part, **㊴** were appalled at the City Council's encroachment on personal dietary choices. In fact, many restaurants reported a tremendous spike in foie gras sales in the months between when the bill was passed and the date on which it took effect.

㊵ What's more, after the ban became active—much like in the old days of prohibition—enterprising Chicagoan restaurateurs, diners, and chefs found ways around the legislation. Some restaurants, such as Har-De-Har-Har and Copperblue, simply continued to sell foie gras, claiming the ㊶ enormous livers were sourced either from chickens or from naturally fed ducks. Bin 36 offered a salad of figs, honey, and apricots at what appeared to be the exorbitant price of thirty ㊷ dollars—until one realized the salad included a "complimentary" serving of foie gras. Bin 36, being the most cavalier of the culinary rebels, was investigated by the Health Department, who nonetheless declined to issue a citation. Following that decision, attempts to enforce the ban essentially ㊸ vivified, and any restaurant in Chicago wishing to serve foie gras could do so without a serious fear of reprisal.

39. Which choice best expresses that restaurant patrons had the opposite attitude about the foie gras ban than the chefs described in the previous sentence?

(A) NO CHANGE
(B) considered moving away from this oppressive society.
(C) just wondered what all the fuss was about.
(D) felt that artists should be able to paint whatever they would like.

40. (A) NO CHANGE
(B) Conversely,
(C) However,
(D) In contrast,

41. Which wording gives the most logical and vivid description based on the context of the sentence?

(A) NO CHANGE
(B) suspiciously large and luscious
(C) grotesquely unappetizing
(D) poultry

42. (A) NO CHANGE
(B) dollars, until one, realized the salad
(C) dollars: until one realized, the salad
(D) dollars; until one realized the salad

43. (A) NO CHANGE
(B) congealed,
(C) checked,
(D) froze,

Two years after the ban was passed, it was repealed. Chefs hailed the action as a victory to personal freedom. Many animal rights advocates decried it as surrender to wealthy special interest groups. Mayor Richard Daley reflected on the council's decision to ban foie gras in the first place as "the silliest thing they've ever done."

44. (A) NO CHANGE
    (B) since
    (C) for
    (D) on

STOP

IF THERE IS STILL TIME REMAINING, YOU MAY REVIEW YOUR ANSWERS.

MATH TEST (NO CALCULATOR)

25 Minutes, 20 Questions

Turn to Section 3 of your answer sheet to answer the questions in this section.

Directions: For questions 1–15, solve each problem and choose the best answer from the given options. Fill in the corresponding circle on your answer document. For questions 16–20, solve the problem and fill in the answer on the answer sheet grid.

Notes:
- Calculators are NOT PERMITTED in this section.
- All variables and expressions represent real numbers unless indicated otherwise.
- All figures are drawn to scale unless indicated otherwise.
- All figures are in a plane unless indicated otherwise.
- Unless indicated otherwise, the domain of a given function is the set of all real numbers x for which the function has real values.

Reference Information

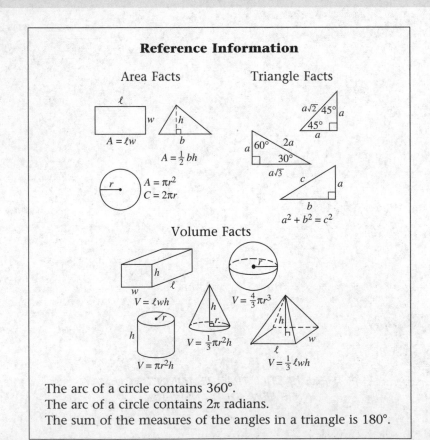

Area Facts

$A = \ell w$

$A = \frac{1}{2} bh$

$A = \pi r^2$
$C = 2\pi r$

Triangle Facts

$a^2 + b^2 = c^2$

Volume Facts

$V = \ell wh$

$V = \frac{4}{3}\pi r^3$

$V = \pi r^2 h$

$V = \frac{1}{3}\pi r^2 h$

$V = \frac{1}{3}\ell wh$

The arc of a circle contains 360°.
The arc of a circle contains 2π radians.
The sum of the measures of the angles in a triangle is 180°.

Year	1990	1991	1992	1993	1994	1995
Number of tournaments	4	5	10	6	9	12

1. The chart above shows the number of tennis tournaments that Adam entered each year from 1990 through 1995. In what year did he enter 50% more tournaments than the year before?

   (A) 1991
   (B) 1992
   (C) 1994
   (D) 1995

2. Which of the following statements is true concerning the equation below?

   $$5(x + 1) + 3 = 3(x + 3)$$

   (A) The equation has no solutions.
   (B) The equation has one positive solution.
   (C) The equation has one negative solution.
   (D) The equation has infinitely many solutions.

3. What is the slope of the line whose equation is $3x + 4y = 24$?

   (A) $-\dfrac{4}{3}$

   (B) $-\dfrac{3}{4}$

   (C) $\dfrac{3}{4}$

   (D) $\dfrac{4}{3}$

4. A, B, and C are three cities in New York State. The distance between A and B is m miles, and the distance between B and C is n miles. If on a map of New York, A and B are c centimeters apart, on that map how many centimeters apart are B and C?

   (A) $\dfrac{cn}{m}$

   (B) $\dfrac{cm}{n}$

   (C) $\dfrac{mn}{c}$

   (D) $\dfrac{c}{mn}$

5. At North Central University, students need at least 120 credits to graduate. Most courses are three credits, but all lab sciences courses, as well as some advanced courses that require more work, are four credits. Which of the following inequalities represents a possible number of three-credit courses, x, and four-credit courses, y, that a student could take to have enough credits to graduate?

(A) $\dfrac{3}{x} + \dfrac{4}{y} > 120$

(B) $\dfrac{3}{x} + \dfrac{4}{y} \geq 120$

(C) $3x + 4y > 120$

(D) $3x + 4y \geq 120$

6. If at Lake Hollow High School the ratio of boys to girls in the French club is 2:3 and the ratio of boys to girls in the Spanish club is 3:5, which of the following statements must be true?

(A) The number of girls in the French club is equal to the number of boys in the Spanish club.
(B) The number of boys in the Spanish club is greater than the number of boys in the French club.
(C) The percent of Spanish club members who are girls is greater than the percent of French club members who are girls.
(D) If new members join the French club (and no old members leave) and if the ratio of boys to girls among those new members is 3:2, then the club will have an equal number of boys and girls.

7. John and his sister Mary each drove the same route from their uncle's house in Boston to their home in New York, a distance of 200 miles. For the entire trip, John averaged 25 miles per gallon of gasoline and Mary averaged 20 miles per gallon. How far, in miles, was Mary from their home when she had used exactly as much gasoline as John had for his entire trip?

(A) 20
(B) 40
(C) 80
(D) 160

8. If the lines whose equations are $2x + 3y = 4$ and $y = 2x$ intersect at the point (a, b), what is the value of $a + b$?

(A) 1
(B) 1.5
(C) 2
(D) 2.5

9. Container I is a rectangular solid whose base is a square 4 inches on a side, and container II is a cylinder whose base is a circle with a diameter of 4 inches. The height of each container is 5 inches. How much more water, in cubic inches, will container I hold than container II?

   (A) $4(4 - \pi)$
   (B) $20(4 - \pi)$
   (C) $80(\pi - 1)$
   (D) $80(1 - \pi)$

10. Pam is a potter who sells the vases she creates to Carl, who then sells them in his crafts boutique for 60% more than he pays Pam for them. To attract customers into his store over the July 4th weekend, Carl runs a special sale on Pam's vases, selling them for 20% less than he pays her for them. A customer who buys one of these vases during the sale is receiving a discount of what percent off Carl's normal selling price?

   (A) 25%
   (B) 48%
   (C) 50%
   (D) 80%

$$y = x^2 + 1$$
$$y = -x^2 + 3$$

11. If (a, b) and (c, d) are solutions of the system of equations above, what is the value of $a + b + c + d$?

   (A) 1
   (B) 2
   (C) 3
   (D) 4

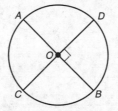

12. In Circle O above with radius r, $\overline{AB}$ and $\overline{CD}$ are a pair of perpendicular diameters. If the area and perimeter of square $ADBC$ (not shown) are a square inches and b inches, respectively, and if $a = b$, what is the length, in inches, of r?

   (A) $\sqrt{2}$
   (B) 2
   (C) $2\sqrt{2}$
   (D) $4\sqrt{2}$

13. The members of the varsity baseball team at Meadowlawn High School are all juniors and seniors. There are 5 more seniors on the team than juniors. If 40% of the team members are juniors, how many students are on the team?

(A) 18
(B) 24
(C) 25
(D) 30

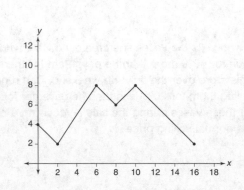

14. The complete graph of $y = f(x)$ is shown above. If $f(3) = a$, what is the value of $f(3a)$?

(A) 3.5
(B) 5.5
(C) 7.5
(D) 10.5

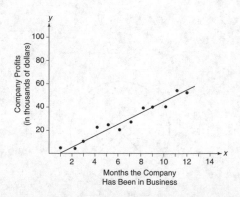

15. The scatter plot diagram above shows the profits of a start-up company during its first year of business. If the company's profits continue to grow at the same rate as predicted by the line of best fit, which has been drawn in, which of the following will be closest to the company's monthly profit after it has been in business for a year and a half?

(A) $40,000
(B) $60,000
(C) $80,000
(D) $85,000

Grid-in Response Directions

In questions 16–20, first solve the problem, and then enter your answer on the grid provided on the answer sheet. The instructions for entering your answers follow.

- First, write your answer in the boxes at the top of the grid.
- Second, grid your answer in the columns below the boxes.
- Use the fraction bar in the first row or the decimal point in the second row to enter fractions and decimals.

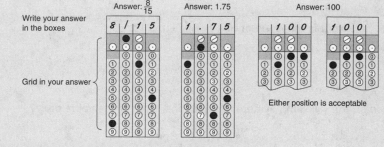

- Grid only one space in each column.
- Entering the answer in the boxes is recommended as an aid in gridding but is not required.
- The machine scoring your exam can read only what you grid, so you **must grid-in your answers correctly to get credit**.
- If a question has more than one correct answer, grid-in only one of them.
- The grid does not have a minus sign; so no answer can be negative.
- A mixed number *must* be converted to an improper fraction or a decimal before it is gridded. Enter $1\frac{1}{4}$ as 5/4 or 1.25; the machine will interpret 11/4 as $\frac{11}{4}$ and mark it wrong.

- **All decimals must be entered as accurately as possible.** Here are three acceptable ways of gridding

$$\frac{3}{11} = 0.272727\ldots$$

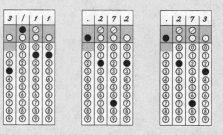

- Note that rounding to .273 is acceptable because you are using the full grid, but you would receive **no credit** for .3 or .27, because they are less accurate.

16. What is the value of $8^{-\frac{1}{3}}$?

17. If the cosine of the larger acute angle in a right triangle is 0.6, what is the cosine of the smaller acute angle in that triangle?

18. If $i = \sqrt{-1}$, what is the value of $\left(7 + i\sqrt{7}\right)\left(7 - i\sqrt{7}\right)$?

19. Based on the following system of equations, what is the value of xy?

$$3x + 4y = 4x + 3y$$
$$x + y = 5$$

20. Consider the parabola whose equation is $y = x^2 - 8x + 16$. If m represents the number of times the parabola intersects the y-axis and n represents the number of times the parabola intersects the x-axis, what is the value of $m + n$?

STOP

IF THERE IS STILL TIME REMAINING, YOU MAY REVIEW YOUR ANSWERS.

MATH TEST (CALCULATOR)

55 Minutes, 38 Questions

Turn to Section 4 of your answer sheet to answer the questions in this section.

Directions: For questions 1–30, solve each problem and choose the best answer from the given options. Fill in the corresponding circle on your answer document. For questions 31–38, solve the problem and fill in the answer on the answer sheet grid.

Notes:
- Calculators **ARE PERMITTED** in this section.
- All variables and expressions represent real numbers unless indicated otherwise.
- All figures are drawn to scale unless indicated otherwise.
- All figures are in a plane unless indicated otherwise.
- Unless indicated otherwise, the domain of a given function is the set of all real numbers x for which the function has real values.

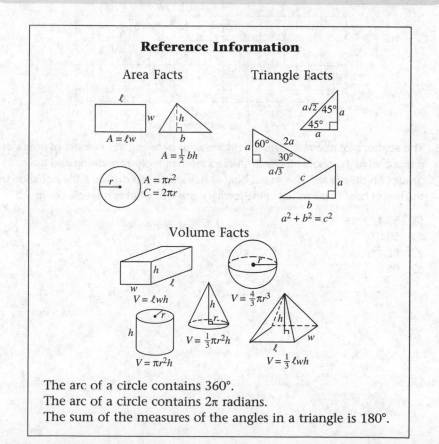

Reference Information

Area Facts

$A = \ell w$

$A = \frac{1}{2} bh$

$A = \pi r^2$
$C = 2\pi r$

Triangle Facts

$a\sqrt{2}$, $45°$, a, $45°$, a

a, $60°$, $2a$, $30°$, $a\sqrt{3}$

c, a, b
$a^2 + b^2 = c^2$

Volume Facts

$V = \ell w h$

$V = \frac{4}{3}\pi r^3$

$V = \pi r^2 h$

$V = \frac{1}{3}\pi r^2 h$

$V = \frac{1}{3}\ell w h$

The arc of a circle contains 360°.
The arc of a circle contains 2π radians.
The sum of the measures of the angles in a triangle is 180°.

1. Water is pouring at a constant rate into a tank that is a 4-foot-high rectangular solid. If the water was turned on at 11:00 and if at 11:25 the depth of the water in the tank was 4 inches, at what time was the pool full?

   (A) 3:35
   (B) 4:00
   (C) 4:25
   (D) 5:00

2. Which of the following statements is true concerning the equation below?

   $$\sqrt{x+7} = -4$$

   (A) The equation has no solutions.
   (B) The equation has one positive solution.
   (C) The equation has one negative solution.
   (D) The equation has more than one solution.

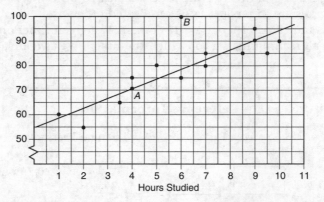
Hours Studied

3. The scatter plot above shows the relationship between the number of hours that a group of high school students studied for their biology midterm and their grades on their tests. The line of best fit has also been drawn. If the equation of the line of best fit is written in the form $y = mx + b$, what is the value of $m + b$?

   (A) 55.4
   (B) 59.0
   (C) 62.4
   (D) 65.0

4. On a recent exam in Mr. Walsh's chemistry class, the mean grade of the b boys in the class was 82, and the mean grade of the g girls in the class was 88. If $b \neq g$, which of the following must be true about the mean grade, m, of all the students in the class?

(A) $m = 85$
(B) $m \neq 85$
(C) $m < 85$
(D) $m > 85$

5. Brigitte is translating children's books from French into English. On average, it takes her 45 minutes to translate a page. If Brigitte works 8 hours a day for 5 days per week, how many pages can she translate in 6 weeks?

(A) 180
(B) 240
(C) 320
(D) 480

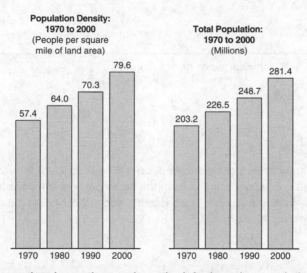

6. In the bar graphs above, the graph on the left gives the population density of the United States (number of people per square mile of land area) from 1970 to 2000. The graph on the right shows the population of the United States in millions for the same period of time. Which of the following is closest to the total land area of the United States, in square miles?

(A) 2,500,000
(B) 3,000,000
(C) 3,500,000
(D) 4,000,000

Questions 7–8 are based on the following information.

On January 1, 2014, Michael put d dollars into an empty safe deposit box. Then on the first day of every month, he put e dollars into the box. No other money was put into the box, and none was taken out. After 3 monthly deposits, the box contained $175. After 8 monthly deposits, it contained $300.

7. Which of the following equations gives the amount, a, of money in the box, in dollars, after m monthly deposits have been made?

   (A) $a = 100 + 25m$
   (B) $a = 100 + 25(m - 1)$
   (C) $a = 25 + 50m$
   (D) $a = 25 + 50(m - 1)$

8. What was the amount of money, in dollars, in the box on December 25, 2015?

   (A) $650
   (B) $675
   (C) $725
   (D) $750

---

9. If $f(x) = 4x^4 - 4$, for what value of x is $f(x) = 4$?

   (A) 1
   (B) 1.19
   (C) 1.41
   (D) 1.68

10. A car going 40 miles per hour set out on a 80-mile trip at 9:00 A.M. Exactly 10 minutes later, a second car left from the same place and followed the same route. How fast, in miles per hour, was the second car going if it caught up with the first car at 10:30 A.M.?

    (A) 45
    (B) 50
    (C) 55
    (D) 60

11. If the product of the two complex numbers $a + 4i$ and $9 - bi$ is a real number and if $a = 6$, what is the value of b?

    (A) 3
    (B) 4
    (C) 6
    (D) 9

12. If Eli flips five fair coins and if, for each of them, Max guesses whether it landed heads or tails, what is the probability that Max makes at least one correct guess?

(A) 0.03
(B) 0.50
(C) 0.80
(D) 0.97

Questions 13–15 are based on the information in the following graphs.

College Enrollment, by Age and Gender
1975 and 1995

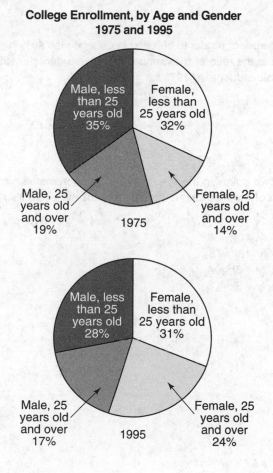

13. If there were 10,000,000 college students in 1975, how many more male students were there than female students?

   (A) 400,000
   (B) 600,000
   (C) 800,000
   (D) 1,000,000

14. In 1975, approximately what percent of female college students were at least 25 years old?

   (A) 14%
   (B) 30%
   (C) 45%
   (D) 76%

15. If the total number of students enrolled in college was 40% higher in 1995 than in 1975, what is the ratio of the number of male students in 1995 to the number of male students in 1975?

   (A) 5:6
   (B) 6:7
   (C) 7:6
   (D) 6:5

16. A and B are two points in the xy-plane. If their coordinates are $A(1, 1)$ and $B(5, 5)$, which of the following is the equation of the circle for which $\overline{AB}$ is a diameter?

   (A) $(x - 3)^2 + (y - 3)^2 = 4$
   (B) $(x - 3)^2 + (y - 3)^2 = 8$
   (C) $(x + 3)^2 + (y + 3)^2 = 4$
   (D) $(x + 3)^2 + (y + 3)^2 = 8$

17. At a national educational conference, all of the participants are teachers or administrators. If there are 584 teachers at the conference and 27% of the participants are administrators, how many administrators are attending the conference?

    (A) 158
    (B) 216
    (C) 312
    (D) 800

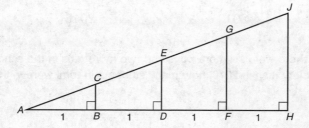

18. In the figure above, what is the ratio of the area of △*AHJ* to the area of △*ABC*?

    (A) 4:1
    (B) 8:1
    (C) 12:1
    (D) 16:1

The graphs below show the percent of boys and girls in the National Honor Society at Central High School in 2010 and 2015.

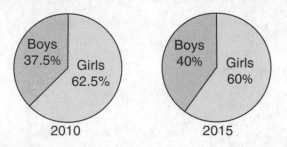

2010   2015

19. If in 2015 there were six more boys and two more girls in the school's National Honor Society than in 2010, how many students in total were in the society in 2015?

    (A) 48
    (B) 72
    (C) 112
    (D) 120

20. All general admission tickets for an upcoming concert are the same price and are available only online. The online agency handling ticket sales charges a processing fee for all orders, regardless of how many tickets are purchased. If the charge for four tickets is $107.95 and the charge for seven tickets is $181.45, how much is the processing fee?

    (A) $6.95
    (B) $7.95
    (C) $8.95
    (D) $9.95

Use the information below and the data in the following chart in answering Questions 21 and 22.

A survey was conducted of 82,184 citizens of the four Scandinavian countries—Denmark, Sweden, Norway, and Finland—concerning their vacation plans for next summer. The chart below shows where, if anyplace, the people surveyed plan to travel.

Country	Travel within Europe	Travel outside of Europe	Not planning to travel	Total
Denmark	10,321	6,244	5,388	21,953
Sweden	13,644	5,881	4,465	23,990
Norway	11,222	5,369	3,468	20,059
Finland	8,196	2,662	5,324	16,182
Total	43,383	20,156	18,645	82,184

21. According to the survey, in which country did the highest percentage of people say that they would be traveling outside of Europe?

   (A) Denmark
   (B) Sweden
   (C) Norway
   (D) Finland

22. When a random sampling of 1,000 of the people who said they planned to travel outside of Europe were asked during a follow-up survey if they planned to visit the United States, 168 said "yes." Based on the data in the chart and the follow-up survey, which of the following statements is most likely to be accurate?

   (A) Of the 82,184 people in the original survey, fewer than 3,000 plan to visit the United States this summer.
   (B) Of the 82,184 people in the original survey, between 3,000 and 5,000 plan to visit the United States this summer.
   (C) Of the 82,184 people in the original survey, between 5,000 and 10,000 plan to visit the United States this summer.
   (D) Of the 82,184 people in the original survey, more than 10,000 plan to visit the United States this summer.

---

23. What is the total surface area of a cube if the length of each main diagonal is 9?

   (A) 81
   (B) 162
   (C) $27\sqrt{3}$
   (D) $81\sqrt{3}$

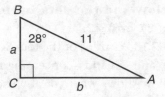

Note: Figure not drawn to scale.

24. In the figure above, what is the value of $\dfrac{b}{a}$?

   (A) 0.47
   (B) 0.53
   (C) 0.67
   (D) 0.88

25. If $i^2 = -1$ and if $(1 + 2i) \div (3 + 4i) = (a + bi)$, what is the value of $a + b$?

   (A) 0.25
   (B) 0.52
   (C) 6
   (D) 10

26. On January 2, 2016, the official rate of exchange for one United States dollar was 16.56 Mexican pesos and 9.47 Argentinian pesos. On that date, to the nearest hundredth, how many Mexican pesos could be exchanged for one Argentinian peso?

   (A) 0.57
   (B) 0.75
   (C) 1.57
   (D) 1.75

27. In a large urban high school, all students are assigned to a homeroom. One of those homerooms has 30 students in it, and all the others have 27. In each homeroom with 27 students, three students were chosen at random to participate in a survey. In the one homeroom with 30 students, 4 students were chosen. If the school has exactly 3,000 students, how many of them took part in the survey?

   (A) 333
   (B) 334
   (C) 336
   (D) 337

Questions 28–30 are based on the information in the following graph.

Motor Vehicle Theft in the U.S.
Percent Change from 1994 to 1998

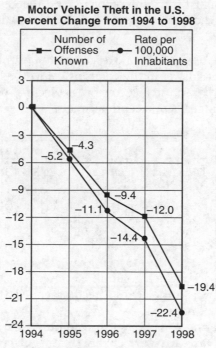

Source: U.S. Department of Justice,
Federal Bureau of Investigation.

28. If 1,000,000 vehicles were stolen in 1994, how many were stolen in 1996?

(A) 889,000
(B) 906,000
(C) 940,000
(D) 1,094,000

29. To the nearest tenth of a percent, by what percent did the number of vehicles stolen decrease from 1997 to 1998?

(A) 7.4%
(B) 8.0%
(C) 8.4%
(D) 12.0%

30. To the nearest percent, by what percent did the population of the United States increase from 1994 to 1998?

(A) 1%
(B) 2%
(C) 3%
(D) 4%

Grid-in Response Directions

In questions 31–38, first solve the problem, and then enter your answer on the grid provided on the answer sheet. The instructions for entering your answers follow.

- First, write your answer in the boxes at the top of the grid.
- Second, grid your answer in the columns below the boxes.
- Use the fraction bar in the first row or the decimal point in the second row to enter fractions and decimals.

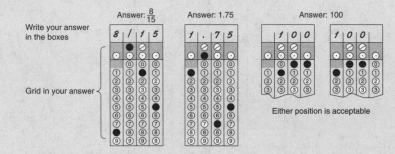

- Grid only one space in each column.
- Entering the answer in the boxes is recommended as an aid in gridding but is not required.
- The machine scoring your exam can read only what you grid, so you **must grid-in your answers correctly to get credit**.
- If a question has more than one correct answer, grid-in only one of them.
- The grid does not have a minus sign; so no answer can be negative.
- A mixed number *must* be converted to an improper fraction or a decimal before it is gridded. Enter $1\frac{1}{4}$ as 5/4 or 1.25; the machine will interpret 11/4 as $\frac{11}{4}$ and mark it wrong.

- **All decimals must be entered as accurately as possible.** Here are three acceptable ways of gridding

$$\frac{3}{11} = 0.272727\ldots$$

- Note that rounding to .273 is acceptable because you are using the full grid, but you would receive **no credit** for .3 or .27, because they are less accurate.

31. If $-\dfrac{3}{7} < a - b < -\dfrac{3}{8}$, what is one possible value of $2b - 2a$?

32. At North Central High School, the only foreign languages taught are Spanish, French, and Chinese, and every student is required to take a language course. The table below shows how many sophomores, juniors, and seniors took classes in those languages last year.

	Sophomores	Juniors	Seniors	Total
Spanish	170	200	190	560
French	125	98	106	329
German	35	42	14	91
Totals	330	340	310	980

What fraction of the juniors and seniors did not take a Spanish class last year?

33. To the nearest thousandth, what is the cosine of the angle formed by the line whose equation is $y = 2x$ and the positive x-axis?

34. If the graph of $y = 10x^2 + bx + c$ has x-intercepts at 1.4 and 1.5, what is the value of $c - b$?

**Use the data in the following diagram
in answering <u>Questions 35 and 36</u>.**

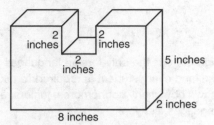

35. The figure above represents a block of wood in the shape of a rectangular solid from which a rectangular groove has been removed. What is the volume, in cubic feet, of the block?

36. Given that the density of Honduran mahogany is 41 pounds per cubic foot and the density of Spanish mahogany is 53 pounds per cubic foot, how much more, in pounds, would the block weigh if it were made of Spanish mahogany than if it were made of Honduran mahogany?

<u>Questions 37 and 38</u> are based on the data in the following graphs that give information about the 500 campers who attended the New England Music Summer Camp for Teens in 2015. The bar graph gives the breakdown by age of the campers, and the circle graph shows the musical specialties of the 15-year-old campers.

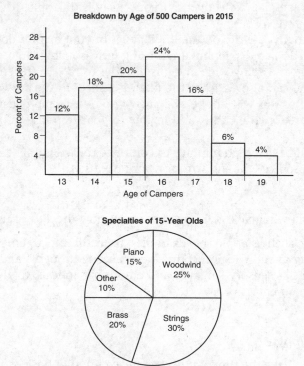

Breakdown by Age of 500 Campers in 2015

Specialties of 15-Year Olds

37. How many of the campers were 15-year-old pianists?

38. In 2015, 12 of the 13-year-olds, 18 of the 14-year-olds, and 12% of the campers aged 16 to 19 were pianists. What percent of all the campers were pianists? (Enter your answer without a percent sign. For example, if the answer were 50%, you should grid in 50.)

IF THERE IS STILL TIME REMAINING, YOU MAY
REVIEW YOUR ANSWERS.

ESSAY (OPTIONAL)

Directions: This assignment will allow you to demonstrate your ability to skillfully read and understand a source text and write a response analyzing the source. In your response, you should show that you have understood the source, give proficient analysis, and use the English language effectively. If your essay is off-topic, it will not be scored.

Only what you write on the lined paper in your answer document will be scored—avoid skipping lines, using unreasonably large handwriting, and using wide margins in order to have sufficient space to respond. You can also write on the planning sheet in the answer document, but this will not be evaluated—no other scrap paper will be given. Be sure to write clearly and legibly so your response can be scored.

You will be given 50 minutes to complete the assignment, including reading the source text and writing your response.

Read the following passage, and think about how the author uses:

- Evidence, such as applicable examples, to justify the argument
- Reasoning to show logical connections among thoughts and facts
- Rhetoric, like sensory language and emotional appeals, to give weight to the argument

Healthy Is Happy

1   I just don't have the time. An inveterate excuse that has postponed physical activity for decades past, it is commonly used by busy parents, exhausted students, and overworked professionals, along with the mastermind procrastinators themselves. Not to worry—one workout won't make or break you. However, as studies continue to confirm, a lifestyle sans regular physical activity can do irreparable damage, and not just to your body. Get this: there is a definite and direct correlation between sound health and fitness and success in career and personal life. The denizens of the bodybuilding and triathlon worlds are hardly the only ones with something at stake. Physically active persons are more successful in their academic endeavors, career ambitions, and relationships, period.

2   Regular exercise releases endorphins that enhance mood, and increase energy and mental sharpness. Acute minds make for better retainment and prolonged focus, a recipe for improved grades and better career prospects. Take the average college student: stressed, anxious, overworked, and fatigued, grabbing processed foods from convenient stops on the way to and from class. Participating in just 45 minutes of rigorous activity three days a week leaves one with cardiovascular endurance, restored alertness, and appropriate serotonin levels to defend against anxiety and depression. The *Journal of Pediatrics* published a report of 12,000 Nebraska schoolchildren that proved better fitness was linked to higher achievement scores regardless of body type. And in 2010, ABC News detailed a study of students at Naperville Central High School who doubled their reading scores on standardized testing after participating in a dynamic morning exercise regimen. It's not just six pack abs but your intellect that you're working for.

3   Advantages of attentiveness and conviviality extend beyond your years in the classroom. Increased productivity and discipline accompanied by reduced stress ensue the active lifestyle of the boss's favorites. A recent survey found that 75% of executives making six-figures listed physical fitness as critical to their career success. They cited better sleep, diligence, and concentration as their favorite advantages to leading a healthy lifestyle; making better diet choices and maintaining higher attendance rates were just icing on the cake, so to speak. Likewise, the survey didn't only postulate the benefits of the fit and ambitious, but deliberated on the faults of the unhealthy and lax, conceding that obesity is a serious career impediment. The word has spread: many employers are now offering incentives for healthier employees and even investing in at-work gyms and cardio machines. Those who would blame their careers for mitigating their gym time should beware—the former suffers without the latter.

4   Nonetheless, your mediocrity was hardly noticed in school, and your humdrum job doesn't deserve you at your best anyway. At least you have someone special to come home to. Or do you? Physical fitness, in all its breadth, extends to relationships as well. You guessed it: those who are happy with themselves are much better friends and companions. An opposite strength, commitment, is valuable in tough workout routines and tougher intimacies. Not only are the lively and fit elect more likely to communicate better, but they are also known to lead active lifestyles outside the gym and the office, spending time in new activities and hobbies with their loved ones. The *Journal of Personality and Social*

Psychology found that couples who maintain a healthy self-image and try new things together, stay together. Yet again, contradiction arises when one lists family as the reason behind his or her physical concession; you invest in your family when you invest in yourself.

5   If health and appearance aren't motivation enough to make time for a jog, hike, or swim, perhaps scholastic, career, and relational aspirations can do the trick. An active lifestyle is vital to rather than incongruous with a swamped day-to-day—it should be, like food and sleep, just another necessity, and an enjoyable one at that. For you weight lifters, a combination of strength training and aerobic exercise is proven to generate the fastest results. For all others, your indignation with the crowded, sweaty gym doesn't have to be a hindrance; you're more likely to continue your routine if you have fun doing it, so get a bike, shoot some hoops, join a challenge, or take a dance class. Do yourself a favor, and pave the way for success.

Write a response that demonstrates how the author makes an argument to persuade an audience that physical fitness should be a priority. In your response, analyze how the author uses at least one of the features from the essay directions (or features of your own choosing) to develop a logical and persuasive argument. Be certain that your response cites relevant aspects of the source text.

Your response should not give your personal opinion on the merit of the source text, but instead show how the author crafts an argument to persuade readers.

ANSWER KEY

Test 2

Section 1: Reading

1. A	14. C	27. C	40. B
2. D	15. A	28. D	41. D
3. B	16. A	29. B	42. B
4. D	17. B	30. B	43. D
5. B	18. A	31. C	44. C
6. C	19. C	32. C	45. A
7. B	20. A	33. D	46. B
8. B	21. D	34. B	47. B
9. B	22. D	35. D	48. C
10. A	23. C	36. A	49. A
11. C	24. D	37. D	50. D
12. B	25. C	38. A	51. B
13. C	26. C	39. B	52. D

Number Correct _____

Number Incorrect _____

Section 2: Writing and Language

1. C	12. B	23. A	34. D
2. A	13. B	24. D	35. A
3. A	14. C	25. A	36. C
4. A	15. C	26. B	37. A
5. C	16. D	27. C	38. B
6. D	17. A	28. B	39. C
7. D	18. D	29. B	40. A
8. B	19. A	30. C	41. B
9. D	20. C	31. B	42. A
10. C	21. D	32. C	43. D
11. B	22. A	33. B	44. C

Number Correct _____

Number Incorrect _____

Section 3: Math (No Calculator)

1. C	5. D	9. B	13. C
2. B	6. C	10. C	14. C
3. B	7. B	11. D	15. D
4. A	8. B	12. C	

16. 1/2 or .5

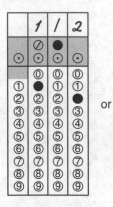

17. 4/5 or 8/10 or .8   18. 56

19. 25/4 or 6.25

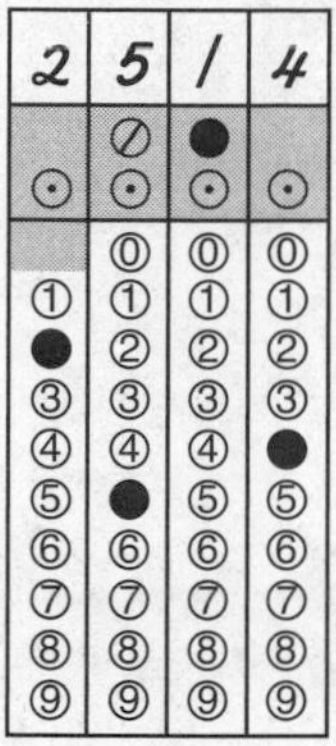

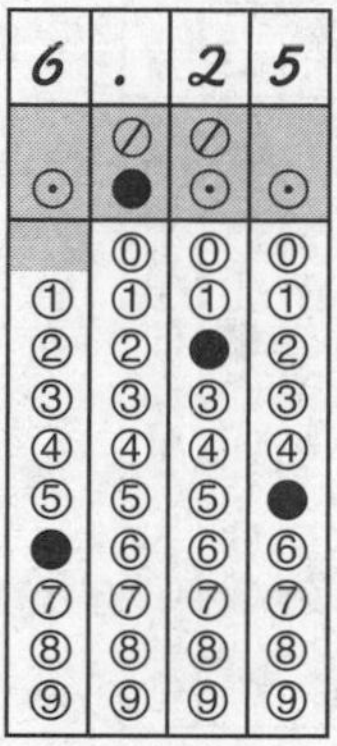

20. 2

or

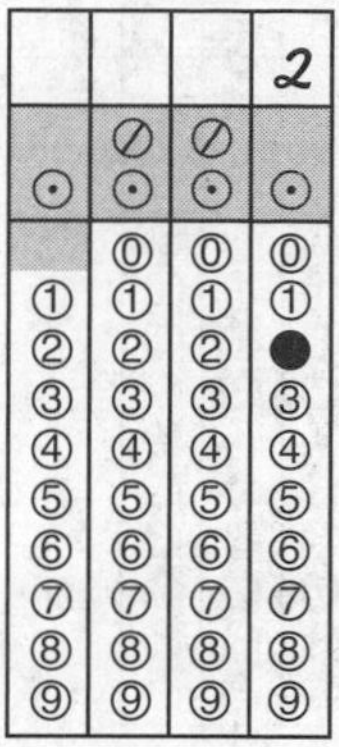

Number Correct _____
Number Incorrect _____

Section 4: Math (Calculator)

1. B	7. A	13. C	19. D	25. B
2. A	8. B	14. B	20. D	26. D
3. B	9. C	15. C	21. A	27. B
4. B	10. A	16. B	22. B	28. B
5. C	11. C	17. B	23. B	29. C
6. C	12. D	18. D	24. B	30. D

31. .8

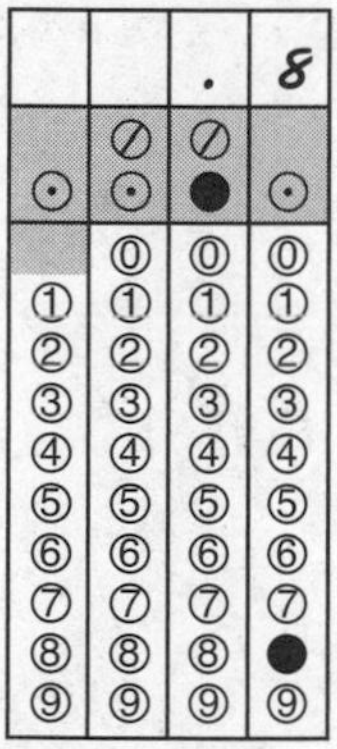

32. 2/5 or 4/10 or .4

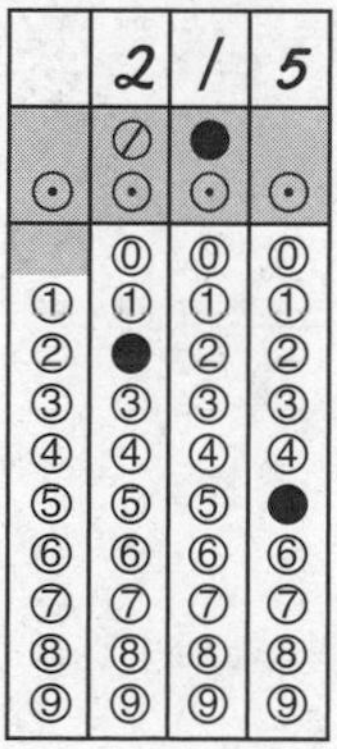

or

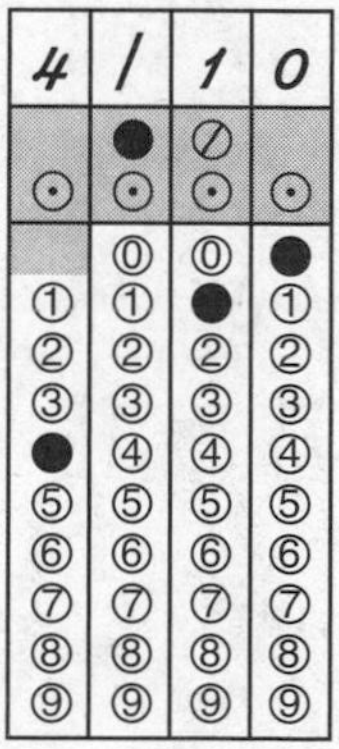

or

.75 < x < .857

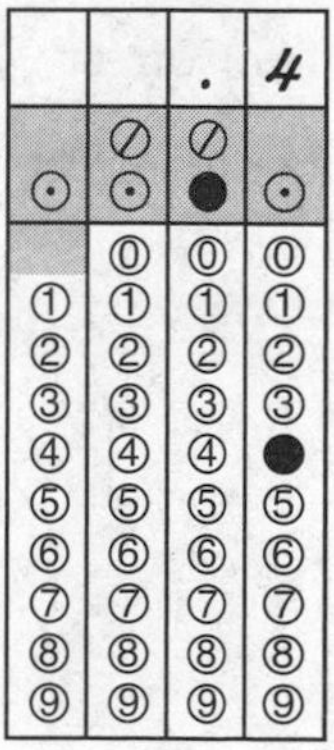

33. .447

34. 50

35. 1/24

36. 1/2 or .5 or

37. 15

38. 15

Number Correct _____

Number Incorrect _____

SCORE ANALYSIS

Reading and Writing Test

Section 1: Reading _____ = _____ (A)
 # correct raw score

Section 2: Writing _____ = _____ (B)
 # correct raw score

To find your Reading and Writing test scores, consult the chart below: find the ranges in which your raw scores lie and read across to find the ranges of your test scores.

$$\frac{}{\substack{\text{range of reading} \\ \text{test scores}}} + \frac{}{\substack{\text{range of writing} \\ \text{test scores}}} = \frac{}{\substack{\text{range of reading + writing} \\ \text{test scores}}} \text{(C)}$$

To find the range of your Reading and Writing Scaled Score, multiply (C) by 10.

Test Scores for the Reading and Writing Sections

Reading Raw Score	Writing Raw Score	Test Score
44–52	39–44	35–40
36–43	33–38	31–34
30–35	28–32	28–30
24–29	22–27	24–27
19–23	17–21	21–23
14–18	13–16	19–20
9–13	9–12	16–18
5–8	5–8	13–15
less than 5	less than 5	10–12

Math Test

Section 3: _____ = _____ (D)
 # correct raw score

Section 4: _____ = _____ (E)
 # correct raw score

Total Math raw score: (D) + (E) = _____

To find your Math Scaled Score, consult the chart below: find the range in which your raw score lies and read across to find the range for your scaled score.

Scaled Scores for the Math Test

Raw Score	Scaled Score	Raw Score	Scaled Score
50–58	700–800	20–25	450–490
44–49	650–690	15–19	400–440
38–43	600–640	11–14	350–390
32–37	550–590	7–10	300–340
26–32	500–540	less than 7	200–290

ANSWERS EXPLAINED

Section 1: Reading Test

1. **(A)**

In the course of this passage, you learn that Sir Walter is a conceited fool whose late wife, a sensible woman, had tried to protect him and their daughters from the consequences of his foolishness. You learn that he values his oldest daughter (who in looks and snobbery resembles him), but disregards his youngest daughter Anne (who in character and good sense most resembles his late wife). The author's intent here is to give you background information about this family in order to set the stage for the plot developments to come. Thus, the main purpose of the passage is to *provide an overview of the interrelationships of the members of* Sir Walter's *family*.

2. **(D)**

The first paragraph opens by stating that Sir Walter was vain about two things: he exhibited both "vanity of person and of situation." The paragraph then goes on to explain both terms. Sir Walter, still handsome in his fifties, prides himself on his personal appearance; that is, his vanity of person. In addition, he takes pride in his baronetcy, the place he holds in society; that is, his vanity of situation. Thus, "situation" here most nearly means *social standing*.

3. **(B)**

The first paragraph establishes Sir Walter as a vain and foolish character. The second paragraph establishes Lady Elliot as a sensible woman whose death leaves her three young daughters in their foolish father's care. Thus, *A vain and foolish character is left to care for three daughters after the death of his sensible wife* best summarizes the first two paragraphs of the passage. Choice (A) is incorrect. Nothing in the first two paragraphs suggests that Sir Walter was devastated by his wife's death. Choice (C) is incorrect. Lady Elliot abandons her family by dying, not by running away from a husband she can no longer endure. Choice (D) is incorrect. It sums up part of the story, but it fails to include vital information (Sir Walter's vanity, Lady Elliot's death, the relationship of the daughters with their father, etc.). Thus, it does not provide the *best* summary of the first two paragraphs.

4. **(D)**

Throughout the second paragraph, the narrator describes the late Lady Elliot as "an excellent woman," one whose judgment and conduct was beyond reproach. Only one action of hers might be viewed critically: *her decision to marry Sir Walter*. Infatuated by his good looks and his rank, she chose to marry a man far inferior to her in character and disposition. If one "pardoned the youthful infatuation which made her Lady Elliot," there was nothing in her life to criticize.

Use the process of elimination to answer this question. Does the narrator view Lady Elliot's *concealment of Sir Walter's shortcomings* critically? No. In concealing Sir Walter's shortcomings, Lady Elliot had "promoted his real respectability." The narrator is not criticizing this action of Lady Elliot. Therefore, choice (A) is incorrect. Does the narrator view Lady Elliot's *choice of an intimate friend* critically? No. The narrator's comments about this friend, Lady Russell, are entirely positive. Therefore, choice (B) is incorrect. Does the narrator view Lady Elliot's *guidance of her three daughters* critically? No. According to the narrator, Lady Elliot had been providing her daughters with "good principles and instruction." She had been guiding them admirably. Therefore, choice (C) is incorrect. Only choice (D) is left. It is the correct answer.

5. **(B)**

In the years following Lady Elliot's unwise marriage, her judgment and conduct demonstrated the superiority of her character; no one had to make any allowances for any foolishness or misbehavior on her part. Her infatuation with Sir Walter and subsequent marriage represent the only misjudgment in her otherwise blameless life.

6. **(C)**

The narrator's statement that Lady Elliot was "not the very happiest being in the world herself" is preceded by a list of all Lady Elliot had to do to cover up for her "conceited, silly" husband. Thus we can infer that the cause of her unhappiness was the difference or *disparity* between her character and that of her husband. Choice (A) is incorrect. Nothing in the passage suggests Lady Elliot lacks beauty. Indeed, we suspect that Sir Walter, so conscious of his own beauty, would not have chosen an unattractive wife. Choice (B) is incorrect. Lady Elliot's best friend had moved to be near her; they were not separated. Choice (D) is incorrect. Nothing in the passage suggests that *over the years* Lady Elliot had been unable to teach her daughters good principles. She regrets being unable to continue teaching them good principles in the years to come.

7. **(B)**

The "awful charge" that Lady Elliot must entrust to her foolish husband is his *responsibility* for the guidance of their daughters. Choices (A), (C), and (D) are incorrect. Although "charge" can mean *accusation* ("a charge of attempted murder), *official instruction* ("the judge's charge to the jury"), or *headlong rush* ("a cavalry charge"), that is not how it is used here.

8. **(B)**

Choice (B) is correct. The narrator tells little directly of Lady Elliot's feelings about dying. However, such phrases as "Three girls. . . . was an awful legacy to bequeath" and "anxiously giving her daughters [instruction]" show us something of her mind. Her concern centers not on herself but on those she must leave behind: her daughters. Her emotions as she faces death are complicated by *anxieties over her daughters' prospects*. Choice (A) is incorrect. Nothing in the passage suggests resignation or pious submissiveness on her part. Choice (C) is incorrect. There is no evidence in the passage to suggest that Lady Elliot has any concerns about her husband's possible remarriage. Choice (D) is also incorrect. Lady Elliot clearly has faced the reality of her approaching death: she recognizes its inevitability and realizes that she is leaving her daughters to the care of her conceited, silly husband.

9. **(B)**

Worry complicated Lady Elliot's emotions regarding her approaching death. She worried about what would happen to her daughters once she was no longer there to guide them. Which lines best support this answer? Lines 18–21: "Three girls, the two eldest sixteen and fourteen, was an awful legacy for a mother to bequeath, an awful charge rather, to confide to the authority and guidance of a conceited, silly father."

10. **(A)**

Lady Elliot in "quitting" her family is not simply taking a trip: she is dying. We expect a person facing death to react strongly, emotionally. Instead, the narrator states that Lady Elliot was merely attached enough to life to make dying "no matter of indifference to her." That is clearly an *understatement*. It is an example of *irony*, the literary technique that points up the contradictions in life, in this case the contradiction between the understated expression and the deeply felt reality.

11. **(C)**

Sir Walter's applications have been *marital* ones. In his conceit, he has applied for the hand in marriage of some women who were far too good for him (his applications were *unreasonable*). Sensibly enough, these women have turned him down (he has been *disappointed* in his proposals of matrimony). However, his conceit is undiminished: he prides himself on remaining single for his dear daughters' sake.

12. **(B)**

By stating that the public loves a simple explanation and by commenting on how much easier it is for schoolchildren to ignore what happened on the American continent from 1492–1620, the historian-author reveals a *condescending,* superior attitude toward the public at large, who are content with easy answers.

13. **(C)**

Throughout this passage, the author is making the point that it is wrong to consider the Mayflower Compact a cornerstone of American democracy. Instead of presenting his thesis immediately, the author uses the opening paragraph to *capture the reader's attention* with some light, humorous comments about why people foolishly continue to harbor this belief.

14. **(C)**

Those who mark the start of democracy in 1620 are *designating* or specifying 1620 as the year democracy originated in America.

15. **(A)**

Note the phrase set off in commas: "to be sure." It is a synonym for the adverb *admittedly* and is used to acknowledge that something is true. The author has just been lightly casting doubt on the idea of associating the Mayflower Compact with the birth of democracy. Here, he *concedes the point* that the compact did establish a form of self-government and thus had some relationship to democracy.

16. **(A)**

According to the author, the Pilgrims "spurned democracy." In other words, they rejected it. Their attitude toward democracy was one of *complete rejection*.

17. **(B)**

The democracy-rejecting Pilgrims would have been amazed to find themselves held up or *cited* as defenders of democracy.

18. **(A)**

The Pilgrims had been given a royal patent that legally empowered them to settle in a certain area. Because they had decided to colonize a different area, some of the group felt that once they were ashore no laws would bind them. The compact bound the signers to obey the laws of the colony. It thus served to *establish legal authority within the colony*. That was its primary purpose.

19. **(C)**

In these two sentences, the author sums up the situation on board the Mayflower that led to the signing of the compact. The Pilgrims had been granted a royal patent to form a colony in a specific area. If they had settled in that particular area, they would have been constrained to follow the terms of that patent; they would have been under the jurisdiction of the British crown, obeying British law. However, they "had decided to settle in an area outside the jurisdiction of their royal patent," and it was unclear what laws and rules would govern them. By signing the compact, the Pilgrims promised to abide by the laws of their new colony. This supports the claim that the compact's primary purpose was to *establish legal authority within the colony*.

20. **(A)**

According to the passage, the Pilgrims signed the Mayflower Compact in order of rank: first, the gentlemen; next, the "goodmen" or yeoman-farmers; finally, the servants. In doing so, they showed their *respect for the social hierarchy*.

21. **(D)**

These four brief sentences sum up the order in which the Pilgrims signed the compact. They signed in order of their class or rank. They were very aware of their position in the social hierarchy, and showed their *respect for the social hierarchy* by signing in their proper places.

22. **(D)**

This bar graph represents the composition of those aboard the Mayflower who went on to found the colony. Look at the different shaded segments of the bar graph. The smaller the segment, the fewer people it represents. Of the four passenger categories given, the smallest is choice (D), *Female minor farmers*. These were children of farming families who had not been indentured as servants.

23. **(C)**

The passage reports on *recent experiments regarding brain activity during sleep* and discusses their results and implications. Choice (A) is incorrect. Even though the passage indicates that humans sleep a great deal, it merely explains one reason why they need to sleep. It does not explain why they need to sleep more than other animals. Choice (B) is incorrect. It is well known, and assumed in the passage, that sleep is beneficial to humans. This does not need to be proved. The questions are why and how it is beneficial. Choice (D) is incorrect. The passage focuses on the "glymphatic" system in the brain, not the lymphatic system. In order to explain the function of the glymphatic system, the author compares it to the lymphatic system, but that is a supporting point and not the main focus of the passage.

24. **(D)**

The passage indicates that one of the functions of the glymphatic system is the clearing out of toxic metabolic byproducts from the brain. The lymphatic system performs a similar function for the rest of the body: "the lymphatic system clears out metabolic waste products from the rest of the body." Thus, one of its functions is the *drainage of waste*. Choice (A) is incorrect. The *glymphatic* system is associated with the brain; the *lymphatic* system is not. Choice (B) is incorrect. The regulation of temperature is not mentioned in the passage. Choice (C) is incorrect. According to the passage, the *glymphatic* system transports cerebrospinal fluid, while the *lymphatic* system transports metabolic waste products from the rest of the body.

25. **(C)**

Scan the passage to find the word "lymphatic." It appears solely in line 20, in which the workings of the lymphatic system in clearing out metabolic waste products from the body are compared to the workings of the so-called glymphatic system in clearing out cellular waste from the brain.

26. **(C)**

According to the passage, sleep serves to drain toxic chemical waste products from the brain, in addition to carrying out other functions that are not yet understood fully. Choices (A), (B), and (D) are clearly incorrect because they do not include the cleaning function that is the main consideration described in the passage.

27. **(C)**

The passage reports the long-standing hypothesis that sleep *promotes* recovery. In other words, sleep leads to, contributes to, or helps bring about recovery. The term *fosters* best captures this meaning. Choices (A), (B), and (D) are incorrect. Although "promotes" can have the meaning *exchanges a pawn* ("She wanted to promote her pawn into a queen"), *raises in rank* ("promoted to sergeant"), or *publicizes* ("ads promoting products"), that is not how the word is used here.

28. **(D)**

The expansion of the glial channels by 60 percent created significantly more room for fluid in the channels. This was a significant result: the increased volume *suggested that the flow of cerebrospinal fluid increased during sleep*, resulting in an increased ability to wash waste chemicals out of the brain. Choice (A) is incorrect. Nothing in the passage suggests that the overall size of the brain increases. Choice (C) is incorrect. No information is provided about the effects of sleep on other organs. Choice (D) is incorrect. Less sensory information is processed during sleep. The scientists hypothesized that the cleaning function and the processing of sensory information are in a sense competing: the brain cannot maximize both at the same time.

29. **(B)**

As used in the passage, "distinguish" means to differentiate the two dyed fluids or to *tell* them *apart*. Choices (A), (C), and (D) are incorrect. Although "distinguish" can mean *characterize* ("Her Brooklyn accent distinguishes her"), *make prominent* ("She distinguished herself on the ski slopes"), or *discern* ("In the dark cellar he couldn't distinguish anything"), that is not how it is used here.

30. **(B)**

The passage makes it clear that the point of using the dyed fluids is to differentiate between the fluid that circulates while the mice are asleep from the fluid that circulates while the mice are awake. Choice (A) is incorrect. The passage never mentions any different types of molecules that might make up the cerebrospinal fluid. In addition, the dyes are associated not with different types of molecules, but with different batches of cerebrospinal fluid that are essentially identical in composition. Choice (C) is incorrect. Lymph was not dyed in the experiment. Choice (D) is incorrect. The experiment focused on the glymphatic system exclusively, not on the lymphatic system.

31. **(C)**

The sentence: "By tracking the movements of red and green dye throughout the brain, the team found that large amounts of CSF flowed into the brain during sleep, but not during the waking state" reveals the reason the different-colored dyes were used: to differentiate between fluid that flowed into the brain during sleep from fluid that flowed into the brain during the waking state. Choice (A) is incorrect. This sentence merely describes the preliminary work Lulu Xie had to do to make the experiment possible. Choice (B) is incorrect. This sentence reports that the two-photon microscope could distinguish the red dye from the green dye, but it does not explain why that was important for the success of the experiment. Choice (D) is incorrect. This sentence reports a concrete result of the experiment, but it does not reveal the specific logical steps that led the scientists to that conclusion.

32. **(C)**

The passage compares what the brain does during sleep to what a human does during the weekend. The point is to suggest not only that cleaning is one function performed by both, but also that both carry out other functions in addition to cleaning. Sleep therefore most likely provides the brain time both to clean itself and to perform several other functions, just as the weekend provides a human the opportunity to clean the house, visit friends, and perform other functions. Choice (A) is incorrect. This statement sounds true. However, even though one could use this comparison to make the point that, just as sleep is essential for the health of the brain, the weekend is essential for the (mental and physical) health of the human, it is not the point the author is making here. Choice (B) is incorrect. There is no suggestion of ranking different activities and deciding which one is most beneficial. Choice (D) is incorrect. As with choice (A), the point sounds plausible, but that is not the focus of the comparison here.

33. **(D)**

The primary focus of this passage is the contradiction between traditional beliefs about the frailty of women and the manner in which black women were treated under slavery. Though there may be other examples of women's strength in this passage, the best answer is choice (D) because it reflects the central theme of the passage. Choice (A) is incorrect. Though the passage mentions, "women at the North . . . talking about rights," this is done as an aside and is not a central part of Truth's argument. Choice (B) is incorrect. Though Truth mentioned having, "born thirteen children," she does this as a demonstration of her treatment under slavery, rather than as proof of the hard work that women do as mothers. Choice (C) is incorrect. Though childbirth is certainly physically challenging, Truth makes no mention of this in the passage.

34. **(B)**

This is the section of the passage in which Truth recounts many of the details of her hard treatment as a slave, including hard physical labor and beatings. It comes immediately after she cites a man's argument that women need to be "helped into carriages" and is intended as evidence against this argument regarding women's weakness. Choice (A) is incorrect. As the explanation of question 33 states, the actions of northern women are mentioned as an aside; they are not a central part of Truth's argument. Choice (C) is incorrect. This sentence is a request for kindness and makes no mention of the strength of women. In fact, this sentence argues that even if women are weaker than men are, that does not justify denying them rights. Choice (D) is incorrect. Though this sentence does mention the strength of biblical women, it is not as strong an answer as choice (B). Why not? First, the sentence provides only one example of female strength. Second, the example is given in order to urge men to meet women's demands, rather than to contradict traditional depictions of women's frailty.

35. **(D)**

"Fix" is used in informal English as a synonym for *predicament*. Though Truth is giving a speech, her style is down-to-earth and casual. One good way to test possible answers is to substitute them in the sentence for the word in question and see if the sentence makes sense with the substitution. In this case, saying that the white men will be in a predicament makes sense. Choice (A) is incorrect. Though repair is one meaning of *fix*, this sentence is not about fixing something that is broken. Additionally, if you substitute the word *repair* in the sentence, it does not make sense. We do not talk about being *in* a repair. Choice (B) is incorrect. While it is common to talk about being "in a rut," this figure of speech refers to being stuck in a particular way of doing things. Talking about rights for women and blacks is not going to cause white men to be unable to change. Choice (C) is incorrect. Although it is common to talk about being *in* a battle, a *battle* is a far more extreme conflict then a predicament or *fix*.

36. **(A)**

The primary focus of this passage is the inevitability of progress toward women's rights because the equality of women is a fundamental truth. Douglass begins by pointing out that slavery, which had been legal for 200 years, was ended. He then refers to the ultimate triumph of Galileo's observation that the Earth revolves around the sun, despite the church's insistence to the contrary. Finally, he predicts a victory for women's rights because, "When a great truth gets abroad in the world, no power on earth can imprison it." Choice (B) is incorrect. The church is mentioned in regards to Galileo, not in regards to women. Choice (C) is incorrect.

Though Douglass argues that women should receive the "rights of American citizenship," he does not argue that their citizenship is a reason that they will win those rights. Choice (D) is incorrect. Douglass argues that the truth always wins out but he does not explain why this occurs. Choice (D) might explain why, but Douglass does not make that argument.

37. **(D)**

In this sentence, Douglass states his primary claim, which is that the truth cannot be stopped. This is for him the fundamental reason that women will be victorious in their struggle for equal rights. Choice (A) is incorrect. This sentence cites a barrier to winning women's suffrage rather than a reason that the movement will succeed. Choice (B) is incorrect. This sentence grants that belief in traditional roles for women is still powerful, despite its obvious falsehood. It states the opposite of Douglass's overall claim. Choice (C) is incorrect. This sentence grants that even when women achieve equal rights, some will still refuse to accept the change.

38. **(A)**

Authorized is a synonym of "sanctioned." It is the best answer in this case because Douglass is speaking about the legislation that allowed slavery, despite the truth that "man cannot hold property in a man." He is describing Henry Clay's bold claim that the law defines what rights people have, rather than a theory of natural rights. Legislation *authorized* slavery, despite its violation of natural rights. Choice (B) is incorrect. The legislation that Douglass refers to allowed slavery rather than penalizing it. Choice (C) is incorrect. The legislation that Douglass refers to allowed slavery rather than prohibiting it. Choice (D) is incorrect. Douglass makes no mention of whether the legislation in question describes slavery as praiseworthy.

39. **(B)**

The story of Galileo's conflict with the Church regarding the Earth's orbit of the sun is one of the most well-known historical examples of an organization's attempting to hold fast to its beliefs despite evidence to the contrary. Douglass uses this example to demonstrate that the truth will always be victorious, despite powerful opposition. Choice (A) is incorrect. Douglass does not believe that there is any basis, scientific or otherwise, for treating women unequally. Choice (C) is incorrect. Though Douglass believes that women's rights are important, he makes no mention of the state of women's rights and their acceptance in other parts of the world. Choice (D) is incorrect. The "unveiling of the statue of Galileo" in a location where the church was very strong demonstrates that the truth will triumph despite powerful opposition, not that this opposition was incorrect.

40. **(B)**

In Passage 1, Sojourner Truth makes a strong argument that women should receive the same rights as men. In Passage 2, Douglass, who supports equal rights for women, argues that women will be victorious in the struggle for equal rights because the struggle is based on the truth that women are men's equals. Choice (A) is incorrect. Douglass is a supporter of Sojourner Truth's cause. Choice (C) is incorrect. Douglass takes no position on how rapidly progress should be made on this issue. He simply argues that progress is inevitable. Choice (D) is incorrect. Though Douglass notes that progress was made on the legality of slavery, he does not mention whether any progress has been made toward recognizing equal rights for women.

41. **(D)**

"That man" argues that women are weak and require assistance. Douglass disagrees with this argument and likens it to the church's insistence that the sun revolves around the Earth. Both are examples of people vociferously advocating old beliefs despite evidence to the contrary. Choice (A) is incorrect. Douglass does not agree with the man's argument. Choice (B) is incorrect. Douglass does disagree with the man, but he fully agrees with the author of Passage 1. Choice (C) is incorrect. Though Douglass disagrees with the man and *might* be angered by his arguments, there is no evidence in the passage proving that he is angered. As a result, though choice (C) could be correct, choice (D) is the best answer.

42. **(B)**

In this sentence, Douglass strongly implies that the "two hundred years of legislation" mentioned previously no longer authorize slavery. These laws were not able to "keep life" in the institution of slavery. Douglass is speaking in 1888, two decades after the Emancipation Proclamation. It is, therefore, a fact, that slavery is no longer legal at the time he is speaking. Choice (A) is incorrect. This is Henry Clay's argument for slavery. Douglass uses it as evidence of a powerful belief or argument that has been defeated by truth. Choice (C) is incorrect. In this sentence Douglass grants that incorrect beliefs still have significant power. Choice (D) is incorrect. This sentence argues that the march of progress toward equal rights will not be reversed, but it makes no claim about what has occurred in the past.

43. **(D)**

Note that the caption on the chart is "Metabolic middle ground." The dinosaurs and the shark are in the middle of the chart. This graphically reinforces the concept that, like sharks, dinosaurs are neither cold-blooded ectotherms nor warm-blooded endotherms, but have metabolisms that fall somewhere in between. Thus, the chief purpose of the chart is to illustrate that *in metabolic rate dinosaurs are most akin to sharks.*

44. **(C)**

The author of the passage succinctly summarizes the competing theories that categorize dinosaurs as ectotherms, endotherms, or mesotherms. Clearly he is *well-informed about* these *competing theories* based on studies of dinosaur metabolic rates. Choices (A) and (D) are incorrect. Nothing in the passage suggests that the author is an active researcher or involved in the development of mathematical equations. Choice (B) is also incorrect: his presentation of the ectotherm theory is objective; nothing suggests he has any bias in its favor.

45. **(A)**

In both the title of the article ("Dinosaur metabolism neither hot nor cold, but just right") and its opening sentence, the author is alluding or referring to the classic children's tale of Goldilocks and the three bears, with the three bowls of porridge. By calling this latest theory about dinosaurs a Goldilocks solution, he hints that this time the researchers may have gotten things "just right."

46. **(B)**

First, the conventional wisdom was that dinosaurs were cold-blooded ectotherms. Then researchers came up with the heretical notion that dinosaurs were hot-blooded endotherms. Now Grady and his fellow researchers have come up with a third idea, in the process establishing an entirely new metabolic category. In admitting that what they have done is audacious (daring), Grady is *acknowledging* how *radical* or revolutionary their suggestion is and how profound a change it makes in the way we think of dinosaurs.

47. **(B)**

Note the references to time with which paragraphs four and five open: "For the first 150 years" and "Beginning in the late 1960s." Paragraph 4 describes the theory that dinosaurs were cold-blooded; paragraph 5, the alternate theory that they were warm-blooded. Taken together, the two paragraphs *give an overview of previous theories about the body temperature and activity level of dinosaurs.*

48. **(C)**

The scientists conducting this research are trying to figure out into which category dinosaurs fit. Are they cold-blooded ectotherms? Are they warm-blooded endotherms? Is there yet another category into which they can fit? By studying the dinosaurs' metabolic and growth rates, the researchers are attempting to *characterize dinosaurs* as cold-blooded, warm-blooded, or something in-between.

49. (A)

Lines 11–13 sum up the conclusion reached by Grady and his fellow researchers: dinosaurs "belonged to an intermediate group that can raise their body temperature but don't keep it at a specific level." Their goal was to figure out into which category dinosaurs fit. In discovering that dinosaurs belonged to an intermediate group, they achieved their goal.

50. (D)

To say that growth rates scale with metabolic rates is to say there is a *correlation* between the two rates. Creatures with a high metabolic rate have more energy to expend. Thanks to this extra energy, they can reach their adult size faster: they have a high growth rate. Choices (A), (B), and (C) are incorrect. Although scale can mean *flake* ("paint scaling from the banister"), *reduce* ("they scaled back their plans"), or *ascend* ("she scaled a 30-foot flagpole"), that is not how the word is used here.

51. (B)

To lay down bone is to build up a deposit of bone tissue. Thus, rings of bone were laid down or *deposited* each year. Choices (A), (C), and (D) are incorrect. Although laid down can mean *rested* ("laid down for a nap"), *sacrificed* ("laid down his life"), or *formulated* ("laid down strict rules"), that is not how it is used here.

52. (D)

The *Harbrace College Handbook* states that "[w]ords used in a special sense are sometimes enclosed in quotation marks." What is the usual sense of the word "defend"? Its primary meaning is to protect someone or something from harm, as in defending our country. Here, however, it *is being used in an unusual sense*. The author is not saying that sharks, tuna, and giant sea-turtles do not resist attacks on their body temperature. He's saying that their bodies do not maintain a constant set temperature. Choice (A) is incorrect. Although the word "defend" is not being used in its usual sense, it is not being used to create *an ironic* (satirical or wryly amusing; paradoxical) *effect*.

Section 2: Writing and Language Test

1. (C)

The key phrase in the question is "not quite the most widespread." Stating that bats are "second only to rodents" means that bats are almost the most widespread but come in second place. Choice (A) does the opposite of what the question asks. Choice (B) gives a percentage without a frame of reference. Choice (D) is too vague because we would need information about the numbers of humans relative to those of other mammals.

2. **(A)**

"Although" gives the needed contrast between the first part of the sentence and the second part. Choices (B) and (D) show cause and effect. Choice (C), "however," would work if a contrast was needed between the previous sentence and the current sentence but does not work to provide a contrast within a sentence like this.

3. **(A)**

"Do" is numerically consistent with the plural subject "roles." Choice (B), "does," is singular. Choice (C), "don't," causes a double negative given the "not" that follows. Choice (D), "do's," is not a word.

4. **(A)**

This is a complete sentence that requires no breaks. The phrase "bodies approximately one inch long" is relatively long, but it should remain a unified phrase without any pauses. The other options unnecessarily break up the sentence.

5. **(C)**

This word refers to "echolocation," which is best described as a "phenomenon" since it is a process that allows bats to navigate. The other options are all associated with physical items.

6. **(D)**

Notice that the footnote beneath the graph states that the population numbers are tabulated at the end of each year. According to the graph, the bat population decreased from around 6,000,000 at the time of the outbreak of the illness at the end of 2007 to about 2,000,000 in 2010. This is a decrease of roughly $\frac{2}{3}$, which equates to about 65%.

7. **(D)**

The word "while" earlier in the sentence already provides the transition needed. So omitting any word at this point makes the most sense.

8. **(B)**

"Effect," which is choice (B), is typically a noun. However, "affect" in choice (A) is typically a verb. In this sentence, the farmers are feeling the consequences of these changes, and "consequences" is a noun like "effect." Even though "affectedness" in choice (C) is a noun, it means having a pretentious attitude. Choice (D), "effectively," is an adverb.

9. **(D)**

"Bats'" correctly shows possession by plural bats. Choice (A), "bats," is a noun. Choice (B), "bat's," shows possession by a single bat. Choice (C), "bat is," has a noun and a verb.

10. **(C)**

The sentence states that this is a species "already on the endangered list." So the most logical choice is the bat species that has the smallest population. Since the paragraph is speaking from a more recent perspective, look at the bat species that has the smallest population in the most recent year, i.e., gray bats.

11. **(B)**

Consider what immediately follows the insertion point—"so preservationists can make the necessary interventions." Preservationists would naturally be most interested in helping those species in need of intervention because the species were in danger of becoming extinct. So the statement "are learning which species are in the most danger" most logically connects to this. Choice (A) is the opposite of what is needed. Choice (C) is irrelevant. Even though choice (D) relates a bit to the information that follows, it does not give as strong a connection as choice (B) does. Preservationists would more likely find information about which bat species most need help more useful than information about bat predator locations.

12. **(B)**

This choice uses consistent punctuation, dashes, to set aside the parenthetical phrase. Choices (A) and (D) are inconsistent; a parenthetical phrase that begins with one form of punctuation should end with the same type. Choice (C) does not have a needed pause before the start of the parenthetical phrase with the word "as."

13. **(B)**

What follows are two general ways that married couples in *The Canterbury Tales* are dysfunctional, so choice (B) gives the best transition. Choice (A) is incorrect because the listed items are not quotations. Choice (C) is incorrect because these themes are consistent with the text, not ironic. Choice (D) is incorrect because the listed items lead to conflict, not resolution.

14. **(C)**

The subject comes after the underlined portion. The subject is the plural "marital troubles," so the plural verb "are" works. Choices (A) and (B) are both singular, and choice (D) uses "them" incorrectly.

15. **(C)**

There is no need to repeat the name of the story, as choice (A) does, since it is mentioned immediately before this sentence. Choice (B) is not correct because it is wordy and adds no substance to the sentence. Choice (D) is incorrect because the current sentence is simply expanding on the previous one, not showing cause and effect.

16. **(D)**

This is a direct quotation from Lord Walter, as indicated by the word "stating" immediately beforehand and by the use of old English spelling. Choices (A) and (B) give factual reasoning, but it is necessary to leave the quotation marks for clarity. Choice (C) is not correct because these words are not coming from the narrator but from a character.

17. **(A)**

This choice is parallel to the structure of the previous phrase "a false order for . . ." and is logical. Choice (B) is illogical, choice (C) is too choppy, and choice (D) is too wordy and is not parallel.

18. **(D)**

This phrase completes the idiomatic expression "is not so much . . . as he is." The other options do not connect appropriately to this earlier phrasing.

19. **(A)**

It is correct to say "contributes . . . through," making choice (A) correct. The other options do not work in conjunction with "contributes" to make a sensible phrase.

20. **(C)**

The key word in this question is "limited." Therefore "only that" makes sense since it minimizes the extent of her request. The other options do not limit the request in any way.

21. **(D)**

The entire phrase "at what she believes to be the end of their marriage" is parenthetical. Choice (D) is the only option that both leaves this phrase intact and places a comma at the end of it so that it is set aside from the rest of the sentence.

22. **(A)**

Even though this story is from long ago, the paragraph is referring to the events as though they were read in a present-day perspective. Therefore, choice (A) works to give a present-tense verb that matches the singular subject "concern." Choices (B) and (C) indicate past events, and choice (D) is plural.

23. **(A)**

Choices (C) and (D) do not use the required possessive form "its." Choice (B) incorrectly uses the plural verb "are." Choice (A) gives appropriate pauses with the commas, uses the singular "is" to match the singular subject "workforce," and correctly uses the possessive "its" to show that school teachers are a part of the singular society.

24. **(D)**

Choices (A) and (B) do not indicate a wide time span since they limit the instructional influence to the confines of a day. Choice (C) refers to places, not time. Choice (D) works best since it indicates that teachers can influence students from the early years of school all the way through postsecondary education.

25. **(A)**

The first word in the underlined portion must be "your" since it refers to the reader's possession of "best," making choices (B) and (D) incorrect. Choice (C) is incorrect because it jumps to using "one" partway through instead of being consistent in the use of "you." Choice (A) uses the correct form of "your" to show possession and uses "you're" to stand for "you are."

26. **(B)**

"So," gives a logical transition from the previous paragraph to the rhetorical sentence that starts this paragraph. Choices (A) and (C) incorrectly show contrast, and choice (D) shows a causal connection that is too direct.

27. **(C)**

You won't have a calculator at your disposal on the Writing and Language section. However, you can estimate the average, especially given that the answer choices are reasonably far apart from one another. Based on the different salaries in each of the five cities, $55,000 comes closest to the average, making choice (C) correct.

28. **(B)**

This choice properly indicates that a singular teacher owns a workday. Choice (A) indicates plural teacher ownership. Choice (C) indicates plural teachers as a subject. Choice (D) inserts unnecessary verbs.

29. **(B)**

"Than" completes the comparative phrase "better . . . than." Choice (A) can work for comparisons but not in this context. Choice (C) is for time, and choice (D) does not lead to a comparison.

30. **(C)**

"Furthermore," provides an appropriate transition into the continued explanation of the education and training of teachers. Choice (A) indicates confusion, choice (B) indicates an assumption, and choice (D) does not provide a transition.

31. **(B)**

"Prospective" means "preparing to do so in the future," which applies to teachers who are being trained since they are not yet licensed professionals. "Perspective" in choice (A) indicates a point of view. "Prospecting" in choice (C) indicates searching. "Previewing" in choice (D) does not apply to people in the process of learning their profession, although it could refer to what the trainees themselves will be doing with respect to professional skills.

32. **(C)**

The data in the chart give an approximate salary range between $52,000 and $62,000, making the variation about $10,000.

33. **(B)**

The colon is appropriate because it indicates a clarification to follow. Choice (A) results in a comma splice, while choices (C) and (D) result in run-on sentences.

34. **(D)**

"Dubious," which can mean "suspicious," correctly refers to the unsavory and illegal happenings mentioned in the beginning of the sentence. The activities are not best described as "transparent," choice (A). Since these activities were associated with lawbreaking, they were not likely done in a way that was easily seen. Choice (B) is incorrect since events from just a few decades past could not be accurately characterized as "ancient."

Choice (C) is associated with speakeasies but not necessarily with a person or a massacre.

35. (A)

"Because" functions to show a cause-and-effect relationship between the first part of the sentence and the second part. Choices (B) and (C) show contrast, and choice (D) shows a continuation of the same thought.

36. (C)

This is the only option that leaves the unified phrase "force-feeding of corn to ducks" completely intact.

37. (A)

This is the only choice that shows ownership by the singular city of Chicago of the City Council. Choices (B) and (D) do not show possession, and choice (C) shows plural possession.

38. (B)

A break between the independent clauses in the sentence is needed, which choices (A) and (D) do not have. Choice (C) needs a comma after the introductory phrase "not surprisingly," and also needs to show that "Chicago" possesses the "chefs." Choice (B) uses a semicolon to break up the two independent clauses and uses the correct possessive form of "Chicago."

39. (C)

The emotions expressed in the previous sentence are extreme and intense, so writing "just wondered what all the fuss was about" demonstrates a clear contrast in attitude. Choices (A), (B), and (D) all indicate some degree of agreement with the attitudes of the chefs mentioned in the previous sentence.

40. (A)

"What's more" correctly indicates a continuation of the ideas from the previous paragraph. The other options all illustrate a contrast. Sometimes similarities among the answers can help you eliminate choices.

41. (B)

Choices (A) and (D) do not provide vivid descriptions. Choice (C) is inconsistent with the type of food one wants at a restaurant. Choice (B) is both logical and vivid.

42. **(A)**

The dash serves to provide a long pause before the closing thought in the sentence. Choice (B) is too choppy and creates a run-on. Choice (C) has an unnecessary comma. Choice (D) is incorrect because there is not a complete sentence after the semicolon.

43. **(D)**

The context indicates that the Health Department stopped enforcing this ban, making "froze" the most logical option. "Vivified," choice (A), conveys an increase in the liveliness of the ban, which is inconsistent with the context. "Congealed," choice (B), means "to take shape." Choice (C), "checked," is illogical. Stating "were checked" could possibly work, but "checked" by itself doesn't make sense.

44. **(C)**

The proper idiomatic phrase is "victory for." The other options join "victory" with prepositions that don't agree given the phrasing needed in this context.

Section 3: Math Test (No Calculator)

For some of the problems, an alternative solution, indicated by two asterisks (**) follows the first solution. When this occurs, one of the solutions is the direct mathematical one and the other is based on one of the strategies discussed in Chapter 6.

1. **(C)**

Test the choices. In **1994**, Adam entered 3 more tournaments than in 1993, an increase of $\frac{3}{6} = \frac{1}{2} = 50\%$. (From 1990 to 1991 the increase was 25%, from 1991 to 1992 it was 100%, and from 1994 to 1995 it was $33\frac{1}{3}\%$.)

2. **(B)**

$5(x + 1) + 3 = 3(x + 3) \Rightarrow 5x + 5 + 3 = 3x + 9 \Rightarrow 5x + 8 = 3x + 9 \Rightarrow 2x = 1 \Rightarrow x = \mathbf{0.5}$

**A solution to the equation $5(x + 1) + 3 = 3(x + 3)$ is the x-coordinate of the point of intersection of the straight lines $y = 5(x + 1) + 3$ and $y = 3(x + 3)$. Since these lines intersect at the point (0.5, 10.5), the original equation has one solution, $x = \mathbf{0.5}$.

3. **(B)**

Rewrite the given equation in $y = mx + b$ form.

$$3x + 4y = 24 \Rightarrow 4y = -3x + 24 \Rightarrow y = -\frac{3}{4}x + 6$$

So the slope, m, is $-\frac{3}{4}$.

**Find two points on the given line and use the slope formula. For example, when $x = 0$, $y = 6$, and when $y = 0$, $x = 8$. Therefore, $(0, 6)$ and $(8, 0)$ are points on the line, and the slope of the line is $\dfrac{6-0}{0-8} = \dfrac{6}{-8} = -\dfrac{3}{4}$.

4. **(A)**

To answer any question about maps or scale drawings, set up a proportion and cross-multiply:

$$\frac{\text{miles}}{\text{centimeters}}: \frac{m}{c} = \frac{n}{x} \Rightarrow mx = cn$$

So $x = \dfrac{cn}{m}$.

5. **(D)**

Multiplying (not dividing) the number of courses a student takes by the number of credits each course is worth gives the total number of credits the student earns. (Clearly, taking 5 three-credit courses earns $5 \times 3 = 15$ credits, not $5 \div 3 = 1.66$ credits.) So the answer is either choice (C) or choice (D). Since "at least 120 credits" means "120 credits or more," the desired inequality is "greater than or equal to" 120: **$3x + 4y \geq 120$**.

6. **(C)**

When you have to determine which of four statements is true, just treat each one as a true-false question.

- The French club could have 2 boys and 3 girls, and the Spanish club could have 30 boys and 50 girls. Statement (A) is false.
- The Spanish club could have 3 boys and 5 girls, and the French club could have 20 boys and 30 girls. Statement (B) is false.
- 3 out of every 5 members of the French club, or 60%, are girls; 5 out of every 8 members of the Spanish club, or 62.5%, are girls. Statement (C) is true.
- Once you know that Statement (C) is true, you don't have to waste your time testing Statement (D); it must be false. For example, if the French club originally had 2 boys and 3 girls and if among the new members there were 30 boys and 20 girls, then the number of boys and girls would *not* be equal.

7. **(B)**

Since John averaged 25 miles per gallon for the 200-mile trip, he used $200 \div 25 = 8$ gallons of gas. At the point that Mary had used 8 gallons of gas, she had traveled $8 \times 20 = 160$ miles. So she was still $200 - 160 = 40$ miles from home.

8. **(B)**

If (a, b) is a point on each line, then $2a + 3b = 4$ and $b = 2a$. Replacing b by $2a$ in the first equation, we get $2a + 3(2a) = 4 \Rightarrow 8a = 4 \Rightarrow a = \dfrac{1}{2}$. Since $b = 2a$, $b = 1$. Finally, $a + b = \dfrac{1}{2} + 1 = \dfrac{3}{2} = \mathbf{1.5}$.

9. **(B)**

The formulas for the volumes of a rectangular solid and a cylinder are $V = lwh$ and $V = \pi r^2 h$, respectively. (Remember that these formulas are given to you on the first page of every math section.) The volume of container I is $(4)(4)(5) = 80$ cubic inches. Since the diameter of container II is 4, its radius is 2, and so its volume is $\pi(2^2)(5) = 20\pi$. The difference in volumes is $80 - 20\pi = \mathbf{20(4 - \pi)}$.

10. **(C)**

The simplest way to answer this type of question is to plug in a simple number. Since this is a question involving percents, the easiest number to use is 100. Assume that Pam sells her vases to Carl for $100. Since 60% of 100 is 60, he sells them for $160. Since 20% of 100 is 20, during the July 4th sale Carl sells the vases for $80, $20 less than he pays for them. Since $80 is exactly half of $160, the customer is receiving a **50%** discount.

If you didn't think to plug in a number, you should have proceeded in exactly the same manner. If Pam sells Carl her vases for x dollars, he normally sells them for $1.6x$ dollars. During the July 4th sale, he sells them for $0.8x$, which is exactly **50% of $1.6x$.

11. **(D)**

If $y = x^2 + 1$ and $y = -x^2 + 3$, then $x^2 + 1 = -x^2 + 3 \Rightarrow 2x^2 = 2 \Rightarrow x^2 = 1$. So $x = 1$ or $x = -1$.

If $x = 1$, then $y = 2$. If $x = -1$, then $y = 2$. So the two solutions are $(1, 2)$ and $(-1, 2)$, and $a + b + c + d = 1 + 2 + (-1) + 2 = \mathbf{4}$.

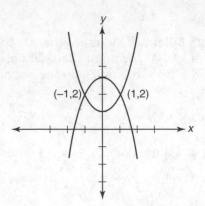

12. (C)

Each of the four triangles in the diagram below are 45-45-90 right triangles.

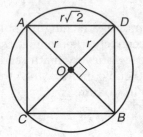

The sides of each triangle are r, r, and $r\sqrt{2}$. So each side of square $ADBC$ is $\sqrt{2}$, and its perimeter, b, is $4r\sqrt{2}$. The area, a, of square $ADBC$ is $\left(r\sqrt{2}\right)^2 = 2r^2$.

Since $a = b$, we have $2r^2 = \mathbf{4r\sqrt{2}} \Rightarrow r = \mathbf{2\sqrt{2}}$.

13. (C)

Let x represent the number of juniors on the team. Then the number of seniors on the team is $x + 5$, and the total number of students on the team is $2x + 5$. So the fraction of the team that are juniors is $\dfrac{x}{2x+5}$. However, it is given that the juniors make up 40% or $\dfrac{4}{10}$ of the team. So,

$$\frac{x}{2x+5} = \frac{4}{10} \Rightarrow 10x = 8x + 20 \Rightarrow 2x = 20 \Rightarrow x = 10$$

So the team consists of 10 juniors and 15 seniors, a total of **25** students.

**You are told that 40% of the team members are juniors and 60% of them are seniors. The 20% difference is due to the fact that there are 5 more seniors on the team than juniors. So those "extra" 5 seniors make up the 20% difference. If those 5 seniors represent 20% or one-fifth of the team, the entire team consists of $5 \times 5 = \mathbf{25}$ players.

14. **(C)**

The slope of the straight line segment connecting (2, 2) and (6, 8) is

$$\frac{8-2}{6-2} = \frac{6}{4} = \frac{3}{2} = 1.5$$

Therefore, as x goes up 1 from 2 to 3, y goes up 1.5 from 2 to 3.5. Therefore, the point (3, 3.5) is on the graph. So $a = 3.5$, and $3a = 3 \times 3.5 = 10.5$. To evaluate $f(10.5)$, consider the straight-line segment connecting (10, 8) and (16, 2). The slope of that segment is

$$\frac{2-8}{16-10} = \frac{-6}{6} = -1$$

So as x goes up 0.5 from 10 to 10.5, y goes down 0.5 from 8 to **7.5**.

15. **(D)**

Since the profit is increasing linearly, we need to find the slope of the line of best fit. The points that are easiest to read exactly are the lattice points. We see that the line passes through (3, 10) and (9, 40). So the slope of the line is $\frac{40-10}{9-3} = \frac{30}{6} = 5$. So the company's profit is increasing by approximately $5,000 per month. A year and a half is 18 months. In the 9 months from the time the company was in business 9 months to when it will be in business 18 months, the profit is expected to increase by $45,000 from $40,000 to **$85,000**.

16. $\dfrac{1}{2}$ **or .5**

This problem would be trivial if you could use a calculator. But, since this question is in the non-calculator section, you need to know how to manipulate fractional and negative exponents.

$$8^{-\frac{1}{3}} = \frac{1}{8^{\frac{1}{3}}} = \frac{1}{\sqrt[3]{8}} = \frac{1}{2}$$

17. $\dfrac{4}{5}$ **or** $\dfrac{8}{10}$ **or .8**

Draw a right triangle. Label it ABC, with C as the right angle, and let the cosine of B be $0.6 = \frac{6}{10} = \frac{3}{5}$. Then label the side adjacent to angle B as 3 and the hypotenuse as 5.

Clearly, this is a 3-4-5 right triangle, so side $\overline{AC}$ is 4, and $\cos A = \dfrac{4}{5}$ **or** $\dfrac{8}{10}$ **or .8.**

18. **56**

$$\left(7+i\sqrt{7}\right)\left(7-i\sqrt{7}\right) = 49 - 7i^2 = 49 - 7(-1) = 49 + 7 = 56$$

19. $\dfrac{25}{4}$ **or 6.25**

Subtracting $3x$ and $3y$ from both sides of the first equation gives $x = y$. Since $x + y = 5$, we see that $x = y = 2.5$. So $xy = 2.5 \times 2.5 = \mathbf{6.25}$.

**Alternatively, since $x + y = 5$, we have that $x = 5 - y$. Then replacing x by $5 - y$ in the first equation, we get that

$$3(5-y) + 4y = 4(5-y) + 3y \Rightarrow 15 + y = 20 - y \Rightarrow 2y = 5 \Rightarrow y = \frac{5}{2}$$

So, $x = 5 - \dfrac{5}{2} = \dfrac{5}{2}$. Finally, $xy = \dfrac{5}{1}\dfrac{5}{2} = \dfrac{25}{4}$.

20. **2**

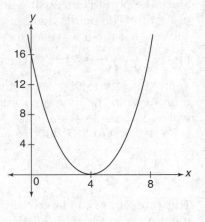

First of all, every parabola whose equation is of the form $y = ax^2 + bx + c$ intersects the y-axis exactly once, at the point where $x = 0$. Here, it is at the point $(0, 16)$. So $m = 1$. In general, such a parabola can intersect the x-axis once, twice, or not at all. It happens wherever $y = 0$. To know how many times this parabola intersects the x-axis, we have to solve the equation $0 = x^2 - 8x + 16 = (x - 4)(x - 4)$. This equation has only one solution: $x = 4$. The parabola intersects the x-axis once, at the point $(4, 0)$. So $n = 1$ and $m + n = \mathbf{2}$.

Section 4: Math Test (Calculator)

For some of the problems, an alternative solution, indicated by two asterisks (**) follows the first solution. When this occurs, one of the solutions is the direct mathematical one and the other is based on one of the strategies discussed in Chapter 6.

1. **(B)**

Convert 4 feet to 48 inches, and set up a proportion:

$$\frac{\text{depth of water in inches}}{\text{time in minutes}} : \frac{4}{25} = \frac{48}{x}$$

By cross-multiplying, we get $4x = (25)(48) = 1200$, and so $x = 300$. So the tank will be full 300 minutes, or exactly 5 hours, after 11:00, which is **4:00**.

**Equivalently, you could reason that if it takes 25 minutes to fill the tank to 4 inches, it would take 3 times as long (75 minutes) to fill the tank to 12 inches, or 1 foot. So it would take $(4)(75) = 300$ minutes to fill the tank to 4 feet.

2. **(A)**

The value of a square root can never be negative So there is no value of x that could make $\sqrt{x+7}$ equal to -4. **The equation has no solutions.**

If you didn't see that, you should have proceeded as follows: If $\sqrt{x+7} = -4$, then squaring both sides gives $x + 7 = 16$. So $x = 9$. So 9 is the only possible solution. However, before choosing choice (B), we have to check that 9 is, in fact, a solution; i.e., it is not extraneous. Does $\sqrt{9+7} = -4$? No, $\sqrt{9+7} = \sqrt{16} = 4$, not -4.

3. **(B)**

It appears that the y-intercept of the line of best fit, the grade that would correspond to not studying at all (0 hours), is 55. So $b = 55$. The slope of the line is obtained by using the slope formula. Since the line of best fit passes through the points $(4, 70)$ and $(9, 90)$, the slope of the line is $\frac{90-70}{9-4} = \frac{20}{5} = 4$, and $m = 4$. So $m + b = 4 + 55 = $ **59**.

4. **(B)**

Since the average of 82 and 88 is 85, the only way that the mean grade, m, of all the students in the class could be 85 is if $b = g$. Since it is given that $b \neq g$, m cannot be 85; $\boldsymbol{m \neq 85}$.

**The weighted average, m, of all the students in the class is $\frac{82b+88g}{b+g}$.

So if $m = 85$, then $\frac{82b+88g}{b+g} = 85 \Rightarrow 82b+88g = 85b+85g \Rightarrow 3b = 3g \Rightarrow b = g$.

Since it is given that $b \neq g$, m cannot be 85.

5. **(C)**

Since 45 minutes is $\frac{3}{4}$ of an hour, a rate of 1 page per 45 minutes is a rate of 1 page per $\frac{3}{4}$ of an hour, which is equal to $1 - \frac{3}{4} = \frac{4}{3}$ pages per hour.

So in an 8 hour day Brigitte can translate $8 - \dfrac{4}{3} = \dfrac{32}{3}$ pages. In a 5-day

week, she can translate $5 - \dfrac{32}{3} = \dfrac{160}{3}$ pages. Finally, in 6 weeks, she can

translate $6 - \dfrac{160}{3} = \mathbf{320}$ pages.

6. **(C)**

Note that (population) ÷ (population per square mile) = area, in square miles.

Since the area of the United States didn't change between 1970 and 2000, subject to rounding errors in approximating both the population density and the population, the answer should be the same for each of the years. For example,

- 1970: 203,200,000 people ÷ 57.4 people per square mile = 3,540,000 square miles ≈ **3,500,000**.
- 2000: 281,400,000 people ÷ 79.6 people per square mile = 3,535,000 square miles ≈ **3,500,000**.

7. **(A)**

After m monthly deposits have been made, the box contained $d + me$ dollars. From the given information, we have

$$175 = d + 3e \quad \text{and} \quad 300 = d + 8e$$

Subtracting the first equation from the second one gives $125 = 5e$, and so $e = 25$. Then $175 = d + 3(25) = d + 75$. Therefore, $d = 100$, and we have that $a = \mathbf{100 + 25m}$.

8. **(B)**

Since after the initial deposit in January 2014 deposits to the box were made on the first of each month, 11 monthly deposits were made in 2014 (on the first of February through the first of December) and 12 monthly deposits were made in 2015 (on the first of January through the first of December). Therefore on December 25, 2014, the amount in the box was the amount of the initial deposit on January 1, 2014 plus 23 times the amount of the monthly deposits. From the solution to the preceding question, we have that the amount in the box on December 25, 2014 was $100 + 23 \times \$25 = \$100 + \$575 = \mathbf{\$675}$.

9. **(C)**

$$f(x) = 4x^4 - 4 = 4 \Rightarrow 4x^4 = 8 \Rightarrow x^4 = 2 \Rightarrow x = \sqrt[4]{2} \approx 1.189$$

**Use TACTIC 5: backsolve. Clearly 1, choice (B), doesn't work, so try choice (C). $f(1.19) = 4(1.19)^4 = 4.02$. That is so close to 4 that it must be the answer. The small difference is due to rounding in the answer choices. The real value of x is closer to 1.1892, and $4(1.1892)^4 - 4 = 3.9998$.

10. **(A)**

At 10:30 A.M. the first car had been going 40 miles per hour for 1.5 hours, and so had gone $40 \times 1.5 = 60$ miles. The second car covered the same 60 miles in 1 hour and 20 minutes, or $1\frac{1}{3} = \frac{4}{3}$ hours. Therefore, its rate was $60 \div \frac{4}{3} = 60 \div \frac{3}{4} = \textbf{45}$ miles per hour.

11. **(C)**

The product $(a + 4i)(9 - bi) = 9a - abi + 36i - 4bi^2 = 9a + 4b + i(36 - ab)$. Since the product is a real number, the coefficient of i must be 0. So $36 - ab = 0$. Then $ab = 36$, and since $a = 6$, b is also equal to **6**.

12. **(D)**

For each coin, the probability that Max guesses wrong is $\frac{1}{2}$. So the probability that he guesses wrong 5 times in a row is $\frac{1}{2} \times \frac{1}{2} \times \frac{1}{2} \times \frac{1}{2} \times \frac{1}{2} = \frac{1}{32}$. The probability that he does not guess incorrectly each time (and hence the probability that he is correct at least once) is $1 - \frac{1}{32} = \frac{31}{32} \approx \textbf{0.97}$.

13. **(C)**

From the top graph, we see that in 1975, 54% (35% + 19%) of all college students were male and the other 46% were female. So there were 5,400,000 males and 4,600,000 females—a difference of **800,000**.

14. **(B)**

In 1975, of every 100 college students, 46 were female—32 of whom were less than 25 years old, and 14 of whom were 25 years old and over. So, 14 of every 46 female students were at least 25 years old. Finally, $\frac{14}{46} \approx 0.30 = \textbf{30\%}$.

15. **(C)**

From the two graphs, we see that in 1975 54% (35% + 19%) of all college students were male, whereas in 1995 the corresponding figure was 45% (28% + 17%). For simplicity, assume that there were 100 college students in 1975, 54 of whom were male. Then in 1995 after a 40% increase in enrollment, there were 140 college students, 63 of whom were male (45% of 140 = 63). So the ratio of the number of male students in 1995 to the number of male students in 1975 is 63:54 = **7:6**.

16. **(B)**

The standard form for the equation of a circle whose center is the point (h, k) and whose radius is r is $(x - h)^2 + (y - k)^2 = r^2$. The center of the circle for which $\overline{AB}$ is a diameter is (3, 3), which is the midpoint of segment $\overline{AB}$. The radius of the circle is the distance from a point on the circle, say $A(1, 1)$ to the center (3, 3).

$r = \sqrt{(3-1)^2 + (3-1)^2} = \sqrt{8}$. So $h = 3$, $k = 3$, and $r^2 = 8$.

The equation of the circle is $(x - 3)^2 + (y - 3)^2 = 8$.

17. **(B)**

If the administrators constitute 27% of the total, then the teachers are 100% – 27% = 73% of the total. So if T is the total number of participants:

$$0.73T = 584 \Rightarrow T = 584 \div 0.73 = 800$$

Therefore, there are 800 – 584 = **216** administrators at the conference.

18. **(D)**

Since $\angle A$ is an angle in both $\triangle AHJ$ and $\triangle ABC$ and since each triangle has a right angle, the triangles are similar. Since $AH = 1$ and $AB = 4$, the ratio of similitude is 4:1, which means that the ratio of their areas is $4^2:1 = $ **16:1**.

**Since $AH = 4 \times AB$, $HJ = 4 \times BC$. Assume $BC = 2$; then $HJ = 8$. Then the area of $\triangle ABC = \frac{1}{2}(1)(2) = 1$, and the area of $\triangle AHJ = \frac{1}{2}(4)(8) = 16$.

19. **(D)**

Let x represent the number of students in the society in 2010. Then the number of students in the society in 2015 was $x + 8$. The number of boys in the society in 2010 was $.375x$ and the number of boys in the society in 2015 could be expressed both as $0.375x + 6$ and $.4(x + 8)$. Therefore,

$$0.375x + 6 = 0.4(x + 8) \Rightarrow 0.375x + 6 = 0.4x + 3.2 \Rightarrow 2.8 = 0.025x \Rightarrow x = 112$$

So, in 2010 the society had 112 members. In 2015, it had 112 + 8 = **120**.

20. **(D)**

If P represents the processing fee and t is the cost of each ticket, we have

$$107.95 = P + 4t \quad \text{and} \quad 181.45 = P + 7t$$

Subtracting the first equation from the second one gives $73.50 = 3t$. So $t = 24.50$. Then $107.95 = P + 4(24.5) = P + 98$. Therefore, $P = 107.95 - 98 = \mathbf{9.95}$.

21. **(A)**

For each of the four countries, you can just divide the number in the column headed "Travel Outside of Europe" by the number in the column headed "Total." However, if you notice immediately that the answer can't be Finland since there were fewer than half as many people in Finland planning to travel outside of Europe than people from any of the other countries, then you can just do the division for the other three countries.

• Denmark: $6{,}244 \div 21{,}953 = 0.284 = 28.4\%$
• Sweden: $5{,}881 \div 23{,}990 = 0.245 = 24.5\%$
• Norway: $5{,}369 \div 20{,}059 = 0.268 = 26.8\%$

The answer is (A), **Denmark**.

22. **(B)**

Of the 1,000 people in the sample, 16.8% ($168 \div 1{,}000$) of them plan to travel to the United States. Since the sample was random, it is likely that about 16.8% of all the original respondents who said they planned to travel outside of Europe would travel to the United States: $0.168 \times 20{,}156 = 3{,}386$. So it is highly likely that the actual number of people would be **between 3,000 and 5,000**.

23. **(B)**

Draw and label a cube with a main diagonal of 9 and a side of s.

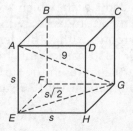

By KEY FACT J8, the length of $\overline{EG}$, a diagonal of the square base, is $s\sqrt{2}$. Then by the Pythagorean theorem (KEY FACT J5), in right $\triangle AEG$:

$$s^2 + \left(s\sqrt{2}\right)^2 = 9^2 \Rightarrow s^2 + 2s^2 = 81 \Rightarrow 3s^2 = 81 \Rightarrow s^2 = 27$$

Since a cube has 6 faces, each of which has area s^2, the formula for the total surface area of a cube is $A = 6s^2$. So $A = 6 \times 27 = \mathbf{162}$.

24. **(B)**

In $\triangle ABC$, $\dfrac{b}{a} = \tan 28^\circ = 0.53$.

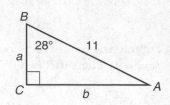

**$\sin 28^\circ = \dfrac{b}{11} \Rightarrow b = 11 \sin 28^\circ = 5.164$.

$\cos 28^\circ = \dfrac{a}{11} \Rightarrow a = 11 \cos 28^\circ = 9.712$.

So $\dfrac{b}{a} = \dfrac{5.164}{9.712} = \mathbf{0.53}$.

25. **(B)**

Express the quotient as a fraction. Then multiply the numerator and denominator by the conjugate of the denominator:

$$(1+2i) \div (3+4i) = \frac{1+2i}{3+4i} = \frac{1+2i}{3+4i} \cdot \frac{3-4i}{3-4i} = \frac{3-4i+6i-8i^2}{9+16} = \frac{11+2i}{25} = \frac{11}{25} + \frac{2}{25}i$$

So $a = \dfrac{11}{25}$ and $b = \dfrac{2}{25}$ and $a+b = \dfrac{13}{25} = \mathbf{0.52}$.

26. **(D)**

16.56 Mexican pesos and 9.47 Argentinian pesos have the same value (namely, 1 U.S. dollar). Set up a proportion:

$$\frac{\text{Mexican pesos}}{\text{Argentinian pesos}} = \frac{16.56}{9.47} = \frac{x}{1} \Rightarrow x = 1.7486 \approx \mathbf{1.75}$$

27. **(B)**

Since $3{,}000 \div 27 = 111.1111\ldots$, the school has 111 homerooms. (110 of the homerooms have 27 students each, which accounts for $27 \times 110 = 2{,}970$ students. The remaining 30 students are in the 111th homeroom.) Since each of the 110 homerooms with 27 students has 3 participating students, there were a total of 330 participants from those homerooms. The total number of students participating in the survey was those 330 students plus the 4 students in the homeroom with 30 students, a total of **334** students.

28. **(B)**

From 1994 to 1996 there was a 9.4% decrease in the number of vehicles stolen. Since 9.4% of $1{,}000{,}000 = 94{,}000$, the number of vehicles stolen in 1996 was $1{,}000{,}000 - 94{,}000 = \mathbf{906{,}000}$. If you get stuck on a question such as this, you have to guess. But since the number of stolen vehicles is clearly decreasing, be sure to eliminate choice (D) before guessing.

29. **(C)**

For simplicity, assume that 1,000 vehicles were stolen in 1994. By 1997, the number had decreased by 12.0% to 880 (12% of 1,000 = 120, and 1,000 − 120 = 880); by 1998, the number had decreased 19.4% to 806 (19.4% of 1,000 = 194 and 1,000 − 194 = 806). So from 1997 to 1998, the number of vehicles stolen decreased by 74 from 880 to 806. This represents a decrease of $\dfrac{74}{880} = 0.084 = \mathbf{8.4\%}$.

30. **(D)**

Simplify the situation by assuming that in 1994 the population was 100,000 and there were 1,000 vehicles stolen. As in the solution to question 29, in 1998 the number of stolen vehicles was 806. At the same time, the number of thefts per 100,000 inhabitants decreased 22.4% from 1,000 to 776. So if there were 776 vehicles stolen for every 100,000 inhabitants, and 806 cars were stolen, the number of inhabitants must have increased. To know by how much, solve the proportion:

$\dfrac{776}{100,000} = \dfrac{806}{x}$. By cross-multiplying, we get $776x = 80,600,000$ and

$x = 80,600,000 \div 776 \approx 103,900$. Then for every 100,000 inhabitants in 1994, there were 103,900 in 1998, an increase of 3.9% or approximately **4%**.

31. **any number between .75 and .857**

Since $2b - 2a$ is −2 times $a - b$, multiply each term of the given inequality by −2, remembering to change the order of the inequalities since you are multiplying by a negative number:

$$\frac{6}{7} > -2a + 2b > \frac{6}{8} \Rightarrow \frac{6}{8} < 2b - 2a < \frac{6}{7} \Rightarrow 0.75 < 2b - 2a < 0.857$$

**Alternate solution. Pick values for a and b that satisfy the original inequality. Since $-\dfrac{3}{7} = -0.428$ and $-\dfrac{3}{8} = -0.375$, let $a = 0$ and $b = 0.4$ so that $a - b = -0.4$. Then $2a - 2b = -0.8$ and $2b - 2a = 0.8$.

32. $\dfrac{2}{5}$ **or** $\dfrac{4}{10}$ **or .4**

There are a total of 650 juniors and seniors (340 juniors and 310 seniors). Of those, 260 took a language other than Spanish (98 + 42 + 106 + 14 = 260). So, the desired fraction is $\dfrac{260}{650} = \dfrac{4}{10} = \dfrac{2}{5}$.

33. **.447**

Sketch the line $y = 2x$. Label two points on the line, such as $(0, 0)$ and $(1, 2)$.

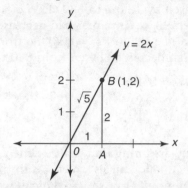

Use the Pythagorean theorem to find the length of $\overline{OB}$, the hypotenuse of $\triangle OAB$:

$$(OB)^2 = 1^2 + 2^2 = 5 \Rightarrow OB = \sqrt{5} \approx 2.236$$

Then $\cos \angle BOA = \dfrac{\text{adjacent}}{\text{hypotenuse}} = \dfrac{1}{2.236} \approx 0.447$.

34. **50**

Since the graph of $y = 10x^2 + bx + c$ has x-intercepts at 1.4 and 1.5, $(x - 1.4)$ and $(x - 1.5)$ are factors of $10x^2 + bx + c$. So $y = 10(x - 1.4)(x - 1.5) = 10(x^2 - 2.9x + 2.1) = 10x^2 - 29x + 21$. Then $b = -29$ and $c = 21$. So $c - b = 21 - (-29) = 21 + 29 = $ **50**.

35. $\dfrac{1}{24}$

The volume of the rectangular block is the area of its face multiplied by its depth. Of course, we must use consistent units; since we want the volume in cubic feet, we have to convert the dimensions given in inches to feet:

$$8 \text{ inches} = \frac{8}{12} = \frac{2}{3} \text{ feet}; \quad 5 \text{ inches} = \frac{5}{12} \text{ feet}; \quad 2 \text{ inches} = \frac{2}{12} = \frac{1}{6} \text{ feet}$$

The face of the block is a rectangle with a square removed. The area of the rectangle is $\dfrac{2}{3} \times \dfrac{5}{12} = \dfrac{10}{36}$ square feet. The area of the square is $\dfrac{1}{6} \times \dfrac{1}{6} = \dfrac{1}{36}$ square feet. So the area of the face is $\dfrac{10}{36} - \dfrac{1}{36} = \dfrac{9}{36} = \dfrac{1}{4}$ square feet. So the volume of the solid is $\dfrac{1}{4}$ square feet $\times \dfrac{1}{6}$ feet $= \dfrac{1}{24}$ cubic feet.

36. $\dfrac{1}{2}$ **or .5**

Since the density of an object is its weight divided by its volume, the weight of an object is the product of its volume times its density. From the solution to question 35, we know that the volume of the block is $\dfrac{1}{24}$ cubic feet.

So calculate the densities:

- Spanish mahogany: $(\dfrac{1}{24}$ cubic feet$) \times (53$ pounds per cubic foot$) =$ 2.208 pounds.

- Honduran mahogany: $(\dfrac{1}{24}$ cubic feet$) \times (41$ pounds per cubic foot$) =$ 1.708 pounds.

So a block made of Spanish mahogany would weigh 2.208 – 1.708 = **.5** pounds more than a block made of Honduran mahogany.

37. **15**

From the bar graph, we see that 20% of the 500 campers were 15 years old. Since 20% of 500 is 100, there were 100 15-year-old campers at the camp. From the circle graph, we see that 15% of the 15-year-olds were pianists. So the number of 15-year-old pianists at the camp in 2015 was 15% of 100, which equals **15**.

38. **15**

Since 12 of the 13-year-olds and 18 of the 14-year-olds were pianists, 30 of the campers under the age of 15 were pianists. From the solution to question 37, we know that 15 of the 15-year-olds were pianists. Finally, from the bar graph, we know that 24% + 16% + 6% + 4% = 50% of the 500 campers, or 250, were 16 or older. Since 12% of those 250 campers were pianists, there were 30 pianists aged 16 or more. Finally, the total number of pianists was 30 + 15 + 30 = 75. So 75 of the 500 campers were pianists, and 75 ÷ 500 = .15 = **15%**.

SAT Essay Scoring

SAT Essay Scoring Rubric

	Score: 4
Reading	Excellent: The essay shows excellent understanding of the source. The essay shows an understanding of the source's main argument and key details and a firm grasp of how they are interconnected, demonstrating clear comprehension of the source. The essay does not misinterpret or misrepresent the source. The essay skillfully uses source evidence, such as direct quotations and rephrasing, representing a thorough comprehension of the source.
Analysis	Excellent: The essay gives excellent analysis of the source and shows clear understanding of what the assignment requires. The essay gives a complete, highly thoughtful analysis of the author's use of reasoning, evidence, rhetoric, and/or other argumentative elements the student has chosen to highlight. The essay has appropriate, adequate, and skillfully chosen support for its analysis. The essay focuses on the most important parts of the source in responding to the prompt.
Writing	Excellent: The essay is focused and shows an excellent grasp of the English language. The essay has a clear thesis. The essay has a well-executed introduction and conclusion. The essay shows a clear and well-crafted progression of thoughts both within paragraphs and in the essay as a whole. The essay has a wide range of sentence structures. The essay consistently shows precise choice of words. The essay is formal and objective in its style and tone. The essay demonstrates a firm grasp of the rules of standard English and has very few to no errors.
	Score: 3
Reading	Skillful: The essay shows effective understanding of the source. The essay shows an understanding of the source's main argument and key details. The essay is free of major misinterpretations and/or misrepresentations of the source. The essay uses appropriate source evidence, such as direct quotations and rephrasing, representing comprehension of the source.
Analysis	Skillful: The essay gives effective analysis of the source and shows an understanding of what the assignment requires. The essay decently analyzes the author's use of reasoning, evidence, rhetoric, and/or other argumentative elements the student has chosen to highlight. The essay has appropriate and adequate support for its analysis. The essay focuses primarily on the most important parts of the source in responding to the prompt.

Score: 3	
Writing	Skillful: The essay is mostly focused and shows an effective grasp of the English language. The essay has a thesis, either explicit or implicit. The essay has an effective introduction and conclusion. The essay has a clear progression of thoughts both within paragraphs and in the essay as a whole. The essay has an assortment of sentence structures. The essay shows some precise choice of words. The essay is formal and objective in its style and tone. The essay demonstrates a grasp of the rules of standard English and has very few significant errors that interfere with the writer's argument.

Score: 2	
Reading	Limited: The essay shows some understanding of the source. The essay shows an understanding of the source's main argument, but not of key details. The essay may have some misinterpretations and/or misrepresentations of the source. The essay gives only partial evidence from the source, showing limited comprehension of the source.
Analysis	Limited: The essay gives partial analysis of the source and shows only limited understanding of what the assignment requires. The essay tries to show how the author uses reasoning, evidence, rhetoric, and/or other argumentative elements the student has chosen to highlight, but only states rather than analyzes their importance, or at least one part of the essay's analysis is unsupported by the source. The essay has little or no justification for its argument. The essay may lack attention to those elements of the source that are most pertinent to responding to the prompt.
Writing	Limited: The essay is mostly not cohesive and shows an ineffective grasp of the English language. The essay may not have a thesis, or may diverge from the thesis at some point in the essay's development. The essay may have an unsuccessful introduction and/or conclusion. The essay may show progression of thoughts within the paragraphs, but not in the essay as a whole. The essay is relatively uniform in its sentence structures. The essay shows imprecise and possibly repetitive choice of words. The essay may be more casual and subjective in style and tone. The essay demonstrates a weaker grasp of the rules of standard English and does have errors that interfere with the writer's argument.

Score: 1	
Reading	Insufficient: The essay shows virtually no understanding of the source. The essay is unsuccessful in showing an understanding of the source's main argument. It may refer to some details from the text, but it does so without tying them to the source's main argument. The essay has many misinterpretations and/or misrepresentations of the source. The essay gives virtually no evidence from the source, showing very poor comprehension of the source.
Analysis	Insufficient: The essay gives little to no accurate analysis of the source and shows poor understanding of what the assignment requires. The essay may show how the author uses reasoning, evidence, rhetoric, and/or other argumentative elements that the student has chosen to highlight but does so without analysis. Or many parts of the essay's analysis are unsupported by the source. The support given for points in the essay's argument are largely unsupported or off-topic. The essay may not attend to the elements of the source that are pertinent to responding to the prompt. Or the essay gives no explicit analysis, perhaps only resorting to summary statements.
Writing	Insufficient: The essay is not cohesive and does not demonstrate skill in the English language. The essay may not have a thesis. The essay does not have a clear introduction and conclusion. The essay does not have a clear progression of thoughts. The essay is quite uniform and even repetitive in sentence structure. The essay shows poor and possibly inaccurate word choice. The essay is likely casual and subjective in style and tone. The essay shows a poor grasp of the rules of standard English and may have many errors that interfere with the writer's argument.

Top-Scoring Sample Student Response

People these days seem to be busier than ever between work, school, family, and other commitments. This often doesn't leave times for the things we know we SHOULD do, but don't really want to. Other activities seem to get in the way that seem more important. Often, the first objective that drops from our "to-do" lists is exercise. In "Healthy Is Happy," the author argues that time should be made for exercise because there is such a high correlation between being physically active and success. The author relies on citing professional, scientific studies, relatable examples, and a casual tone through diction that appeals to a wide variety of readers, in order to convince them that exercise and success are closely linked.

It's often hard to convince a skeptical reader. Citing professional studies is often a foolproof way to show people that your opinion or idea is, in fact, backed up by science. This is exactly what the author did. The author makes a grand claim that exercise and success are inextricably linked. She then backs this claim with a study published in a well-known journal (The Journal of Pediatrics) which found that "fitness was linked to higher achievement scores regardless of body type." This also speaks to naysayers who may argue that only "fit" children were tested. Another study cited by the author appeared on ABC News and showed that high school students doubled their reading scores on standardized tests if they "[participated] in a dynamic morning exercise regimen." These findings are quite significant when thinking of achievement and success in the classroom.

Just when the reader begins to wonder, "but what about those outside the classroom," the author references a recent study which "found that 75% of executives making six-figures listed physical fitness as critical to their career success." It's hard to argue that health is only related to success in school when high paid business men and women place such a high value on fitness. The executives said fitness helped them across the following areas: sleep, diligence, and concentration.

High paying business executives are great role models, but it may be hard for the average Joe to relate to them. As such, the author made great use of more relatable examples. Throughout the essay, the author seems to speak to the lay reader through problems experienced by people in all walks of life. The author offers up complaints like their careers making it hard to get to the gym, being a stressed out college student, and even someone busy with family commitments. These are pretty universal experiences that allow the reader to put themselves in the shoes of the essay, so to speak. The author draws in the reader, making them think "yeah, that's me!" then gives examples of how fitness could help them improve their lives in a variety of ways.

Relatability can make or break a persuasive paper. If a reader disagrees with your point and also feels like they are being personally attacked, they will often disregard it regardless of the evidence behind the argument. Throughout "Healthy Is Happy," the author maintains a casual tone that is appealing to readers. He/she references widespread roles like "busy parent," "exhausted student," "overworked professional." Additionally, the author uses colloquial phrases like "take the average college student," "six pack abs," "the word has spread," "or do you?" The insertion of these colloquials helps balances out the sometimes verbose, extended vocabulary. This strategy and use of diction allows the essay to appeal to the widest variety of readers, and thereby sways the most amount of people toward exercise.

Many studies have proven the link between exercise and success. Some of these studies have even been published by reputable sources like the The Journal of Pediatrics and ABC News. Scientific studies lend more credibility to arguments than generalized, broad statements. Additionally, using smart diction and applicable examples makes the author seem like a credible, but relatable resource. Overall, the author's use of scientific studies, pertinent examples, and casual tone make for a solid argument.